Reading Hume's Dialogues

Indiana Series in the Philosophy of Religion
Merold Westphal, general editor

Reading
Hume's
Dialogues

A VENERATION FOR
TRUE RELIGION

WILLIAM LAD SESSIONS

Indiana
University
Press

BLOOMINGTON AND INDIANAPOLIS

This book is a publication of
Indiana University Press
601 North Morton Street
Bloomington, IN 47404-3797 USA

http://iupress.indiana.edu

Telephone orders 800-842-6796
Fax orders 812-855-7931
Orders by e-mail iuporder@indiana.edu

*The paper used in this publication meets the minimum
requirements of American National Standard for Information
Sciences—Permanence of Paper for Printed Library
Materials, ANSI Z39.48-1984.*

MANUFACTURED IN THE UNITED STATES OF AMERICA

Library of Congress Cataloging-in-Publication Data

Sessions, William Lad.
Reading Hume's Dialogues : a veneration for true religion / William Lad Sessions.
p. cm. — (Indiana series in the philosophy of religion)
Includes bibliographical references and index.
ISBN 0-253-34116-7 (cloth : alk. paper) — ISBN 0-253-21534-X (pbk. : alk. paper)
1. Hume, David, 1711–1776. Dialogues concerning natural religion.
2. Religion—Philosophy. I. Title. II. Series.
B1493.D523 S47 2002
210—dc21

2001006741

1 2 3 4 5 07 06 05 04 03 02

In memoriam

William George Sessions
April 12, 1919–May 17, 2000

John William Elrod
January 21, 1940–July 27, 2001

But in proportion to my veneration for true religion,
is my abhorrence of vulgar superstitions . . .
—Philo to Cleanthes, Part 12.9

CONTENTS

PREFACE AND
ACKNOWLEDGMENTS

THIS BOOK HAS had a long gestation. I was introduced to the rudiments of Hume's *Dialogues* in the late '60s in graduate school at Yale, where I audited a course on Hume from James Dickoff and Patricia James, while also struggling, along with fellow graduate student Eugen Bär, to put the design argument into "regular form." From the outset, this text stoutly resisted my efforts to extract neat summaries, clean-cut positions, and exact arguments. Later on, when I began using Hume's text in my philosophy of religion courses, I encountered new complications on every page, and I began to think more and more of how the "literary" aspects of the text might relate to its philosophy.

I also began reading the secondary literature, eventually compiling a bibliography that extended to nearly 500 items (many but not nearly all of which are contained in the "List of Sources" below). This reading disclosed an almost bewildering variety of divergent interpretations, indicating at the minimum that the Humean scholarly community was as perplexed by this text as I was. Moreover, to my mind, most treatments of the *Dialogues* seemed either too narrowly focused on discrete parts, ignoring or dismissing the organic unity of the work, or too broadly concerned for external, historical links to the text, ignoring or dismissing its internal dynamics.

Gradually I came to two realizations: First, there is great need of a comprehensive treatment of the *Dialogues*—for some reason or other, piecemeal approaches abound, but no one has yet bothered to write a commentary on the whole. Second, few readers employ what I call an "internal" hermeneutic (see Chapter 1 below) on a text that goes out of its way to provide tools for its own analysis—far too many of the text's intricately related details and nuances are usually overlooked. I concluded that a new reading of the whole could add something important to the voluminous scholarly literature as well as help new readers enjoy the delectations of Hume's most "artful" creation.

As I was poised in the early '90s to begin writing, a four-year sojourn in academic administration put the project on hold. A timely sabbatical leave in the fall of 1996 enabled me to write most of a first draft, which has since grown, altered, and, most recently, condensed into the present version. The process has benefited enormously from the comments and advice of many people, who of course bear no responsibility for the errors and problems that remain. I am most grateful for their wonderful assistance and encouragement.

Ed Craun, Ben Eggleston, and Jack Wilson read earlier versions of the entire manuscript and provided extremely helpful suggestions from their quite different perspectives. In addition, Harlan Beckley, Jamie Ferreira, and Bob Sessions graciously commented on parts of the manuscript, and the members of the Society for Philosophy of Religion were equally generous with thoughtful criticism when I presented parts of my project to their annual meetings in 1998 and 2001. An undergraduate seminar in the spring of 1998 worked through a draft alongside Hume's text, and I benefited from comments by Jeremy Adams, Charlie Alm, Chris Dewhurst, John Farringer, Dré Fleury, Schuyler Marshall, Whit Polley, Trevor Reed, Josh Solot, Jennifer Strawbridge, and Alex Taylor. I also presented some ideas before Alex Brown's Religion 282 class. The positive experience of all these undergraduates suggests that my reading will be as useful to students as to scholars.

I am grateful to Kluwer Academic Publishers for permission to reprint portions of my article, "Natural Piety in the *Dialogues*," which appeared in the *International Journal for Philosophy of Religion* volume 49 (2001), pages 49–62; these portions, somewhat revised, appear in Chapter 16, sections 4–6.

Washington and Lee has provided ideal conditions for scholarly work, including time (summers and a sabbatical leave), money (Glenn Grants), encouragement (from administration and colleagues alike), and resources (especially computing and library resources such as Betsy Brittigan at interlibrary loan but also the essential services of Karen Lyle). If you love teaching good students in a beautiful setting, there is no better spot on earth than "this old place," and thoughtful provision for scholarship is an essential component of that teaching.

Indiana University Press has given wonderful assistance and support at every step of the way; it has been a particular pleasure to work with series editor Merold Westphal, sponsoring editor Dee Mortensen, and copy editor Kate Babbitt. Adrienne Hall Bodie is an excellent indexer.

As always, my greatest debt is to my wife, Vicki Sessions, who has borne me on her wings of care more times than I can count.

Finally, and not least, this book is dedicated to my father Bill Sessions, veterinarian, citizen, seeker, and to my good friend John Elrod, philosopher, colleague, leader. Both lived exemplary lives and deserve to be remembered with the greatest affection.

Reading Hume's Dialogues

1

Introduction

HUME's *Dialogues concerning Natural Religion* is widely recognized as perhaps his finest work from a literary standpoint and a seminal classic in the philosophy of religion. Yet, astonishingly, it has never received a book-length reading in English. This absence is particularly surprising because Hume's text has raised many interpretive problems and spawned hundreds of scholarly publications over the past century. But these scholarly comments are partial or circumscribed; none is a full-fledged commentary on the whole.[1]

At the same time, many other important philosophical works—particularly masterpieces in Greek, German, and French—have often received extended commentaries in English, and there have been a number of commentaries or quasi-commentaries on other works by Hume, particularly on his *A Treatise of Human Nature.*[2] But there are no thoroughgoing commentaries on the *Dialogues,* which Hume considered his most "artful" work, which many philosophers regard as "beyond any question the greatest work on philosophy of religion in the English language" (Penelhum 1975, 171), and which some even hold to be "the finest dialogue written in English" (Morrisroe 1970, 95; see also Mossner 1977, 2).

A general reason why there has been no full-scale commentary on the *Dialogues* is that, as Barry Smith points out, "The commentary-tradition is not to be found within the world of English-speaking philosophy," which is "oriented not around schools and school texts, but around ideas, arguments and problems" (Barry Smith 1991, 7). To be sure, Smith employs a special sense of "commentary"—a work whose order of exposition is determined by the order of its "master text" and which "will strive to do justice to this text as a unitary object to be taken as a whole. A work of secondary literature, in contrast, will treat its object atomistically, as a source to be mined at will" (Smith 1991, 1–2).

To extend Smith's mining metaphor: Twentieth-century philosophy in English has generated an extensive secondary literature on Hume by prospecting his texts for veins—or even isolated nuggets—of argumentative ore that are of current interest; this ore is then extracted from its literary matrix and processed by elaborate analytical machinery into the metal of clear and distinct propositions, often compressed into symbolic form, and then cleverly refuted or otherwise put to use, while the textual slag is unceremoniously dumped outside the mine. More charitably put, and minus the mining metaphor, many English-language philosophers have used classic texts such as Hume's *Dialogues* as a kind of virtual discussion partner—to engage in philosophical argument with views and inferences drawn from the text with varying degrees of reformulation—thereby "doing philosophy" with (and sometimes upon!) a text via exegesis and isogesis, drawing the text into the customary "dialectic" of late-twentieth-century philosophical discussion. Consequently, scores of philosophical articles take up and take issue with some proposition or argument detectable in Hume's *Dialogues*, sometimes indeed worrying over what is actually said in the text or what Hume or one of his literary characters might have meant by what they say, or seem to say, but chiefly concerned with the truth or rational support for what they, or someone, might possibly *mean* by the extracted and processed claims and conclusions.

Increasingly over the last three decades, a contrary tendency has gained ascendancy in Hume scholarship. This tendency is opposed to and even dismissive of analytic mining operations[3] but has itself been no more productive of commentaries on the *Dialogues*. It typically seeks to situate Hume's thought and writings within its eighteenth-century Scottish social and intellectual context.[4] Of course, this context is itself usually more or less restricted—to other writings by Hume; to Hume's life; to those persons, books, and ideas that influenced Hume; or to those about whom or to whom Hume wrote. But in principle, historical contextualization may be extended to any item with a plausible causal or genetic relation to Hume's text. Even an entire tradition of thought such as classical skepticism may be proposed as a proper context for understanding Hume's writings.[5]

Interestingly enough, such historical approaches to understanding Hume share with analytic approaches a concern for contextualizing. The analytic tradition inserts a classic text into a twentieth-century philosophical conversation (interpreting its meaning in terms of what comes later, like reader-response critics), while the historicist tradition tethers a text to its contemporary situation or personal, social, or historical antecedents (interpreting its meaning in terms of what went before, like new-historicist critics). It may be coincidence, but the fact remains that neither analytic nor historical contextualizing has yet produced a full-scale, self-standing commentary on Hume's *Dialogues* as a whole. The present reading aims to remedy that lack, and in doing so it departs—or rather prescinds—from the desire to contextualize. It naturally rides on the flood of secondary literature and responds to the varied insights and interpretations of that literature. But its central responsibility is to interpret the text itself—not to place the text in context.

The present work is unique not simply because it offers the first thorough and detailed commentary upon the *Dialogues* as a whole. It also presents a distinctive, though somewhat unfashionable, kind of interpretation of Hume's text—what I will call an *internal* interpretation.[6] Both analytic extraction and historical contextualization provide *external* interpretations; they seek to understand a text by means of tools that are not given by the text itself but rather drawn from other sources. External interpretations doubtless shed some light on the *Dialogues,* but this light always comes, more or less distantly, from "outside" the text itself. I think it is worth exploring a text's—and particularly *this* text's—self-luminescence. Of course, many would regard a merely internal interpretation of the *Dialogues* as confining and reactionary, a naive abstraction, suspect politically, an impossible ideal, a return in these deconstructive days to the discredited New Criticism of the '40s and '50s. I wish to dispute all these disparaging suspicions and to suggest contrariwise that the *Dialogues* is well-suited, perhaps uniquely suited, to an internal hermeneutical approach. Such an approach begins with two principles:

First, *close reading* of a text *on its own terms* is the essential first step in textual criticism of any sort, but particularly for an internal interpretation in which the text itself is its own most important hermeneutic tool and context. Ideally, therefore, *nothing* in the text should escape notice—neither in itself nor apart from its relations with (at least potentially) everything else in the text. This places internal criticism of Hume's *Dialogues* under a stern discipline; it means not simply comparing words (especially not just statements or propositions) spoken by one character with words spoken by another, but also seeing how what a character says connects with what he and other agents do, with how he speaks and acts, with the dramatic setting, personal relationships, and so on. It's a complicated and demanding responsibility, but I believe it is an ultimately rewarding one.

Second, an internal interpreter should inquire under the defeasible *presupposition of unity* in and of the text.[7] One should begin by supposing that a text possesses a very high level of organic unity, where nothing in the text is extraneous—not even apparent or actual contradictions, for they may find their place in a larger harmony. This presupposition is indeed defeasible; the quest for unity may disclose that some parts of the text are after all only loosely or contrarily connected to the others—extraneous accretions and disruptions, not integral tensions. The maxim should not be "Seek and you will find" but rather "Seek or you will not find"—seeking unity is a necessary, not a sufficient, condition for finding unity. Further, the injunction to seek unity can surely be misused or abused, particularly if it prevents recognition or appreciation of tensions, inconsistencies, and bare loose ends or if a text's unities are thought to be its only or its supremely valuable elements. Still, loose ends and inconsistencies are not incompatible with organic unity; indeed, such tensions and oppositions can be useful or essential to the overall harmony of a text, deepening its intensity through what Whitehead called "contrast."

It is worth remarking on this latter point, for the quest for unity may seem quaint and naive to deconstructionists and other postmoderns, who seek rather to ferret out a text's unwitting contradictions and hidden disunities so that text, author, and unsuspecting reader can be "unmasked." We live in an age of suspicion—suspicious of claims to unalloyed perfection and seamless unity, suspicious of the motives lurking just under the surface in author and audience alike, and deeply suspicious of the ways in which power is illegitimately maintained and manipulated by idealized text and idealizing authors. No doubt such suspicion is often "rewarded" by finding exactly what it seeks, and perhaps the discontinuities and inconsistencies require suspicion to be noticed at all. Yet a hermeneutic of suspicion remains fundamentally an *external* approach to most texts because of the ways it uses a text's disunities to "subvert" the text, the reader, and society. It is therefore unhelpful to an internal commentary, which requires a hermeneutic more trusting of its text. As a guide to inquiry, suspicion stultifies the search for unifying connections: What is suspected not to exist will likely not be found even should it happen to exist. As a posture, suspicion produces a certain kind of ironic satisfaction, for (should one be surprised at this?) it makes the interpreter not the text's student or servant but rather its teacher or master: The suspicious interpreter approaches a text not to enlarge herself but rather to shrink the text. No doubt a trusting willingness to be instructed by a text can degenerate into textual idolatry, with the interpreter blinded by imagined perfections and unmindful of the flaws readily apparent to suspicious eyes. Since the present commentary employs a hermeneutic of textual trust, I do wish to record my awareness of the potential dangers of this approach. (Suspicious readers are entitled to suspect even this admission.) Nevertheless, I believe the potential rewards in a trusting approach to a classic text such as the greatest philosophical dialogue in English are well worth the risks.[8]

Still, let me admit quite openly that a fully internal interpretation is impossible, and this for reasons as much in the interpreter as in the text. Clearly every interpreter brings to a text more than just a desire to understand it, and this is true even for those resolving to understand a text internally. The interpreter is willy-nilly a person who has developed his or her interpretative skills and tools not only from reading the text at hand. In particular, no interpreter can escape all influence of others who have addressed the same text. Even if those others have proffered differing interpretations, or even different kinds of interpretation, still their readings leave traces. As well they should. Any interpreter should be responsible not only to the text but also to his or her contemporary community of readers of the text, and this community today is composed of prolific critics of the text, a scholarly community. I have therefore sought to take account of the billowing secondary literature on Hume's *Dialogues,* in part to learn from it (even, and perhaps especially, when I disagree with it), but also to point out some dominant and deviant readings of parts and the whole, in service to this scholarly community. So while the present interpretation seeks to ground its interpretations in the text of the *Dialogues,* it is not unmindful of the cloud of external witnesses.

In addition, no text can be *entirely* self-contained. Not only will it normally refer to particulars in the world by means of proper names or definite descriptions,[9] but the very words and grammar it employs—not to mention many of its phrases, idioms, and tropes—belong to a particular natural language at a definite point in its historical development. As Nicholas Capaldi notes, "The text cannot be fully understood without understanding the intellectual climate in which it was conceived" (Capaldi 1989, 28). Since Hume intended to communicate to his contemporaries, even to understand the bare literal meaning of the language of the *Dialogues* requires some going "outside" the text to see how words and figures and phrases were used and understood by these contemporaries. Fortunately, the language Hume used is largely comprehensible to speakers of English today. Still, twenty-first-century readers of Hume are occasionally brought up short, or even misled, by eighteenth-century meanings of apparently innocuous words. To cite just one example, Pamphilus mentions Hermippus's judgment of Philo's "careless scepticism" (PH.6.),[10] but "careless" here need not mean, as it usually does today, "unconcerned," "not taking care," or "thoughtless" (and therefore "inaccurate") but may rather have the quite proper eighteenth-century senses of "free from care," "cheerful," or "undisturbed" (i.e., without anxiety).

For all these and many other reasons, it is impossible to understand the *Dialogues* without going outside the text to some extent—after all, the man David Hume undisputably wrote the *Dialogues,* so there are real causal connections from the text via his creative authorship to the world in which he lived and to its historical antecedents. That is why an internal interpretation can never be more than an ideal to be approximated, never consummated. Nonetheless, it is, I believe, an ideal well worth pursuing, for the following reasons.

1. Most obviously, the *Dialogues* has notoriously received a number of conflicting interpretations. Prominent among disputed issues is the question of what beliefs *Hume* intended to convey and endorse through the discourses

of his characters—an issue focused in the common queries, "Who speaks for Hume?," "Who represents Hume?," or even "Who is Hume's mouthpiece?"[11] The possible candidates, in rough order of popularity, are Philo, Cleanthes, no one, everyone, and everyone but no one in particular.[12] Henry D. Aiken expresses the majority view: "In general, I think we may say that Philo comes closer to representing Hume than any of the other characters, especially when he is attacking the arguments of Cleanthes and Demea, and that Cleanthes represents him only when he is agreeing with Philo against Demea" (Aiken 1948, xiii). Most arrive at such assignment of views to Hume by first gleaning Hume's views from other texts, then applying them to the *Dialogues*.[13]

Now, in one sense an internal interpretation simply brackets such issues, seeking instead to determine more closely what the *Dialogues* says on its own terms. But in another sense the present interpretation may serve as a prolegomenon to external interpretations interested in questions of Hume's ownership of the views expressed in the *Dialogues*. It is always possible that, even when we have understood *this text's* intentions, we will still be unable to determine what *Hume's* own views were, for perhaps the work does not express those views or does not express them clearly and unambiguously or was not intended to express the author's views but rather to provoke readers into examining their own views.

Further, there are textual puzzles aplenty quite apart from discovering what Hume believed, or intended, in the text. For instance, there are the famous worries over Philo's apparent "reversal" in Part 12. For most of the preceding Parts, Philo subjects the argument from design to withering criticism, but in Part 12 he not once but thrice declares his (indeed everyone's!) adherence to this centerpiece of natural theology. How is his apparent about-face to be explained, particularly if, as most commentators suppose, Philo and Philo alone is Hume's "spokesman" (Mossner 1977, 8)? Jonathan Dancy considers Philo's "volte-face" as "one of the crucial features of the *Dialogues,* success in the explanation of which is a test of any interpreter" (Dancy 1995, 30).

In addition, what weight should a reader give to the opinions of Pamphilus, who relates the dialogues to his friend Hermippus and who is made to "confess" at the end "that, upon a serious review of the whole, I cannot but think, that PHILO's principles are more probable than DEMEA's; but that those of CLEANTHES approach still nearer to the truth" (12.34.Pamphilus to Hermippus). And there are many other puzzles, on which commentators have taken divergent positions. For example, why is Philo "a little embarrassed and confounded" in Part 3.10? Why does Demea leave at the end of Part 11 (and why not at some other time or not at all), and what, if anything, changes following his departure? Why do both Cleanthes and Philo take turns, in that order, in refuting Demea's *a priori* argument in Part 9? Often external interpretations, far from resolving such puzzles, actually cause or exacerbate them; by using an outside context for understanding the text, many readers fail to see, or to appreciate, just what is *in* the text, in all its complexity.

My hope is that the closer reading of Hume's text engendered by an internal interpretation will clarify and perhaps resolve many of these puzzles. Internal interpretations, therefore, may be allies rather than competitors to external approaches. At any rate, if readers more accustomed to external interpretations will but suspend judgment for the duration, they may be surprised at the self-clarification of Hume's text.

2. The *Dialogues* is an exceedingly well-constructed book. Hume, whose "ruling passion" was "literature" (see Hume's "My Own Life"), wrote at the end of his life to Adam Smith that upon revising this work "I find that nothing can be more cautiously and more artfully written."[14] He worked on the manuscript for some twenty-five years, with an initial draft (at least through Part 3) completed by 1751, a revision ten years later, and further extensive revisions in 1776, the year of his death. Moreover, Hume was a model stylist in his own age. From these facts, I draw two boundary conditions for interpreters of the *Dialogues*: At the minimum, we should not readily ascribe to authorial incompetence or haste any difficulties we encounter in the text. At the maximum, we should entertain the possibility that these difficulties are intended by a master craftsman of the English language and that it is our responsibility to discover how they contribute to the text's overall design.[15]

3. The *Dialogues* contains a remarkably large number of aids to its own interpretation (no accident, I believe, but an aspect of its "artful" construction). External interpreters usually rush over these aids, which are contained mostly in the preface ("Pamphilus to Hermippus") and in Parts 1 and 12, in their haste to get to the "arguments" of Parts 2–11.[16] This is, I believe, a great mistake. The *Dialogues* contain considerable comment on its own saying and doing (in particular, what is said and shown about education, piety, and dialogue), and understanding this self-commentary is essential for understanding the text, at least on an internal approach. At the bare minimum, an internal hermeneutic should seek to discover how far the text's own proffered terms of self-understanding can be applied to itself.

4. We must remember that the *Dialogues* is, after all, a set of dialogues.[17] Readers familiar with Plato's *Dialogues* will have no trouble comprehending the weighty ramifications of this apparently innocuous remark; and indeed Platonic commentaries are one source of inspiration for the present reading.[18] In dialogues more than in any other philosophical/literary genre, the literary form is inseparable from, and indeed essentially contributory toward, its philosophical content, intended effect, and overall meaning. What is said is

said by someone, who speaks in a distinctive voice from a distinctive point of view, using language not simply to convey abstract propositions but to further other ends as well, often producing effects unintended by the speaker (if not, perhaps, by an "artful" author). In short, in a dialogue, rhetoric of all kinds is no mere window dressing but is vital to structure, content, and meaning.

Further, not only what is said (in all a dialogue's ways of saying) needs to be taken into account in an internal interpretation. For dialogue is a dynamic *activity*, involving a sequence of various actions and reactions of several characters as well as the changing nature of their relationships and interactions—in short, a dialogue has both character and plot. Dialogues are, like dramas, stories of agents acting. To be sure, in a philosophical dialogue the actions are mostly speech-acts, and stage directions normally consume only a small number of the words of the text. But quantity is no true measure of importance. On the contrary, deeds often speak louder than words, and this is true even when the "deeds" are no more than a raised tone of voice, a momentary embarrassment, or an unusual display of self-confidence. Moreover, the speech-acts that bulk so large are not usually, nor even simply, lectures or creedal recitations; typically more is going on than the bland delivery of propositions or beliefs. Who is being addressed, explicitly or implicitly, in what kinds of language, with what intentions, who is aware of what is going on, and at what level—all are necessarily further concerns in a dialogue. "Arguments" in a dialogue are not strings of propositions but series of points and shadings that take different meanings as they are made by and to different people. Action springs from, expresses, and affects personality and character.

But a good dialogue is not confined to its characters. It reaches out from its pages to ensnare the reader, who no doubt is antecedently interested in the topics but finds herself drawn into the conversation—evaluating the comments and the character of various speakers in turn, wondering about what and how she would reply to someone's remarks or what she would or should have done instead of or in reaction to some character's actions. In short, an artful author finds ways to involve his reader in a dialogue's unfolding drama.

All these many and varied elements, moreover, are in Hume's *Dialogues* not merely stated nor externally related. Rather, they are most skillfully depicted, indicated, and delicately suggested (even at times by what is *not* said or done) as they are woven into an intricate whole. Here we are in the extraordinarily nuanced realm of a master dialogue-writer, in the very same league as Plato. In reading this most "artful" philosophical dialogue in English, therefore, we should never forget the many elements and dimensions of a dialogue—who is speaking to whom, on what occasion, in what kind(s) of language, with what aims and intentions, to what effect, and so forth. An internal interpretation can more readily take notice of such dialogic elements than an external interpretation intent on relating a text to some context. In the present commentary, the literary form of Hume's *Dialogues* is therefore viewed as a golden opportunity, not an obstacle, to its own understanding.

In putting forth these reasons for working against the current interpretative grain and seeking an internal interpretation of Hume's *Dialogues,* let me reiterate that I do *not* think that external interpretations are misguided or unhelpful. On the contrary. Understanding is many-faceted and unending, and external approaches to a text have their rightful place. But no interpretation is all-sufficing, and the recent near-monopoly of external interpretations in scholarship on Hume's *Dialogues* produces its own reaction. Hence, paradoxical as it sounds, I believe the current interpretive situation can be enriched by *eliminating* context—by attending solely (so far as possible) and carefully to the *Dialogues'* own self-interpreting resources.[19]

Several general themes will emerge in the course of this reading. First, the *Dialogues* possesses much more coherence and unity, as well as richer complexity and perplexity, than has often been supposed. Of course, since an internal interpretive approach initially assumes and searches for such unity, we must take care not to ignore disunity. We must be prepared to notice inconsistencies where they do exist and not to imagine coherence where it is absent. But a close reading of the text shows, I believe, that many supposed Humean inconsistencies are not inconsistent at all, while other, mostly unnoticed, real inconsistencies serve important textual purposes and contribute toward larger harmonies.

Second, the "literary" quality and form of the *Dialogues* is more ingredient in its philosophically interesting content and "message" than many philosophers have believed. If I have given extended treatment to such matters as the title, the characters and their actions, and the preface, this is not just because other commentators have given them almost no treatment at all. It is also because I believe due attention to these aspects genuinely illuminates the *Dialogues.* No doubt the literary elements complicate the philosophy, but then the philosophy of "natural religion" *is* complicated—especially for Hume. Hume's views on this heading are considerably more subtle than those perceived by readers such as A. J. Ayer, who claims that "Hume, without ever openly displaying his hand, intended the discerning reader to conclude that he adopted Philo's position. In my view, indeed, the discrediting not only of the more superstitious types of theism but of any form of religious belief was one of the principal aims of Hume's philosophy" (Ayer 1980, 23). To cite but one large contrary complication: While Parts 2–11 are indeed mostly concerned with religious belief, it is a profound mistake to think that the *Dialogues* is about nothing more than this, as if "natural religion" meant only "natural theology," and as if the Preface and Parts 1 and 12 were merely peripheral—interesting literary flourishes, perhaps, but having little or nothing to do with the central issues and overall interpretation of the work.

Third, contrary to Ayer, Hume—or rather Philo—did *not* forever "discredit" theological design arguments, either in fact[20] or in logic.[21] Certainly Philo's exposé of the limits and inutility of a certain form of analogical argument made its impact not only on Cleanthes but also on philosophers of religion in the nineteenth and twentieth centuries, even if it did not have, *pace* Penelhum, "the effect of destroying a whole tradition of theological reflection" (Penelhum 1975, 163). Still, in the end even Philo concedes the persistence of deep-seated human tendencies to anthropomorphize the world, to perceive (or project) teleology, and to presume agent causality, tendencies which can and do survive in the absence of argument and which continue to seek argument rendering themselves intelligible and respectable.

Fourth, on my internal reading of the *Dialogues,* there are broader or deeper issues at stake than theological design arguments, and they have more a practical than a theoretical aspect. The *Dialogues,* it turns out, is more about piety than theology. Given that humans have an ineradicable teleological bent, how does our species' sense for cosmic design comport with our natural "common life"? For both Cleanthes and Philo, discerning an Author of Nature must be consonant with living harmoniously with others, realizing human capacity, and fulfilling human aspiration. They both seek, in their divergent ways, to make natural religious thinking ("theology") commensurate with natural religious practice ("piety") and to make both contribute to a humane life in a human society. Even today, more than two centuries after Hume's most artful work was finally placed before the reading public, we still have much to learn from its treatment of these issues.

2

Scene-Setting

Dialogue . . . has been little practiced in later ages, and has seldom succeeded in the hands of those, who have attempted it.

—Pamphilus to Hermippus, ¶1

The setting and structure of the *Dialogues* are deceptively simple: Three gentlemen of leisure, Cleanthes, Philo, and Demea, discuss the subject of "natural religion" amid the pleasant surroundings of the library in the summer home of Cleanthes, their every word and sometime gesture or action reported faithfully by the youthful Pamphilus to his equally youthful friend Hermippus. In his prefatory comments to Hermippus, Pamphilus explains why dialogues[1] are especially appropriate to the topic at hand and mentions Hermippus's views of the principal speakers. Hermippus has formed the opinion, based on an earlier "imperfect account" of the conversations given him by Pamphilus, that Cleanthes has an "accurate philosophical turn," Philo a "careless scepticism" and Demea a "rigid inflexible orthodoxy" (PH.6.Pamphilus to Hermippus). Whether these tags are accurate, they do make a first, and sometimes a lasting, impression upon the reader.

Then follow twelve "Parts" of varying length (the shortest is Part 9, with 11 paragraphs; the longest is Part 12, three times longer with 34 paragraphs), with the following rough structure:

In Part 1, Demea, Cleanthes and Philo all discuss natural religion and religious inquiry (particularly skepticism). The basic themes of education, friendship, natural theology and piety, reason, common life, and true religion are introduced (1.1–2),[2] the drama begins (1.3–4), and the varieties and difficulties of skepticism, particularly in religious subjects, are discussed (1.5–16), as are the relations of faith and reason and of religion and life (1.17–20).

In Parts 2–8, Cleanthes introduces an *a posteriori* argument from the world's "design" to the "hypothesis" of the "Being" of an "Author of Nature" with certain "natural" attributes (chiefly intelligence and power), and Philo explores in great detail the many "inconveniences" of this argument and manner of thinking. In Part 2, Demea presents his "pious" view of the being and nature of God (2.1–4) just before Cleanthes sets forth his argument from design (2.5). Demea and Philo offer initial objections (2.6–10), followed by a longer critique from Philo (2.11–28). In Part 3, Cleanthes replies to Philo (3.1–9), who suffers a momentary "embarrassment" (3.10), rescued by Demea's objections to Cleanthes' form of argument (3.11–13). In Part 4, after some name-calling by Cleanthes and Demea (4.1–3) and a sly syllogism by Philo (4.4), Philo begins to show the "inconveniences" of Cleanthes' argument, focusing first on where to stop in finding the causes of nature (4.5–14). In Part 5, a second inconvenience is raised—that one can't infer infinite or perfect attributes (5.1–12)—with a weak reply by Cleanthes (5.13).

In Parts 6–8, Philo alleges a third inconvenience: Various alternative hypotheses are equally likely/unlikely, to wit: (1) God is the soul of the world (6.2–6); (2) order is inherent to the world (6.12–13); (3) the world originates by generation or vegetation (7.1–15); (4) the world was spun from a giant spider (7.16–17); or, dearest to Philo's heart, (5) the refined Epicurean hypothesis: A finite eternal universe is its own best explanation (8.1–10). Philo then claims "a complete triumph for the sceptic" (8.11–12).

In Part 9, Demea produces an *a priori* argument to prove both the existence and the infinite nature of the deity (9.1–3), and Cleanthes (9.4–9) and Philo (9.10–11) take turns refuting him.

In Parts 10–11, Cleanthes, Demea, and (chiefly) Philo confront the existence and extent of earthly suffering in relation to the moral attributes of God (goodness, benevolence, providence). First, Demea and Philo wallow in human misery (10.1–19), in contrast to Cleanthes' Panglossism (10.20); Philo then presses the problem of evil and the rejection of an inference to a moral deity (10.21–27) and, despite a rebuttal by Cleanthes (10.28–31), Philo claims yet another "triumph" for the skeptic (10.32–36). Cleanthes then proposes a limited or "finitely perfect" deity (11.1). Philo critiques this proposal (11.2–17), mentioning four "circumstances" of natural evil (11.5–12), for which the "most probable" cause is "a blind nature" (11.13–15), with moral evil introducing still more difficulties (11.16–17). At this point Demea detects betrayal and leaves the conversation (11.18–21).

Finally, in Part 12, Philo and Cleanthes are free to discuss "true religion" in a new "manner" of dialogue (12.1). Philo confesses his own "sense of religion" (12.2–4) and offers his "unfeigned sentiments" (12.6–9). Both Cleanthes (12.10–12) and Philo (12.13–23) then reflect on religious piety and moral practice, variously contrasting "true religion" with "vulgar superstition." Philo closes the conversations with his final view of piety (12.27–32) and theology

(12.33). Part 12 then concludes with a brief paragraph by Pamphilus to Hermippus, summing up the strong impressions made on him by the speakers:

> I confess, that, upon a serious review of the whole, I cannot but think, that PHILO's principles are more probable than DEMEA's; but that those of CLEANTHES approach still nearer to the truth. (12.34)

This outline is a very rough one indeed, and it affords small sense of the full range of topics discussed or the manner and outcome of their discussion, but it will suffice for now; when we deal with each Part we will have occasion to detect more subtle and complicating structures.

While the conversations reported by Pamphilus supposedly occur all on one summer's day, three other events need to be placed in relation to them: Pamphilus's giving of the (presumably oral) "imperfect account" to Hermippus; the writing down of the "more exact detail" which constitutes the body of Parts 1–12; and the writing of a cover letter, entitled "Pamphilus to Hermippus," which conveys the text of the *Dialogues* to Hermippus.

A relative time line can be easily reconstructed from the last paragraph of "Pamphilus to Hermippus": First come the actual conversations, then the oral "imperfect account," then the "more exact detail," and finally the cover letter. But the lapse of time between (and during) each event is problematic. The actual conversations occur during "the summer season" and consume half a day, perhaps a long afternoon (to speak the recorded words without interruption takes just under four hours at my own pace). But then how much time passed before Pamphilus delivered his "imperfect account" to Hermippus? According to his own account, Pamphilus comes to write his cover letter only after the summer season has already "passed"—albeit just "lately"; that is, recently. Likewise, the oral report to Hermippus had also been made "lately." Putting these clues together, it seems that Pamphilus did not relate either his oral or his written accounts to Hermippus while he was spending the summer season at Cleanthes' country place but did so shortly thereafter. So some time—perhaps a month or more—must have lapsed between the actual conversations and Pamphilus's double recital of them. Probably the gap between his first oral report and his second written recital is shorter: Hermippus was "so excited" by the former that he pressed Pamphilus to quickly write down the latter. The writing itself need not have taken much longer than a day or two, but it did occur well after the events recited. Pamphilus claims the original conversation was "deeply imprinted in my memory," but this imprint must have endured for well over a month.

Each word of the title of this book bears careful thought. We noted earlier the considerable ambiguity of "*dialogue*." Initially, a dialogue is both form and content—a certain literary form and an actual or imagined conversation described, reproduced, or invented within that conventional form. Rather than a third-person, indirect report of a conversation, a dialogue is the depiction of a conversation firsthand, with two or more speakers speaking directly, in their own voices. This depiction may be preceded by more or less elaborate scene-setting, typically by means of a narrator who adds an additional voice and further levels of complexity. Plato's *Dialogues*, for example, sometimes begin abruptly and supply their own context as the conversation unfolds (*Meno, Gorgias*), but they often include a narrator who is sometimes Socrates himself (*Republic*). At other times the narrator is another principal to the original conversation (*Phaedo*) or some non-participating auditor who relates the conversation to yet another party (*Symposium*). In short, a dialogue seldom begins abruptly but provides its own literary context, thereby introducing the characters and setting to a reader.

The literary form of a dialogue naturally draws a reader into its content —as Pamphilus says, it "carries us, in a manner, into company" with the text and its characters (PH.4). By depicting people conversing, it not only entices readers into listening, it also invites us to participate in that conversation, to join in the argumentative give-and-take that constitutes the great bulk of a philosophical dialogue. We are induced to take sides, to extend or amend claims and rebuttals, to comment on remarks, to evaluate judgments, and to wonder why the conversation goes the way it does and not in some other direction or fashion. In short, we are drawn into the written dialogue in such a way that we open up a further dialogue, this time between text and reader. To be sure, any text engages its reader at some level or it would not be read with understanding. But a dialogue form excites such engagement more than other literary forms such as essay, history, treatise, or enquiry (all forms used by Hume). A dialogue's discourse is more like ordinary human conversation, flowing from topic to topic not *more geometrico* but somewhat more loosely, even haphazardly, according to the whims and fancies of the speakers. This looseness—as well as the conversational tone, the non-technical vocabulary, and the appealing imagery—contributes to reader involvement with the text.

There is a fourth possible sense of "dialogue." As an author sets about making his "artful" creation, he may find that he is no arbitrary despot with regard to his characters but at times more like a fellow conversationalist. His characters begin to emerge with minds of their own with their own idiosyncratic styles, arguments, attitudes, and agendas, and the author must at times conform his will to theirs. Perhaps not all artworks come about in this way, but it is frequent in fiction-writing, and there is reason to think that Hume's *Dialogues* were constructed through at least a partial dialogue of this kind. We know that Hume not only returned at least twice to the text for extensive revisions but sent around the partial manuscript to his friends, seeking their advice as to how it might be improved. In particular, he sought help in shaping the character of Cleanthes. While the character of Philo came naturally to him, Hume confessed to particular difficulty imagining "formal & regular" arguments in support of Cleanthes even while admitting his strong "Propensity of the Mind" toward Cleanthes' conclusion of an Author of Nature. At one point he toyed with the "thought, that the best way of composing a Dialogue, wou'd be for two Persons that are of different Opinions about any Question of Importance, to write alternately the different Parts of the Discourse, & reply to each other."[3] Of course, different authors for different characters wouldn't guarantee excellent or even different opinions or arguments, and surely literary unity would be endangered by a plurality of authors. Nevertheless, Hume's "thought" in this letter of 1751 does indicate that he was struggling to imaginatively fashion his *Dialogues*—that he was, in an important sense, in dialogue with his growing text. Though considerations of authorial intent are no immediate concern of the present internal interpretation, they should give pause to any external commentator who rushes to credit (or discredit) Hume with any of the views expressed in the text, for a literary character can easily come to have a limited independence of its author, *even when* the author is temperamentally close to his creation.

At any rate, we should keep in mind the multiple ambiguity of "dialogue" when reading Hume's title. But in addition we should be puzzled by the use of "dialogues" in the plural: Is there indeed more than one dialogue? If so, just how many dialogues are there? What is comprehended in "one" dialogue?

Let us quickly dispatch several mistaken ways of regarding the plural title. First, has Hume perhaps simply made a typographical error? No; over twenty-five years of writing and rewriting, the title is always "Dialogues" and never "A Dialogue."[4] It is also a mistake to think of the *Dialogues* as comprising only one dialogue with twelve "sections"[5] and an equal error to regard the twelve Parts of the *Dialogues* as constituting twelve dialogues.[6] Hume didn't merely number these divisions; he gave them the bland and unhelpful labels of "Part 1," "Part 2," and so forth. Another, more fanciful error grows from suspicion of the narrator, Pamphilus: Perhaps the youthful and impressionable Pamphilus recollected, confused, or collated a number of conversations he had overheard on different occasions. But this view is contradicted by Pamphilus's concluding comments, where he speaks of "the reasonings *of that day*" (12.34.Pamphilus to Hermippus, emphasis added) as well as by the fact that it has no textual evidence in its favor save the need to account for a plural title.

A better view of the plural title is that there are exactly two dialogues in the *Dialogues*, one with three speakers in Parts 1–11 and another with two speakers in Part 12. After Demea departs at the end of Part 11, the tenor and subject of the discussion do significantly change, in ways we will later note. But the first words of Part 12 read: "After DEMEA's departure, CLEANTHES and PHILO continued *the conversation,* in the following manner" (12.1.Pamphilus to Hermippus; emphasis added). More important, the number two is suspiciously exact and surprisingly small. If there were indeed exactly two dialogues, why didn't Hume entitle his work "Two Dialogues concerning Natural Religion"?[7] Still, this answer seems headed in the right direction, as does a further suggestion that there is a new dialogue whenever a new pair of speakers takes up the conversation (there are three available pairs in Parts 1–11—Cleanthes/Philo, Cleanthes/Demea, and Philo/Demea—but only one in Part 12). On this view, in Part 9, for example, there would be two dialogues, one between Demea and Cleanthes and another between Demea and Philo. But this suggestion seems arbitrary and constricted. Not all conversations are two-sided, and even when different pairs of speakers converse they can continue a conversation on the same topic and in the same manner as previous speakers.

What these views are leading us toward, I think, is the position that the *Dialogues* does indeed contain many dialogues but that there is no easy or unique way of individuating them, for there are multiple criteria of individuation at work. Sometimes it is indeed a different conversation when the *speakers* change; but also sometimes it is a new conversation when the *topic* changes or when the *manner,* tone, and tenor alter or when the participants change *roles* or when the *audience* changes. Sometimes, but not always, for these conditions do not always coincide. When they do coincide, individuation is relatively easy. For example, despite what Pamphilus says at the outset of Part 12, it *is* a different conversation after Demea leaves, not just in speakers and audience but also in manner, topic, and the roles played by Cleanthes and Philo toward each other (and toward their auditor Pamphilus). But often only some of the criteria coincide: for example, just the topic changes (skepticism per se versus particular skeptical arguments); or changes under one description (*a priori* versus *a posteriori* argument) but not under another (natural theological argument); or the speakers alter their roles (now on the attack, now defending; now allied with one, now with another). Then there may be equal reason for saying either that a new dialogue begins or that the old dialogue continues but in an altered form.

Moreover, the *Dialogues* is rich in different *kinds* of dialogue. It would be a dreary dialogue—and an unimaginative author—if all conversations were of the same type and form. Part of Hume's genius as an author is in moving skillfully from one kind to another. Consider, for example, just these four types: In Part 7, Philo and Demea discuss an idea of Philo's, while Cleanthes listens to their interchange and then contributes, in the Part's last paragraph, some comments of his own. In Part 9, Demea (with some prodding by Cleanthes) presents his *a priori* argument; Cleanthes and then Philo take turns offering critiques, with only silence from Demea in reply. In Part 10.16–19, Philo converses with an "adversary" of his own imagining. In Part 11, in the first paragraph Cleanthes invites Philo's opinion, then Philo launches into a monologue that consumes the remainder of the Part. Such examples could be multiplied, and they contribute to the multiple ambiguity of "dialogue" in our text.

So there are many dialogues in the *Dialogues,* but we cannot pin down the exact number. Nevertheless, we should be alert to the often important changes of speaker, topic, manner, role, audience, and form—changes which may, but need not, signal a transition from one dialogue to another.

All the dialogues in the *Dialogues* are, in some way or other, "*concerning* natural religion." "Concerning" seems such an innocuous word. Its firsthand meaning to modern Americans is "relating to, having to do with, in regard to, with reference to, about."[8] So all the various dialogues seem unproblematically *about* natural religion. But possibly more is involved.[9]

First, look closely at the paragraph where Pamphilus indicates that the "subject" of the conversation he recites is natural religion (PH.5), for it contains further and deeper resonances of "concerning"—further and deeper *concerns.* The "Being of a God," Pamphilus says, is a "truth so obvious, so certain, . . . so important." "But in treating of this obvious and important truth," he continues,

> what obscure questions occur, *concerning* the *nature* of that divine being. . . . *Concerning* these, human reason has not reached any certain determination: But these are topics so interesting, that we cannot restrain our restless enquiry *with regard to* them; though nothing but doubt, uncertainty and contradiction have, as yet, been the result of our most accurate researches. (PH.5; emphases added)

Here "concerning" and its neighbor "with regard to" reside in a context of restless but obscure and fruitless questioning and summon forth other senses of "concern": concern for and care about this subject, involving active interest and attention but also anxiety and unease. Clearly this is a subject that touches and affects "us," as Pamphilus would have it. These questions are not just about us, they concern us because they belong to us, they interest us, they trouble us; and our "restless" pursuit of them does not seem to allay our concerns but only heightens them. Given this semantic field opened up by Pamphilus, these other meanings of "concern" reverberate with the bland "concerning" of the title.

So the title's "concerning" does more than indicate the subject matter of the dialogues to come; it also nods to its participants' interest in this subject and perhaps also hints at their anxiety attendant upon something not only unresolved but unresolvable. Everyone, from Pamphilus and Hermippus to Cleanthes, Demea, and Philo, talks and thinks about "natural religion," is interested in it, is concerned *with* it. But everyone is concerned *about* it as well; it is both important to them and yet unresolved and uncertain. Of course, natural religion means something quite different to all three speakers, but for all it is more than just a topic for polite conversation; it affects their lives. It also affects any reader who is drawn into the conversations: We start thinking "concerning" natural religion and find ourselves being concerned with, about, and by the subject. When Pamphilus says "we cannot restrain our restless inquiry" regarding such topics (PH.5), the "we" includes ourselves.

It is best to explore the genus "Religion" before considering the species that is "Natural." Here it is vitally important not to be too narrow. "Religion" in the *Dialogues* should be treated as a very broad category indeed. To be sure, it is Christian religion that primarily concerns our discussants, and there is no equal time or regard for other world religions.[10] But within this somewhat constricted compass, "Religion" is quite an encompassing term. In particular, even if religion is taken to deal only with God or gods, it should not be limited to "*theism*"—a set of particular theological doctrines—nor equated with "*theology*"—a set of beliefs, claims, propositions, arguments, evidence, and so forth about the divine. That would make of religion a wholly theoretical or intellectual affair, and it would make of Hume's *Dialogues* no more than what so many analytic philosophers have presumed it to be, a narrow examination of arguments.

To be sure, it is tempting to see things in this narrow way, for the text itself gives much aid and comfort. Pamphilus, for example, in his prefatory comments to Hermippus, has his eye fastened on "topics" (PH.1), "subjects" (PH.2), "doctrine" (PH.3), and "question of philosophy" (PH.4) as the appropriate "subject of NATURAL RELIGION" (PH.5). No wonder, then, that he fastens on the "obvious and important truth" of the "*Being* of a God" as well as the "obscure questions" about this being's "nature" (PH.5). That is why Pamphilus views the "conversations" among Cleanthes, Philo, and Demea as a matter of "reasonings" and "systems" (PH.6).

Further, this youthful impression seems to be reinforced by Demea's opening words in Part 1. In talking about education, Demea says he follows the advice of "an ancient" (Chrysippus) in studying last of all subjects, "this science of natural theology" (1.1.Demea to Cleanthes). It is this "science" that interests Pamphilus above all others, to the point where he notices little else, just like an analytic philosopher.

But we should not rush to join Pamphilus and Demea here, for Philo immediately prods Demea (and not for the last time) with a double-edged worry: Should not the "principles" of religion be taught earlier rather than later, for fear that they might not take hold in children's impressionable minds? Demea sees the problem and beats a quick retreat:

> It is only as a science, replied DEMEA, subjected to human reasoning and disputation, that I postpone the study of natural theology. To season their minds with early piety is my chief care; and by continual precept and instruction, and I hope too, by example, I imprint deeply on their tender minds an habitual reverence for all the principles of religion. (1.2.Demea to Philo)

This is a remarkable speech. First it introduces an important distinction between theology and "habitual reverence"—that is, piety—a distinction we shall find ingredient throughout the entire *Dialogues*. Second, if the ensuing discussion were solely instruction in natural theology, "subjected to human reasoning and disputation," then what about Pamphilus? Is he old enough to listen to such a theological discussion at all, according to Demea? Or is he not still young enough to require instruction in and about something more important than theology? Third, piety "season[s]" a youthful mind and "imprint[s]" in that mind a certain habitual attitude, or set of attitudes, toward "the principles of religion." Fourth, this seasoning or imprinting of piety is produced as much by example as by "precept and instruction." Fifth, while the piety Demea seeks to imprint is "a proper submission and self-diffidence" (1.2.Demea to Philo), we should not necessarily expect others to share in the same piety, even if they should agree to (some of) the same principles to be imprinted—they may be imprinted in different ways. Putting these points together, it is clear that even Demea, the least perceptive and self-aware of all the speakers in the *Dialogues,* recognizes a distinction between theology and piety and sees not only that piety is a precursor of theology but also that education in piety is more important than education in theology.

Several questions now arise: (1) Does Pamphilus in his observing role see that piety (in particular his own piety) as well as theological principle is at stake in the day's conversations? (2) Does Demea in his participating role see this? (3) Do Cleanthes and Philo see this? (4) *Are* both piety and theology in fact at stake in the *Dialogues?* (5) Is *education* in both piety and theology also at stake?

Putting Pamphilus's perceptions aside, we should distrust Demea's erratic observation and authoritarian judgment. Demea, as we shall see, is a most inaccurate guide, not only concerning how to think (in natural theology) and what to feel and do (in piety) but also concerning what is actually happening in the conversation (in "real life"), for it is not until the end of Part 11 that he finally perceives the fundamental gulf yawning between him and Philo, despite early and frequent hints to the contrary, a gulf that is evident to Philo and to Cleanthes. Still, Demea does start off Part 1 with expressions of concern for seasoning in early piety and presumably is alert enough to apply this to the present situation involving Pamphilus. Cleanthes' concern for piety is evident to Demea in "the great care" and "the pains" which he takes in educating Pamphilus as well as in the (adopted) filial piety Pamphilus feels toward Cleanthes.

Philo at least nods perfunctorily to piety: "Your precaution . . . of seasoning our children's minds with early piety, is certainly very reasonable; and no more than is requisite in this profane and irreligious age" (1.3.Philo to Demea). But his true concern for education in piety is displayed by his fervor throughout the *Dialogues* in pursuing his skeptical course—it is this whole production that Philo refers to at the end in hoping that "Cleanthes will forgive me for interposing so far in the education and instruction of his pupil" (12.33.Philo to Cleanthes). Philo's education and instruction of Pamphilus are not in theology alone but also in piety, attempting to inculcate a passionate and committed life of inquiry into theological questions and the total impact of religion. Philo's piety is centrally expressed in his skeptical questioning, and it is this approach to religion that he wishes to "interpose" in Pamphilus's education, even at so early an age that Demea might not think it appropriate. So even should we think that Pamphilus and Demea are not aware, or not fully or initially aware, of the stakes in the day's conversations, I do think Cleanthes and Philo realize that the piety of at least Pamphilus hangs in the balance and that education in piety greatly matters.

Still, the bulk of the book (Parts 2–11) *is* given over to theology—doesn't this mean that theology is more important than piety both in the discussion and to the discussants? Not at all. Although it is not possible to elaborate the evidence quite yet, I shall here issue some promissory notes, to be repaid in the detailed commentary on the appropriate Parts:

1. Part 1 is chiefly a discussion of philosophical method (both in theology and in general), particularly of philosophical skepticism (the method of Philo), but the purpose always in view is the kind of life this method is consonant with and conduces to—that is, in the case of religion, the kind of piety it both exemplifies and produces. The *Dialogues* is a case study in religious education, and theological argument is a large part but by no means all of that education. Further, education is a means to a form of life, and a means should not be mistaken for an end; theology therefore is not life. But piety *is* life, the way one lives one's life.

2. Throughout Parts 2–11 there are glimpses of the characters of Demea,

Cleanthes, and Philo; their habits of mind and temperament that precisely constitute their "season[ing]" of piety. How someone is seasoned to view education, morality, and even argument in religious subjects is a window onto his piety. In a dialogue we learn about more than positions; we learn about persons, and persons are more important than positions.

3. Piety is distinct from theology, and they may be separated as well. Persons with different pieties (Demea and Philo) can share a theology, and persons with very similar pieties (Cleanthes and Philo) can diverge on theology. But in the end it is piety that is the more fundamental concern—at least for the characters in Hume's *Dialogues*. Cleanthes and Philo are fundamentally friends in piety at a level and in ways in which Demea and Philo, for example, can never be in harmony, despite their apparent mutual embrace of "mysticism." All this is shown vividly by how the characters interact differently in Parts 1–11 (when Demea is present) and in Part 12 (when he is absent).

4. Part 12 is largely a discussion of "true religion" and its contrary (or contraries). Theology here turns out to be of rather small concern, a matter of merely verbal disagreement between Cleanthes and Philo, but piety is of vital concern to both; the question remaining between the two friends who "live in unreserved intimacy" (12.2.Philo to Cleanthes) is how to characterize and evaluate the kind of natural piety they more or less share.

So while one joins a sizeable company in viewing the "Religion" about which the *Dialogues* are concerned as nothing more than philosophical theology, the present commentary takes a contrary view and commends attention to the parts as well as the Parts of the *Dialogues* that display how piety is also a vital part of religion, and a more important part at that.[11]

Fortunately we need not canvass the overwhelming ambiguity of "*natural.*"[12] Here we will consider only three points, taking our bearings from within the text.

First, Pamphilus from the very outset of his covering letter to Hermippus displays a deep concern for what is natural.[13] He notes first the difficulties of writing dialogues: Using contemporary standards of "accurate and regular argument" quite "naturally throws a man into the methodical and didactic manner," but "to deliver a *System* in conversation scarcely appears natural." On the other hand, while dialogue-writing is "peculiarly adapted" to certain topics, one of which is natural religion, nonetheless to follow completely a "dispute in the natural spirit of good company" sacrifices the virtues of "order, brevity, and precision" (all PH.1–2). So Pamphilus is concerned about what is natural in actual human discourse about certain subjects and about what is natural in writing down such discourse. There is thus a double claim of naturalness in Pamphilus's recital: A certain kind of human conversation is natural to the subject of natural religion, and the natural written form of this kind of conversation is dialogue.[14]

Second, Pamphilus notes not only Hermippus's curiosity about the conversations he heard but also his own curiosity—indeed, he finds such curiosity "natural to the early season of life" (PH.6).[15] Young persons are naturally interested in natural religion and enjoy its discussion, either as participants or observers. This interest is independent of the results of the discussion—the discussion is interesting because the topic is interesting. Even so, a vicarious listener's interest can be enhanced by conveying the discussion in dialogic form: A natural curiosity in natural religion may be stimulated by hearing the kind of human conversation (dialogue) most natural to the topic, whether firsthand (Pamphilus's observation) or secondhand (his dialogue-recital).

Third, at the very end of the *Dialogues,* consider the final paragraph of Philo's famous, or infamous, concluding speech (12.33), where he reduces "the whole of natural theology" to "one simple, though somewhat ambiguous, at least undefined proposition, *that the cause or causes of order in the universe probably bear some remote analogy to human intelligence.*" Philo then remarks that "some contempt of human reason [will naturally arise], that it can give no solution more satisfactory with regard to so extraordinary and magnificent a question." So natural theology is what "human reason" (later, "natural reason") can discern about "God or the gods," and it contrasts with what lies beyond human reason and comes to humans, if at all, only through being divinely given; that is, revealed. In short, natural theology seems to be the opposite of revealed theology, and so to derive its sense.

But Philo goes on to make an important qualification to this distinction:

> The most natural sentiment, which a well disposed mind will feel on this occasion, is a longing desire and expectation, that heaven would be pleased to dissipate, at least alleviate this profound ignorance, by affording some more particular revelation to mankind, and making discoveries of the nature, attributes, and operations of the divine object of our faith.

What a "well disposed mind" wants and hopes for is not revelation per se but "some more particular revelation." The contrast Philo is making between natural theology and something else is not between revelation and reason but between "some more particular revelation" and "some more general revelation." What do "particular" and "general" mean here? They have reference, I believe, not to the scope of what is known (the propositions) but rather to how widely it is known (by a few, many, or all), on what basis (evidence available to some or to all), and by what means (human efforts sufficient or insufficient to obtain it).

Does Philo's additional comment circumvent the revealed versus natural theology dichotomy? I think not, but it does add an interesting interpretative twist. The contrast between more particular and more general revelation makes sense only from a certain standpoint of religious piety, one that views all truth as revealed truth, as truth that comes from and via God. If all truth is God's truth, authored by God—whether this truth is received and known in experiences or thoughts had by a few ("some more particular revelation") or by many ("some more general revelation") or even by all ("thoroughly general revelation")—then *all* knowledge is revealed theological knowledge. In a sense, this is what Cleanthes hopes the argument from design will establish, or at least support: a mind well-disposed to perceive and credit divine authorship in all things. By the same token, this viewpoint seems to be what Philo has strenuously avoided and resisted throughout Parts 1–11. But no one in the *Dialogues* has sought to deny the "Being" of God or gods.[16] So one can hardly escape something like the position Philo expresses: If there is an Author (or Authors) of Nature, then every truth (at least every contingent truth) is an authored truth, and in that sense every truth is a "revealed" truth to anyone who comes to know it, whether the revelation is more general or more particular.

So while from an abstract vantage point, or one external to the *Dialogues,* the term "natural theology" may seem utterly disjoint from "revealed theology," within the context of the *Dialogues* it is better to adopt Philo's terminology: "Revealed theology" is "some more particular revelation," while "natural theology" is some more general revelation, some revelation of truth by the Author of Nature to a more general audience from a more generally available basis via a more generally available means.

To sum up the significance of the title: Hume's *Dialogues concerning Natural Religion* is the "artful" depiction of a number of conversations, variously individuated, about issues of religion by persons who are variously concerned with and about these issues. These issues concern all of natural religion—both piety and theology—and seek what can be known of the Author or Authors of Nature more widely than only by the believers in some more particular revelation.

Prescinding from questions of philosophical topology[17] and historical identification,[18] four aspects of the characters are of primary interest to an internal interpretation: personality, character (both moral and intellectual), relations to one another, and roles in the *Dialogues.*[19] Let us begin with Pamphilus and Hermippus, who play important roles in the *Dialogues* (the report of the conversations), even though they are not quite *in* the dialogues (the conversations reported).

Both are young, and they are friends. *Hermippus* never speaks in his own voice but is said by Pamphilus to be interested in two aspects of the twice-reported conversations: first, the "various systems, which they [Cleanthes, Philo, Demea] advanced with regard to so delicate a subject as that of natural religion," and second, "the remarkable contrast in their characters" (PH.6). Hermippus is intrigued not only by the thoughts but also by the thinkers—is this double curiosity misguided, or is it thoroughly appropriate to the subject matter?

What are we to make of the impressions Hermippus has already formed of the three speaking characters? His abbreviated descriptive tags—"the accurate philosophical turn of Cleanthes," "the careless scepticism of Philo," and "the rigid inflexible orthodoxy of Demea" (PH.6)—give readers of the *Dialogues* their first impressions of these three characters, and many have been so impressed as to consider them Hume's own judgments or, more subtly, Pamphilus's views.[20] At the minimum, we should be on our guard about accepting these memorable characterizations, for they are founded on youthful hearsay, and we will need to check them against what the characters actually do and say.

Pamphilus is no less impressed than Hermippus by the "conversations."[21] Indeed, they have been "deeply imprinted in my memory" (PH.6). But should we suspect this "recital" of Pamphilus? After all, he is young, he is deeply affected by the conversations ("nothing ever made greater impression on me" [12.34.Pamphilus to Hermippus]), and strong impressions are not necessarily accurate ones. Moreover, and crucially, Pamphilus has a certain interest in who "wins" the arguments, for he has very special ties of affection and loyalty to Cleanthes. Cleanthes, we learn from Demea in Part 1, was once the "intimate friend" of Pamphilus's father, and he treats Pamphilus as an "adopted son," taking "great care" in Pamphilus's education (1.1.Demea to Cleanthes). Indeed, Pamphilus customarily spends part of the summer at Cleanthes' country home (PH.6), and he is free to wander about Cleanthes' house and into his library when Cleanthes is conversing with other adults. Moreover, we also learn in Part 1 that the conversations not only are for the intrinsic joys of arguing theoretical questions and participating in lively "company" but also are crucially aimed by each participant in different ways at the education of the youthful Pamphilus. He is an audience of one, but each speaker has him in mind throughout; his education is at least as important to them as the topics they discuss.

For all these reasons, then, we should not expect Pamphilus to be a particularly unbiased observer. Yet Pamphilus obviously expects Hermippus to credit his account as an accurate depiction of the day's entire conversation. Should we follow the "excited" and curious lead of Hermippus and accept the "recital" as though transcribed by a totally accurate recording device, or should we rather regard the whole as a performance by Pamphilus, tinctured with his youthful enthusiasm and filial piety? There are two issues: Does Pamphilus leave anything out, and does he alter anything he puts in? Pamphilus tries to assure Hermippus on both counts: He has "so deeply imprinted in my memory the whole chain and connexion of their arguments, that, I hope, I shall not omit or confound any considerable part of them in the recital" (PH.6). Beyond Pamphilus's own word, we do have the following line of indirect evidence for his veracity: It is hard to see how a mere youth could have concocted so sophisticated a story and so clever a set of arguments and how an admiring adopted son of Cleanthes could have given so many more, and such triumphant, words to Philo, his mentor's intellectual antagonist. If we are to tax Pamphilus for his youth and partiality, we must not then credit him with the extraordinary powers needed to author the details of the conversation he claims he merely reports. Even if we may still suspect him of having comprehensible motives for shading his "recital," the suspicion must remain an empty one, for there is nothing in the text to sustain it.

Cleanthes is the host of the dialogues, father/mentor to Pamphilus, and friend of Demea and Philo.[22] We have just explored his relation to Pamphilus, but what kind of a friend is he to Demea and Philo? He is at least polite to Demea, who correctly comments on Cleanthes' "unwearied perseverance and constancy in all his friendships" (1.1.Demea to Cleanthes)—*all* his friendships, whether deep or shallow. Cleanthes not only desires good form and proper manners but has a conciliating disposition, seeking to smooth over social awkwardness and to avoid conflict. He has a sunny and optimistic personality, perceiving in himself "little or nothing" (10.20.Cleanthes to Philo) of the unhappiness and misery so colorfully and elaborately painted by Demea and Philo as endemic to "all men" (10.16f.Philo to Demea and Cleanthes). He would rather talk separately with Demea and Philo "on a subject, so sublime and interesting" (12.1.Cleanthes to Philo) than risk confrontation and embarrassing disagreement. Cleanthes' friendship with Demea, we infer, is shallow and limited, but his friendship with Philo is of long duration and considerable depth—at least so judges Philo, who says, when they are quit of Demea, that he and Cleanthes "live in unreserved intimacy" (12.2.Philo to Cleanthes), a trusting personal relationship that allows Cleanthes and Philo to speak from the heart when they are by themselves, without the troubling presence of Demea.

As to his views, Cleanthes is enamored of "experimental theism," which seeks to make of theology a science resembling the "natural philosophy" of Copernicus and, especially, Newton, basing its "hypothesis" of "deity" upon evidence open to all and employing common forms of argument. This is the manner in which Cleanthes presents his famous version (or versions, as we shall see) of the so-called design argument for God. In addition, he is a staunch defender of what he regards as "true religion," which encompasses not only theology but also piety. To judge from his specific references,[23] he is knowledgeable not only about contemporary natural philosophy but also about "the ancients" and slightly cosmopolitan to boot (though only in generalities). If one is typecasting, Cleanthes plays the "dogmatist" to Philo's "sceptic" in that the former puts forth a theological argument that the latter pretty thoroughly dismantles. But we should not be blinded by these labels to the deep *agreements* between Cleanthes and Philo: By Part 12, we will see that these good old friends are in considerable (though not complete) harmony not only in theology but also, and more importantly, in piety. To Demea, however, Cleanthes appears not dogmatic at all but scandalously undogmatic—in fact, heterodox and therefore the enemy of Demea's brand of religious authoritarianism. Demea above all wants certainty from philosophy and theology, whereas Cleanthes puts forth his view, in perfect consistency with its profession as empirical "science," only with some degree of probability less than certainty.

Hermippus (working from Pamphilus's earlier brief account) thinks Cleanthes has an "accurate philosophical turn" (PH.6). There is some reason to doubt the accuracy of Cleanthes, and hence the accuracy of this label. Every reader of the *Dialogues* quickly forms the distinct impression that Philo gets the better of (nearly) every argument with Cleanthes and that Cleanthes never expends the effort Philo does in thinking clearly. So if we think of philosophy as argument and clear expression, it is Philo, not Cleanthes, who best fits Hermippus's label. But perhaps Hermippus was referring not to arguments at all but rather to "principles," thinking that Cleanthes' philosophical stance is "accurate" in the sense of being on target regardless of whether his arguments are good ones. In particular, if Hermippus is a fan of teleology, he might think Cleanthes is more accurate in his steadfast loyalty to design arguments, while Philo only comes round to (at least nominal) acceptance of this kind of argument in Part 12 after opposing it with as many "cavils" as he can invent up to that point.

About *Demea*, Hermippus is both right and wrong in thinking of "rigid inflexible orthodoxy" (PH.6.Pamphilus to Hermippus). Demea does indeed possess an authoritarian temperament—he clings tenaciously to what he regards as true religious piety, and his bristling readiness to force others into conformity with his views is almost palpable. But his theological principles, however heartfelt, are suspect from the standpoint of Christian orthodoxy (they smack of "mystical" aberration, as Cleanthes points out, and are morally repugnant as well), and Demea is anything but rigid and inflexible when it comes to theological argumentation. In fact, the ease with which Demea takes up and abandons one form of argument after another indicates that he is not really tied to "reasoning" at all but rather to persuasion (or to coercion, should persuasion prove ineffective). What matters fundamentally to Demea is having a certain cast of character, a kind of piety, that is from one point of view domineering and tyrannical (toward presumed "inferiors"), from another submissive and obeisant (toward perceived "superiors"); the two are different sides of the same coin, jointly enabling hierarchical relationships and institutions.[24]

Cleanthes and Philo treat Demea with civility, as befits the comfortable occasion, but they do not at all agree with his views and are rightly disturbed by his piety, which is an intrusion into their accustomed "intimacy." Philo plays with Demea from the outset,[25] enticing him to think that Philo's skepticism about the limits of human reason is in the service of the same ends and piety as Demea's. (Cleanthes twice tries to warn Demea [1.5; 1.17], but to no avail.) That it takes Demea so long to realize that Philo is more enemy than ally measures another aspect of Demea's character—his enormous obtuseness. Demea is as unperceptive in judging persons and situations as he is bumbling in argument and reasoning. He is taken in by the surface of the social situation, not realizing the deeper significance of what people say or their reasons for saying so. Cleanthes tries to be nice to Demea (as to everyone), but in exchange Demea gives Cleanthes gratuitous ingratiation at the outset and opposition as to an infidel thereafter; in 4.1–3, Demea even projects the labels "common bigots and inquisitors of the age" upon his host.

From the outset, we see Demea as a fawning guest and a shabby thinker. But the more worrisome aspects of his character emerge more gradually: a totalitarian streak, coupled with a deep self-loathing. There are hints in Part 2, but clear evidence awaits Part 10, where Demea gives as his deepest-felt support for "the truth of religion"—that is, for his kind of religious piety—the sense of "melancholy" he has when faced with the "imbecility and misery" of human life (10.1, 3.Demea to Philo). Again Philo appears to agree with Demea against Cleanthes' optimism, but the reasons Philo has for pointing out human misery, as well as the kinds of misery he points out, are worlds apart from Demea. Demea wants to force his piety upon others and to delight in their slavery to his cause, while Philo merely(!) wants to show that we have little reason for thinking God good—no more than for thinking God bad and less than for supposing God indifferent. Demea seeks practical religious conquest, Philo theoretical suspense of judgment.

Philo is the longtime good friend of Cleanthes. They "live in unreserved intimacy," in the sense that they can, when alone together, speak their heartfelt minds to one another without worrying about slanting their views for an audience that does not share such intimacy. We must take this personal relationship very seriously, for it conditions the vastly different "manner" of the conversations in Parts 1–11 (when Demea is present) and in Part 12 (when he is absent). Consequently, we must take with a grain of salt everything said in trio—not that the speakers are lying, but that they may not be saying all that they believe or saying it in the way that they believe it or saying it out of conviction instead of for impression. Philo especially is prone to speaking for (often dazzling) effect, and the skeptical *role* he plays must not be taken as his entire *character.*

Hermippus sees in Philo a "careless scepticism." Now Philo is certainly a skeptic, but how is he "careless"? Clearly the meaning cannot be "not taking due care, not paying due attention to what one does, inattentive, negligent, thoughtless, inaccurate" (*Oxford English Dictionary* [hereafter *OED*], sense 3), for Philo takes considerable pains in argument, and he makes few mistakes.[26] Moreover, the sense of "unconcerned; not caring or troubling oneself; not solicitous, regardless" (*OED,* sense 2) seems equally inapt; Philo does care about natural religion and not just about his own skeptical prowess, even though he occasionally lets his imagination run riot on this subject (see 12.2.Philo to Cleanthes). So if Hermippus is not simply mistaken in his judgment of Philo, how can we understand the appellation of "careless"? Can his meaning possibly be the one (archaic by the mid-seventeenth century) of "free from care, anxiety, or apprehension" (*OED,* sense 1)? If it is, then Hermippus sees Philo as lacking the ordinary cares of propriety, partisanship, and personal stake; he is therefore free to follow the argument wherever it wanders. Whether or not Hermippus intends this meaning (the suggestion invests him with too refined an intelligence), it is one of the few senses in which Philo is "careless."[27]

Philo is a dashing and inventive intellect, full of energy and enthusiasm, though liable to controversy. Occasionally, however, his "sifting, inquisitive disposition" gets the better of his "natural good sense" (3.9.Cleanthes to Philo). In such a mood, he will probe views and propound arguments simply for their intrinsic interest, regardless of whether anyone—even Philo himself —actually holds them. Philo calls this his "affected scepticism," at least as seen by Cleanthes (2.4.Philo to Cleanthes). In Cleanthes' eyes, Philo goes so far on occasion as to belong to "a sect of jesters or railliers" (1.15.Cleanthes to Philo), for he too readily succumbs to the entertaining temptation of twitting unconsidered opinions and defending untenable views. In short, Philo loves inquiry and argument, intellectual fencing, dialectical dancing; and he is very good at it, as well as confident, sometimes preeningly proud, of his skill. As a result, at times it is hard to know whether to take him seriously or whether he takes himself seriously. It is as if Philo seeks to display *himself* in and through displaying his *arguments,* like a peacock flaring his splendid tail.

Yet Philo the free-floating skeptic is also a man, and like every man he has beliefs of his own, not least on the subject of natural religion. When Demea, the occasion and object of so much of Philo's skeptical surgery, retires from the scene at the end of Part 11, Philo is set free to speak his honest mind to Cleanthes. What he then says in Part 12 is more than a little startling: "No-one has a deeper sense of religion impressed on his mind, or pays more profound adoration to the divine Being, as he discovers himself to reason, in the inexplicable contrivance and artifice of nature" (12.2.Philo to Cleanthes). What exactly we are to make of this and similar utterances in Part 12 we will explore later; here I stress only the possible gap between Philo's skepticism and Philo's beliefs. He has the ability to be seriously skeptical, following the under-cutting argument wherever it may lead, while at the same time possessing the very beliefs under scrutiny. This is no paradox, only the necessary fate of a skeptic who "must act . . . and live, and converse like other men" (1.9.Philo to Cleanthes). While Philo the skeptic is "on the offensive," he has "no fixed station or abiding city, which he is ever, on any occasion, obliged to defend" (8.12.Philo to Cleanthes); but when Philo the man feels no need for debate, he is free to confess his unavoidable beliefs—at least to his friend Cleanthes. In understanding Philo, therefore, we must neglect neither his undoubted skepticism nor his residual beliefs.

3

Pamphilus to Hermippus

The book carries us, in a manner, into company, and unites the two greatest and purest pleasures of human life, study and society.

—Pamphilus to Hermippus, ¶4

Structure:
   ¶¶ 1–5: Pamphilus "observes" the special appropriateness of dialogues for natural theology—both for obvious, certain, and important truths and for obscure, uncertain, but interesting questions
   ¶6: Pamphilus sets the scene; Hermippus labels Demea, Cleanthes, Philo

Prior to his twelve-part "recital," Pamphilus delivers a six-paragraph preface or introduction. It is well to attend most carefully to these paragraphs, although few commentators have done so.[1] Ostensibly, Pamphilus takes the occasion to "observe" the appropriateness of dialogue-writing to the topic of natural religion and then to sketch a dramatic context linking together the three conversationalists with Pamphilus and Hermippus. But much more than this is going on. Important distinctions are made, impressions are given, expectations are raised, and we are handed a small but problematic set of interpretative tools whose coherence, utility, and reliability deserve our scrutiny.

Before examining the content of the preface, we need to ask a prior question: Why do we have a preface at all? Presumably the *Dialogues* could have begun with Part 1 neat, and we can even imagine the *Dialogues* scrubbed of narration altogether. Moreover, if some narrator is needed, why introduce Pamphilus, a mere auditor, instead of using one of the three active discussants? It is no answer even for an external interpretation to note that Hume's *Dialogues* shadows the form of Cicero's *De Natura Deorum*, which likewise has a narrator and three typified characters, Velleius the Epicurean, Balbus the Stoic, and Cotta the Academic skeptic, because Hume is no slavish imitator.

Hume departs from Cicero's model in a number of ways, and even when he follows Cicero, it is for his own purposes.[2] Hume's work is therefore "*original* imitation" (Battersby 1976, 240; emphasis added), the product of deliberate choice, Hume's own artful design. So let us see what purposes are evident in the preface.

¶¶1–5: Pamphilus on dialogue-writing

How oddly this discourse of Pamphilus opens—not with an account of why he is making his "recital" to Hermippus or with setting the scene of the reported conversation (these are not mentioned until the last paragraph) but rather with "observations" on the appropriateness of the dialogue "method of composition" to the subject of natural religion. These five paragraphs are in the third person and are as distancing from the dialogues soon to be recited as they can be. They begin in the passive voice—"It has been remarked"— and we are not told who has so remarked. We are being referred by someone we do not yet know (Pamphilus) to someone so obscure he is anonymous. Moreover, these five initial paragraphs seem to be the musings of a dialogue-*writer* about his craft—not at all what we would expect from someone who supposedly heard, not invented, the dialogues he "recites." They sound like the beginning of an essay or a preface to a book, and not at all like the observations one would expect from Pamphilus.[3] What is going on?

Were we seeking an external interpretation, we would naturally try to locate this odd beginning in Hume's biography, in his actual course of writing: Perhaps the thought of Pamphilus didn't occur to Hume until after he had begun composing in his own voice, à la Cicero; or perhaps he first wrote only the sixth paragraph, realized it was too abrupt a beginning to the conversations, and then decided to insert the first five paragraphs. Perhaps. But such speculations can play no part in an internal interpretation. Besides, to read the *Dialogues* in this way is to view the text as not very artful—in fact as rather clumsy, containing a major breakdown in point of view right at the outset. Surely Hume could do better. So let's look again, trying to make sense of the premise that we are listening to the *auditor* of the dialogues (Pamphilus) and not to the *author* of the *Dialogues* (Hume). What could Pamphilus be up to?

One extreme possibility is that the auditor somehow imagines himself to be an author, the creator of the discussions that follow. He is not merely providing, as he says, a "recital" of previous conversations among Cleanthes, Demea, and Philo; he is in fact inventing them. But to suppose this would effectively upend the entire work, turning a youthful auditor needing education in natural religion into the crafty creator of his would-be mentors' words and thoughts. Moreover, we needn't credit Pamphilus with an infallible memory to believe that he is doing his best to faithfully report "the whole chain and connexion of their arguments." There is ample middle ground between completely making up the conversations or recording them verbatim.

Still, even if Pamphilus didn't create the content of the "recital" he makes, he does give us a *recital* of an event; that is, a repetition and a re-presentation, not the event itself. Our young narrator is no more a tape-recorder of Cleanthes, Demea, and Philo than he is a "mouthpiece" of Hume.[4] Pamphilus himself realizes, and he wants Hermippus to see, that the dialogue form is not only an attractive literary form for conveying conversation but also one particularly well suited to the topic at hand. *Not* to give his "recital" in dialogue form would mean a failure to convey what happened as and how it actually happened.

The first point to notice in a more internal interpretation is that Pamphilus is *writing* to Hermippus, not *speaking* to him. So Pamphilus is a "dialogue-writer" willy-nilly, even if he purports not to be the inventor of the dialogues he conveys to Hermippus. Perhaps we might modify his own term for what he is offering (a "recital") and think of him as a *dialogue-reciter,* to emphasize that he purports to report a real dialogue in and through the form of a literary dialogue. Cleanthes, Demea, and Philo are then *dialogue-speakers,* speakers within the dialogues, while Hume, the undeniable *author* of the *Dialogues,* disappears from view behind his literary creations.

Why does Pamphilus use the *dialogue form* for his recital? My suggestion is that Pamphilus offers to Hermippus two things that are tightly connected: (1) a rationale for dialogue writing (or reciting) as the best way to report from memory a particular philosophical dialogue, and (2) a depiction of natural religion as particularly suited to both senses of "dialogue." By instructing Hermippus about his understanding of dialogue-writing, therefore, Pamphilus is also setting forth his understanding of natural religion as explored in dialogue.

There are many ways to report the memory of a witnessed event. One may state the facts and actions in a variety of third-person narrative orders. Or one may sketch the "gist" of someone's expressed views, with or without quotation. But these kinds of report are deficient when it comes to some conversations, because they omit the full texture of the actual event. When attempting to adequately portray a discussion that occurs "in the natural spirit of good company," it is important to allow all speakers to have their say, in their own words and voices, for each person has something distinctive to add. An adequate report of such conversations must state each speaker's views just as the speaker himself delivered them and must indicate the tone and manner of speech as well as the temperament and character of the speakers and their personal interactions and relationships. In short, a remembered lively conversation comes to life only when its "recital" is another conversation.[5]

When the remembered event is not just any lively conversation but one that concerns the subject of natural religion, there is even greater need for dialogue-writing. Here the literary form of dialogue is more than just a "natural" way of reporting a conversation but turns out to be essential to capturing a conversation about *this* subject—"dialogue-writing is peculiarly adapted" to the subject of natural religion, says Pamphilus (PH.2)—so, conversely, natural religion is peculiarly suited to portrayal in dialogues.

In making the link between dialogue-writing and natural religion, Pamphilus provides some potentially useful, though also problematic, interpretative tools. He opens with a double contrast between "the ancient philosophers" who "conveyed most of their instruction in the form of dialogue" and those "philosophical enquirers" "in later ages" who "naturally" practice in "the methodical and didactic manner." Modern philosophers are expected to produce "accurate and regular argument," to explain intended points and "thence proceed, without interruption, to deduce the proofs on which it is established." Such writing has the virtues of "order, brevity, and precision." But "to deliver a *System* in conversation scarcely appears natural." Moreover, there are problems with dialogue-writing: It is little practiced because almost no one has been able to do it well. It tends to become either tediously didactic, conveying "the image of pedagogue and pupil," or else diffusely conversational, with too wide a variety of topics, too great a balance among speakers, and too much time lost "in preparations and transitions" (PH.1). Yet despite its perils, dialogue-writing still has its place, for there are some "subjects" to which it is "peculiarly adapted" (PH.2). One of those subjects, thinks Pamphilus, is natural religion.

Dialogues are "still preferable to the direct and simple method of composition" where either or both of the following conditions hold: (1) The work presents "any point of doctrine" that is obvious, certain, and important yet requires repeated inculcation; here dialogue-writing may block tedium by placing the point in a "variety of lights," for example, by having different characters "enforce the precepts" in different ways (PH.3). (2) The work presents a "question of philosophy" that is obscure, uncertain, and yet "curious and interesting"; here dialogue-writing allows different speakers to hold different views, and "opposite sentiments, even without any decision, afford an agreeable amusement"—indeed more than amusement, for "the book carries us, in a manner, into company, and unites the two greatest and purest pleasures of human life, study and society" (PH.4).

"Happily," continues Pamphilus, "these circumstances are all to be found

in the subject of NATURAL RELIGION." The "truth" of "the Being of a
God" is obvious, certain, and important, while questions "concerning the *nature* of that divine being" are obscure and uncertain yet still endlessly interesting (PH.5). Dialogues are "peculiarly adapted" to inculcating the first and
to displaying the second.[6]

Let us take note of how many substantive commitments Pamphilus has
made in the course of explaining to Hermippus why his "recital" is appropriately cast in dialogue form:

1. Natural religion (or rather natural theology)[7] has two parts, "the
Being of a God" and "the nature of that divine being." (PH.5)
2. The former part is an obvious, certain, and important truth that
bears repeated inculcation because it "ought never to be a moment absent
from our thoughts and meditations." (PH.5)
3. The Being of a God is important because it is "the ground of all
our hopes, the surest foundation of morality, the firmest support of society." (PH.5)
4. The nature of God is obscure and uncertain to human reason,
which has reached, and can reach, no "certain determination" about such
interesting topics. (PH.5)
5. On such topics, "Reasonable men may be allowed to differ, where
no-one can reasonably be positive." (PH.4)
6. The "company" that discussion of such topics produces—either
firsthand in the reported conversation, secondhand in Pamphilus's absorbed observation, third-hand in Hermippus, or fourth-hand in the
reading of Pamphilus's report to Hermippus—is a great and unalloyed
good, for it "unites the two greatest and purest pleasures of human life,
study and society." (PH.4)

What a remarkable list! As we shall see, not all of these commitments are
shared by all the participants in the reported conversation. Cleanthes and
Philo agree on more of them than either shares with Demea; in particular,
they share the values ingredient in number 6: Both enjoy each other's conversational inquiry and companionship.

We see, therefore, that Pamphilus's first five paragraphs about dialogue-
writing alert not only Hermippus but also the careful reader to the intimate relation of the literary form to the content of Pamphilus's "recital" and
thereby tie together several senses of "dialogue" (literary form, conversation,
and readers' and author's relations to the text). They also contain a rather
extensive view of natural religion (as natural theology). But Pamphilus's point

of view is not privileged; even if his vivid memories are more or less accurate, that does not mean that his judgments are correct.

Let us note one last arresting hint in the very first paragraph: "To deliver a *System* in conversation scarcely appears natural," says Pamphilus, implying that what does appear natural in conversation is not a system. This ties in, of course, with the view of dialogues as appropriate to "restless enquiry" into obscure but interesting questions. But more, a good dialogue-writer should craft a represented conversation so that it "appears natural," containing neither awkwardness nor artificiality. So the design of a dialogue-reciter or author should not seem like artifice! We will see whether this hint can be applied to the natural theological "design" arguments that follow.

¶6: Pamphilus sets the scene

Pamphilus's last paragraph sets the scene not only for the conversations he goes on to recite but also for the meta-context of his recital to Hermippus. Four points deserve notice:

1. Pamphilus has heard the conversations while spending "as usual, part of the summer season with Cleanthes" (6). Perhaps the residence in which the dialogues occur is a "summer place" for Cleanthes as well as for Pamphilus; perhaps it is Cleanthes' country estate, an old family possession. Cleanthes is clearly a gentleman of leisure with the time and inclination to pursue philosophical study and conversation. Understanding Cleanthes' relationship to the youthful Pamphilus is vital for understanding how Pamphilus views the conversations he recites. Pamphilus is the son of an "intimate friend" of Cleanthes, now deceased, and Cleanthes has taken him on as not only a "pupil": He "may indeed be regarded as your adopted son" (1.1.Demea to Cleanthes). Of course, these words are Demea's, and Demea is a sycophant, so one is tempted to discount this opening patter as insincere flattery of a host. But I think there is more to it than that. Pamphilus *is* genuinely partial to Cleanthes, not primarily from theological agreement but rather from a habit of loyalty and goodwill to his mentor, host, and adoptive father.

Pamphilus does have an undeniable affection for Cleanthes. This is most evident in his famous concluding judgment (Cleanthes' principles are most probable; 12.34.Pamphilus to Hermippus), but it is also evident in his rare comments on actions and persons in the midst of his recital of the dialogues,[8] which seem to be slightly anxious attempts to show Cleanthes in a better light. In addition, he is at least partially responsible for the character judgments Hermippus makes (most favorable to Cleanthes, less so to Philo, least of all to Demea [PH.6]). Because of Pamphilus's bias, then, we do well to suspect his judgments about the dialogues' arguments even if we do not doubt the accuracy of his "recital" of those arguments. We are therefore entitled to disagree with Pamphilus as to whose principles "approach still nearer to the truth" (12.34.Pamphilus to Hermippus).

2. Pamphilus had given Hermippus "lately some imperfect account" of these conversations, which had three important effects on Hermippus: The account aroused his desire for "more exact detail," it "raised [his] expectations" for satisfying his "curiosity," and it generated an initial impression about the characters of Cleanthes, Philo, and Demea. Why does Pamphilus give these reactions *of Hermippus* as the moving cause of his dialogue recital? Does he not have his own compelling reactions?

Once again, it does not help much to note that using the excited curiosity of one not present to the conversation as a means of motivating a full and accurate account is a time-honored device.[9] Better to see an internal reason. An obvious one is that it would be odd for Pamphilus to unload such a fulsome account on his friend right at first telling; Hermippus's appetite needs to be whetted first by "some imperfect [i.e., incomplete] account." Next, Pamphilus reveals something of his own character in mentioning these effects: He is sympathetic to his friend's sentiments and seeks to extend to him the pleasures he has experienced firsthand. Third, Pamphilus does, I believe, share Hermippus's reactions; he has, after all, the very same "curiosity natural to the early season of life," and he wishes to share what is "so deeply imprinted" in his memory. By sharing with a like-minded friend, he enjoys those "two greatest and purest pleasures of human life, study and society" (PH.4). Fourth, we may speculate, Pamphilus does not think that he and Hermippus are atypical in their reactions; others will naturally share their curiosity and gain similar pleasure through access to the dialogue recital Pamphilus gives—it is, after all, a *written* dialogue he sends along with his preface to Hermippus, and a conversation once written may be enjoyed by many others.

3. While Pamphilus was "a mere auditor of their dispute," the "arguments" he heard were "so deeply imprinted in my memory" that he hopes to give a full and accurate "recital" to Hermippus. Just as Hermippus excitedly seeks instruction from Pamphilus's recital, so Pamphilus himself eagerly sought instruction from the conversation he later recites. Moreover, all three discussants clearly view Pamphilus as something of a pedagogical project. All speak with him in mind throughout (even though they mention him only three times [1.1.Demea; 2.10.Demea; 12.33.Philo]), and all speak at least implicitly for his benefit as they see it, all the while ostensibly talking to one another. Demea's concern for Pamphilus's education is expressed at the very beginning (1.1–2) and Philo's at the very end (12.33, last sentence), while Cleanthes' instructional care is not only commented upon by Demea and Philo but is also central to the narrative we read: It is only because of Pamphilus's

strong ties to Cleanthes that Pamphilus is writing his "recital" to Hermippus. In fact, the youthful Pamphilus's unobtrusive presence in the dialogues he reports is as important as his presence in the recital he gives of them. Hence we need to notice not merely how Pamphilus shapes his recital of the conversation but also how the conversation recited is shaped to him. We must weigh how, and how much, various remarks are trimmed for his benefit.

4. Although he does note Hermippus's interest in "character" as well as in "reasonings" and "systems," Pamphilus thinks of the "conversations" as "arguments." Having just mentioned in PH.5 "our restless enquiry" about natural theology, Pamphilus goes on in PH.6 to speak of something more combative and confrontational. He will give "a more exact detail of their *reasonings*"; he will display the "*systems*" they "*advanced*"; he was "a mere auditor of their *disputes*"; he remembers "the whole chain and connexion of their *arguments*" (all PH.6; emphases added). This shift from "restless enquiry" to "disputes" deserves explanation.

There certainly *is* a lot of dispute in the *Dialogues*—not only the opposing views and arguments, but also the critical examination (chiefly by Philo) of almost any position held by anyone. But there is more to the *Dialogues* than disputation. There are also revelations of character; gestures toward phenomena; rhetorical appeals to interest, desire, and authority; and much more. Nor are these other elements mere literary "frills" on an argumentative dress. So why doesn't Pamphilus notice anything except argument in referring to his own recital? His inattentiveness here, I believe, reveals the limitations of Pamphilus. Pamphilus, after all, is a young man, and youth—at least male youth—is not always keen on nuance, subtlety, and indirection; it is rather more attracted to conflict and disagreement, bold and colorful strokes, winners and losers. The non-argumentative parts and aspects of the *Dialogues* escape Pamphilus's notice, then, because he is immaturely fixated on "disputes." For that reason, while Pamphilus is arguably a reliable courier of the content of the conversation he recites, he is not necessarily a completely trustworthy guide to (all of) their meaning and importance.[10]

4

Part 1

To season their minds with early piety is my chief care; and by continual precept and instruction, and I hope too, by example, I imprint deeply on their tender minds an habitual reverence for all the principles of religion.

—Demea to Philo, Part 1.2

Structure:

¶¶1–2: Demea displays his piety and introduces the basic themes: education, friendship, natural religion, reason, and "common life"
¶¶3–4: The drama begins
> *¶3: Philo constricts "this frail faculty of reason"*
> *¶4: Demea and Cleanthes react quite differently*
¶¶5–16: The varieties of skepticism
> *¶¶5–7: Cleanthes inveighs against "total scepticism"*
> *¶¶8–11: Philo reinforces the limits of reason and touts the salutary effects of skepticism*
> *¶¶12–16: Cleanthes observes the difficulties of skepticism (in various forms)*
¶¶17–20: Philo and Cleanthes view the history of faith and reason quite differently: "strong symptoms of priestcraft" versus "confirmation of true religion"

Part 1 is a well-contrived introduction to the following eleven Parts, and we must not rush through it in our haste to enjoy the natural theological arguments that follow. Although Part 1 is primarily a discussion of the competency of human reason to explore, much less to settle, the great issues of natural theology, it is much more than that. It also introduces most artfully other primary topics of the *Dialogues,* sets the dramatic terms, puts the plot in motion, and foreshadows a fundamental topic of underlying concern to Cleanthes and Philo: how theology and piety, and what kind of theology and piety, fit together in "true religion."

¶¶1–2: Opening themes

Demea opens the conversation after Pamphilus joins "the company,"[1] and he is given, or rather takes, surprising liberty to introduce the primary topics, if not quite the exact issues, of the ensuing dialogues. He also has occasion to introduce himself. A reader may be discomfited, even alarmed, by what Demea divulges of himself but also intrigued by the topics he broaches.

Demea's first comments are "some compliments" to his host Cleanthes and go beyond polite flattery to obsequiousness, remarking on Cleanthes' "great care" in Pamphilus's education and "his unwearied perseverance and constancy in all his friendships" (1.1.Demea to Cleanthes). Quite plainly Demea is seeking to ingratiate himself with Cleanthes and hence with Pamphilus, and this effort implies that his friendship with both of them is questionable from the outset. Demea is no stranger to Cleanthes, for he knows Cleanthes' relationship to Pamphilus, but his statement of what he knows is gratuitous; such facts do not need mentioning among close friends. Demea is *seeking* Cleanthes' friendship in *commending* it. Moreover, while Cleanthes and Philo later signal their deep and lasting friendship with each other, neither has a friendly word for Demea. What "friendship" the two friends do have with Demea is a matter more of politeness and civility than of loyalty and trust; there is no fundamental affinity, despite Demea's misapprehension to the contrary. (Demea's congenital misperception is part of why Cleanthes and Philo cannot trust him.)

Understanding the relationships among Demea, Philo, and Cleanthes is of utmost importance in understanding their subsequent dialogues. As in life, so in dialogue-writing: Different personal relationships ground quite different discussions. Thus, when Demea is present, the conversations have a constant edge of display and competition—competition for the better argument and more impressive view, to be sure, but also competition for friendship with one another and especially for the attention and allegiance of Pamphilus.[2] Moreover, there is an air of affectation and posturing, even one of "raillery or artificial malice" (1.4.Pamphilus to Hermippus). When Demea leaves, however, at the end of Part 11, the tone and tenor of the discussion alter radically, for only then can Philo and Cleanthes divulge their "unfeigned sentiments" (12.9.Philo to Cleanthes); without the distorting presence of Demea, intimate friends can at last speak openly and genuinely to each other with no need to win over an audience. Along with this transition to greater genuineness in the discourse goes a shift in subject matter: The ostensible topic of Parts 2–11 is natural theology, while that of Part 12 is "true religion," or piety and theology *together,* in relation to life in community with intimate friends.[3]

To be sure, the arguments put forth while Demea is present stand on their own; they are powerful pieces of reasoning, and their speakers intend them to have some impact on their audiences. But we should not ignore the important dramatic fact that Demea's presence distorts the discussion. When he is on hand, things are not necessarily what they seem and are declared to be by anyone. Demea's pretense, posturing, and hypocrisy infect the discourse of others, so that no one can quite say what is on his mind, or say it all, or say it directly. While Demea is present, there is an inevitable air of semblance in the argumentation—not so much a lack of seriousness as a sense that deeper concerns are being carefully avoided.

Let us return to Demea's opening speech. His attempted ingratiation with his host leads him to speak of Pamphilus and the careful education Cleanthes has bestowed on his "adopted son" (1.1.Demea to Cleanthes). But Demea does not limit himself to flattery; he cannot resist offering advice, in the guise of describing how he educates "my own children":[4] In philosophy, one should first learn logic, then ethics, then physics, then the "science of natural theology"; this last is the "most profound and abstruse of any" and requires mature judgment and prior knowledge (1.1.Demea to Cleanthes). Demea not only misdescribes this order of topics as a "method,"[5] he also has the effrontery to question his host Cleanthes about whether Pamphilus is mature enough to be permitted to hear the conversations that are to follow. Since Cleanthes has given Pamphilus free run of his house and conversations, we may presume that he regards such conversation as a useful part of the youth's education. The implications of Demea's remarks, then, are that Cleanthes is irresponsible in his education of Pamphilus, that Pamphilus either has received the wrong piety or not enough proper piety, and hence that Pamphilus is not yet ready for discussions on natural theology. So Demea has moved from overt compliment to veiled reprimand of his host.[6]

Perceiving Demea's bad manners, Philo quickly and sarcastically prods him, not for the last time: Isn't there a danger in waiting too long to teach children "the principles of religion," for fear that they will reject "those opinions of which they have heard so little" in their formative years?[7] Demea hastily corrects (or clarifies) himself and introduces an important distinction: Only natural theology as a "science" is to be postponed in children's education, while "to season their minds with early piety is my chief care" (1.2.Demea to Philo). Theology and piety are the two parts, or aspects, of religion, and formation in piety should precede "human reasoning and disputation" about religious subjects. This seems a useful distinction, useful not only in the conversations but also for interpreting them.[8] But Demea goes beyond the bare distinction to give us a glimpse of his own alarming views of natural theology and piety.

The "seasoning" Demea wants to "imprint deeply on their tender minds" is "an habitual reverence for *all* the principles of religion"; he wants to "[*tame*] their mind [*sic*] to a proper *submission* and *self-diffidence*" (1.2.Demea to Philo; emphases added). A properly "seasoned" mind for Demea is a submissive, obedient, and pliable mind, one totally subservient to the dictates of authority, willing to believe and to do whatever one is told by a superior. Natural theology is but a prop of this piety, and it should always be mindful of its secondary role, else under the name of "philosophy" it should tend to "arrogance." To that end, Demea finds it useful to inculcate a sense of the weakness of human capacity to think and reason, not only in the secular sciences but especially concerning the "mysteries of religion." That is why he points out the uncertainty, disputation, obscurity, and strange and ridiculous conclusions of "mere human reason" in other subjects—so that a tender mind will not worry about these features when he discovers them in theology. Demea's religious piety is authoritarian to the core, and his view of theology and all human reason is severely constricted by and in the service of that piety. Piety provides for him the certainty theology cannot. We have then, in Demea, not a reasoned but a pious view of piety and theology. Moreover, his piety seeks to insinuate itself in others through whatever effective means are available—by "continual precept and instruction" but also by "example." Demea is indeed an excellent example of the piety he professes, but Philo and Cleanthes both reject the oppressive kind of communal life it implies.

We have, then, in the opening discourse of Demea, a concise introduction to the major themes of the entire *Dialogues*: education, friendship, natural religion (including both theology and piety), human reason, and common life. Of these, natural theology will occupy the foreground of the next ten Parts; the scope and reach of human reason are treated in the remainder of Part 1, while the other themes remain in the background, only to step forward again in Part 12.

¶¶3–4: The drama begins

Philo's response to Demea's opening discourse does not dispute the need for early piety but instead focuses on how Demea blocks the "arrogance" of "mere human reason" as part of his program of "early seasoning" in piety (1.2.Demea to Philo). "Philosophy and learning," Philo says, inspire the "pride and self-sufficiency" that "have commonly, in all ages, been found so destructive to the principles of religion." The vulgar are ignorant of science and, observing secondhand the "endless disputes of the learned," develop "a thorough contempt for philosophy"; they thereby "rivet" themselves to the theology imprinted in them. Some know more science, but not enough— a little learning is a dangerous thing, for it presumes that human reason can adequately handle any subject, including "the inmost sanctuaries of the temple." Although ignorance is "the surest remedy" for the "profane liberty" of overconfident philosophy, Philo also recommends an extension of Demea's skepticism about human faculties: "Let us become thoroughly sensible of the weakness, blindness, and narrow limits of human reason . . . even in subjects of common life and practice." There are "insuperable difficulties" in the "first principles in all systems" and "contradictions" in the "object" of science. In short, even when working on materials of "common life and experience" reason is feeble and defective; why then trust "this frail faculty" when confronting such grand subjects as "the origin of worlds"? (all 1.3.Philo to Demea)

How are we to understand Philo's speech? Is it, as it appears to be, literal and facile agreement with Demea, is it sheer irony and mocking disdain, or is it something in between? Note how Demea and Cleanthes perceive it. Both of them *smile* during the speech, but their smiles are worlds apart: Demea's smile "seemed to imply an unreserved satisfaction in the doctrines delivered," while Cleanthes' smile had "an air of finesse; as if he perceived some raillery or artificial malice in the reasonings of Philo" (1.4.Pamphilus to Hermippus). Of course, these are only the observations of young Pamphilus, yet there is no doubt that he is right in light of the ensuing conversations. Demea thinks that Philo is an ally, a fellow skeptic and a co-religionist, while Cleanthes sees in the same words lighthearted teasing or darker sarcasm. Demea thinks that skepticism about "this frail faculty of reason" will support and lead to religion—to *Demea's* religion, submissive in piety and supposedly orthodox in theology—while Cleanthes thinks that Philo is baiting Demea and disguising his own actual "principles" behind an all-corroding skepticism. Given Cleanthes' long association with Philo, we should expect his perception to prove more accurate, and so it does over Parts 2–11. Philo's dim view of the "narrow limits of human reason" (1.3.Philo to Cleanthes) fits not with Demea's authoritarian religion but with the "attenuated deism" (Gaskin 1988, 7) and tolerant piety he shares with Cleanthes. Cleanthes sees this from the outset, Demea not until the end—if then.

At any rate, the different reactions of Demea and Cleanthes do mark important underlying tensions in the ensuing conversation and set the plot in motion. The tension is superficially different reactions to the skeptical use of reason in natural theology, but more deeply it is a tension between different pieties. The primary plot-line winds through various natural theological arguments to a skeptical "triumph" (10.36.Philo to Cleanthes; see also 8.12.Philo to Cleanthes), with a sub-plot involving Demea's dawning dim recognition of Philo's intent and what is at stake in a skeptical approach to religion.

There is even more to learn from the different smiles of Demea and Cleanthes. Demea's smile is smug and clueless while Cleanthes' is subtle and knowing. Demea thinks that anyone who says that Demea's "doctrines" should be "improved and cultivated," as Philo has just proposed to do, must be on his side. Philo seems to him to have the right approach to natural theology because he proclaims the narrow limits of human reason; therefore, thinks Demea, Philo's theology, and hence his piety, must be as orthodox as Demea's. But Cleanthes knows better because he knows Philo better; he knows that Philo's true piety (not to mention his own!) cannot live together with Demea's authoritarian cast of mind. He also knows that any theological disagreements between Philo and himself cannot cloud the "unreserved intimacy" of their friendship.

Cleanthes will now and again try to get Demea to see the true tendency of Philo's skepticism about religion but to little avail until the end of Part 11, and even then it is doubtful that Demea learns from this disclosure the lesson he should—the effect is not to create doubt in Demea about his piety but rather to give him "little inclination to revive this topic of discourse, while you [Philo] are in company" (12.1.Cleanthes to Philo). Demea can participate in the dialogues even while all theological supports are knocked from under him only because he is deluded into believing that Philo is an ally. Cleanthes, on the other hand, can tolerate the "strange lengths" to which Philo goes in his "spirit of controversy" (both 12.1.Cleanthes to Philo), knowing full well what Philo's true religious principles are and knowing that they are not so very distant from his own. Their abiding friendship undergirds their theological disagreement, while Demea's dangerous piety eventually disrupts even the apparent theological alliance Philo dangles before him in Part 1.

¶¶5–16: The varieties of skepticism

Cleanthes and Philo now conduct a small dialogue of their own (Demea is addressed but has nothing useful to say) on the topic of skepticism. This conversation occupies the bulk of Part 1 and consists of three speeches, two by Cleanthes (1.5–7, 1.12–16) sandwiching one by Philo (1.8–11); it is animated more by different rhetorical flourishes than by antagonistic views. To a large extent, they simply talk past each other, and their apparent dispute is only an artful instance of something Pamphilus noted in the preface: A dialogue can "inculcate" an obvious and important "point of doctrine" by the "vivacity of conversation" and the "variety of lights" added by different personages (PH.3). Cleanthes hammers away at the theoretical and practical difficulties of "total scepticism," a label he tries to pin on Philo. Philo declines the offer and instead touts the salutary effects on common life of a more limited and moderated skepticism while still exuding suspicion about subjects that go beyond "the senses and experience" (1.11.Philo to Cleanthes). In all this, there is much semblance of dispute but little real disagreement. Both agree that responsible skepticism must be piecemeal and proportioned to the evidence, as it is in science, and that however fares the inquiry into natural theology, the overarching question that concerns them is the quality of mind produced by skeptical thinking: Is a skeptic a mere "jester or raillier," as Cleanthes worries, or someone more sensible and humble—"like other men" —as Philo urges?

Cleanthes goes first with a ringing attack on "philosophical scepticism," construed in the direst terms. His first point is ad hominem: Philo's own skepticism cannot be "as absolute and sincere as you pretend," or else he would experience grave practical consequences upon leaving the company; even Philo has good reason to exit via the door instead of the window, despite his skeptical doubts[9] about gravity and other facts "derived from our fallacious senses and more fallacious experience" (1.5.Cleanthes to Philo).

Cleanthes then nods (and winks?) to Demea, trying to enlist him in thinking ill of skeptics. Skeptics are not dangerous, no more than an unintentionally "humorous sect," for if they are in earnest, they will meet a bad end at the hands of a recalcitrant nature; while if "only in jest, they are, perhaps, bad railliers" and no threat politically, philosophically, or religiously (1.5.Cleanthes to Demea). Why does Cleanthes so mistake Demea's recently stated positive attitude toward skepticism? To begin with, he is trying to warn Demea, knowing full well how destructive to Demea's principles Philo's skepticism will prove to be, even if Demea does not yet realize it. Perhaps also, Cleanthes' own position on faith and reason simply cannot comprehend why faith would not seek, or at least accept, the aid of reason where it can be found. Skepticism threatens, not supports, religion. Finally, Cleanthes may realize that Demea is an inconsistent skeptic, or rather not really a skeptic at all. Later we shall find Demea offering a variety of decidedly non-skeptical arguments for his views (arguments from authority in Part 2, name-calling in Part 4, and *a priori* reasoning in Part 9). It turns out that what Demea really wants is to be, or at least to feel, certain about his own views, and he will embrace (for the moment) any approach that allows him to remain cloaked in self-assurance. Perhaps Cleanthes knows Demea's temperament, anticipates how Philo's skepticism is incompatible with Demea's certitude, and politely seeks to help Demea realize this sooner rather than later. But to no avail.

Turning back to Philo, Cleanthes continues his attack. Although someone may "entirely renounce all belief and opinion" for a while, no one can "persevere in this total scepticism," for "external objects press in upon him: Passions solicit him." Total skepticism is a "violence upon his own temper," and an unnecessary violence at that. Such doubt undermines itself, particularly when extended to common life (1.6.Cleanthes to Philo). Moreover, ancient Pyrrhonians (skeptics) resemble Stoics (dogmatists), for both hold to "this erroneous maxim, that what a man can perform sometimes, and in some dispositions, he can perform always, and in every disposition." Stoics can indeed on occasion elevate themselves "into a sublime enthusiasm of virtue" so as "even to smile and exult in the midst of tortures," but they cannot sustain this enthusiasm, for "the bent of his mind relaxes . . . and the *philosopher* sinks by degrees into the *plebeian*" (1.7.Cleanthes to Philo). By implication, Skeptics are only occasional enthusiasts for skepticism.

It seems Cleanthes has mustered an impressive attack on "total" or "absolute" skepticism as an "enthusiasm" that is theoretically insupportable and practically unfeasible, being defeated by Nature without ("External objects press in upon him") and Nature within ("Passions solicit him"). But all the while, Cleanthes has been thumping a straw man. Philo claims that his own skepticism is not of this totalizing kind. He grants Cleanthes' "comparison" of Stoics and Skeptics, and by implication also grants Cleanthes' criticism that their attitudes cannot continuously constrain a mind's natural bent. Nonetheless, Philo avers, just as a Stoic's occasional "flights of philosophy" create a "disposition" that has a benign influence on "conduct in common life," affecting "the whole tenor of his actions," so also a habit of "sceptical considerations on the uncertainty and narrow limits of reason" will carry over into "reflection on other subjects," affecting at least one's "philosophical principles and reasoning" if not also one's "common conduct." In short, a skeptically seasoned mind differs importantly from an unseasoned mind, whether it be ignorant and misologistic or excessively enthusiastic over the power of reason (1.8.Philo to Cleanthes). Skepticism may not be total or absolute, but it can be pervasive, persistent, and effective.

Philo grants (in his own voice!) that skeptics "must act, I own, and live, and converse like other men," for no other "reason" than "the absolute necessity" of doing so. He does, however, register his appreciation for the pleasures of philosophical speculation, which he thinks is only an extension of a natural human tendency to form ever "more general principles of conduct and reasoning": "What we call Philosophy is nothing but a more regular and methodical operation of the same kind. To philosophize on such subjects is nothing essentially different from reasoning on common life" (1.9.Philo to Cleanthes).[10]

Having bowed to philosophical speculation, Philo next shores up his earlier (1.3) claim about its narrow limits.[11] When we go beyond "human affairs and the properties of the surrounding bodies" and speculate about "the two eternities," the creation of the universe, spirits, and particularly the "one universal spirit," in this distant realm we are "quite beyond the reach of our faculties." In "trade or morals or politics or criticism" we can appeal to "common sense and experience" to strengthen the principles supported by "subtle or refined" philosophical thinking; but theology's objects "are too large for our grasp." In theology, "We are like foreigners in a strange country, to whom every thing must seem suspicious"; we can no longer trust even in the "kind of instinct or necessity" that guides us in the "province" of common life (1.10.Philo to Cleanthes). Beyond our reach, too large for our grasp, a strange country—so remote is theology from ordinary inquiry!

While skeptics "pretend" that they have "invincible arguments" against reason "in an abstract view," nevertheless Philo admits that these "refined and subtle" skeptical arguments "are not able to counterpoise the more solid and more natural arguments, derived from the senses and experience." Philo here concurs with Cleanthes that common life prevails against total skepticism, even if common life cannot give satisfactory theoretical answers to skeptical questions. But when we "run wide of common life," then our positive reasonings are "on a footing with" skeptical doubts, which "oppose and counterbalance them," leading to a "suspense or balance." This suspense, Philo claims, is "the triumph of scepticism" (1.11.Philo to Cleanthes).

Philo will twice later (8.12 and 10.36) proclaim a skeptical "triumph," so we should be clear on how he defines victory. Skepticism triumphs when it can achieve a balance of arguments or reasons that leads—or at any rate would lead a rational person—to a suspense of judgment or belief. Where p labels some positive view, then skepticism triumphs not in showing, or even being able to show, that p is false, or in getting someone to believe that p is false. Rather, skepticism wins by persuading a person to believe that there is no better reason for believing p than for disbelieving p—that there are equally good (or bad) reasons for and against p. Achieving such a theoretical "suspense or balance" of evidence does not entail that no one believes (or disbelieves) p, for there may be other supports or causes for beliefs than "reasonings." Skepticism's triumph merely means that anyone who holds a counterbalanced view cannot claim evidence or reasons for his belief. Nonetheless, skepticism also seasons the mind to epistemic humility and so tends to undermine certitude in all areas,[12] particularly when one ventures "quite beyond the reach of our faculties." It is possible to go on believing in such an evidential vacuum, with any degree of confidence, but there is simply no good reason to do so.

In apparent reply to Philo, Cleanthes now launches into his second longest speech in the entire *Dialogues*,[13] pointing out some difficulties of particular or partial (versus total) skepticism. Philo and "all speculative sceptics" are theoretically as well as practically inconsistent. Philo adheres as closely to evidence as does any dogmatist, and it would be "ridiculous" for him to remain skeptical about a subject where there is evidence supporting a good theory: Witness "Newton's explication of the wonderful phenomenon of the rainbow" and Copernicus and Galileo on "the motion of the earth." A general skepticism casting doubt on such scientific achievements because of their abstruse subject matter and startling claims would be "brutish and ignorant," an enemy not simply of theology but of knowledge itself. In the night of "brutish" skepticism, witches are as credible as Euclid (all 1.12.Cleanthes to Philo).

Of course, Cleanthes' comments do not touch Philo, whose skepticism is neither brutish nor ignorant. Why then does Cleanthes even bother with a broadside that seems so badly off the mark? Perhaps he thinks that "scepticism" is a single "sect" instead of a loose confederation of postures and arguments. More likely he perceives a tendency in Philo to allow his skeptical bent of mind to run wild; perhaps he has other experience of Philo's skeptical flame torching an entire conversation, consuming even Philo's own cherished beliefs.[14]

But "the refined and philosophical sceptics," Cleanthes continues, are also inconsistent; as they pursue their researches and proportion their assent to the available evidence, they paradoxically discover that there is better evidence for some of "the most abstruse corners of science" (for example, theories concerning light and the solar system) than for such familiar and undoubted realities as the nourishment of food and the cohesion of matter. The point is not that one should not doubt at all but rather that one should not doubt "on the general presumption of insufficiency of human reason, without any particular discussion of the evidence" (1.13.Cleanthes to Philo). Reasonable doubt requires particular reasons for doubt and should be proportioned to those reasons. Hence there should be no blanket suspicion of natural theology or religion; any suspicions should be particular ones, subsequent to and substantiated by particular evidence.

Moreover, adds Cleanthes, while he himself lacks the "capacity" and "leisure" to refute the skeptic's general claims that our ideas "even of the most familiar objects" are "full of absurdities and contradictions," he also thinks it "superfluous" to provide such a refutation, since skepticism is practically self-refuting: "Your own conduct, in every circumstance, refutes your principles; and shows the firmest reliance on all the received maxims of science, morals, prudence, and behaviour" (1.14.Cleanthes to Philo). The sect of skeptics is so inconstant, forever unable to keep words, deeds, and life together, that they seem a comical bunch, and Cleanthes cannot resist a wry but cautious jibe[15]

—skeptics are not so much "a sect of liars" (Arnauld's opinion in *L'Art de Penser*) as they are "a sect of jesters or railliers" whose dialectical forays into "metaphysical subtleties and abstractions" are a poor "amusement" and "entertainment." For his part, Cleanthes would rather read "a comedy, a novel, or at most a history" (1.15.Cleanthes to Philo).

Finally, a skeptic cannot drive a wedge between "science and common life or between one science and another," for the arguments in all "are of a similar nature, and contain the same force and evidence." So argument in natural theology is (in principle) no worse off than reasoning in natural science or common life. In fact, "theology and natural religion"[16] are in some ways better off than science. Science, such as the Copernican system, "contains the most surprising paradox, and the most contrary to our natural conceptions, to appearances, and to our very senses." But on the other hand, "the religious hypothesis" "is founded on the simplest and most obvious arguments, and, unless it meet with artificial obstacles, has such easy access and admission into the mind of man" (1.16.Cleanthes to Philo).[17]

Cleanthes and Philo only apparently disagree. In fact, their views are thoroughly compatible—the two old friends are simply emphasizing different points as though they were disagreeing over something important and substantive. Both reject total skepticism, both approve of partial skepticism where backed by particular reasons, and both accept in philosophy the very same canons of rational thinking used in science and ordinary life. At the same time, Philo constantly emphasizes that theological subjects are very distant from our common life and hence too remote for our faculties, while Cleanthes thinks a simple and obvious line of thought can effectively, though only partially, plumb such depths. In short, they disagree about the *degree* of comprehension humans can achieve in theological subjects.[18] But these initial judgments must be backed by particular arguments to follow.

¶¶17–20: Skepticism, science, and religion

Cleanthes next turns to Demea and opens a new dialogue. At least the line of thought now alters, even though Demea does not respond.[19] Instead, Cleanthes and Philo now discuss the historical relation of faith to reason, particularly the "pretty curious" traditional Christian attitude toward "the sciences."[20] Cleanthes sketches one view of this history in 1.17, Philo gives his dark interpretation of the matter in 1.18–19, and Cleanthes closes in 1.20 with a gentler construal, displaying once more his smoothing disposition.

Early Christian "religious teachers," Cleanthes says, attacked every native human capacity (reason, the senses), presumably in order to discredit human works and allow conceptual room for divine grace to work its miracle of salvation. Hence the Church "fathers" readily adopted the techniques of "the ancient academics"—that is, the Greco-Roman skeptics—and so did the Reformers: "All panegyrics on the excellency of faith were sure to be interlarded with some severe strokes of satire against natural reason." But times have changed. Locke was "the first Christian, who ventured openly to assert, that faith was nothing but a species of *reason*, that religion was only a branch of philosophy, and that a chain of arguments, similar to that which established any truth in morals, politics, or physics, was always employed in discovering all the principles of theology, natural and revealed." Locke's position was only furthered by the "ill use" that Bayle "and other libertines" made of skepticism. So today, "all pretenders to reasoning and philosophy" agree that "atheist and sceptic are almost synonymous"; no one can "seriously maintain" either one (all 1.17.Cleanthes to Philo).

This short account is seriously unfaithful to the actual history of Christian theology. It ignores the considerable number of Biblical (e.g., Acts 17.22–31), Patristic (the Apologists, Athenagoras, Irenaeus, the Cappadocians, Origen, Augustine), and pre-Reformation theologians (Anselm, Abelard, Bonaventure, Aquinas) who had more positive views toward natural human reason.[21] It also overstates Locke's position: Faith is *not* "nothing but" reason, even when religious beliefs are reasonable, and for reason to discover "*all* the principles of theology, natural and revealed" would be to obliterate the distinction between "natural" and "revealed."[22] But let us remember that this parody of "history" is directed at *Demea*—its picture of early Christianity is really Cleanthes' portrait of *Demea's* piety, in contrast with Cleanthes' own more Lockean position.

Philo then engages in a bit of banter with Cleanthes concerning "the excellent saying of Lord Bacon on this head": Cleanthes' guess ("a little philosophy . . . makes a man an atheist: A great deal converts him to religion") is trumped by Philo's memory of another, more obscure passage where Bacon says that atheists are twice over "David's fool" ("who said in his heart there is no God"): both in their hearts and with their lips. "Such people," Philo claims, "though they were ever so much in earnest, cannot, methinks, be very formidable" (1.18.Philo to Cleanthes). Philo is trying to put some distance between his own sensible skepticism and foolish atheism. But Philo really wants to comment on the small history Cleanthes has presented: "It appears to me, that there are strong symptoms of priestcraft in the whole progress of this affair." In ignorant ages, priests perceived atheism or heresy to arise from "the presumptuous questioning of received opinions, and from a belief, that human reason was equal to every thing," and so sought to use education in skepticism to gain "a mighty influence over the minds of men," even though this education does not rely on the skeptic's normal master, the "suggestions of the senses and common understanding." But when men learn to compare religions, "our sagacious divines" change their whole approach, now employing dogmatic instead of skeptical philosophy: "Thus, sceptics in one age, dogmatists in another; whichever system best suits the purpose of these reverend gentlemen, in giving them an ascendant over mankind, they are sure to make it their favourite principle" (1.19.Philo to Cleanthes). In short, it is not rational argument that steers theology but a priestly interest in power and control over the pious masses.

Cleanthes disagrees, as much out of politeness as from principle, and suggests a more charitable interpretation. It is not "priestcraft," but everyone's "very natural" and "reasonable" tendency to adopt whatever principles will best defend one's doctrines; there is no need to suspect motives of power and advantage (1.20.Cleanthes to Philo).

Philo and Cleanthes appear to disagree over the motives of religious thinkers: Philo seems paranoically pessimistic, while Cleanthes appears naively optimistic. Philo thinks these motives are the discreditable ones of getting "an ascendant over mankind," gaining power or control over others; while Cleanthes holds the view that theologians are simply trying to defend as best they can whatever they think true, welcoming help from any quarter. What kind of a disagreement is this?

Neither speaker here mentions any evidence for his claim (though Philo will dilate on this topic in Part 12), so it might seem like just an expression of differing attitudes toward religious people. Yet we do have evidence of a kind within the *Dialogues*: We have Demea, and Demea instances Philo's view, not Cleanthes'. Before he leaves (11.21), Demea shows he is quite prepared to use any and every form of argument (save those, like Cleanthes', that afford no certainty), no matter how bad and mutually inconsistent the forms might be, so long as they will support his authoritarian piety. If Demea is at all typical of religious thinkers, then Philo's seemingly jaundiced view of the history of faith and reason is only a reasonable man's proper suspicion of those who are fundamentally motivated by something other than reason. So Philo's pessimism has supporting evidence ready to hand, while Cleanthes' optimism lacks instance (aside from himself).

In that light, let us turn to the perplexing last sentence of Part 1, where Cleanthes claims that "nothing can afford a stronger presumption, that any set of principles are true, and ought to be embraced, than to observe, that they tend to the confirmation of true religion, and serve to confound the cavils of atheists, libertines, and freethinkers of all denominations" (1.20.Cleanthes to Philo). This comment is at once contextually odd, internally cryptic, and logically suspect. It is odd at this point in the conversation because it seems to abruptly change the subject from religious motives to religion's "confirmation." It is cryptic about what "true religion" is and how confirming it and confounding freethinkers could show the truth of philosophical principles. And as a point of logic, one wonders about the validity of the underlying argument form: *q* is true and *p* confirms *q*, therefore *p* is true.[23] So we have a very puzzling declaration from Cleanthes, whose entire point is unclear.

Is Cleanthes here speaking only from the standpoint of someone who believes her religious principles to be "true" and defends them as best she can (as Cleanthes urged in the preceding sentence)? No, this is no merely hypothetical stance; it is Cleanthes' very own position. "True religion" is vitally important to Cleanthes, and he wants to maintain the legitimacy of using it as a touchstone in accepting or rejecting theological arguments.

In contrast, Philo thinks we should work our way *to* religion, as something strange and foreign, *from* what is more familiar or knowable to us, from "common life" (mentioned in 1.8, 1.9, 1.10, and 1.11), "human affairs" (1.10), "common sense and experience" (1.10), or "the senses and experience" (1.11). Since religion is "a strange country" (1.10), theological views are, or should be, grounded in something closer to home; they should be held on probation of "common life." Cleanthes agrees, but only in part. He does think "the religious hypothesis" can meet this test of common sense and experience via the design argument and thereby establish its credentials in common life. But he also believes this line of argument is neither the only, nor perhaps the firmest, foundation of theology; one can also ground theological principles on "true religion," a basis independent of common life. True religion justifies those theological principles that support it and undermines those that negate it. The logic of this procedure is certainly not absent from science (theories are often sifted by their agreement with well-rooted facts and with practices of the scientific community), and it is often present in common life (ways of life seek principles that will support them).

But the most vital question remains: What *is* "true religion"? Cleanthes' views are undeveloped in Part 1, but this much is clear: True religion is much more than another set of principles, theological or otherwise, and however privileged; it is a way of life, a set of practices, attitudes, and propensities as well as principles. To use the distinction Demea introduced earlier (1.2), religion includes "piety" as well as "theology." Of course, *which* piety and *which* theology are "true" must at this point of the *Dialogues* remain unclear; we can only wait until Part 12, where Philo and Cleanthes return to the topic of true religion after Demea leaves. But we do need to note well Cleanthes' point that what is at issue encompasses considerably more than theological principles. Cleanthes' last sentence in Part 1 in effect cautions Pamphilus (and through him a reader of his recital): Do not think that theology alone is at stake in these conversations; attend also to what a speaker says or implies about the totality of religion in assessing the "truth" of his principles.

Part 1 is indeed an artful introduction and manages to insinuate a whole host of concerns that need to be kept in mind over the next eleven Parts: education in piety as well as in theology, the nature and relevance of skepticism, the limits and procedures of human reason, the nature of natural religion and its role in common life, the practical roots and implications of theological principles. These larger and deeper topics mostly await Part 12 for their explicit discussion and for some measure of resolution. In the meantime, Pamphilus is treated to a three-act drama on natural theology, beginning first with protracted discussion of the design argument for the natural attributes of God, as well as some consideration of our natural affinity for teleology (Parts 2–8), continuing with a brief consideration of "that simple and sublime argument *a priori*" (9.1.Demea to Cleanthes and Philo), and concluding with a discussion of evil and the moral attributes of God (Parts 10–11).

5

Part 2

Look round the world: Contemplate the whole and every part of it: You will find it to be nothing but one great machine, subdivided into an infinite number of lesser machines . . . adjusted to each other with an accuracy, which ravishes into admiration all men, who have ever contemplated them.

—Cleanthes to Demea and Philo, Part 2.5

Structure:

¶¶ *1–4: Demea and Philo "agree" on the being and nature of God*
   ¶¶ *1–2: Demea maintains the being of God is "self-evident" and the nature of God "altogether incomprehensible and unknown" and then appeals to authority (Malebranche)*
   ¶¶ *3–4: Philo holds to the same "truths"—with several twists*
¶¶ *5–10: The design argument is introduced and disputed*
   ¶ *5: Cleanthes presents his "argument* a posteriori*"*
   ¶ *6: Demea attacks anthropomorphism and arguments from experience*
   ¶¶ *7–8: Philo attacks this kind of argument from experience*
   ¶ *9: Cleanthes responds to Philo*
   ¶ *10: Demea cries out and censures Cleanthes*
¶¶ *11–28: Philo rallies Demea, then addresses Cleanthes' argument*
   ¶¶ *11–15: Philo "restates" the argument*
   ¶ *16: Cleanthes assents to the restatement, and Philo pauses*
   ¶¶ *17–24: Philo raises objections to the argument*
   ¶ *25: Pamphilus comments on Philo's attitude, and Cleanthes protests that Philo is treating theology unlike astronomy*
   ¶¶ *26–28: Philo contrasts astronomy and theology*

Part 2 opens with a contrast of theological beliefs and postures: Demea and Philo seem to unite against Cleanthes (though only Demea is fooled), while deeper agreements and disagreements lie just below the surface. Cleanthes cuts short the pious declarations by Demea and Philo and, in one brief paragraph (2.5), presents his own theology bundled into a single "argument *a posteriori*" —the infamous "design argument."[1] Demea and Philo vent their initial reactions to Cleanthes' argument, with a quizzical rejoinder by Cleanthes. Following an impolite and rather menacing outburst from Demea, Philo enlists Demea's interest, if not his aid, in an examination of Cleanthes' argument, an exercise that will consume not only Part 2 but the following five Parts as well. Philo's chief criticism in this Part is the "wide step" the argument takes from parts of the universe to the whole universe, with a resulting very weak analogy or similarity between human mind or intelligence and "the Author of Nature." Philo returns time and again to his earlier theme that the whole "sublime" subject is "so remote from the sphere of our observation," so "vastly beyond the reach of my faculties" (2.24.Philo to Cleanthes), that we should expect, as we find, no useful or definite results from any such argument *a posteriori*.

¶¶1–2: Demea's performance

Once again, and not for the last time, Demea speaks first, in two paragraphs of inconsistent and troubling declamations that reveal more about his piety than about his theology. He begins with a worry addressed to Cleanthes: "The whole tenor of your discourse" seems to give aid and comfort to "atheists and infidels" because it seems to make the being of God an open question. But this is not, Demea hopes, "a question among us. No man; no man, at least of common sense, I am persuaded, ever entertained a serious doubt with regard to a truth so certain and self-evident." The only question concerns "the NATURE of God." But that nature, given "the infirmities of human understanding," is "altogether incomprehensible and unknown to us."

> Finite, weak, and blind creatures, we ought to humble ourselves in his August presence, and, conscious of our frailties, adore in silence his infinite perfections, which eye hath not seen, ear hath not heard, neither hath it entered into the heart of man to conceive them.

Lashing even more piety to his slender reed of theology, Demea holds that the divine nature is not merely unknowable by us, it is "profaneness to attempt penetrating through these sacred obscurities." As a result, Cleanthes is in danger not only of committing the "impiety of denying his [i.e., God's] existence" but also "the temerity of prying into his nature and essence, decrees and attributes" (all 2.1.Demea to Cleanthes).

Having thus ruled the question of divine existence to be self-evident and beyond doubt and the question of divine nature to be mysterious and impenetrable by us and having taxed his host for heterodoxy on both matters, one might suppose that Demea should, in all consistency, lapse into silent adoration. But Demea is never inconvenienced by inconsistency, in thought or in deed. With no hint of self-awareness and only a trace of embarrassment, he hastens next to provide what he regards as an appropriate kind of argument for what he has just declared to lie beyond argument. "But lest you should think, that my piety has here got the better of my *philosophy*, I shall support my opinion" (2.2.Demea to Cleanthes). No doubt we should and do so think, just as we should not be surprised at the kind of support Demea offers: It is an appeal to authority consisting of a lengthy quotation from Malebranche's *De la recherche de la vérité*.[2] Demea doubtless thinks that quoting someone "equally celebrated for piety and philosophy" renders his views more philosophically credible.

A number of points are noteworthy about this opening performance. First, it *is* a performance, and a performance primarily for the benefit of Pamphilus, although the implied threats to Cleanthes (and also to Philo) cannot be ignored. Moreover, it is a performance of which Demea is at least partially aware. He certainly does wish to educate Cleanthes' "adopted son" just as he has educated his own children (1.1–2.Demea to Cleanthes and Philo), and his primary means of instruction requires pious declamation instead of clearheaded thinking. It is less clear how conscious Demea is of the menace contained in his implicit accusation that his host Cleanthes is guilty of impiety and temerity (in 2.1) and of "betraying the cause of a Deity" or at least giving "advantages to atheists" (2.6).[3] These are worrisome charges indeed from "*zealous* defenders of religion" (2.10; emphasis added).

Second, Demea gives what he regards as a *pious* performance, lapsing into language that seems more appropriate to public worship than to private philosophical conversation. His depiction of the divine nature as "altogether incomprehensible and unknown to us" (2.1) uses the figurative language of faith, and he occasionally substitutes confession and adoration for argument. Clearly Demea's personal bent is not philosophical but religious. Moreover, his religiosity is at once authoritarian and conventional. To be sure, Demea is better at exercising authority than obeying it; he relies upon Malebranche's authority only to shore up his own (and amends Malebranche on his own authority). Concerning the object of his piety, he uses platitudinous verbiage —comfortable and consoling but also unexamined and inappropriate. The meaning of this language lies more in its soothing practical effects than in its theoretical cogency.

Third, there is something nearly comical, were it not so seriously freighted, about Demea's expressions of piety—and hence also about his piety. While his language may appear piously orthodox, it strikes a chord with many jarring overtones. Consider once more the sentence from 2.1 quoted above. The archaic verbal forms, the imperative mood, the sonorous patterns—all seem liturgical and quite conventional. Demea seems to be making a kind of public profession of faith and a prayer of confession, adoration, and praise all at once, and one can imagine the words rolling off a cleric's pious tongue. Demea in fact is recycling language from St. Paul,[4] who in turn is interpreting Isaiah.[5] But Demea alters both the referent and the sense of the Biblical language to suit his own designs. To be sure, the meaning of the Isaiah passage is obscure, and Paul's interpretation—the divine mysteries prepared for believers—is but one of several possibilities. The Revised Standard Version,[6] for example, turns it into a statement about other divinities; the Jewish Publication Society[7] puts the emphasis on divine works. But none of these versions apply the restrictive language to God's *nature,* as does Demea.

In Demea's mouth, the whole sentence has the ring of unselfconscious self-parody and recalls another, altogether less pious, appropriation of this same language. In Shakespeare's *Midsummer Night's Dream,* the inimitable Bottom garbles these words as he recalls his "most rare vision"—not of God but of Titania![8] Bottom's malapropic dream of the Queen of the Fairies is only a misplaced adjective or two away from Demea's encomium to God. To be sure, Demea is unaware of his words' antecedents and reverberations; he is merely mouthing pious-sounding words. But often we say more—especially about ourselves—than we consciously intend, and what Demea's language says about him is that he is as thoughtless in his use of sacred tradition as he is in his misuse of scholarship and philosophy. His degree of "orthodoxy" (PH.6.Pamphilus to Hermippus) may be considerably less than Hermippus and others (including himself!) think.

Fourth, consistency is not Demea's strong suit. Either he does not recognize his own inconsistency or he does not care about it. What Demea desires above all else is *certitude*—not epistemological justification but removal of disturbing doubt. The acquiescence of others in his opinions he sees as further confirmation that he is right, so he will seek to bind them to his views, if he can. He therefore readily adopts and adapts any stratagem, line of argument, or even threat that will assure himself, and convince others, of his supposedly orthodox theology and piety. Here a claim of self-evidence, there a recourse to pious phraseology, next an appeal to authority—no matter how mutually incompatible these devices may be, what matters to Demea is that they *work,* that they "support" (preserve if not justify) his own heartfelt positions.

Fifth, after having displayed an unctuously flattering face to his host Cleanthes at the opening of Part 1, Demea here shows a more menacing side: He implicitly criticizes Cleanthes for "impiety" and "temerity"—no small concerns for a religious bigot—and the threatening undertones of his re-proaches cannot go unnoticed by Cleanthes. As we shall later see, there is every reason to believe that Demea is perfectly willing to carry out his threats should argument fail to persuade and should he reckon that force has a chance of success.

Sixth, Demea's distinction between the being and the nature of God should raise our eyebrows—how could one be at all certain that something exists without *some* idea of what is supposed to exist? Of course, this distinction is not new to the *Dialogues;* it was already mentioned by Pamphilus (PH.5) and shortly will be echoed by Philo (2.3). But we should be suspicious of this apparent consensus, for it masks deep disagreements in piety; likewise, apparent disagreement on this point may conceal a deeper agreement. Demea, for example, thinks denying God's existence is impious, while Philo thinks affirming God's existence is nearly useless (cf. Part 12), but despite this apparent agreement they seek to live with others in radically incompatible ways. Cleanthes, on the other hand, does not doubt God's existence, even though he opens both nature and existence to inquiry; still, Cleanthes' conviction here differs vastly from Demea's. Whereas Demea is antecedently and inflexibly certain of God as an object of devotion, seeking arguments only after the fact of belief, Cleanthes puts this question, as he does all questions, to the test of reason and experience, so that his belief in a divine Author of Nature is the result (as he thinks) of finding overwhelming evidence in favor of this "hypothesis." Finally, although Philo appears to agree with Demea in withholding divine existence from questioning because it is self-evident, in fact he does later put forth arguments that call this existence into question (especially in Part 10). Moreover, Philo's underlying acceptance of God's existence is based on experience of the very same kind as that pointed out by Cleanthes. The surface alignment of Philo and Demea against Cleanthes masks the deeper community of Philo and Cleanthes that has no room for Demea. Demea is the real odd man out in these conversations—quite literally after Part 11—and it is only a pious hope on his part that divine existence can be their unexamined Archimedean point.

Seventh, should we take at all seriously the negative theology coiled in Demea's comments? If the nature of God is "altogether incomprehensible and unknown to us," if "the essence of that supreme mind, his attributes, the manner of his existence, the very nature of his duration" are all "mysterious to men," if we are completely "blind" when it comes to divinity, then logically the only alternative is indeed silence, whether adoring or otherwise. But Demea doesn't care about logic. His remarks are pious hyperbole, not serious theology, for he wants above all to preserve a proper sense of "these sacred obscurities," to safeguard the holiness of God (all 2.1.Demea to Cleanthes).

For Demea, the denial of God's existence is *impious,* not *impossible;* and it is temerity, not contradiction, to pry into his nature. Demea does not present a seriously intended negative theology, only its pious-sounding counterfeit.

¶¶3–4: Philo's performance

Following Demea's performance, Philo produces one of his own. To Demea, he offers apparent agreement; to Cleanthes, seeming criticism and expressions of piety. But there is more to Philo's words than his surface meaning.

He tells Demea that "reasonable men" can never question "the *being* but only the *nature* of the Deity," because the former is "unquestionable and self-evident." But the claim of "unquestionable" is circular and uninformative; it amounts to saying that the being of the Deity cannot be questioned because it is unquestionable. The claim of "self-evident" is immediately undermined because, without blinking an eye, Philo provides an argument—not to show that God's being is indeed self-evident but rather to show (and to show *a priori*) that God exists.[9] The argument is simple, albeit enthymemetic: "Nothing exists without a cause, and the original cause of this universe (whatever it be) we call GOD." Anyone who questions the divine being deserves philosophical "punishment"—"to wit, the greatest ridicule, contempt and disapprobation." Everyone else should "piously ascribe to him [i.e., the divine being] every species of perfection." However, we don't comprehend the divine attributes because God's perfections have no "analogy or likeness to the perfections of a human creature." So even though we "justly" attribute such perfections as "wisdom, thought, design, knowledge" to God, we shouldn't think they "have any resemblance to these qualities among men"; we make these attributions only because we have no other language to "express our adoration of him." God is "more the object of worship in the temple than of disputation in the schools" (2.3.Philo to Demea).

Turning to Cleanthes, Philo for a moment drops "that affected scepticism, so displeasing to you" in order to offer the premises of a syllogism—"Our ideas reach no farther than our experience: We have no experience of divine attributes and operations"—and to ask that Cleanthes draw the conclusion himself: presumably, that our ideas do not reach to divine attributes and operations. Philo concludes with the declaration that both "just reasoning and sound piety" concur in establishing exactly what Demea had previously urged—"the adorably mysterious and incomprehensible nature of the Supreme Being" (2.4.Philo to Cleanthes).

So it appears that Philo supports Demea and criticizes Cleanthes, and this is doubtless how Demea understands matters. But anyone paying close attention should be more cautious. Let us assemble some pieces of evidence that all is not as it seems. One striking clue is that Philo, in dropping his "affected scepticism," offers arguments that are not at all what one expects from Philo. First they are arguments *for* something, not *against* it. Second, they are not arguments from experience but rather arguments *a priori*. Third, they support positions and piety altogether too comfortable to Demea.[10]

Next, what Philo is claiming (as self-evident) and arguing for (as "original cause") amounts to very little. If we call this original cause "God" and "piously ascribe to him every species of perfection" (2.3.Philo to Demea), we have said almost nothing, because the terms "God" and his various perfections are only labels for our ignorance. We hold that there must be some original cause of the universe, and we want to affirm only the best of this cause. But divine perfections can be nothing like those applicable to humans. We may, if we piously please, adore such a being in language that is most "honorable among men," but we should not think that we have any idea at all of such a being, whose nature is quite literally "incomprehensible" (2.4.Philo to Cleanthes). This is Demea's stated position, but Philo takes it more seriously than Demea because he takes it literally. Whereas Demea's interest in negative theology is only passing and pragmatic, Philo sees its full and strict implications: If God's nature is truly "incomprehensible," then we comprehend nothing of God, and the terms we ascribe to him in devotion are literally meaningless to us. But this epistemic *via negativa* is of no real help to Demea: Such an unknown "cause" prescribes no actions and devolves no authority because it *has* no authority.

Moreover, Philo says, the "punishment" among "philosophers" due anyone who "scruples" the "fundamental truth" of the divine being is "ridicule, contempt and disapprobation." What sort of *philosophical* punishment is this? Doesn't appropriately philosophical punishment consist in pointing out flaws in reasoning, not ad hominem "ridicule, contempt and disapprobation"? Only Demea, it seems, would understand these kinds of punishments; they are the sort of pedagogical sticks he would use to shape his own children. Precisely. Philo is providing a parody of Demea, not giving his own considered views. First he declares something "self-evident," then he provides an *a priori* argument for what should need no support, then he threatens punishments to anyone who disagrees. This is exactly how Demea the religious fanatic "argues," not how Philo the philosophical skeptic reasons. We expect something better from Philo.

There is also more than meets the eye to Philo's *a priori* argument to Cleanthes, where he patronizingly asks Cleanthes to supply the conclusion. In essence, it is nothing new but only a restatement of Philo's repeated contention in Part 1 that theological inquiries "run wide of common life" (1.11.Philo to Cleanthes). Why would Philo wish to repeat himself once more at this point in the conversations?

A final clue: Philo returns several times to the question of piety. We "piously ascribe to him every species of perfection"; "we have no other language or other conceptions, by which we can express our adoration of him"; he is "more the object of worship in the temple than of disputation in the schools"; "just reasoning and sound piety here concur." But what kind of piety is "sound"? The piety Philo supports seems very tame indeed, an intellectual "adoration" and "worship" of something "infinitely superior to our limited view and comprehension" (all 2.3–4), and it is utter distant from Demea's enthusiastic anti-intellectual piety.

Putting these various strands together, let us ask: What is really going on in Philo's performance? I believe that, under the guise of agreement with Demea, Philo responds in kind to Demea with a performance of his own—a mocking, ironical performance where nothing is as it seems. His apparent support of Demea's piety undermines itself upon reflection, and his apparent critique of Cleanthes is considerably less than devastating. The area of agreement between Philo and Demea is very constricted. They agree there is a deity unknowable by us; beyond that, their paths in thought and in life diverge immensely. At the same time, Philo's disagreement with Cleanthes is negotiable (it concerns the *degree* to which human reason is adequate to theology), and it doesn't affect their friendship, founded as it is on a common piety.

Philo's performance undoubtedly sounds to Demea like an echo of himself, but it is in fact both a caricature of Demea's manner and a clearer statement of the limits of negative theology. Still, Philo does want Demea to think he is on his side in order to keep Demea in the conversations so that others (especially Pamphilus) can learn from them. The yawning chasm between Philo and Demea will gradually become plain to Demea as Philo opens up the "inconveniences" not merely of experimental theism but also of enthusiastic piety. At the same time, Philo's own stance will become clearer, and while his theology in Part 12 will turn out to be not much different from what he states in Part 2, his piety will display itself as antithetical to Demea's piety.

¶5: Cleanthes' design argument

Rather than responding to the pieties of Demea or Philo,[11] Cleanthes abruptly puts forward an "argument *a posteriori*," the famous design argument. This is a key paragraph, for it sketches (somewhat vaguely) the target at which Philo will aim his criticisms over the next five Parts.

Cleanthes begins with a double appeal to consider experience: "Look round the world: Contemplate the whole and every part of it." What you will find in both part and whole, Cleanthes believes, are "*machines*," mechanisms minutely adjusted within themselves and to each other "with an accuracy, which ravishes into admiration all men, who have ever contemplated them." Moreover, this mutual adjustment is also "the curious adapting of means to ends, throughout all nature." These naturally adjusted and adapted mecha-

nisms are greater than, but greatly resemble, "the productions of human contrivance; of human design, thought, wisdom, and intelligence."[12] We may
therefore infer, "by all the rules of analogy," that where effects resemble, "the
causes also resemble," so that "the Author of Nature is somewhat similar to
the mind of man; though possessed of much larger faculties, proportioned
to the grandeur of the work, which he has executed" (all 2.5.Cleanthes to
Demea and Philo).[13]

There are a number of important lacunae in this argument. The first
concerns its conclusion. Cleanthes says his argument proves both the existence
of God and the nature of God to be similar to "human mind and intelligence." But as actually stated, his argument seems not to *prove* but rather to
assume the existence of an Author of Nature. Cleanthes' conclusion, that "the
Author of Nature is somewhat similar to the mind of man," is a conclusion
about the *nature* of "a Deity," not about its *existence.* This is no small matter.
It is one thing to infer by analogy something of the nature of a being known
or assumed to exist; it is quite another to infer by analogy that some being
exists. Cleanthes, despite his claim to prove both existence and nature, is really assuming existence so that he can dilate on the nature of a deity.

Second, Cleanthes begins with a premise that is itself a disguised analogy:
It is not that the parts and whole of the world *are* machines but that they are
like (or at any rate *look like*) machines. Cleanthes doesn't just look and see that
the world and its parts *are* machines; he looks and sees them *as* machines. But
how does he arrive at this interpretative perception, this seeing-as? Cleanthes
needs an argument *to* design (showing that parts and the whole of the world
are like, or seem to be like, machines) as well as an argument *from* design
(showing that the designer[s] of the world-machines is [are] like a human
designer).

Third, Cleanthes conflates the "adjustment" of machines and their parts
with the "adapting" of means to ends. The issues are complicated, but the
general point is clear: Part/whole is not the same as means/end. Of course, a
machine cannot achieve its "ends" or proper functions, or achieve them effi-
ciently, unless its parts are carefully adjusted one to another; similarly, several
machines cannot function well together toward some common end without
mutual adjustment. Moreover, where there are ends and means to them, there
are also wholes with their respective parts. But they are not identical. A whole
is composed of its parts but not necessarily produced by means of its parts;
an end is furthered or produced through its means but is not composed
(either materially or conceptually) of its means. The parts/whole relation has
to do with structure, order, composition; the means/end relation has to do
with purpose, goals, teleology. Cleanthes owes his audience an account of
how the two distinctions are related.

Fourth, there are further ambiguities of part and whole: "Contemplate the whole and every part of it: You will find it to be nothing but one great machine, subdivided into an infinite number of lesser machines, which again admit of subdivisions." Does Cleanthes' argument proceed from the "one great machine" or from "the lesser machines" or from both? Is the argument from features of the whole world or from features of parts of the whole world? Or is the argument first from parts to whole and then from the whole to its "Author"?

Fifth, how great is the resemblance between natural "machines" and human "contrivances"? Cleanthes initially says the "curious adapting of means to ends" "resembles *exactly,* though it much exceeds" human contrivance (emphasis added). But he begins to back off this claim as he proceeds: Since the effects "resemble," we infer that the causes "also resemble," but only that "the Author of Nature is *somewhat* similar" (emphasis added). Clearly there is a lot of play between "exactly" and "somewhat"; these are vague terms of degree.[14]

Sixth, Cleanthes' argument is a probabilistic one, not a demonstrative "proof." It is not just that the conclusion employs the vague "somewhat similar," or even that the premises are dependent upon subjective perception (seeing the world and its parts *as* machines), but also that any arguing by analogy, particularly about causes of like effects, permits only more or less probable inferences, not logically necessary or certain ones.[15] Demea will seize upon this point shortly; if even he can spot the probabilistic character of the argument, it must be plain to view indeed. So why does Cleanthes not state it explicitly?

At the minimum, these lacunae mean that Hermippus's opinion of "the accurate philosophical turn of Cleanthes" (PH.6) demands revision: Even if Cleanthes' views are more or less correct, clearly they are neither transparently expressed nor well supported. Cleanthes just is not good at laying out a philosophical position and its evidence. That is why Philo will have to restate "the" design argument shortly; but first, both Demea and Philo respond to Cleanthes' *kind* of argument.

¶¶6–10: Reactions to Cleanthes' argument

Both Demea (2.6) and Philo (2.7–8) react vigorously to Cleanthes' design argument; Demea is emotionally wrought, eventually exploding in a "censure" of his host (2.10), while Philo is cooler and deeper. Cleanthes responds, weakly, to Philo's criticism (2.9) but not at all to Demea's outbursts. Once again we learn as much of character as of philosophy in this exchange of reactions.

Demea's initial reaction makes two related points: He does not "approve" of Cleanthes' emphasis on similarity between God and humans, and he approves "still less" of the empirical way in which Cleanthes attempts to show this similarity. On this latter point the heat of his emotional response is palpable: "What! No demonstration of the being of a God! No abstract arguments! No proofs *a priori*!" Why is Demea so exercised? It is not that he has a scholarly fondness or personal affinity for abstract argument, but rather that Cleanthes' *a posteriori* method affords only probability, not certainty. Mere probability threatens Demea's pious self-certitude, and he retaliates by threatening Cleanthes: "By this affected candour, you give advantages to atheists" (all from 2.6.Demea to Cleanthes).

Philo's initial reaction is more subtle. He does not reject arguing from experience—in fact he embraces it—but rather worries that the *kind* of argument from experience Cleanthes employs is not "the most certain and irrefragable of that inferior kind." Where we have an "exact similarity of the cases," experience will provide us with "perfect assurance . . . and a stronger evidence is never desired nor sought after." But where cases are dissimilar, we have only "a very weak *analogy*, which is confessedly liable to error and uncertainty." Here Philo cites an intriguing scientific example: the circulation of blood in humans, frogs, and fishes and the circulation of sap in vegetables. The inference is indubitable from other humans to Titius and Maevius, less "strong" from humans and mammals to amphibians and ·fish, and most "imperfect" when applied to plants; as the degree of similarity diminishes, the argument from analogy loses force. How similar, then, *is* a house (or any human artifact) to the universe as a whole? "The dissimilitude is so striking, that the utmost you can here pretend to is a guess, a conjecture, a presumption concerning a similar cause." Finally, Philo wonders how this "pretension" will be received in the world (all from 2.7–8.Philo to Cleanthes).

Cleanthes picks up on Philo's last point; it matters to him how his view will be received "in the world"—particularly by Pamphilus, if not by Demea. Cleanthes wants more from his "proofs of a Deity" than "a guess or a conjecture," but he clearly believes his "argument *a posteriori*" can supply something more. Instead of trying to show this, however, Cleanthes somewhat surprisingly launches his own raft of questions—questions that he may regard as merely rhetorical but that Philo considers open to dispute. The queries are all variations on the same theme: *Is* the "adjustment of means to ends in a house and in the universe so slight a resemblance?" While the inferences that stair steps are contrived for human "mounting" and that human legs are contrived for "walking and mounting" are not "certain and infallible," yet *do* these inferences "deserve the name only of presumption or conjecture" (all 2.9.Cleanthes to Philo)?

Demea can contain himself no longer, and he heatedly, and piously, interjects: "Good God! . . . Where are we?" What bothers him is Cleanthes' admission that his argument produces less than complete certainty. Demea can scarcely believe that "zealous defenders of religion allow, that the proofs of a deity fall short of perfect evidence!"[16] He is so threatened by this line of thought that he lashes out with considerations closer to his heart: alliances and threats. He seeks to enlist Philo in opposing "these extravagant opinions of Cleanthes" and then expresses his "censure" of his host Cleanthes for speaking such thoughts "before so young a man as Pamphilus" (all 2.10.Demea to Cleanthes and Philo). Here as elsewhere, Demea's outbursts are at least impolite, at worst menacing. When things do not go his way, he seems on the verge of disrupting civil discourse and the community of friends.

¶¶11–16: Philo restates the argument—and pauses

Philo reduces the tension a bit by ignoring the menace in Demea's words and reassuring Demea that they are still allies: Philo is working, he claims, against Cleanthes in his own way. Philo here capitalizes on Demea's gullible belief that an enemy of my enemy is my friend; Philo hopes that Demea will not see that his reasons for opposition to Cleanthes serve quite different ends and reach quite different conclusions than do Demea's. Philo takes this opportunity ostensibly to restate the matter, but really to clarify the form, of Cleanthes' argument (2.11–15); then, after Cleanthes assents to the fairness of Philo's characterization (2.16), Philo raises objections to the restated argument (2.17–24). Part 2 closes with an interesting exchange between Cleanthes and Philo on the differences and similarities of astronomy and theology (2.25–28).

In response to Demea's "censure" of Cleanthes in 2.10, Philo not only misleads Demea about their agreement but thoroughly misrepresents Demea's reasons for upset. "But what sticks most with you," Philo says to Demea, is that Cleanthes' representation of his own argument "is likely to escape your hold and vanish into air" because it seems "so disguised." Philo then offers, disingenuously, to restate the argument so that Demea "will entertain no farther scruples with regard to it" (2.11.Philo to Demea). Of course this is nonsense. It is not Demea but Philo who is dissatisfied with the unclarity of Cleanthes' argument; for Demea it is clear enough to arouse his ire. Demea is upset because Cleanthes' argument lacks complete certainty and concludes with a deity too similar to man.[17]

Philo spends the next three paragraphs (2.12–14) not so much recasting Cleanthes' argument as pointing out to Demea how this argument is an experiential one, absolutely dependent upon experience to draw its conclusion. Antecedent to all experience, anything that can be clearly conceived is possible; we have to learn from experience which of these many possibilities are fact and which are fancy and chimera. In particular, "experience alone can point out to him the true cause of any phenomenon" (2.13.Philo to Demea).

This experiential principle plays a vital role in Cleanthes' argument: Cleanthes wants to point to "order, arrangement, or the adjustment of final causes"[18] as "proof of design." But it is proof "only so far as it has been experienced to proceed from that principle"; *a priori*, it is equally possible that order, arrangement, and natural teleology could be due to some internal, unthinking principle: "For ought we can know *a priori*, matter may contain the source or spring of order originally" (2.14.Philo to Demea). It is only experience that settles the question.

Now Philo is in a position to restate Cleanthes' argument, which he does quite economically:

> Experience, therefore, proves that there is an original principle of order in mind, not in matter. From similar effects we infer similar causes. The adjustment of means to ends is alike in the universe, as in a machine of human contrivance. The causes, therefore, must be resembling. (2.14.Philo to Demea)

In effect, Philo hopes to close another loophole in Cleanthes' "argument *a posteriori*." Inferring a designing Author of Nature as the cause of "order, arrangement, or adjustment of final causes" in the universe requires that other possible causes be ruled out and they can be ruled out only by experience, because only experience can reveal "the true cause of any phenomenon" (2.13.Philo to Demea).

Philo next adds a paragraph professing (for Demea's benefit) Philo's shock at Cleanthes' claim of resemblance between "the Deity and human creatures," which must "imply such a degradation of the supreme Being as no sound theist could endure."[19] "With your assistance, therefore, Demea," Philo proposes to refute Cleanthes and defend "the adorable mysteriousness of the divine nature"[20] (2.15.Philo to Demea). This is a transparent attempt to keep Demea involved, and it succeeds, for Demea does remain; in fact, Philo's "assistant" even steps up to "save his [Philo's] countenance" when Philo is "a little embarrassed and confounded" in Part 3 (3.10.Pamphilus to Hermippus).

Philo attends to one apparently minor matter before refuting Cleanthes: Philo must secure Cleanthes' agreement that Philo has given his argument "a fair representation." Cleanthes does indeed assent. But then Philo *pauses*—"a short pause," to be sure, but one noticeable to Pamphilus (2.16.Pamphilus to Hermippus). Since this is one of those rare moments of non-discursive "action" in the *Dialogues,* it is important to understand it. Is Philo merely clearing his head, pausing for dramatic effect, and turning more directly toward Cleanthes? There is more to his gesture than that. Philo is also signaling that he intends to take charge of the ensuing conversations, beginning in Part 2 and continuing until the end of Part 8, with a momentary setback in Part 3.

Philo's dominance is evident in the quantity of his discourse. Until now, each speaker has been prominently represented in the conversations,[21] but in Parts 2–8, Philo does the lion's share of the talking.[22] Moreover, except for Part 3, Philo is in control of the subsequent topics, while Cleanthes and Demea merely offer (mostly feeble) objections and queries—they cannot present competing views of equal cogency. In short, following his short pause, the dialogues on design belong to Philo. Small wonder, then, that at the end of Part 8, Philo will declare "a complete triumph" for his skeptical ways (8.12.Philo to Cleanthes); the "short pause" announces the opening of Philo's eventually triumphal campaign.

¶17: Undisputed principles

Before launching eight paragraphs (2.17–24) of uninterrupted critique of Cleanthes' argument, Philo first lists two things that "I shall not, at present, much dispute with you"[23]: first, that "all inferences . . . concerning fact are founded on experience" and second, that "all experimental reasonings are founded on the supposition, that similar causes prove similar effects, and similar effects similar causes" (2.17.Philo to Cleanthes). If "inferences founded on experience" is equivalent to "experimental reasonings," Philo has provided two premises of a syllogism, the conclusion of which is that all inferences concerning matters of fact are "founded" on a principle of analogical causality. This syllogism raises several interesting questions: Does Philo suppose that Cleanthes believes this conclusion and/or both of its premises? Does Cleanthes so believe? Why does Philo not dispute these principles? And where does Demea stand in these matters?

Philo does indeed think that these principles and the resulting syllogism are at the heart of Cleanthes' case for experimental theism, and he is correct in thinking so. Philo has merely made explicit what Cleanthes had implied by constricting his natural theology entirely to an "argument *a posteriori*" that depends upon an experienced likeness between nature and human contrivances; hence Cleanthes' entire case rests solely on "all the rules of analogy" (2.5.Cleanthes to Philo and Demea). Later we shall see Cleanthes embracing the first premise, that only experience and not *a priori* argument can prove matters of fact (cf. 9.5). Cleanthes also likely accepts both parts of the principle of analogical causality, even though he mentions only the inference from like effects to like causes in 2.5; here he is working toward, not from, a cause, but there is no reason to think that he would exclude "similar causes prove similar effects" from "all the rules of analogy" that he does embrace.

But why does Philo not dispute these principles? One possibility is that he accepts them himself. If so, there would be little to distinguish the kind of empirical reasoning favored by Philo the skeptic from that of Cleanthes the experimental theist, save perhaps in the way they embrace these principles: Philo is willing to "dispute" these principles, while Cleanthes accepts them "dogmatically." But this difference cannot be very great, since Cleanthes provides no more support for his principles than does Philo—instinct and habit ground them as deeply as anything either provides. Second, perhaps Philo rejects these principles himself but is willing to suspend his disbelief for the purposes of the discussion, foreseeing that powerful criticisms can be made of Cleanthes' design argument even granting the soundness and strength of these principles. If so, Philo would be prepared to open a "dispute" on empirical reasoning with Cleanthes in some other context. Third, perhaps Philo neither accepts nor rejects these principles himself, but he just doesn't want to make them an issue at present, preferring to focus instead on the employment of these principles in natural theology. In the end, these three possibilities are indistinguishable on this occasion: The dialogues proceed on the assumption of the validity of analogical causal reasoning, and the only questions concern the application of these principles to natural theology.

Finally, what about Demea? In effect, he has already taken himself out of the ensuing discussion on design by protesting vigorously not only "your conclusion concerning the similarity of the Deity to men" (2.6) but also the kind of analogical reasoning on which this conclusion is based. We now see how tightly the similarity in the conclusion is connected to the manner of reasoning, for analogical principles run from similarity to similarity, while similarities ride best on analogical rails of inference. If one rejects either, one should reject the other, so Demea's rejection of both is, for once, consistent. But in consequence, he has nothing to contribute to the discussion in the next six Parts, save for momentarily holding the fort when Philo is "a little embarrassed and confounded" in Part 3. Demea has declared himself irrelevant to the whole investigation, and he will not make a major reappearance until the topic changes in Part 9.

¶¶17–24: Philo's objections to Cleanthes' hypothesis

Over the next eight paragraphs, Philo launches as many criticisms; it is worth commenting briefly on each of them, noting not only their meaning and logical force but also some attendant jibes, rather unfairly ad hominem, against Cleanthes. It is as if Philo senses he has his man on the ropes and cannot resist a few taunts or even an occasional blow beneath the belt.

1. Philo warns that "just reasoners" should use analogical reasoning with "extreme caution." The implication, of course, is that incautious Cleanthes is not a just reasoner.

Unless the cases be exactly similar, they repose no perfect confidence in applying their past observation to any particular phenomenon. Every alteration of circumstances occasions a doubt concerning the event; and it requires new experiments to prove certainly, that the new circumstances are of no moment or importance.

Philo then contrasts "the slow and deliberate steps of philosophers" with "the precipitate march of the vulgar, who, hurried on by the smallest similitude, are incapable of all discernment or consideration." Again by implication, Cleanthes marches with the vulgar, since he does not deliberate over the many differences between nature and human contrivance (all 2.17.Philo to Cleanthes).

But Philo has laid down an impossibly strict requirement. No two distinct cases are *exactly* similar; resemblance is a question of degree. Doubts are occasioned not in every "alteration of circumstance," only in those where the results of applying the current best account are unexpected, where nature surprises theory. Doubts are correlative to expectations, and expectations are themselves formed by experience. There is nothing wrong with pursuing theory to extremes—that is the only way to tell where it breaks down. So Philo's criticism really boils down to the complaint that Cleanthes is moving too hastily in fastening on the (small) degree of similitude between the world and human artifice without more careful consideration of distance, dissimilarity, and other complications. As for the ad hominem implications, Philo seems himself too hasty in consigning Cleanthes to the vulgar camp: Even if Cleanthes is not a deliberate philosopher, he may still be an accurate one; Cleanthes may well hit the mark even if he has not considered all the complications of doing so.

2. Philo next elaborates perhaps his central concern in this Part, though again he adds something ad hominem:

But can you think, Cleanthes, that your usual phlegm [i.e., calmness and equanimity] and philosophy have been preserved in so wide a step as you have taken, when you compared to the universe houses, ships, furniture, machines;[24] and from their similarity in some circumstances inferred a similarity in their causes?

In moving from parts of the universe to the whole universe, Philo asks, "Does not the great disproportion bar all comparison and inference?" (all 2.18.Philo to Cleanthes).

Philo is not criticizing *all* inferences from parts to whole, only an inference "so wide" as the one from small parts to the whole vast universe. Nor is his complaint a sampling worry. Cleanthes is not attempting to determine the character of the entire universe by interrogating only a few of its parts; his inference is not a generalization of the character of the whole from the character of some parts supposed to be representative (because they are fair samples) of the whole. Rather, Cleanthes thinks that there is an especially strong resemblance between the universe as a whole and certain parts of the universe familiar to him (human contrivances), while Philo thinks the similarity is small because of the "great disproportion." This difference of opinion concerns the *degree* of resemblance, likeness, or analogy.[25]

3. In the same paragraph, Philo also notes that the cause of the part of the universe to which Cleanthes has likened the whole is only one of very many possible causes of other parts. "Thought, design, intelligence, such as we discover in men and other animals, is no more than one of the springs and principles of the universe" (2.18.Philo to Cleanthes). Indeed, Philo later even extends this claim in a bit of typical hyperbole: "Nature, we find, even from our limited experience, possesses an *infinite* number of springs and principles" (2.21; emphasis added).[26]

This criticism is beside the point, or at least beside Cleanthes' main point. Cleanthes is not attempting an inductive inference designed to fasten on thought and eliminate all other possible "springs and principles." For such an induction, it would be well not only to sample widely but also to find ways of ruling out all other causal principles besides thought. But Cleanthes' argument is not an induction; it is an analogy. All that Cleanthes seeks to show—not that it is an easy matter!—is that there is a sufficient analogy between the world (whole or parts) and human contrivances to license belief that their respective causes also resemble one another.

4. Almost as an afterthought, Philo introduces a new distinction and thereby suggests a distinctly new criticism: We cannot take the "*operations* of one part of nature upon another for the foundation of our judgement concerning the *origin* of the whole" (2.19.Philo to Cleanthes). Within nature, one part operates on other parts in making and altering them; but this is quite different from origination of the whole. Philo doesn't mention the traditional theistic distinction between causality within creation and the causality of creation ex nihilo, but that is the locus of his concern. Bringing about the whole of nature may, for all we know, be totally different from bringing about any part of nature, and we cannot infer the one from the other. Here is another "great disproportion" (2.18).

5. Even if we could move from operations of parts to origin of the whole ("which never can be admitted"), Philo holds that reason or design—"this little agitation of the brain which we call thought"—is such a weak principle that our preference for it must be an illusion born of "partiality in our own favour" (2.19.Philo to Cleanthes).

Again Philo sounds the theme of "great disproportion." Reason is "so minute, so weak, so bounded a principle" that we shouldn't "make it the model of the whole universe." But now he adds a new twist: We should suspect our predilection for reason because it is a natural human tendency—indeed a weakness—to project what is near and dear to us onto the wider universe. This is *anthropocentrism,* or human-centered bias, and it fuels, Philo is suggesting, our approval of *anthropomorphism,* the stamping of our likeness on all we find—including the entire universe. Philo's point is well taken as a general suspicion, but it is question-begging in the current case. One should have recourse to this undercutting kind of explanation only to the extent that the evidence for or appearance of anthropic likeness is weak or lacking. If something does indeed resemble us, then noticing that resemblance is not "natural illusion" but discerning perception. So the cogency of this point depends upon taking Philo's side against Cleanthes concerning the *degree* of analogy between the world and human contrivance.

6. Philo extends his "great disproportion" theme from part-to-whole to part-to-part inferences: "I will not allow any one part to form a rule for another part, if the latter be very remote from the former." Hence we cannot conclude that inhabitants of other planets have faculties like humans, for thought may well "be confined merely to this narrow corner" of the universe. How then can we consider human-like thought "the original cause of all things?" Once again, Philo cannot resist a topping of ad hominem: This error is even worse than "the narrow views of a peasant" speculating about governing a whole kingdom. So Cleanthes, by implication, is not only among the vulgar, but worse than a peasant (2.20.Philo to Cleanthes)!

This point seems mostly irrelevant to Cleanthes' argument. If there are cases of thoughtfully contrived artifacts in the universe that are designed by non-human intelligence, that does not strengthen the inference to the character (and existence?) of an Author of Nature; nor, conversely, does lacking such cases weaken Cleanthes' inference. It simply doesn't matter to Cleanthes whether thought is widespread or rare in the universe as a whole. What matters instead is whether there is sufficient likeness between human artifacts and nature. Of course, it might be worrisome if there *were* other forms of intelligence, thought, and reason in other parts of the universe, particularly if they functioned differently from the human variety.[27] But again, Cleanthes' argument is not fundamentally wounded; all he need do is form an analogy based on a wider range of data. The original cause of nature would then be held to resemble either what all the different forms of intelligence have in common or the various ways in which they are alike—a more complex analogy, to be sure, but clearly not the thinking of a "peasant."[28]

7. Philo next switches from space to time: Even if reason did operate throughout the whole vast universe as it is presently "constituted, arranged, adjusted," that would be no guarantee that reason had any similar role in the

world's "embryo-state." Here Philo spins an analogy of his own, one he will develop later (cf. 7.3): The world is like an organism. Observing a "finished animal" does not permit any sure inferences to "the growth of a fetus in the womb" or "still more, to the formation of an animalcule in the loins of its male-parent." Just as there is "an infinite number of springs and principles" scattered throughout space, so we discover still more principles operative at different times. Once again, our experience is too limited to allow us to make just inferences about the whole (2.21.Philo to Cleanthes). Philo summarizes the difficulties inherent in Cleanthes' argument in a rhetorical question:

> A very small part of this great system, during a very short time, is very imper-
> fectly discovered to us: And do we thence pronounce decisively concerning the
> origin of the whole? (2.22.Philo to Cleanthes)

Much of this we have heard before. What is new in this criticism is the idea that different explanatory principles are, or might be, operative at different stages in the development of an organism and therefore also, by analogy, probably operative at different stages in the development of the whole universe. Philo's point is not that the universe *is* an organism or that it is *more like* an organism than anything else but that it is *as like* an organism as anything else, *so far as we can tell.* Cleanthes is fascinated by a perceived likeness between machines and the universe, but he ignores or underappreciates other likenesses with quite different implications. To Philo, the degree of likeness in all such cases is relatively small and approximately equal, and our experience is so limited and our ignorance so vast that the only sensible course is to suspend our judgment.

8. In any event, in speculating about the origin of the universe we are in over our heads. Our total experience is too brief to judge a universe-sized duration (2.21); worse, we have no "experience of the origin of worlds." A normal "argument from experience" requires a number of instances so that when "two *species* of objects have always been observed to be conjoined together, I can *infer,* by custom, the existence of one, wherever I *see* the existence of the other." But there is only one universe, a unique individual, and not only do we lack experience of its origin and much experience of its present constitution and development, we also entirely lack experience of other beings of its kind in any stage of their development. We have nothing to go on in judging the laws of world origination and the kind of causality involved (2.24.Philo to Cleanthes).

Philo runs together several points in this paragraph, though his central thrust is clear: First, we have no experience of the whole (in its spatial extent or temporal origin), only experience of parts of the whole; second, the parts of which we do have experience are small, limited and probably atypical; third, we have no experience at all of other universes to compare with this one. This last difficulty strikes Philo as a key one for Cleanthes' line of argument. Reliable arguments from experience, Philo holds, are based upon *regular* experience, upon experienced regularities. But there is only one universe, and we have no experience of its origin or of the origins of other worlds. So Cleanthes' hypothesis that the world is the product of an intelligent Author of Nature is *merely* speculative, an imaginative projection onto the entire universe of some qualities of some few things in one small region of space-time. Philo's point is not so much that Cleanthes is mistaken in his anthropomorphic hypothesis as that he has no reasonable way of securing conviction; without experiential tether, our speculative imaginations run riot, and the results are completely untrustworthy.

Instead of being so libertine in speculation, we should instead emulate the "prudent reserve of Simonides," who always asked for more time to think of a proper answer to Hiero's question about the nature of God; like Simonides, Philo is "sensible that this subject lay vastly beyond the reach of my faculties," and he expects no success in whatever "feeble conjectures" humans may devise (2.24.Philo to Cleanthes). The subject is so "sublime" and "remote," and our faculties so feeble and limited, that we would do well to find better ways to spend our time.

¶25: Cleanthes protests

What a profusion of perplexities! Quite apart from their cogency as objections to Cleanthes' argument, we can sense how much fun Philo is having at Cleanthes' expense. Indeed, one suspects that Philo's primary concern is not whether the difficulties he raises are genuine or even fully relevant; his joy is more in the process than in the results. Even Pamphilus notices this: "Philo was proceeding in this vehement manner, somewhat between jest and earnest, as it appeared to me, when he observed some signs of impatience in Cleanthes, and then immediately stopped short," allowing time for a brief interjection by Cleanthes (2.25.Pamphilus to Hermippus). In response, Cleanthes rapidly squeezes in several points, all of them surprising and surprisingly ineffectual.

Initially, Cleanthes protests Philo's "abuse" of terms in using "popular expressions to subvert philosophical reasonings." He claims that "the vulgar often distinguish reason from experience," whereas a properly philosophical analysis shows "that it [reason] is nothing but a species of experience" (2.25.Cleanthes to Philo). Usually the vulgar are taxed for *not* making distinctions; Cleanthes here chastises them for making an unwarranted one. Moreover, Cleanthes is unkindly (and uncharacteristically) repaying Philo in kind for his earlier ascription of the term "vulgar" to Cleanthes (2.17). But why does Cleanthes make this complaint? To be sure, Philo has just insisted that we can't evaluate reasoning about the origin of worlds because we lack experience of the origin of worlds (in 2.24). But if Cleanthes thinks that Philo has illicitly traded on the distinction between reason and experience, he is mistaken, for Philo is linking reason and experience every bit as tightly as Cleanthes could wish: Our reason is ineffective where experience is lacking.

Once again in these dialogues, what appears is not necessarily what is the case. What really bothers Cleanthes is Philo's contention that we have no experience of the origin of worlds, for this, if true, would indeed cripple Cleanthes' whole line of argument. So Cleanthes needs to rebut Philo's contention. But his rebuttal is not much help:

> To prove by experience the origin of the universe from mind is not more contrary to common speech than to prove the motion of the earth from the same principle. (2.25.Cleanthes to Philo)

Having just criticized the "vulgar," Cleanthes now makes an appeal to "common speech," and an odd one at that: One thing is "not more contrary" to it than another![29] Moreover, he compares items in two quite different categories —alteration or operation (the motion of the earth) and genesis or origin (the origin of the universe). Finally, if there is any resemblance at all between our experience of the motion of the earth and our experience of the origin of the universe, it licenses inference in either direction. But are both provable by experience (since the motion of the earth is so provable) or are both *not* provable by experience (since the origin of the universe is not)? At any rate, Cleanthes makes bold to assert that "the Copernican system" faces exactly the same difficulties Philo has been urging against Cleanthes' hypothesis: "Have you other earths . . . which you have seen to move?" (2.25.Pamphilus to Hermippus).[30]

¶¶26–28: Philo on astronomy and theology

Philo impolitely cuts off Cleanthes in mid-sentence and plunges into a three-paragraph tutorial on the differences between astronomy and theology —differences that eviscerate Cleanthes' rebuttal. "Yes! . . . we have other earths," Philo interjects with a renewed "vehement manner." The moon and the planets are "other earths" for astronomical purposes, and analogies among them are "the sole proofs of the Copernican system" (2.26.Philo to Cleanthes).[31] In fact, affirms Philo, the whole of modern (post-Galilean) astronomy shows that our experience can indeed reach other, celestial worlds and that the distinction in the "schools" between "elementary and celestial substances" has no foundation in fact. After Galileo demonstrated the earth's similarity to the moon and the planets, these latter "became proper objects of experience" (2.27.Philo to Cleanthes). But theology is totally different: Its proper object "exceeds all human reason and enquiry" and can never be made a proper object of experience. It is impossible for us to observe the whole universe in its current arrangement, much less at its origin. Thus, in theology, unlike astronomy, we have no evidential support for any empirical theory at all, much less for one theory over any other (2.28.Philo to Cleanthes).

So ends Part 2: with Cleanthes smarting from the critical blows Philo has administered to his "argument *a posteriori*" (though some of these blows are only glancing ones) and perhaps stung by Philo's jabs to his person; with Philo still vehement in his skeptical sallies, resting on a fundamental conviction that theology is too vast for our weak and narrow capacities; and with Demea an agitated spectator in a ringside seat. What kind of a "dialogue" is this? Is there any reason to continue exploring the design argument, much less anything remaining to be said?

6

Part 3

Tell me, from your own feeling, if the idea of a contriver does not immediately flow in upon you with a force like that of sensation.

—Cleanthes to Philo, Part 3.7

Structure:

¶¶ *1–9: Cleanthes refines his argument*
    ¶ *1: Similarity is "self-evident and undeniable"*
    ¶¶ *2–3: First example: "an articulate voice in the clouds"*
    ¶¶ *4–6: Second example: "natural volumes" of a "universal language"*
    ¶¶ *7–8: The force of natural teleology*
    ¶ *9: Alleged counterexamples are deflected*
¶ *10: Philo is "a little embarrassed and confounded"*
¶¶ *11–13: Demea saves Philo's "countenance"*

Following his bruising in Part 2, one would not be surprised to see Cleanthes change the subject in Part 3. Instead, undaunted, he summons up a long rejoinder that nonpluses Philo for once (indeed, for the *only* time in the *Dialogues!*), and as a result (and for once), Demea must step in to help Philo instead of the reverse. Demea reiterates his earlier view of divine incomprehensibility and human infirmity that appears consonant with Philo's skepticism but is in fact utterly different in motivation and implication. Part 3 is the only Part in which Philo sits entirely on the sidelines and listens to the other two speakers; what he is thinking we shall learn only in Part 4 after Cleanthes and Demea finish their conversation, though by then their dialogue has degenerated into name-calling.

¶1: Cleanthes refines his argument

Cleanthes, it turns out, has not given up on Copernicus; but now he wants to contrast, not compare, theology with astronomy. He professes astonishment at Philo's "ingenuity and invention" in giving "an air of probability" to "the most absurd argument." Copernicus needed to "prove the similarity of the terrestrial and celestial matter" because some denied it; but theists have no need to "prove the similarity of the works of nature to those of art" because this is "self-evident and undeniable"—"the same matter, a like form." Philo's objections therefore are merely "abstruse cavils"[1] and need to be refuted by "illustrations, examples, and instances, rather than by serious argument and philosophy" (3.1.Cleanthes to Philo).

Clearly Cleanthes is returning to his previous design argument (stated in 2.5 as an argument from analogy), but with a different focus. In fact, he makes two distinct refinements.[2] These seek to circumvent Philo's chief criticism in Part 2 (the "great disproportion" between our faculties and the whole universe) by concentrating on what Cleanthes claims is a perfectly natural and normal inference from ordered entities such as organisms to the thought of an artificer as cause of their distinctive order. In short, Cleanthes dwells not on the relations of parts to whole but rather on the *inference to design*—or the *recognition of design,* as he would have it—whether in parts or in the whole. Cleanthes first produces two hypothetical examples (in 3.2–3 and 3.4–6) that are intended to show how natural, immediate, and justified is the inference to an author or artificer, thinking that if this inference is justified in such hypothetical examples, it is likewise justified in relevantly similar actual cases. The difficulty, of course, lies in establishing the relevant similarity. He then goes on (in 3.7–9) to appeal to Philo's own perception of artifice and inference to artificer when he experiences things that display "the curious adjustment of final causes" (3.7.Cleanthes to Philo). The difficulty here lies in ascertaining the objectivity of this experience of teleology.

In producing his two famous (or infamous) examples, Cleanthes seeks imaginary works of nature that are obviously and undeniably like works of art or artifice; he thinks that such examples would "prove the similarity of the works of nature to those of art; because this similarity is self-evident and undeniable" (3.1.Cleanthes to Philo). He cannot point to such self-evident examples in the actual course of nature, for that would beg the fundamental question whether nature as we presently observe it *is* in fact (sufficiently) similar to works of human artifice. Hence Cleanthes produces not *actual* "illustrations, examples, and instances" but two rather bizarre *hypothetical* thought-experiments that are supposed to have the following properties: They describe (1) undoubtedly real and objective works of nature (not hallucinations or subjective delusions) that (2) we would immediately see as works with an intelligent origin, and that (3) are so like ordinary works of nature that (4) we would transfer our inference of intelligent causality from the imagined case to the actual one. It is not, however, a matter of *inferring* from the imagined to the actual case; rather, Cleanthes intends that we *credit our natural appre-hension* of agent causality not only in the imagined case but also in the every-day world—thereby vivifying our immediate sense of intelligent design in the natural world. In other words, Cleanthes is using these imaginary examples to redirect Philo's gaze—asking, in effect, "Don't you see?"

Both of Cleanthes' examples are introduced with the word "suppose," indicating that imagination and not rhetoric or logic plays the crucial role in directing apprehension. Cleanthes' appeal to imagination surely has promise, if indeed the challenge is to open one's eyes to unnoticed aspects and pros-pects. But there is a large potential for error, for seeming to see what is not there, for seeing what we want to see, for projecting our self-image upon the universe. We shall find, in fact, that Cleanthes's appeal is equivocal on pre-cisely this score.

There is a further aspect to Cleanthes' hypothetical examples: Both of them involve language.[3] The first is an articulate voice in the clouds, the sec-ond a living book; both insert into nature discourse that is widespread and cogent, a discourse clearly authored by a superior being. Cleanthes wants Philo (and not just Philo) to see the actual world as like his hypothetical worlds, rich in examples of divine discourse in both ordered whole and or-ganized parts. In Cleanthes' examples, to grasp that certain phenomena are linguistic is the crucial step in recognizing that they have an intelligent cause. It is not just that organisms and other parts of nature are teleologically con-stituted (possessing "the curious adjustment of final causes") but that they *say something*. A *mute* teleological world would not support the theism Cleanthes seeks.[4]

¶¶2–3: "An articulate voice"

Suppose then, first, that "an articulate voice were heard in the clouds" with the following properties: It is "much louder and more melodious than any which human art could ever reach," it is "extended in the same in-stant over all nations," it speaks "to each nation in its own language and dia-lect," and it conveys not merely "a just sense and meaning" but also "some instruction altogether worthy of a benevolent Being, superior to mankind." Cleanthes then asks of this heavily laden example: "Could you possibly hesi-tate a moment concerning the cause of this voice? And must you not instantly ascribe it to some design or purpose?" The emphasis is on the almost percep-tual immediacy of one's natural reaction—still an inference, but one not de-liberatively drawn. Given such an amazingly articulated voice, Philo, in con-cert with all humans, would infer without hesitation that the phenomenon is clearly designed and implies a designer. Cleanthes concludes by claiming that this imagined case is exactly parallel to theism in the actual world: Any objections against the one are objections against the other (3.2.Cleanthes to Philo). In particular, although the "extraordinary voice" differs greatly from ordinary human speech ("by its loudness, extent, and flexibility to all languages"[5]), we wouldn't hesitate to attribute such speech to an intelligent author, not to "some accidental whistling of the winds" or to an unknown and unknowable cause (3.3.Cleanthes to Philo).[6]

Is the example a coherent one? It seems physically possible, however remote, but several of its features work against Cleanthes' purposes. The voice is supposed to be "in the clouds"—probably Cleanthes means it is heard as *coming from* the sky and is not resident solely in the upper atmosphere, for otherwise we would have a non-obvious inference. Second, Cleanthes' example includes a number of features that cannot be immediately perceived, only inferred. The voice is heard "in the same instant over all nations" and speaking everywhere the local dialect. Perhaps these features could be inferred later as local reports timed by previously synchronized clocks came in from around the world. But neither property could be immediately perceived by any one person—all that an observer in one place could witness would be a voice from above speaking in her own native language; the rest is testimony. Third, the author(s) of such a phenomenon need not be divine, nor benevolent, nor thought to be such. This seems obvious today, suffused as we are with fictional images of aliens broadcasting their stories over all the earth. But it would not have been beyond the reach of an Enlightened citizen of the eighteenth century—non-divine superior beings such as angels (good and bad) were at least conceivable; in addition, of course, there is always the possibility of mass hallucination.

More to Cleanthes' point, does this example do its intended job of being a work of nature that is obviously of intelligent origin? The example is loaded to display intelligence, indeed intelligence superior to the human kind, in a self-evident way. But in doing so, it loses connection with ordinary actual works of nature. We have never heard such a voice, save in a work of imagination, and were we to do so, we would count it as the most extraordinary event in all of human history.[7] That we would immediately infer intelligence in this case seems irrelevant to whether we would or should do so in the ordinary run of nature, because the cases are so dissimilar. Ordinarily, we do not think that nature literally "speaks" in an "articulate," "rational," and "benevolent" voice, even though we recognize that some may see the world as something like divine discourse—but discourse quite unlike a natural human language. In short, as the inference from the imagined case to an intelligent author becomes more and more "self-evident and undeniable," it grows less and less able to "prove the similarity of the works of nature to those of art" and, conversely, as the similarity increases the inference grows less and less "self-evident." Cleanthes cannot have it both ways.

¶¶4–6: "Natural volumes"

Cleanthes recognizes that his first example is too remote from ordinary works of nature; and so, "to bring the case still nearer the present one of the universe," he introduces a second and even more imaginative supposition:

> Suppose, that there is a natural, universal, invariable language, common to every individual of human race; and that books are natural productions, which perpetuate themselves in the same manner with animals and vegetables, by descent and propagation.

No longer is there local dialect; there is but one tongue for all humans, and this language is spoken, or rather written, in or by books that naturally propagate—parts of nature that communicate to us in a language we all understand. The idea of a universal language is not far-fetched, Cleanthes thinks, because "several expressions of our passions contain a universal language," nor is the idea of books naturally propagating at all impossible, because books have "infinitely fewer parts and less contrivance" than "the coarsest organized body" (3.4.Cleanthes to Philo).

Cleanthes goes on to extend his imagined example: The "natural volumes" contain not just any discourse but "the most refined reason and most exquisite beauty." Could anyone doubt, Cleanthes rhetorically asks, that the "original cause" of such extraordinary volumes "bore the strongest analogy to mind and intelligence?" Even Philo, despite his well-known "obstinacy" in skeptical inquiry, could not continue raising doubts in the face of such an obvious display of intelligent design (3.5.Cleanthes to Philo). Moreover, if there are differences between "our vegetating library" and the actual world, "it is all to the advantage of the latter," since animal anatomy displays "many stronger instances of design" than books by Livy or Tacitus.[8] Inconclusive queries about "the first formation of worlds" have no tendency to disprove intelligent design in either the actual or the imagined case. Cleanthes is so confident of his example that he offers Philo a bold challenge: "Assert either that a rational volume is no proof of a rational cause, or admit of a similar cause to all the works of nature" (3.6.Cleanthes to Philo).[9]

Once again the efficacy of Cleanthes' example may be doubted, though not because of its incoherence. The initial supposition of a "vegetating library" would not startle a modern geneticist, although the language of his "volumes" is written in a minuscule four-letter alphabet coiled tightly within each cell. So the analogy with living organisms is actually a good deal stronger than Cleanthes could have known. There is indeed "a natural, universal, invariable language" for life on earth. Moreover, even the simplest bacterium is extraordinarily complicated, well beyond the works of any human author, so that an author of bacteria inferred by Cleanthes' method must possess a proportionally superior intelligence. But of course modern biologists have an alternative account of the design of life forms: Their "original cause" is no intelligent contriver but a thoroughly "blind" process of evolution by natural selection.

Perhaps anticipating that a language of life might well be thought opaque to human minds or indifferent to human values, Cleanthes makes one further extension to his supposition: The "natural volumes" bespeak "the most refined reason and most exquisite beauty," appealing not only to "the pure intellect" but also to "the affections." This multiple appeal shores up the obviousness of inference to design (or the perception of design); natural books that are both rational and beautiful more readily excite our apprehension of intelligence. But once again Cleanthes has purchased obviousness of intelligent design at the cost of remoteness from the ordinary run of nature. Our "vegetating library" is now so very like a real library that it has become very *un*like a living organism. A *rational* living volume would indeed be proof of a rational cause, but nature "speaks" a vastly different "language."

¶¶7–9: Natural teleology

But Cleanthes is not finished; he adds two paragraphs about our natural sense of teleology and a concluding paragraph rebutting some objections.[10] First Cleanthes holds that what he now calls "this religious[11] argument" is not at all weakened but rather strengthened by Philo's skeptical inquiry. Recurring to his position in Part 1, Cleanthes maintains that *wholesale* skepticism is "either affectation or madness"; instead,

> the declared profession of every *reasonable* sceptic is only to reject abstruse, remote and refined arguments; to adhere to common sense and the plain instincts of nature; and to assent, wherever any reasons strike him with so full a force, that he cannot, without the greatest violence, prevent it. Now, the arguments for natural religion are plainly of this kind; nothing but the most perverse, obstinate metaphysics can reject them. (3.7.Cleanthes to Philo; emphasis added)

Cleanthes thinks such "arguments" are found in the anatomy of the eye, in matching male and female sexual organs, and in "millions and millions" of other instances. Here Cleanthes asks Philo to consider such examples and "tell me, from your own feeling, if the idea of a contriver does not immediately flow in upon you with a force like that of sensation." One can, of course, conjure up "abstruse" objections, but they are "frivolous" and impotent in the face of such striking examples of design. Indeed, "no language can convey a more intelligible, irresistible meaning, than the curious adjustment of final causes" (3.7.Cleanthes to Philo). Such an appeal, Cleanthes admits, may seem "contrary to rules," constituting an argument of an "irregular nature." None-theless, "whatever cavils may be urged; an orderly world, as well as a coherent, articulate speech, will still be received as an incontestable proof of design and intention" (3.8.Cleanthes to Philo).

But if natural teleology is so "universal" and "irresistible" in its theistic implications (3.8), why is not everyone a devout theist? Cleanthes' answer is intriguing: Two types of people are not properly affected.[12] One type is "an ignorant savage and barbarian" who has not asked the right questions about origin and causality: "But this is neither dogmatism nor scepticism, but stu-pidity." The other is the "sifting, inquisitive disposition" of people like Philo. Philo's problem is not the barbarian's "barrenness of thought and invention" but rather "too luxuriant a fertility, which suppresses your natural good sense, by a profusion of unnecessary scruples and objections" (3.9.Cleanthes to Philo).

In these three paragraphs, Cleanthes shifts his appeal. In Part 2, he made an abstract argument that relied upon considerations available to anyone: *Any-one* can "look round the world"; find it filled with "machines" resembling, though exceeding, "human contrivance"; and infer an Author of Nature "somewhat similar to the mind of man; though possessed of much larger fac-ulties" (2.5). Likewise his imaginative examples earlier in Part 3 (the articulate voice and the vegetative library) are thought-experiments that anyone can undertake. But now Cleanthes appeals directly to *Philo,* to Philo's own first-hand experience, to the phenomena as *he* actually experiences them and not to arguments abstracted from his concrete experience.

Further, although Cleanthes calls it an "argument," it is not, initially, a piece of reasoning but rather an appeal to something prior to reasoning—not an inference (certainly no "abstruse, remote and refined" argument), but evi-dence or data upon which an argument can be built. It is an appeal to some-thing Philo (allegedly) already experiences but fails to notice because of his monomania for disputation. Moreover, this "something" is to be felt or re-ceived, not imagined or analyzed. Indeed, it is supposed to be felt with "a force like that of sensation." Cleanthes, knowing his friend Philo well, thinks Philo simply avoids noticing this forceful experience in his zeal for skeptical critique.[13]

Philo's mind is, or should be, naturally poised to receive this inflowing "sensation"-like experience. He can of course invent objections to what may be legitimately inferred from this experience in an effort to block or deflect its power; but these objections are "frivolous" and carry no conviction. Such experiences are "natural" and utterly "convincing" (3.7). It is therefore (part of) Philo's nature to discern and appreciate "the curious adjustment of final causes" and to explain this adjustment by intelligent authorship.

But, Cleanthes continues, Philo's nature is everyone's nature. This "argument for theism" has a "universal" and "irresistible" influence, affecting everyone who considers it properly. Natural theism is thus a response to Nature by our natures. Perhaps this human tendency is "irregular," as logicians define the regular principles of logic, but that in no wise renders it ineligible for our acceptance. On the contrary, logical rules and principles must answer to our natural human tendencies.

Such is Cleanthes' appeal to Philo—and ultimately to everyone. The major question is whether this appeal to an alleged natural human tendency is any more successful than Cleanthes' earlier hypothetical examples. In one way, it is quite successful: It succeeds in silencing Philo, at least for the moment (until 4.4), and it will later reverberate in Philo's famous "confession" in Part 12.2. To be sure, Demea is not persuaded, but it is not clear that he has even understood Cleanthes' appeal, much less consulted his own experience or devised any compelling criticism of this approach. Demea is simply bent upon reiterating his earlier contentions of divine incomprehensibility and human inadequacy, and he has no time for natural teleology.

But what, then, does Cleanthes' appeal establish? At best only that some humans are so fashioned, or conditioned, as to be struck by "the curious adjustment of final causes" they find in nature and to respond immediately to them as most everyone responds to artifacts. For such persons, theists do not need to "prove the similarity of the works of nature to those of art; because this similarity is self-evident and undeniable" (3.1.Cleanthes to Philo). That is to say, when they regard nature, it is *evident to them*—they have neither desire nor reason to deny—that there is a "curious adjustment of final causes" that calls forth immediately "the idea of a contriver" with a power "like that of sensation" that is thoroughly "convincing," provided we are neither barbarously ignorant nor extravagantly imaginative (3.7.Cleanthes to Philo). But does this conviction prove that there is indeed an artificer of nature? Well, to one who is seized by this inflowing sentiment, no argument can persuade otherwise; while to one who lacks this sense for design or who has reason to discount or distrust this sense or can explain it away,[14] the "argument" is totally unpersuasive. In the end, Cleanthes' "religious argument" is not a question of logic or rhetoric but an interrogation of experience: Do you find within yourself a sense for design?

¶10: Philo's embarrassment

Following Cleanthes' appeal to Philo's feelings, Pamphilus reports that "Philo was a little embarrassed and confounded," hesitating so long in reply that, "luckily for him, Demea broke in upon the discourse, and saved his countenance" (3.10.Pamphilus to Hermippus). Whether Demea does indeed "save" Philo we shall consider shortly. But why is Philo embarrassed, and how is he confounded?[15] This is one of those rare moments of (reported) action in the *Dialogues,* and we are obliged to take it most seriously, even though any interpretation of its significance is bound to be somewhat speculative.

One possibility is that Philo is startled into silence by the dramatic way Cleanthes has shored up his argument. In Part 2, Cleanthes had given an "argument *a posteriori*" that identified the parts and whole of nature as machines, resembling though exceeding "the productions of human contrivance." Since the effects resemble one another, their causes must do likewise, so that "the Author of Nature is somewhat similar to the mind of man" (2.5.Cleanthes to Demea and Philo). We noted earlier that this argument has many holes, one of which is that Cleanthes offers no support for thinking that things in nature are (or are like) machines. But now, in Part 3, Cleanthes seems to have addressed this lack: We see things with "the curious adjustment of final causes" as machines or designed artifacts (immediately implying an intelligent author) because we are naturally constituted to see things in this way. Theistic conviction therefore rests not on logical inference but on a kind of immediate apprehension. But why should an appeal to experience confound Philo any more than an appeal to argument?

Further, Cleanthes does seem to have blocked one obvious line of criticism —namely, that this experience is not universal—by discussing two categories of persons to whom it does not appeal (ignorant "barbarians" and too-clever skeptics). But this is ad hominem—to Demea as well as to Philo—and perhaps Philo does not wish to continue in this vein.

But the most likely cause of Philo's awkward silence is the very personal quality of the appeal that Cleanthes has made: He has asked Philo to consider such natural objects as the eye and "tell me, *from your own feeling,* if the idea of a contriver does not immediately flow in *upon you* with a force like that of sensation" (3.7.Cleanthes to Philo; emphasis added). Such an appeal would not embarrass a disingenuous or oblivious skeptic, who could forge ahead with critical questions regardless of how he felt personally. But Cleanthes knows Philo all too well, and he has put Philo on the spot: Philo cannot dissemble *to Cleanthes* when asked to report his own feelings. Philo does indeed feel within himself the power of *teleological thinking*; he too has a tendency to see design in nature. Philo is therefore embarrassed and confounded precisely because Cleanthes' appeal resonates in his heart.

Further, both Philo and Cleanthes genuinely share this teleological sense of the works of nature as somehow like the works of human contrivance,[16] while once again Demea is the odd man out because he is tone-deaf to natural teleology. We may go even farther. Perhaps this shared teleological sense is integral to the friendship of Philo and Cleanthes, one very deep reason why they are friends; certainly it is a vital part of their shared natural religious piety, and it is thoroughly consonant with their human virtues. Demea's teleological insensitivity mirrors the rest of his authoritarian personality and constitutes one more disqualification from true society with Cleanthes and Philo.

¶¶11–13: Demea to the rescue

Pamphilus next reports that "while he [Philo] hesitated in delivering an answer, luckily for him, Demea broke in upon the discourse, and saved his countenance" (3.10.Pamphilus to Hermippus). This is the judgment of a youth, and whether Demea does indeed save Philo's face—or if he does so, how "lucky" it is for Philo—demands scrutiny.

Demea first notes his own reaction to Cleanthes' appeal and fastens upon its reliance on language: "Your instance . . . drawn from books and language, being familiar, has, I confess, so much more force on that account." But what Demea reads in the Book of Nature is not insight into divine attributes and intentions but rather *mystery*: "This volume of nature contains a great and inexplicable riddle, more than any intelligible discourse or reasoning." This is an old and favorite theme of Demea's. He constantly points out the dangers of thinking that "the Deity"[17] can be comprehended by the human mind— that is, he harps on the perils of anthropomorphism, with several variations:

1. Cleanthes' line of argument contains the "danger" of rendering us "presumptuous, by making us imagine we comprehend the Deity, and have some adequate idea of his nature and attributes." By reading a volume, we "enter into the mind and intention of the author: I become him, in a manner, for the instant." But we cannot do this with the Book of Nature: "His ways are not our ways. His attributes are perfect, but incomprehensible" (3.11.Demea to Cleanthes).[18]

2. Demea once again appeals to authority, but to a very odd authority— "the ancient *Platonists*," particularly Plotinus—for support of even odder claims: "that intellect or understanding is not to be ascribed to the Deity; and that our most perfect worship of him consists, not in acts of veneration, reverence, gratitude or love; but in a certain mysterious self annihilation or total extinction of all our faculties." Here Demea is willing to throw out the central Christian conception of God as love as well as typical Christian acts of piety (worship, prayer, veneration, reverence, gratitude, love) in favor of mystical self-abnegation or "annihilation," all in order to controvert Cleanthes. Demea seems to realize how heterodox[19] this position is: "These ideas," he says, "are, perhaps, too far stretched." Yet Demea is willing to make use of Plotinus as a counterweight to Cleanthes in order to avoid "the grossest and most narrow partiality, and make ourselves the model of the whole universe" (3.12.Demea to Cleanthes).

3. Finally, there is a certain logical problem in transferring human attributes to "a supreme existence." Human thinking can be divided into two aspects, its "materials" and its "manner"; the former consists of two sorts of ideas, derived from internal sentiment and from external sensation. But none of these aspects of human thinking can properly belong to a supreme being. As for the materials, the internal "sentiments of the human mind" such as "gratitude, resentment, love, friendship, approbation, blame, pity, emulation, envy" can scarcely be ascribed to the deity. Nor can "all our ideas, derived from the senses," for these are "confessedly false and illusive." As for manner, human thinking is "fluctuating, uncertain, fleeting, successive, and compounded," whereas divine thought can be none of these; and if we remove these temporal features of human thought "we absolutely annihilate its essence, and it would, in such a case, be an abuse of terms to apply to it the name of thought or reason." There may still be reasons of piety to apply such terms to God, but, Demea concludes,

> We ought to acknowledge, that their meaning, in that case, is totally incomprehensible; and that the infirmities of our nature do not permit us to reach any ideas, which in the least correspond to the ineffable sublimity of the divine attributes. (3.13.Demea to Cleanthes)

Once again Demea has arrived at a kind of negative theology, but this version is no better thought out than before. For what is the basis upon which Demea claims that these various features of human thinking are *not* found in the deity? How could Demea know that the supreme being is "totally incomprehensible"? How could he grasp that divine attributes possess "ineffable sublimity"? One suspects that Demea would like to appeal to revelation[20] or some other authority (perhaps private intuition) outside the tests of common experience and reason to which both Cleanthes and Philo appeal. But he does not produce such an extraordinary appeal, and in its absence all we have are his unsupported—and insupportable—claims to incomprehension.

One final point: Demea's efforts to save Philo's "countenance" do not help Philo, aside from giving him time to regain his composure and determine how best to respond to Cleanthes. Philo may agree with Demea on our incomprehension of divine attributes, but his grounds, aims, and motivations are altogether different.

For Demea, divine incomprehensibility is due to certain attributes *of God*: divine sublimity and perfection. We cannot know God because God is great and lifted up, immense, supreme, transcendent. Demea's language expresses the point nicely: It is not that God is perfectly incomprehensible but that He is "perfect, but incomprehensible" (3.11.Demea to Cleanthes). Such incomprehensibility logically ought to yield to silence. But there is need for discourse to rightly orient young newcomers to Demea's piety—that is, to train them in submissiveness. So Demea aims to squelch natural theological speculation in order to make way for an authoritative piety and theology that will command obedience without taxing anyone's intellect. A doctrine of divine mystery plays easily into his hands, for by humbling our capacities in the face of divine sublimity, we are made submissive to divine fiat and hence more compliant for the deity's earthly mouthpieces.

For Philo, on the other hand, divine incomprehensibility is due to certain properties *of us*: our weakness and imperfection. We cannot know God because our native human capacities are so frail and infirm that they plunge us into perplexity even within the realm of ordinary experience. Philo therefore aims to turn attention from God to Man. The notion of divine incomprehensibility expresses skepticism of our limited ability to know and leads us into the paths of humility. By making us less, not more, certain about ultimate matters, it allows us to form a human community more tolerant of theological disagreement.

Part 3's dialogue seems unfinished—not unpolished, but incomplete. Cleanthes has for once "embarrassed and confounded" Philo, and Demea's face-saving intervention is no substantive help to Philo. We therefore expect Philo to rejoin the conversation at any moment and to issue a direct rejoinder to Cleanthes' "irregular" argument as well as a correction to Demea. He will indeed return to the discussion in Part 4, but whether he will engage Cleanthes' appeal to personal experience remains to be seen; certainly he will pay no attention at all to Demea. Meanwhile, we shall first hear Cleanthes and Demea sparring over the possibility, and the appropriateness, of an incomprehensible deity, for the current conversation between them continues into the first three paragraphs of Part 4.

7

Part 4

I shall endeavor to show you, a little more distinctly, the inconveniences of that anthropomorphism, which you have embraced.

—Philo to Cleanthes, Part 4.5

Structure:

¶¶ *1–4: Name-calling*

¶ *1: Cleanthes: Demea is a "mystic"*

¶ *2: Demea: Cleanthes is an "anthropomorphite" and an atheist*

¶ *3: Cleanthes: Mystics are atheists*

¶ *4: Philo: Is everyone an atheist?*

¶¶ *5–14: Philo considers the first "inconvenience" of anthropomorphism: A divine plan is non-explanatory*

¶¶ *5–12: Philo shows the inutility of supposing a divine plan of the world*

¶ *13: Cleanthes protests: "I have found a Deity, and here I stop my enquiry"*

¶ *14: Philo would stop sooner, with the material world*

The first four paragraphs of Part 4 continue the dialogue started in Part 3 by Demea's insinuation that Cleanthes' design argument is "presumptuous, by making us imagine we comprehend the Deity" (3.11). Though both Cleanthes and Demea do have points to make, their exchange deteriorates into name-calling until Philo resumes control of the conversation (4.4). First he shows the futility (and perhaps lack of seriousness) of such badinage, for it reduces everyone to a position no one wants to hold: atheism. Then (in 4.5) he begins a line of inquiry that will continue for several Parts, pointing out to Cleanthes various "inconveniences" of the anthropomorphism ingredient in his design arguments. Philo's first point is that recourse to a divine design, plan, or idea in creating the world is non-explanatory, for either it launches an infinite search for causes of causes or it should not be taken in the first place. Both Cleanthes and Philo reject the *regressus ad infinitum*, but Cleanthes wants to take just one more explanatory step than does Philo; this kind of disagreement between the two friends persists until the very end of the *Dialogues*.

¶¶1–3: Name-calling

In the previous Part, Demea had "saved" Philo's "countenance" by attacking Cleanthes' presumption in comparing the divine mind to our human minds (3.13.Demea to Cleanthes). Now Cleanthes replies to Demea, leading with an ad hominem jab to Demea's piety and continuing with some body blows against maintaining the "absolute incomprehensibility of the deity." The jab is this: How can "you, Demea, who are so sincere[1] in the cause of religion," insist that the Deity has no resemblance to human creatures? Cleanthes' worry is that if human ideas either do not apply or cannot be known to apply to God, then (theistic) religious piety has neither object nor basis; without partial divine-human resemblance, any words of praise, supplication, petition, "sublime eulogies," and the like would be without meaning.[2] Cleanthes readily concedes that we don't comprehend *all* of the "many powers and attributes" of divinity. "But if our ideas, so far as they go, be not just, and adequate, and correspondent to his real nature, I know·not what there is in this subject worth insisting on. Is the name, without any meaning, of such mighty importance?" In sum, Cleanthes asks, "How do you *mystics*, who maintain the absolute incomprehensibility of the deity, differ from sceptics or atheists, who assert, that the first cause of all is unknown and unintelligible?" (4.1.Cleanthes to Demea).[3] So Demea is not only a "mystic" with an incomprehensible God, he is also an "atheist" who denies the existence of any deity whom humans can conceive, discuss, and worship. In short, Demea's theology subverts (what is for Cleanthes) proper piety.

This is an important line of questioning, for it asks how theistic language could possibly be meaningful if common human experience and reason are rejected because they make God too much like a human being. In all fairness, Demea could respond by defending the meaningfulness of his pious discourse, perhaps by citing some special backing for his claims (e.g., private experiences, *a priori* argument, revealed authority). But he doesn't, for all he hears in Cleanthes' discourse is the name he has been called, and that is the level on which he responds, in like kind but greater quantity. Not only does he chastise Cleanthes for being like "the common bigots and inquisitors of the age" in having "recourse to invective and declamation, instead of reasoning," he immediately proceeds to "retort" with some name-calling, "invective and declamation" of his own (thereby establishing his own company with "the common bigots and inquisitors of the age"). Cleanthes is an "anthropomorphite," and this "invidious" name "implies as dangerous consequences, as the epithet of *Mystic,* with which he has honoured us" (4.2.Demea to Cleanthes).[4] By "dangerous," Demea primarily means threatening to what he regards as orthodox theology, but there is also an undercurrent of threat to Demea's own piety, against which he will retaliate. Hence the danger is double-edged: not just to (Demea's) religion but also to any challenger of that religion. Demea's label of "dangerous" is a clear threat to the one who threatens him.

Demea follows his "invidious" name-calling by presenting an interesting view of divine attributes, albeit a derivative one. The human "soul," he says, is composed of various distinct faculties united in one self; these faculties give rise to one arrangement of ideas, passions, and affections after another, and these swiftly cascading contents "continually diversify the mental scene." But God is supposed by "all true theists" to be immutable and simple, comprehending all time in "one individual operation"; since there is "no succession, no change, no acquisition, no diminution" in God, "He stands fixed in one simple, perfect state" utterly unlike the human condition (4.2.Demea to Cleanthes). Cleanthes opposes this traditional view of the divine nature, so he denies God and is an atheist. Demea has thus repaid Cleanthes completely in kind.

Insult aside, it is by no means clear how Demea thinks he is in a position to know the supposed divine immutability and simplicity if he still clings to the total incomprehensibility of the deity. Is divine incomprehensibility only partial? Is Demea taking divine simplicity and immutability on authority, as the reference to "all true theists" suggests?[5] But Demea is singularly unconcerned with consistency, and it is no use trying to reconcile his present view with any earlier ones, except as they connect with and protect his piety.

Cleanthes rejoins that those who hold this view of divine simplicity and immutability are "complete *mystics*" and, whether they realize it or not, atheists. For Cleanthes, "intelligent nature" is "essential" to divinity, and any view incompatible with this doctrine should be rejected:

> A mind, whose acts and sentiments and ideas are not distinct and successive; one that is wholly simple, and totally immutable; is a mind, which has no thought, no reason, no will, no sentiment, no love, no hatred; or in a word, is no mind at all.

So once again "it is an abuse of terms" to call immutable simplicity "mind," as contradictory as "limited extension without figure, or . . . number without composition" (4.3.Cleanthes to Demea).[6]

¶4: Philo on name-calling

At this point Philo finally steps in and reflects back to Cleanthes the outcome of all this name-calling: What Cleanthes is calling "atheist" includes "all the sound, orthodox divines almost, who have treated of this subject." Cleanthes is in danger of reckoning himself "the only sound theist in the world." Worse, "if idolaters be atheists, as I think, may justly be asserted, and Christian theologians the same; what becomes of the argument, so much celebrated, derived from the universal consent of mankind?" (4.4.Philo to Cleanthes). Cleanthes, according to Demea, is an idolater for fashioning a concept of God in human form. So Philo is pointing out, if adherents of divine simplicity, immutability, and incomprehensibility are atheists (according to Cleanthes), and if adherents of divine-human similarity are also atheists (according to Demea), then all are atheists (according to both). This means the traditional theistic appeal to "the universal consent of mankind"[7] backfires, not because there is no universal consent but because what universal consent there is points to atheism!

Implicit in Philo's banter are several important points. There is of course the obvious historical moral that (in certain cultures) imputations of "atheism" are powerful weapons, but they are no party's private possession, for they can be wielded by anyone who thinks another's conception of God is mistaken. An "atheist" is one who denies the existence of God—but which God? Demea, Cleanthes, and Philo all believe there is a God; no one would regard himself as an atheist. Yet each has a different idea of God's nature. To crystallize the essential quarrel, let's abbreviate Demea's God, or God as conceived by Demea, as God_D, Cleanthes' God as God_C, and Philo's God as God_P and assume that God_D, God_C, and God_P all differ. In particular, Demea supposes that God's nature is different from what Cleanthes and Philo maintain. Were this discussion among friends, at this point they could perhaps agree to disagree, maybe even adding some account of how their disagreement is possible or even likely. This is indeed how Philo and Cleanthes resolve the issue between them in Part 12. For these good friends, belief in God_C does not entail disbelief in God_P, and conversely; theists (at least their kind of theists) can and should tolerate a range of alternative conceptions of the nature of God.

But Demea is another matter altogether. Demea's religion is competitive and exclusionary. Demea believes that God = God_D and that others' views are mistaken; others not only mistakenly believe that, for example, God = God_C or that God = God_P but also, because God ≠ God_C and God ≠ God_P, they misbelieve that God ≠ God_D.[8] It follows, on Demea's principles, that to believe in God_C or God_P is to disbelieve in God, because to do so is to disbelieve in

God$_D$, and God$_D$ *is* God. So Cleanthes and Philo are atheists, because they do not believe that God *as conceived by Demea* exists. Thus, Demea's piety makes atheists out of those who do not share his conception of deity. In conceiving of God differently than Demea, they believe *against him*. Further, in Demea's eyes, this is no mere intellectual error but a serious soteriological failing, and Demea is willing to use any necessary means to alter their minds to save their souls.

¶¶5–12: The first "inconvenience" of anthropomorphism

But Philo does not find name-calling profitable, so he swiftly moves on to his major task over the next several Parts: showing Cleanthes "the inconveniences of that anthropomorphism, which you have embraced." This, at last, is Philo's formal and extensive reply to the "irregular" argument Cleanthes presented in Part 3 that so "embarrassed and confounded" Philo. Philo will use the remainder of Part 4 to focus on only one aspect of Cleanthes' argument —its effort to explain the structure, order, or arrangement of the material world via "a plan of the world to be formed in the divine mind, consisting of distinct ideas, differently arranged; in the same manner as an architect forms in his head the plan of a house which he intends to execute" (4.5.Philo to Cleanthes).[9]

Philo's initial criticism of this view is that postulating a divine plan to account for the world's order is non-explanatory, in either of two ways. First, the order in a divine plan itself requires explanation, but this launches an infinite regress of explanations of explanations, and an infinite regress is non-explanatory. Second, Cleanthes regards the divine plan's order as satisfactorily *self*-explanatory, but "self-explanatory" is as applicable to the material world as to a mental world of ideas. In either case, nothing is gained by postulating a divine plan or set of divine ideas. Philo reinforces this point over several largely redundant paragraphs with different emphases, as if needing to hammer home something that is far from obvious to Cleanthes—or to Pamphilus.

First, he says that the "supposition" of a divine plan is non-explanatory either to reason or to experience. Philo makes this distinction between reason and experience, even though Cleanthes had earlier (2.25) called it an abuse of terms. Cleanthes does not demur now, however, for what Philo is showing is that whether one stresses the abstract or the sensory aspects of experience (or indeed combines them) the result is the same. *Reason* ("I mean abstract reason, derived from enquiries *a priori*") is "mute" regarding causality, but even if it were not, it would find no difference between mental and material worlds: Both worlds require causes, and they require similar causes if the worlds have similar "arrangements" of their respective elements (4.7.Philo to Cleanthes).[10] *Experience* goes "beyond her sphere" in judging the origin of whole worlds (the "great disproportion" theme once again). But within her reach, experience finds "these two kinds of worlds . . . to be governed by similar principles." In miniature, our own mind resembles the divine mental world, while "a vegetable or animal body" resembles the material world. But then we find by experience that neither is "more delicate with regard to its causes"; neither "depend[s] upon a greater variety or more curious adjustment of springs and principles" (4.8.Philo to Cleanthes).

But then there is no need to explain the material world in terms of an "ideal world." "Have we not the same reason to trace that ideal world into another ideal world, or new intelligent principle? But if we stop, and go no farther; why go so far? Why not stop at the material world?" To block this fruitless regress of causes of causes, "it were better, therefore, never to look beyond the present material world. By supposing it to contain the principle of its order within itself, we really assert it to be God; and the sooner we arrive at that divine Being so much the better" (all 4.9.Philo to Cleanthes).

What about the alleged self-explanatory character of the ideal mental world? It is unclear just what it means to say that "the different ideas, which compose the reason of the supreme Being, fall into order, of themselves, and by their own nature," but it is equally meaningful, and as unclear, to say that "the parts of the material world fall into order, of themselves, and by their own nature" (4.10.Philo to Cleanthes). Indeed, we have experience of apparently self-ordering matter in "all instances of generation and vegetation," and we have experience of apparently intrinsic disorder in mind ("madness") and in matter ("corruption"). So far as we can tell, then, matter and mind are equally ordered or disordered, of and by themselves. Hence it does no good to explain the material world's order by removal to a world of ideas; and if we take but one step, we are unable to keep from stepping without end. "It were, therefore, wise in us, to limit all our enquiries to the present world, without looking farther" and to remain within "the narrow bounds of human understanding" (4.11.Philo to Cleanthes).

Philo concludes with a reference to "the Peripatetics,"[11] who gave only apparent explanations with their "faculties or occult qualities," as if bestowing the name "nutritive faculty" on the causal power of bread to nourish provided any explanatory assistance. Similarly, it does not explain the order of ideas in the divine mind to say that their cause is "a *rational* faculty, and that such is the nature of the Deity." But if order in the world of ideas provides no real explanation of order in the material world, and if there is no real explanation of the former, why not just accept that there is "a faculty of order and proportion" in the nature of the material world? Both removal to the world of ideas and embrace of the material world's order "are only more learned and elaborate ways of confessing our ignorance" (4.12.Philo to Cleanthes).

Philo here accepts analogies drawn from ordinary experience for thinking about cosmological causality, even though this is precisely what Cleanthes proffered in his design argument and what Philo earlier criticized as beyond the reach of our limited faculties. Moreover, both use human minds as proper analogues to a divine world of ideas. There is, however, a major rift when it comes to analogues to the material world: Cleanthes focuses on living bodies as they resemble "machines" of human contrivance, while Philo considers living bodies as they are self-regulating natural entities. The difference is vital. For Cleanthes, if the world resembles a human artifact, their respective causes also resemble each other, so the Author of Nature has a mind like ours. For Philo, living bodies only remotely resemble artifacts, and there is no obvious inference from mental to material microcosm; hence the Author of Nature does not resemble human intelligence. But we should not make too much of Philo's embrace of analogy here. Philo is using analogical thinking to disabuse Cleanthes of the profitability of an analogical leap to a divine plan; even if analogical inference is natural, Philo does not find compelling the kind of analogy that licenses projecting teleology from human artifacts onto the entire universe.

¶13: Cleanthes' stopping point

Cleanthes finally replies to Philo's much-reiterated critique, dryly noting that Philo has "displayed this argument with great emphasis" and affirming that an answer to it is "easy." He claims that assigning a cause to an event is proper even when we cannot discern the cause of that cause "and answer every new question, which may incessantly be started." Even philosophers— or rather, especially philosophers—should know that in the end they will run up against "principles" that are as inexplicable to them as are the "phenomena" with which they began to "the vulgar." For Cleanthes, the design argument clearly signals a Creator:

> The order and arrangement of nature, the curious adjustment of final causes, the plain use and intention of every part and organ; all these bespeak in the clearest language an intelligent cause or author.

Of course, Philo may start "abstruse doubts, cavils, and objections" concerning the cause of this "intelligent cause or author." But Cleanthes' inability to answer these cavils does not shake his fundamental confidence: "I have found a Deity, and here I stop my inquiry. Let those go farther, who are wiser or more enterprising" (4.13.Cleanthes to Philo).

Cleanthes' brief retort has clarified how he views his design argument: It is an amalgam, and it centrally employs the metaphor of language. He cites three quite different kinds of premise, all pointing toward the same conclusion of divine authorship: the order and arrangement of nature, the curious adjustment of final causes in nature, and the internal teleology of living bodies. Whether in his view the premises are separable or even distinct is unclear; likewise unclear is whether an argument from each distinguishable premise considered separately would succeed. What matters for him is that they all "bespeak" an intelligent Author of Nature—the kind of inference from these premises is the kind involved in inferring language from sound. Moreover, all "bespeak in the clearest language"—the inference is as natural and obvious as discerning the intelligence of a human author from comprehending her discourse. Nature is the lucid language of God, and we are naturally equipped to comprehend that language.[12]

¶14: Philo's stopping point

In the final paragraph of Part 4, Philo makes two points in reply to Cleanthes. First, instead of going farther than Cleanthes in search of a cause of the natural world, Philo would rather not go so far, particularly since the answer Cleanthes gives faces the very same explanatory problems as Philo's proposal. Cleanthes thinks the material world is not self-explanatory but requires explanation in terms of something outside itself—a divine action—even though he cannot account for the order in this external cause either on its own terms or in terms of anything else.

Here Philo neatly encapsulates his central disagreement with Cleanthes concerning our desire for a teleological explanation of the natural world—and shows how small and unimportant this disagreement is. Cleanthes wants to discover the Author that the world "bespeaks"; Philo does not want to "go so far."[13] Cleanthes finds the material world inexplicable on its own terms, so he seeks an external cause—a mighty creator with an intelligent mind somewhat like our own—even if he cannot explain the cause of this cause. Philo finds the material world no more inexplicable, and no more in need of explanation, than the deity, so he holds that if one is eventually going to appeal to inexplicability anyway, one might as well remain within this mysterious world. For Cleanthes, a degree of understanding is achieved by our completely natural, indeed unavoidable, inference from the world to God, while for Philo, the world is just as explanatorily good as God: Both are proximately intelligible, ultimately inexplicable. Their disagreement, then, boils down to a question of *degree*—how much (or how little) understanding is gained by recourse to an external deity? Hence the difference between them is not great: *some* understanding for Cleanthes, *not much,* if any, for Philo. Such a disagreement of degree is unlikely to threaten their friendship, particularly when, as we shall see (in Part 12), there are deeper solidarities.

Second, Philo chooses this moment to make a completely new point, contending that there is an important difference between the causal regress Cleanthes proposes and the kind used by natural scientists: "Naturalists indeed very justly explain particular effects by more general causes," however inexplicable the latter may be, whereas Cleanthes proposes "to explain a particular effect by a particular cause," itself inexplicable.[14] Philo concludes Part 4 with this statement:

> An ideal system, arranged of itself, without a precedent design, is not a whit more explicable than a material one, which attains its order in a like manner; nor is there any more difficulty in the latter supposition than in the former. (4.14.Philo to Cleanthes)

This point is more problematic than the first. Why should an inexplicable particular cause of a particular effect be less "satisfactory" than an inexplicable general cause? Philo recounts "the story of the *Indian* philosopher and his elephant" (4.9.Philo to Cleanthes), where the earth remains where it does in space by resting on the back of an elephant—and the elephant on the back of a tortoise, and the tortoise on something else, and so forth. Clearly this line of explanation is unsatisfactory, because the need for support which started the series is retained at every level: If the earth needs support, so does the elephant, the tortoise, and every other member of the stack, and each needs support in exactly the same way. So to explain a particular effect by a particular cause that itself requires the very same sort of explanation seems futile. But what about a "more general cause"? Is, say, the law of universal gravitation any less unsatisfactory if we cannot account for gravity? What have we gained by shifting from a non-self-explanatory particular to a non-self-explanatory general law? Perhaps Philo is thinking that we have at least gained generality and therefore the potential of explaining "other earths"[15] in the same way; a general cause can explain not only this particular but others of the same kind, while usually a particular cause can explain only its particular effect. To be sure, general causes by themselves cannot explain particular events qua particular at all.[16] But when they are ingredient in a theory and combined with descriptions of particulars (antecedent events and background conditions), general factors may provide a more powerful explanation than just the particulars alone. This is hardly a reason for preferring naturalism over theism, however, as neither can provide either general laws or particular antecedents that explain the origin of worlds.

One last point deserves comment. Philo assumes that God must be a particular and not a general cause. But this is problematic. God is a strange kind of particular being—thoroughly and superlatively unique, with causal powers quite unlike those of any other being. Divine action (on a traditional view) acts everywhere immediately; its power and scope are unbounded; it creates (and can remove or alter) conditions, such as natural laws, that affect everything else. Divine creation is also ex nihilo, working without material (and other?) antecedents. Even so, there might well be general laws of divine agency, and perhaps we could know them, gaining some degree of explanation of divine effects. So, all in all, Philo's point about general and particular causes adds little or nothing to his critique of Cleanthes' design argument.

By the end of Part 4, Demea and Cleanthes have ceased their name-calling, at least for a while, and Philo has settled into pointing out the "inconveniences" of Cleanthes' "anthropomorphism." The particular inconvenience he examines in this Part is that recourse to a divine mental world is non-explanatory, because it either launches an infinite regress of causes or provides a double of the physical world that is no less mysterious than the world itself. This inconvenience seems less than devastating to anthropomorphites such as Cleanthes. In part this is because Philo's favored material world-system, "arranged of itself, without a precedent design" (4.14.Philo to Cleanthes), differs little from Cleanthes' preferred divine intelligent causality—and not just because, on Philo's view, we are equally ignorant of both! But we shall return, in Chapters 15 and 16, to the question of the kind and depth of disagreement between Cleanthes and Philo.

8

Part 5

Like effects prove like causes. This is the experimental argument; and this, you say too, is the sole theological argument.

—Philo to Cleanthes, Part 5.1

Structure:

¶¶ *1–12: Philo elaborates a second inconvenience of anthropomorphism: The divine attributes are undermined*

    ¶ *1: The fundamental principle of "experimental theism"*

    ¶¶ *2–4: Do scientific discoveries support "the true system of theism"?*

    ¶¶ *5–12: How experimental theism denies traditional attributes of "the Deity"*

        ¶ *5. Infinity*

        ¶¶ *6–7. Perfection*

        ¶¶ *8–9. Unity*

        ¶ *10. Immortality*

        ¶ *11. Immateriality*

        ¶ *12: Summary and Demea's reaction*

    ¶ *13: Cleanthes' response: The "hypothesis of design" is nonetheless "a sufficient foundation for religion"*

Part 5 consists almost entirely of a learned and captivating monologue by Philo—quoting Lucretius and Cicero from the Latin and inventing clever tales of possible deities while fastening upon the essential principle of Cleanthes' "experimental theism"—punctuated only twice (in 5.4 and 5.13) by some feeble comments from Cleanthes. We should get used to this type of one-sided conversation, for it sets a pattern for most of the following Parts. The fact is that Philo has taken over, and others can manage only infrequent interjections, usually to very weak effect. It is chiefly Philo's domination of the discussion from here on that creates for so many readers the vivid impression that Philo is the "victor" in the *Dialogues* and therefore Hume's hero, his alter ego, even Hume himself. However, we should be wary of equating quantity of discourse with finality of statement or author's credo; Philo's dominance certainly is important, but his skeptical "triumphs" (as he labels them) need to be placed in the larger context of the *Dialogues* as a whole.

At any rate, in Part 5, Philo continues his recitation of the "inconveniences" of Cleanthes' anthropomorphism, focusing this time on the divine attributes. He first isolates the fundamental principle of Cleanthes' reasoning —"Like effects prove like causes"—and then gives two versions of how applying this principle has untoward consequences for Cleanthes. Initially, he shows how using this principle on recent scientific evidence bolsters "the true system of theism" in opposition to Cleanthes' "experimental theism," and then, in an about-face, he shows how Cleanthes' principle undermines the traditional infinite attributes of God. Demea reacts with "horror" to the finitistic implications, but Cleanthes is nonplussed, noting that even Philo's indulgent imagination can "never get rid of the hypothesis of design."

¶1: Philo restates Cleanthes' principles

Philo opens Part 5 by claiming to "take a new survey" of Cleanthes' "principles." It is a very short survey indeed, for it fastens on only a single principle: "*Like effects prove like causes.*" This *principle of causal analogy*,[1] Philo asserts, is not only vital to Cleanthes' theological argument; in some sense it *is* "the experimental argument,"[2] and indeed it is "the *sole* theological argument," the only kind Cleanthes accepts. The strength of Cleanthes' design argument therefore depends upon the *degree* of likeness: The more alike the observed effects, the more alike the inferred causes. "Every departure on either side diminishes the probability, and renders the experiment less conclusive" (5.1.Philo to Cleanthes). Before examining the supposedly embarrassing "consequences" Philo claims to follow from this principle, let us ask two questions: Is this a fair characterization of Cleanthes' position? What are Philo's own views on these matters?

Cleanthes offers no objection to Philo's swift "survey of your principles," and we may take his silence as assent (as it was earlier; cf. 2.16). Still, one should note how extreme is the position Philo ascribes to Cleanthes. It holds that (1) only "experimental" arguments are acceptable in theology, and (2) the sole principle of all experimental inference is causal analogy.[3] Cleanthes clearly is eager to put theology on what he regards as a "scientific" empirical basis, so he is committed to any necessary and proper (acceptable, valid, truth-preserving) principles of empirical reasoning. Moreover, even if analogical inference or recognition of resemblance were not the whole of Cleanthes' experimental theism, it would surely be its heart, for it grounds his design argument, and "the hypothesis of design in the universe" is "a sufficient foundation for religion" (5.13.Cleanthes to Philo).

But there are problems with these principles. For one, "experimental" for Philo and Cleanthes means "relating to experience" (*OED*, sense 1), not "of or pertaining to experiments" (*OED*, sense 6). It borrows the prestige of natural science's appeal to experience without the labor of painstaking experimental design, instrumentation, and measurement. Philosophical "hypotheses" are "tested" by widespread human experience, and although such experience is said to make the hypotheses more or less likely, there is no rigorous logic of confirmation—or disconfirmation. "Like effects *prove* like causes" only in the weak sense of "make trial of, try, test" (*OED*, sense 1), not in the strong sense of "to establish as true; to make certain; to demonstrate the truth of by evidence or argument" (*OED*, sense 5). Second, Cleanthes does not consider the possibility that experimental reasoning might yield evidence for cosmological hypotheses other than design. Third, causal analogy is not the only principle of ordinary reasoning about experience. Not all causes are, or can be, analogically inferred; some are directly observed (cf. 6.2) and others are inferred via other empirical principles such as contiguity and regularity.

Philo, of course, enjoys pointing out to Cleanthes the unwelcome consequences of "experimental" principles; lashing oneself to the principle of causal analogy casts one adrift on an ocean of speculation and leads to a "wild and unsettled" theology (5.12.Philo to Cleanthes). But what does Philo himself think? During the present conversation he is arguing with Cleanthes "in his own way," working with and from principles *Cleanthes* accepts. These principles therefore need not be embraced by Philo (2.11.Philo to Demea). So we cannot work directly from the arguments Philo provides to Philo's own views—he is trying to refute Cleanthes, not to represent Philo. We shall have to wait until Part 12 to learn Philo's own principles. There we shall find that he does indeed embrace arguments from experience as our best hope of obtaining reliable, though not absolutely certain, beliefs about matters of fact and existence, and he also accepts the principle of causal analogy. So there is less disagreement with Cleanthes than meets the ear in Part 5; both Philo and Cleanthes accept the same principles of inference and share an appreciation for scientific as well as ordinary evidence. It is just that they differ on how far these principles and evidence carry one; that is, on the *degree of likeness* of an Author of Nature to a human agent.

¶¶2–12: Philo's double game

Philo is playing a curious double game in his critique of the principle of causal analogy. In 5.2–4, he first tries to show, a bit lamely, that modern scientific discoveries of "the immense grandeur and magnificence of the works of nature" point away from Cleanthes' "experimental theism" and toward something he calls "the true system of theism" (5.2.Philo to Cleanthes)—a more expansive and unlimited deity than Cleanthes' God. Cleanthes objects to this reading of the scientific evidence and holds that the sciences "only discover new instances of art and contrivance" that more closely resemble human artifice (5.4.Cleanthes to Philo). Philo then abruptly changes course and proceeds in 5.5–11, "with an air of alacrity and triumph," to "mark the consequences" of Cleanthes' finitistic and anthropomorphic construal of the evidence: Traditional attributes of deity are incompatible with Cleanthes' method.

Why does Philo play the evidence both ways? He cannot, of course, have it both ways, for (assuming that analogical inference from empirical evidence to divine cause is even possible), either the evidence (1) is ambiguous (i.e., it equally supports a traditional unlimited deity and Cleanthes' limited deity), or (2) it supports one more than the other. One possible interpretation is that Philo seeks to entrap Cleanthes into theological unorthodoxy, first baiting him by using the principle of causal analogy to infer a deity more to Demea's and Philo's liking, and then closing the trap when Cleanthes insists on a different construal of the evidence. But Philo doesn't need to induce Cleanthes to accept the principle of causal analogy—that *is* Cleanthes' principle! Moreover, Philo does not really insist on nature as providing evidence of infinity. He does not himself endorse this approach, and he wouldn't accept a conclusion so congenial to Demea.

Another possibility is that Philo is as committed as Cleanthes to experimental theism and the principle of causal analogy, their only difference being that Cleanthes thinks intelligent design is the most probable hypothesis, while Philo wants to consider other possibilities. This interpretation has the merit of seeing that the target of Philo's critique is not so much the principle of causal analogy as the principle's uncertain and "unsettled" use in theology. Also, it makes sense out of Cleanthes' final remark in Part 5: "I see, that, by the utmost indulgence of your imagination, you never get rid of the hypothesis of design in the universe" (5.13.Cleanthes to Philo). Cleanthes' conciliatory disposition fastens on agreement about the principle of causal analogy. But there a problem: This interpretation commits Philo to the principle of causal analogy, and this is premature, for there is no evidence in this Part that he does in fact accept it. In fact, he says that he would rather embrace no theology at all than to hold the "wild and unsettled" theology that Cleanthes experimentally rests on finite evidence (5.12.Philo to Demea).

Most plausibly, Philo wants to show that "experimental theism" is in trouble no matter how the evidence is construed: No matter how like or unlike finite humanity nature turns out to be, using the principle of causal analogy will result in theological "inconveniences" to Cleanthes: Either support for traditional theism or denial of attributes usually considered essential to the divine nature. But of course it is open to Cleanthes to take, as he does, the latter horn of Philo's dilemma, to argue that the empirical evidence does indeed support only a limited deity and hence to deny the traditional divine attributes. In that case, Philo's critique would serve chiefly to highlight how different Cleanthes' "experimental theism" is from traditional theism—here tendentiously and perhaps teasingly labeled "the true system of theism." But that result would come as no surprise to Philo and Cleanthes, nor would Cleanthes (and maybe Philo) find it unacceptable. The only real impact of Philo's double game is to make clearer just how different is Cleanthes' anthropomorphic God from Demea's mysterious or "mystical" God. This is progress, though not necessarily a refutation of Cleanthes—save perhaps in the eyes of Demea.

¶¶2–4: Science and theism

Philo begins the first part of his double game with the science of astronomy. Recent telescopic discoveries "prove the immense grandeur and magnificence of the works of nature"—works so vast that they remove "the effect still farther from all resemblance to the effects of human art and contrivance." Of course, continues Philo, such grandeur could be learned even from "the old system of the world," as related by Lucretius and Cicero. These ancients clearly saw with naked eye the "vast" and "boundless" character of the starry night sky and by using the principle of causal analogy inferred an appropriately cosmic creator quite beyond the anthropomorphic infirmities of Cleanthes' deity. But the age-old awe of the heavens has been deepened by recent discoveries: "The bounds of nature are so infinitely enlarged" as to make it "still more unreasonable to form our idea of so unlimited a cause from our experience of the narrow productions of human design and invention" (5.2.Philo to Cleanthes). This is an odd line of argument for Philo to take, for all along he has insisted on the limitations, not the expansiveness, of human experience and reason, and perhaps that is why he quotes ancient authorities to make his points.[4]

Nevertheless, Philo presses on, from the large to the small: Microscopes "open a new universe in miniature" and lead us "to infer the universal cause of all to be vastly different from mankind, or from any object of human experience and observation" (5.3.Philo to Cleanthes). Philo is on the verge of introducing similar anti-anthropomorphic evidence from anatomy, chemistry, and botany when Cleanthes interjects: On the contrary, these sciences "only discover new instances of art and contrivance. It is still the image of mind reflected on us from innumerable objects" (5.4.Cleanthes to Philo). A memorable phrase, but does Cleanthes realize what he is saying? No matter how brightly illuminating, a *reflection* after all is not a *source* of light. Shouldn't Cleanthes ask himself whether the "new instances of art and contrivance" he perceives are *given to* him by the sciences—or rather *projected by* him upon what science discovers?

But Philo does not pick up on this point, seeking instead only to secure Cleanthes' agreement that the image of mind "reflected on us" is a mind "like the human" and "the liker the better" (5.4.Philo to Cleanthes). Cleanthes readily assents, and Philo proceeds to "mark the consequences" with "an air of alacrity and triumph." This is the first, though it will not be the last, of Philo's "triumphs."[5] Philo takes considerable pleasure in these triumphs, because they are more than winning positions or arguments; they are also vindications of himself. Philo is a competitive man who enjoys argument because he is good at it; he delights in the exercise of his fecund imagination and critical acumen. But Philo also likes to *win* arguments; by disputing with others and disabling their views he *triumphs over* them and displays his superiority. At least, Philo is competitive in this way *when Demea is present*. After Demea leaves at the end of Part 11, we see a rather different Philo, more concerned to signal agreement with a friend than to proclaim triumph over an adversary. It is as if Demea brings out the worst side—the most contentious, critical, and combative side—of Philo.

¶¶5–12: Divine attributes

The consequences Philo "marks" over the next seven paragraphs (5.5–11) concern five traditional divine attributes: infinity, perfection, unity, immortality, and immateriality.[6] Just as these attributes together form a monotheistic picture of one infinite, perfect, undying spirit, so the denial of each attribute fashions a polytheistic view of a group of finite, imperfect, mortal, and corporeal deities. Two of the traditional attributes, perfection and unity, receive two paragraphs each, with the second paragraph for each inserted in a later revision by Hume that introduces some sophisticated but tangential points.

1. *Infinity*: By using the principle of causal analogy, Philo holds, Cleanthes must "renounce all claim to infinity in any of the attributes of the Deity."[7] This is because the cause can only be like the effect, and the effects we observe are finite (5.12.Philo to Cleanthes).[8] This is an important point in theology, for infinity traditionally functions as a meta-attribute, qualifying other attributes, and a negative attribute, blocking finite qualities and meaning "unlimited." Thus, an infinite God is infinitely good, powerful, wise, and so forth, and not limited in goodness, power, wisdom, and so forth. By Cleanthes' "method of reasoning," infinity cannot be affirmed of the deity, so God must

in some sense be limited. But this does not mean that Cleanthes must set any particular limits on the deity; indeed, in principle he could even claim that God is limited but that those limits surpass human comprehension. What Cleanthes seeks is likeness to human mind or intelligence, "the liker the better," and this principle of likeness takes over for him the role of infinity, acting both as meta-attribute and as negative attribute: It is a test for any divine attribute and a way of blocking features incompatible with a divine intelligence like unto human intelligence.

2. *Perfection*: Cleanthes cannot ascribe perfection to his deity,[9] not even a finite perfection.[10] In particular, this god cannot be supposed "free from every error, mistake, or incoherence in his undertakings." An *a priori* theology with a perfect God perhaps could account for the "many inexplicable difficulties in the works of nature"[11] as due to "the narrow capacity of man, who cannot trace infinite relations." But for Cleanthes these must be real difficulties—unless, Philo adds with biting sarcasm, these imperfections are "insisted on, as new instances of likeness to human art and contrivance"! Moreover, without a divine standard of perfection, there is no way to tell whether the world "contains any great faults, or deserves any considerable praise, if compared to other possible, and even real systems" (5.6.Philo to Cleanthes). Cleanthes' God must be an imperfect god—no doubt less imperfect than humans, but imperfect nonetheless.

Philo then adds the tangential point (in a paragraph inserted in a later revision) that even were the world perfect, "it must still remain uncertain, whether all the excellencies of the work can justly be ascribed to the workman." Perhaps the deity has a different job—no longer a designer or author of the world but rather a workman following someone else's plan. Or perhaps God is not even a master craftsman but only "a stupid mechanic," new to "the art of world-making," who merely imitates others or blindly copies their craft; or perhaps the world-making workman is in the early stages of learning through trial and error; or perhaps . . . —but there are far too many possibilities. "In such subjects, who can determine, where the truth; nay, who can conjecture where the probability, lies; amidst a great number of hypotheses which may be proposed, and a still greater number, which may be imagined?" (5.7.Philo to Cleanthes) We simply lack empirical evidence to ascertain the nature of the deity; we have far too many possible analogies with human contrivance to fasten on any one of them as the proper analogue for the creator. Author, designer, workman, apprentice—how are we to judge?

3. *Unity*: The unity of the deity is also at risk—not the internal coherence of a single being's various attributes but the uniqueness of the instantiation of the divine attributes. Cleanthes' method seems unable to settle the dispute between monotheism and polytheism, although Philo gives reason to

think that it tilts toward the latter. By human analogy, works of art are often joint products; a ship, for example, is produced by many people. "Why may not several deities combine in contriving and framing a world? This is only so much greater similarity to human affairs." Philo also points out, mock-helpfully, that polytheism has the further advantage of limiting the power, knowledge, and other attributes of each divinity (5.8.Philo to Cleanthes), thereby securing greater coherence in Cleanthes' conception of God—but of course at the cost of heterodoxy.

Another inserted paragraph follows, addressing once again a peripheral issue: Though Cleanthes has not done so, an opponent of polytheism might argue that one God is explanatorily preferable to many gods because it is a simpler explanation, appealing to Occam's razor. But Philo deflects the razor: Its use would be appropriate if one had antecedent proof of a deity causally sufficient to produce the world; the razor would then cut off needless supposition of other deities. But the razor cannot be used without begging the question "while it is still a question, whether all these attributes are united in one subject, or dispersed among several independent beings."[12] Once again, we lack sufficient evidence to settle the question, though since the power to cause the universe must be so very much greater than the power of any single human maker, the presumption should be that the cosmic creative power is shared by several beings and is not the monopoly of one deity (5.9.Philo to Cleanthes).

Once again Philo cannot resist singing his "great disproportion" theme song: "An intelligent being of such vast power and capacity, as is necessary to produce the universe, or to speak in the language of ancient philosophy, so prodigious an animal, exceeds all analogy and even comprehension" (5.9.Philo to Cleanthes). Despite his criticism of Cleanthes' use of analogy to speak of the universe and its creator, however, Philo finds it proper to speak at least of the universe in analogical terms—not as a machine, à la Cleanthes, but as an animal.[13]

4. *Immortality*: If God is analogous to humans, how can Cleanthes overlook the essential human attributes of mortality and sexuality? Indeed, "all living creatures" die "and renew their species by generation"—so quickly are we plunged into "the theogony of ancient times," with gods living, breeding, and expiring like earthly creatures (5.10.Philo to Cleanthes).[14] Implicit in this point is the uncontrollable spread of analogy: Once one begins to contemplate the likeness of human maker to divine creator, *any* human feature becomes a potential ground for a similar divine feature, unless it is ruled out on other grounds; for example, incompatibility with other (and better entrenched) attributes.

5. *Immateriality*: If Cleanthes believes that the gods are mortal, "why not

become a perfect anthropomorphite" and assert they have bodies too, with full humanoid features?[15] This, for Philo as for Cicero, is a complete reductio ad absurdum of Cleanthes' theology (5.11.Philo to Cleanthes).

Two major outcomes are claimed for this exploration of divine attributes: First, Cleanthes' experimental theism supports not "the true system of theism" but some polytheistic and heterodox rival. But second, there really is not enough evidence to choose between these, or many other, alternatives. The only legitimate result of Cleanthes' experimental theism is a spare and obscure conjecture;[16] anything more rides solely on the whims of imagination. Philo summarizes this result for Cleanthes' benefit in 5.12: "A man, who follows your hypothesis, is able, perhaps, to assert, or conjecture, that the universe, some time, arose from some thing like design: But beyond that position he cannot ascertain one single circumstance, and is left afterwards to fix every point of his theology, by the utmost licence of fancy and hypothesis" (5.12.Philo to Cleanthes). To drive this point home, Philo mischievously allows his own fancy to take flight, imagining three more monotheistic possibilities, each presenting a view of divinity that is repugnant to all present. Perhaps, he says, the world

> was only the first rude essay of some infant deity, who afterwards abandoned it, ashamed of his lame performance: It is the work only of some dependent, inferior deity; and is the object of derision to his superiors: It is the production of old age and dotage in some superannuated deity; and ever since his death, has run on at adventures, from the first impulse and active force, which it received from him. (5.12.Philo to Cleanthes)

Philo gets the reaction from Demea he doubtless expected—a visceral "horror" at "these strange suppositions"—but he deflects the blame from his own fevered imaginings to Cleanthes' experimental method. If analogy reigns, seemingly anything is permitted, producing "so wild and unsettled a system of theology" that it is not preferable to no theology at all (5.12.Philo to Demea).[17]

¶13: Cleanthes fixates on design

Cleanthes concludes Part 5 with a terse and puzzling paragraph. First he vehemently "disown[s]" Philo's imaginative "suppositions"; they are not Cleanthes' own views,[18] however speculatively possible they may be. Still, unlike Demea, he is not at all horrified by their suggestion, for he detects in Philo's "rambling" a certain lack of seriousness. So rather than attempting to refute or qualify anything Philo has alleged about the divine attributes, Cleanthes remarks only on Philo's apparent embrace of "the hypothesis of design," viewing this as a "concession" by Philo. Acceptance of this hypothesis is all-important for Cleanthes, since he regards it as "a sufficient foundation for religion" (5.13.Cleanthes to Philo).

This is a strange paragraph, both for what it says and for what it leaves unsaid. Cleanthes is so fixated on the fact but not the details of design that once he detects, or thinks he detects, Philo's allegiance to the design hypothesis, he does not bother to counter any of the finitistic suggestions or wild "suppositions" Philo says follow from the use of causal analogy, thereby ignoring Philo's claim that these suppositions "are Cleanthes's suppositions, not mine" (5.12.Philo to Demea). Instead, Cleanthes fastens on Philo's earlier assertion that "the universe, some time, arose from some thing like design," and he ignores Philo's further qualification that "beyond that position he cannot ascertain one single circumstance, and is left afterwards to fix every point of his theology, by the utmost licence of fancy and hypothesis" (5.12.Philo to Cleanthes). Cleanthes, once again, is seeing what he wants to see, finding "the image of mind reflected on us" (5.4.Cleanthes to Philo) now in Philo's discourse as well as in the world.

What about the content of Cleanthes' theology? By using his experimental method and his construal of the evidence, can he accept traditional divine attributes such as infinity and perfection? If not, what is to replace these attributes in Cleanthes' theology? Is Cleanthes committed to some form of polytheism? Not necessarily. In the remainder of the dialogues Cleanthes will continue to speak of "theism" and "the Author of Nature," even while entertaining the "theory" of a "finitely perfect" deity in Part 11. Cleanthes has a surprising lack of concern about theological detail; once the design hypothesis is conceded and he reaches "the existence of a Deity, and his similarity to human mind and intelligence" (2.5.Cleanthes to Philo and Demea), the particulars simply don't concern him.[19]

But further, Cleanthes asserts that "the hypothesis of design in the universe" is "a sufficient foundation for religion." This is an even larger claim than first appears. Cleanthes does not say design is sufficient to found *theology* but rather to found *religion*, which includes piety as well as theology. But in Part 5 he provides little theology beyond the vague thought of an Author of Nature; and he provides no characterization of the correspondent piety at all. So we are unable to understand, much less to assess, Cleanthes' claim that the hypothesis of design is a "sufficient foundation for religion" until we learn more about his account of "true religion," to be delivered in Part 12.

Thus ends Part 5, rather inconclusively. Cleanthes' fundamental principle of "experimental theism"—that "like effects prove like causes"—leads to no determinate divine attributes, not necessarily even to a finite and imperfect deity instead of an infinite and perfect one. It all depends upon what the evidence shows, on the actual kinds and degrees of likeness, and Cleanthes is disinclined to debate the details. The principle of causal analogy simply transfers degree of likeness from effect to cause (or causes). If, as Demea claims, the universe is vastly unlike human contrivance, then there is little likeness in their causes, and God is transcendently mysterious; while if, as Cleanthes believes, the likeness is palpable, and "the liker the better," then God becomes quite similar to "human mind and intelligence"—and perhaps, as Philo tries to remind Cleanthes, similar in other ways as well. Philo's main contention, then, is not that Cleanthes is necessarily committed to some particular heterodoxy but rather that there is no way, following his method, to commit to *any* particular theology. There are many kinds of human contrivance that might serve as analogues to the world and hence a large array of possible design hypotheses, but there are also many other analogues than human contrivance and hence a very large array of possible non-design hypotheses. In addition, there are differences as to the degree of likeness. In sum, theology on Cleanthes' principles is irredeemably "wild and unsettled."

9

Part 6

All these systems, then, of scepticism, polytheism, and theism you must allow, on your principles, to be on a like footing.

—Philo to Cleanthes, Part 6.13

Structure:

¶1: Demea questions the religious value of experimental theism; he is ignored by Philo and Cleanthes

¶¶2–6: Philo raises a "new species of anthropomorphism": God is the world's soul

¶¶7–11: Cleanthes oddly critiques Philo's new anthropomorphism

    ¶7: Cleanthes is modestly mum, but Philo inveigles his reply

    ¶8: The world is more like a vegetable than an animal

    ¶¶9–11: The world is not eternal

        ¶9: The "vulgar" argument

        ¶10: The "better" argument

        ¶11: More "convincing proofs"

¶¶12–13: Philo criticizes Cleanthes' critique, defends inherent order, and pronounces a stalemate among "scepticism, polytheism, and theism"

Following an opening paragraph by Demea that looks back to Part 5, most of Part 6 is given over to a mini-drama in three acts: First, Philo explores another hypothesis that appears, on Cleanthes' own principles of inference, to be no less likely than Cleanthes' favored design hypothesis: The world is like "an animal or organized body," so "the Deity is the SOUL of the world, actuating it, and actuated by it" (6.3). Second, Cleanthes is induced to offer some odd criticisms of Philo's view, thereby implicitly criticizing Cleanthes' own design hypothesis and calling into question his philosophical acumen. Third, Philo returns (not for the last time) to two important themes: Were he forced to choose any world-system, it would be one that "ascribes an eternal, inherent principle of order to the world"; even so, and more important, no system is preferable to any other *on Cleanthes' principles*. Part 6 therefore exposes a third important "inconvenience" of experimental theism: On the evidence of experience, the design hypothesis is no more likely than other hypotheses. Cleanthes' fondness for design must have other sources than evidence.

¶1: Demea's piety

Cleanthes closed Part 5 strongly proclaiming not only that "the hypothesis of design" cannot be avoided, not even by Philo, but also that it constitutes "a sufficient foundation for religion" (5.13.Cleanthes to Philo). Demea now opens Part 6 by expressing his astonishment at the latter claim. Far from being sufficient for religion, Demea holds, the design hypothesis is too "tottering a foundation" on which to erect anything substantial or satisfying. It cannot, for example, settle such vital religious questions as whether there is one god or many or whether "the deity or deities, to whom we owe our existence, be perfect or imperfect, subordinate or supreme, dead or alive." Moreover, it cripples such central theistic attitudes as trust, confidence, devotion, worship, veneration, and obedience. Finally, and for Demea most important, it is useless, in a practical sense, "to all the purposes of life" (6.1.Demea to Cleanthes). In sum, Cleanthes' theology is religiously inadequate as well as speculatively uncertain.

While Demea is aware of the speculative uncertainty of Cleanthes' hypothesis, his overwhelming concern is a *practical religious* one: "All the purposes of life" rest on *piety*. This overriding concern for piety is characteristic of Demea—it was, for example, his major interest in Pamphilus' education at the very outset of the *Dialogues*—and he brings it up without much regard for its appropriateness to the conversation at the moment. That his interjection here is unsuccessful (Philo and Cleanthes simply ignore it) does not mean that he will not try again.

In addition, Demea's piety is fixated on certainty—or rather on *certitude,* the feeling of complete and unwavering self-assurance. What bothers him most of all about Cleanthes' line of thought, even more than its claimed result of a finite designer, is that it yields no certitude. Demea is interested in theoretical support for his piety if, but only if, it promises an absolutely confident result. But Cleanthes' principle of causal analogy, even if it were completely successful, would not and could not guarantee a conclusion one could embrace without doubt, perplexity, or qualification. Demea requires certitude for "all the purposes of life." So any argument failing to generate *perfect* certitude is for him "*totally* precarious and unsatisfactory" (6.1.Demea to Cleanthes; emphasis added).

Neither Cleanthes nor Philo, however, takes up Demea's point about the practical significance of the design hypothesis. Why? In part, Philo and Cleanthes each have their own reasons. Philo is interested in pursuing his own agenda—displaying his dialectical skills through a wide-ranging and penetrating critique of speculative theology—and not in exploring Demea's concerns. The kind of practical religious critique Demea would like to make differs enormously from Philo's theoretical critique. Moreover, Philo controls the conversation at this point, and he has no desire to shift the spotlight to Demea, for that might impress the wrong principles upon the youthful Pamphilus. Cleanthes, for his part, is having enough difficulty handling Philo's logical points without being asked to worry about Demea's pietistic ones. Additionally, his mannered civility prevents him from entering into a three-person conversation he knows will prove contentious and emotionally draining. As he says to Philo after Demea leaves the dialogues, "I should rather wish to reason with either of you apart on a subject, so sublime and interesting" (12.1.Cleanthes to Philo).

But Philo and Cleanthes also share other reasons for not taking up Demea's challenge. It is an open secret of these conversations that the three speakers no more share a common piety than they share a common theology.[1] In fact, their differences in piety are more extensive and more important than their all-too-apparent differences in theology. To delve into piety at this point, therefore, would plunge the conversation into a tangled, confusing, and possibly impolite dispute. Yet Cleanthes and Philo do find it possible to talk about piety—their *shared* piety—when they are alone together in Part 12. So the real problem for both Philo and Cleanthes is—Demea. Philo cannot join Demea in a pietistic critique of Cleanthes' design hypothesis because neither he nor Cleanthes shares Demea's piety. Rather than turn a theological argument into something more personal and dangerous, Philo and Cleanthes simply ignore Demea's attempt to strike up a dialogue on piety.

There is one further important reason for ignoring Demea: Pamphilus. Philo and Cleanthes both wish to steer their protégé away from the dark depths of Demea's piety and into a sunnier form of piety—namely, their own. Keeping the discussion focused on theological argument while Demea is present, and reserving conversation on religious piety until he is absent, keeps Pamphilus's gaze on what both Philo and Cleanthes believe is more salutary for his soul.

¶¶2–6: Is God the world's soul?

Philo is only too glad to introduce yet another "inconvenience" of Cleanthes' experimental theism: It licenses any number of plausible alternatives to the design hypothesis. One alternative in particular Philo considers even more probable[2] than Cleanthes' design hypothesis: The world is (like) an animal body, so God is (like) its soul.[3] The world is like an animal's body because its continual changes produce no disorder, it repairs itself, there is "the closest sympathy" among parts, and each part "operates both to its own preservation and to that of the whole" (6.3.Philo to Cleanthes). God is to the world as an animal's soul is to its body—an internal principle of animation distinct from the operation of the organism but not a separate, transcendent entity.

Prior to reaching this conclusion, Philo discusses what is supposed to be its principle of inference. It is a puzzling principle. Philo supplements Cleanthes' principle of causal analogy—"that like effects arise from like causes"—with "another principle of the same kind, no less certain, and derived from the same source of experience; that where several known circumstances are *observed* to be similar, the unknown will also be *found* similar" (6.2.Philo to Cleanthes) This statement is not pellucid, but from the examples Philo gives (observe human limbs/infer head; observe part of sun/infer whole) it might appear that the principle is a mereological one:[4] Where we have found through experience certain parts always or usually conjoined with other parts (as parts of the same whole), when we experience the former we expect we will be able to observe the latter as well. But this mereological interpretation cannot be right, for it is irrelevant to reaching Philo's conclusion, simply because the relation of soul to body is not a mereological one. Is the relation then a causal one? But if so, how would Philo's new principle differ from Cleanthes' principle of causal analogy?

Let us try a different tack. Philo says an animal's organized body is "actuated" with "a principle of life and motion," and "the Deity" as the world-soul both actuates and is actuated by the world (6.3.Philo to Cleanthes). Whether or not "actuation" is the same as causation, it at least involves some minimal sense of association: In our everyday experience, bodies and souls go together, so experience of the former allows one to infer the existence of the latter. On this reading, Philo's principle of association commits one to even less than Cleanthes' principle, and in a case such as that of the puzzling relation of soul to body, it can be very useful—just what the skeptic ordered.

Following his brief argument in 6.3 to the conclusion of a divine world-soul, Philo next bolsters his world-soul hypothesis with an appeal to "almost all the theists of antiquity," who often considered the world to be God's body. Philo still is troubled by the pretensions of cosmic speculation, but "if our limited analogy could ever, with any propriety, be extended to the whole of nature, the inference seems juster in favour of the ancient [God is the world's soul] than the modern theory [God is the world's author or artificer]." This is because "the universe resembles more a human body than it does the works of human art and contrivance" (6.4.Philo to Cleanthes).

Philo clearly holds some naturalistic version of his analogy, where the soul is a principle of order and life of a natural body. "Nothing [is] more repugnant to common experience," he claims, "than mind without body; a mere spiritual substance" (6.5.Philo to Cleanthes). But his exact position is more than a little unclear. He leaves it open whether a particular mind/soul is inseparably connected to some one particular body or whether transmigration of souls is possible. Also, he holds that mind and body are "co-eval" principles, neither one prior to the other; both have "order and arrangement naturally inherent in them, and inseparable from them" (6.5.Philo to Cleanthes). This is an odd form of naturalism—neither pantheism (where God just is the world, in a certain aspect) nor animism (where God animates the world, but is a separable entity), but some kind of dualism (where God and world are distinct but inseparable natural entities).

At any rate, Philo commends his world-soul hypothesis to Cleanthes because it stays closer to "common experience" than does the hypothesis of a divine spirit capable of existing without a body, "a mere spiritual substance." The "ancient theologians" also held this view of purely non-physical beings, "of which they had not observed one single instance throughout all nature" (6.5.Philo to Cleanthes). In conclusion, he appeals to Cleanthes to rise above his "*systematical prejudices*" to see that order can be as easily intrinsic to mind as to body and to be more sympathetic to "the *vulgar prejudice*" that "body and mind ought always to accompany each other," because this latter prejudice "is founded on *vulgar experience,* the only guide which you profess to follow in all these theological enquiries." Were Cleanthes to balk at following vulgar experience, then "you entirely abandon your own hypothesis, and must thenceforward adopt our mysticism, as you call it, and admit of the absolute incomprehensibility of the divine nature" (6.7.Philo to Cleanthes). So Philo's concluding appeal is ad hominem but not fallacious. Cleanthes has put his theological raft into a river of experimental reasoning, and he must navigate solely within its banks.

¶¶7–11: Cleanthes' lame reply

Cleanthes' response to Philo's cosmic animism is incredibly lame. Initially he professes never to have thought about this "theory" before, although he admits it is "a pretty natural one," and he has nothing to say about it "upon so short an examination and reflection." Philo, sensing that Cleanthes is merely playing dumb out of politeness, encourages him to conduct an examination of Philo's world-soul hypothesis, just as Philo has been examining Cleanthes' design hypothesis. Philo provides two shrewd inducements, and from their effectiveness we can infer something about Cleanthes. First, Philo flatters Cleanthes for his "caution and reserve" as contrasted with Philo's own impulsiveness. Second, he invites Cleanthes to speak "if anything occur to

you."[5] Philo sees that Cleanthes likes to appear a man of "caution and reserve," in contrast to the precipitous Philo, even while he itches to respond in
kind to Philo's sallies; Cleanthes' reticence to "deliver any opinion" is more
manners than deep conviction. Philo's flattery of Cleanthes, his polite self-
deprecation, and his provision of an easy opening to speak all strike a chord
in Cleanthes, who conducts an examination of Philo's hypothesis that becomes a parody of proper argumentation, an unintentional critique of his
own design argument, and an embarrassing reflection on himself. Cleanthes
has been receiving worse than he has been giving in recent Parts, and it is
natural for him to want to retaliate in kind—Philo's kind—but he is simply
unable to pull it off. Cleanthes is a polite conversationalist but a wretched
dialectician.

Cleanthes has two major criticisms to make of Philo's world-soul hypothesis: The first undercuts his own design hypothesis, the second damages
his credibility as a critic. The first criticism is that while the world resembles
an animal body, the resemblance is slight—there are in the world "no organs
of sense; no seat of thought or reason; no-one precise origin of motion and
action"—so that in fact the world bears a greater resemblance to a vegetable
than to an animal. Cleanthes seems blissfully unaware that his own world-
analogy is threatened by this line of thought. If, as Philo has urged, the world
is more like an animal than a human contrivance, and if, as Cleanthes now
argues, the world is more like a vegetable than an animal, then contrivance
becomes the weakest analogy around.[6] At the very least, there are a number
of different possible analogies, each with a modicum of resemblance, but each
"defective in many circumstances, the most material" (all 6.8.Cleanthes to
Philo). Parity of reasoning, and simple fairness, should extract from Cleanthes
the recognition that his design hypothesis is as flawed and vulnerable as any
of them.

Next, Cleanthes claims that "your theory seems to imply the eternity of
the world" and sets about refuting this implication "by the strongest reasons
and probabilities." Before giving reasons, however, Cleanthes should have
asked two prior questions: Why should thinking of the world as (like) an
animal body imply its eternity? Why should eternity be more closely connected to an animated world than to an artifactual one? Cleanthes doesn't
seem to realize that refuting the eternity of the world cuts as much, or as
little, against his own hypothesis as against Philo's. Nor does he recognize how
the arguments he presents undermine his own credibility, for they are comically weak. He gives two such arguments; the second one he considers to be
original to himself:

Cleanthes first discusses a "vulgar argument" that "wants not force" but
also "seems a little precarious." This argument points to "the late origin of arts

and sciences": If the world were eternal and the human race equally long-lived, they would have occurred much earlier. But Cleanthes thinks this inference is "refuted" by considering "the nature of human society, which is in continual revolution . . . so that it is impossible for us, from our limited experience, to foretell with assurance what events may or may not be expected." He then provides a thumbnail sketch of the narrow escape "ancient learning and history" made through the "convulsions" of the Middle Ages, with some counterfactual speculation about what might have happened had the popes not "preserved a little jargon of LATIN" in order to render the West "in a fit disposition for receiving the GREEK language and learning." Here Cleanthes seems to be running together human arts and our knowledge of them. On the one hand, perhaps these human arts were invented long ago (perhaps more than once) but then vanished during one or another of the periodic upheavals of human society. On the other hand, perhaps our knowledge of when they were invented is defective, so that "it is easily imagined, that fable or tradition might ascribe to them a much later origin than the true one" (6.9.Cleanthes to Philo). On any hand, however, the reasoning is more than just "a little precarious"—it is completely hopeless and inspires no confidence in anyone who accepts it.

Yet Cleanthes thinks he can build "a better argument" along the same lines. His prime example is the introduction of cherry trees from Asia to Europe! Cherry trees naturally thrive in European climes, but they were only introduced within historical times.[7] If the world is eternal, how could this species fail to have been introduced earlier than it was and, once introduced, continued to thrive to this day? This odd horticultural argument is not "affected by the revolutions of human society" (6.10.Cleanthes to Philo), for these human activities could not have extinguished the trees once introduced.[8]

As if the late introduction of cherry trees were not bizarre enough, Cleanthes proceeds to pile on other biological examples of what he regards as "convincing proofs of the youth, or rather infancy, of the world": Within historical times, grapevines were introduced to France and "horses, cows, sheep, swine, dogs, corn" to America. If the world were eternal, there would be no reason why these introductions would not have occurred much earlier. And then comes the clincher: "We may as well imagine, that all men would wear stockings for ten thousand years, and never have the sense to think of garters to tie them" (6.11.Cleanthes to Philo). From cherry trees to garters—a veritable comedy of criticism, a spoof of disproof!

Cleanthes' whole line of argument is so preposterous that it is hard to take it seriously. How can *any* fact or event within human history (memory *or* event) count for or against the eternality of the world? And what does eternality have to do with deciding between Philo's and Cleanthes' hypotheses? Cleanthes would have done better to remain silent and preserve at least the appearance of that "caution and reserve" Philo charitably ascribed to him.

¶¶12–13: Philo's stalemate

Philo graciously does not dwell on the many weaknesses of Cleanthes' arguments or on Cleanthes' own argumentative shortcomings,[9] but he does briefly mention one fatal flaw of the argument. Cleanthes assumes that the earth's history has been uniform over geological time, that it has not been subject to "a total convulsion of the elements" that would extinguish species locally or globally. Cleanthes admits "convulsions" in human affairs but not in nature. But Philo is aware of geological evidence for terrestrial catastrophes in the distant past, such "that every part of this globe has continued for many ages entirely covered with water." Further, he sees no reason why matter itself may not "be susceptible of many and great revolutions, through the endless periods of eternal duration" (6.12.Philo to Cleanthes).[10]

At any rate, Philo quickly moves on to something more fundamental: He is concerned with Cleanthes' principles themselves, when used in a theological context. Arguments from experience using such principles as causal analogy or association are useless in theology, Philo contends, because experience cannot decide among a host of possible alternative explanatory hypotheses. Because each hypothesis is more or less equally plausible on the evidence available to us, overall, each is thoroughly *im*plausible.

Philo says that "were I obliged to defend any particular system of this nature (which I never willingly should do) I esteem none more plausible, than that which ascribes an eternal, inherent principle of order to the world; though attended with great and continual revolutions and alterations."[11] This theory is too general to satisfy, but at least it addresses a problem any worldview must finally face: Whatever the ultimate explanatory principle, it must possess "an original, inherent principle of order," for "chance has no place, on any hypothesis, sceptical or religious. Every thing is surely governed by steady, inviolable laws." These laws at base must rest on nothing other than absolute necessity, or so Philo supposes; he imagines that, "were the inmost essence of things laid open to us," we would see that things could not be other than they are (6.12.Philo to Cleanthes). Of course, such a glimpse of absolute necessity is neither revealed to us nor naturally possible for us, in Philo's view, but his point is not about whether we can discern such necessity in things; rather, he holds that we must imagine that something like it *resides* in whatever ultimate explanatory principle we propose, whether it be the heart of nature or the mind of God. Once chance has been ruled out, Philo contends, such necessity is the only way to block a dispiriting regress of explanations, each unsatisfying on its own terms.

Because absolute necessity can be supposed resident in the material world, the theory of the ultimacy and eternality of the world is as plausible as Hesiod's polytheism (a society of "30,000 deities"), and "a numerous society of deities [is] as explicable as one universal deity." The overall point is that *all* these systems are, on Cleanthes' empirical principles, "on a like footing," and "no-one of them has any advantages over the others. You may thence learn the fallacy of your principles" (6.13.Philo to Cleanthes).[12] It is not that Cleanthes' principles are generally unreliable; on the contrary, we use them all the time in everyday life, and with justified confidence. It is only when we seek to extend such principles to *theology* that we run into irremediable difficulties. When an ordinarily reliable principle of reasoning licenses inference from the available evidence to any number of alternate and incompatible hypotheses, then something has gone wrong: Either we lack enough evidence to give the principle purchase, or the principle is inapplicable in that domain. Theology has both kinds of problem: Given the empirical evidence and the divine domain, experimental reasoning can yield no determinate theology. On the evidence, an intelligent Author of Nature is no more plausible than a society of deities, or a world-soul, or material necessity. And where all are equally plausible, no one is very plausible at all.

Part 6 presents Philo's treatment of the third great "inconvenience" of Cleanthes' experimental theism, joining the non-explanatoriness of a divine plan (Part 4) and the undermining of traditional divine attributes (Part 5). In fact, it mates with these other inconveniences. Recourse to a divine world of ideas only postpones coming to grips with the need for intrinsic necessity or self-explanatoriness, which may be attributed with equal lack of justification to the material world as to a divine mental world; and Cleanthes' principles yield only indeterminate divine attributes as indiscriminate explanatory hypotheses. All three inconveniences converge on a central point: Cleanthes' experimental theism with its hypothesis of design is vastly *under*-determined by the evidence, and it is no more plausible than any number of competing hypotheses. The next two Parts of the *Dialogues* reinforce this point by proposing still more bizarre world hypotheses that, Philo alleges, receive as much support from Cleanthes' principles as any yet suggested.

10

Part 7

You must be sensible, that common sense and reason is entirely against you, and that such whimsies, as you have delivered, may puzzle, but never can convince us.

—Cleanthes to Philo, Part 7.18

Structure:

¶¶ 1–17: Philo and Demea discuss Philo's "new idea" in front of Cleanthes

¶1: Philo states the general conditional: If the world resembles an animal or plant, it is due, on Cleanthes' principles, to generation or vegetation

{¶2: Demea asks for more}

¶3: Philo affirms the antecedent: The world "plainly resembles more an animal or vegetable" than a machine

{¶4: Demea asks about the mechanism of cosmic generation and vegetation}

¶¶5–6: Philo fantasizes that comets are seeds or eggs

{¶7: Demea concedes only slight resemblance and asks for data}

¶8: The data are limited, agrees Philo, but the world resembles living beings more than human artifacts

{¶9: Demea asks for an explanation of generation and vegetation}

¶¶10–11: Philo maintains that all ultimate principles are quite unknown and inexplicable

{¶12: Demea asks whether order doesn't imply design}

¶¶13–15: Philo claims that, on the basis of experience, "the matter seems entirely arbitrary," although generation has a slight advantage

¶¶ *16–17: Philo cites ancient authorities and adds one last analogy:*
"The world arose from an infinite spider"
¶ *18: Cleanthes, puzzled but unconvinced, responds ad hominem*

Part 7 is a new dialogue, not simply with new participants but with a new and unusual form, even though the theological subject and interpersonal effects are familiar. Whereas Part 6 consisted of a three-act drama between Philo and Cleanthes, Part 7 is mostly a catechetical series of Demea's questions and Philo's answers, all supposedly for Cleanthes' benefit. Although this kind of exchange is new to the *Dialogues*, it does not present new content but merely explores the attractiveness of alternative analogies to humanly designed artifacts—in particular, animal and vegetable (and even insect) analogies. Perhaps the novel elements are designed simply to "enforce the precepts" (PH.3). What is truly odd is that the views and principles Philo and Demea are discussing actually belong to Cleanthes, who sits mutely on the sidelines. Only in the last paragraph does Cleanthes step into the conversation, confessing his inability to reply to the arguments Philo presents while also dismissing Philo's queries as a symptom of Philo's unique temperament, unanswerable yet unconvincing to the deep "common sense and reason" all humans share.

¶¶1–17: Philo's "new idea"

Philo announces to Cleanthes a "new idea" he has had "all on a sudden,"[1] an idea which he thinks "must go near to subvert all your reasoning, and destroy even your first inferences, on which you repose such confidence." As it develops, the idea is not really new,[2] but it is simple enough: If the universe is more like a great animal or plant than a human contrivance, then probably, *on Cleanthes' principles,*[3] its cause resembles generation or vegetation more than reason or design (7.1.Philo to Cleanthes). Cleanthes' experimental theism manufactures theology from the best analogy available to us from our experience, and in Part 7 Philo makes clear to Cleanthes that our experience provides us with some alternative analogies for the world that are at least as good as, if not better than, human contrivance. But since none of these alternatives requires intelligence or consciousness, an author of the world who uses them is something less, not more, than a human mind. Even worse, although Philo marginally prefers at least one of these alternatives to design, in truth "the matter seems entirely arbitrary" (7.14.Philo to Demea). Using Cleanthes' empirical method, we are simply unable to reach any determinate theological conclusion, so that the strife of alternative analogies can only "prepare a complete triumph for the sceptic" (8.12.Philo to Cleanthes).

Philo has an assistant in setting up his argument: Demea provides five brief leading questions in 7.2, 7.4, 7.7, 7.9, and 7.12, while Philo dilates upon the answers. No doubt Philo could do well enough without Demea's assistance; after all, the principles on trial clearly belong to Cleanthes, who is quite capable of asking his own questions of Philo. So why is Demea involved? Perhaps Demea is restless—after all, he has not spoken since the opening paragraph of Part 6. Perhaps he feels compelled to ask these questions because Cleanthes will not ask them because of his "caution and reserve" (6.7). Perhaps Cleanthes would look foolish to Pamphilus in asking them. Perhaps the questions are such setups that only a supposed ally such as Demea would fail to be embarrassed in asking them. Whatever the reason, we have a catechetical rhythm with the following roles: Demea naively asks the questions, Philo authoritatively answers, and Cleanthes is a silent witness.

¶¶2–3: Question 1

Demea's initial question is a simple request for Philo to say something more, but it is interesting what Philo chooses to say about the principles of "our friend, Cleanthes."[4] First, he says that on Cleanthes' principles, all questions of fact can be proved only from experience and that whether God exists is a question of fact (7.3.Philo to Demea). Cleanthes, we recall, had earlier claimed that his "argument *a posteriori*" proves "at once the existence of a Deity, and his similarity to human mind and intelligence" (2.5.Cleanthes to Demea and Philo), although in practice Cleanthes has worried much more about divine nature than about divine existence. Cleanthes takes for granted that the world has a cause or causes, and he looks to experience to provide a characterization of the world from which to infer the nature of the world's author. Philo does not call Cleanthes to account on the question of divine existence here, but we shall find Cleanthes undercutting himself in Part 9 as he responds to Demea's *a priori* argument by wondering whether everything need have a cause.

Second, Philo notes that human works are only a "very small part" of nature (7.3.Philo to Demea). This should be obvious to all, but Cleanthes seems oblivious to such facts. Philo is engaged in improving Cleanthes' vision, not only enlarging the domain of possibility he considers but also sharpening his sense of what is likely to be actual.

Third, Philo claims there are other parts of nature that "plainly" bear "a greater resemblance [than human works] to the fabric of the world, and which therefore afford a better conjecture concerning the universal origin of this system" (7.3.Philo to Demea). This claim is key to his disagreement with Cleanthes, but Philo provides no more proof for his position than Cleanthes does for his. Indeed, hardly any evidence is cited by either. Philo says that "the world plainly resembles more an animal or vegetable than it does a watch or a knitting loom," but this is hardly plain to Cleanthes; for Cleanthes, the world plainly resembles a human contrivance much more than an animal or vegetable. In short, they disagree over where the greater resemblance "plainly" lies. But what kind of a dispute is this, and how is it to be settled? We shall have to wait until Part 12 for a partial resolution. At this point, all we have are claim and counterclaim, different perceptions of what is "plainly" obvious.

Fourth, Philo holds that "the cause, therefore, of the world, we may infer to be something similar or analogous to generation or vegetation" (7.3.Philo to Demea). The argument proceeds on an extension of Cleanthes' experimental principles: If x is more like y than z is like y, then the cause of x is more like the cause of y than the cause of z is like the cause of y. So if the world is more like an animal or plant than it is like a human artifact, then the world's cause(s) must resemble more the originating principles of animals or plants (i.e., generation or vegetation[5]) than the originating principle of human artifacts (reason or intelligence). Presumably Cleanthes would regard this argument as valid but unsound, for he would not concede the crucial premise that the world is indeed more like an animal or plant than a human contrivance. Philo spends little time trying to persuade Cleanthes that this premise is true; his deeper point is that there is no real way for us to tell from our experience whether it is true or false.

¶¶4–6: Question 2

Next, prodded by Demea to conceive how the world could originate from generation or vegetation—that is, how something like these local principles of reproduction could serve a cosmic function—Philo gives two answers. If the world is like a plant, then it may reproduce like a plant or a tree, producing within itself seeds of its world-progeny; if it is like an animal, then it may reproduce like an ostrich, laying a cosmic egg. In either case, we can imagine that a comet or some other celestial object serves as the required reproductive agent—"the seed of the world" (7.5.Philo to Demea) or "the egg of this animal [i.e., the world]" (7.6.Philo to Demea).[6] Also, in both cases a suitable environment is required to nourish the germ of a new world, and for this role Philo imagines "the surrounding chaos" or "the unformed elements, which every where surround this universe" (7.5.Philo to Demea). His proposals are no doubt outlandish even by the standards of eighteenth-century astronomy, and so they seem to Demea.

¶¶7–8: Question 3

Demea calls into question Philo's "wild, arbitrary suppositions" on three grounds. First, he asks, "What *data* have you for such extraordinary conclusions?" Second, he queries whether the evidence, slender as it is, is as good for the world-vegetable analogy as for the world-animal analogy.[7] And third, he asks whether objects "so widely different" from each other could possibly be "a standard for each other."[8] These three grounds come to the same point: Philo is skating on thin evidential ice and has no good reason to be confident in proposing generation or vegetation as cosmogonic principles (7.7.Demea to Philo).[9]

Philo shares Demea's concerns. In fact, Demea is making *Philo's* own major point: "We have no *data* to establish any system of cosmogony" because our experience is so imperfect and limited. If, contrary to Philo's better judgment, one *were* to hazard a cosmic hypothesis, one should then be guided only by the "greater similarity of the objects compared"—that is, the stronger experienced analogy. In that case, he asks rhetorically, is not the world more like a plant or animal than like a humanly designed "artificial machine" (7.8.Philo to Demea)? In short, Philo is not strongly committed to generation and vegetation as cosmogonic principles; although they seem to him preferable to design on Cleanthes' own principles, he finds the whole "experimental" procedure irreparably handicapped by inability to show that *any* object of experience provides a good analogy to the entire universe, much less that one or another is the best of the lot.

¶¶9–11: Question 4

Demea next asks Philo for an explanation of the "operations" and the "fine internal structure" of the principles of generation and vegetation (7.9.Demea to Philo). The question seems straightforward and reasonable, yet it causes Philo to retreat a bit from his earlier claims and to hold not that his alternative hypotheses are *more likely* than Cleanthes' hypothesis of design but only that they are *just as unlikely.* Philo's first response is to link his fate to Cleanthes. Cleanthes' principle of reason faces the very same difficulty as Philo's principles of generation and vegetation, and, strikingly, Philo can only repeat the very same solution Cleanthes offered earlier (2.5, 3.1): When Philo sees an animal, he immediately infers or just believes "that it sprang from generation," just as when Cleanthes sees a house, he immediately infers or perceives that it was "reared by design" (7.10.Philo to Demea). Philo, just like Cleanthes, has proposed an ultimate explanatory principle that is itself inexplicable.

Philo then retreats even further from his earlier claim that generation and vegetation are superior to reason and design on Cleanthes' principles; now all such principles are *equally* ineffective in explaining "such extraordinary and such magnificent subjects." On a "larger" view of the matter, Philo notes that in "this little corner of the world alone, there are four principles, *reason, instinct, generation, vegetation,* which are similar to each other, and are the causes of similar effects."[10] Doubtless there are many more ultimate principles elsewhere "in the immense extent and variety of the universe." Each principle, when pumped up via analogy, is capable of affording some "theory" of the origin of the world, so we should not be partial to the principle by which our own minds operate. Reason is as inexplicable and "little known" as instinct, generation, or vegetation; while the experienced effects of each may be known somewhat, in itself each is "totally unknown." So when we rely upon our tiny experience plus Cleanthes' rule of analogical inference, we are completely unable to shed any light on which, if any, theory is more adequate (all 7.11.Philo to Demea).

¶¶12–17: Question 5

Demea's last question raises a concern that could well have come from Cleanthes: A vegetative power that "could sow the seeds of new worlds into the infinite chaos" would seem to imply design, since ordered effects proceed from a principle of order, and "How can order spring from any thing, which perceives not that order which it bestows?" In sum, doesn't order imply intelligent design (7.12.Demea to Philo)?

In response, Philo borrows Cleanthes' trick of asking Demea (and implicitly Cleanthes) to look again to the world: Everywhere there are examples of organisms (trees, birds) unconsciously but effectively bestowing order on their offspring and surrounding parts of the world (e.g., bird nests). To say that one does not see this and to continue to insist that order *must* spring from reason and intelligence only begs the question. Whether all order in fact "proceeds ultimately from design" can only be proved *a priori*, if at all.[11]

Philo next maintains that Demea's "objection" cannot consistently be made by Cleanthes,[12] who earlier registered his decision to halt the explanatory regress at God: "I have found a Deity, and here I stop my enquiry" (4.13.Cleanthes to Philo). Philo thinks he can use the same escape mechanism and call an equally plausible halt to explanation at an ultimately vegetative or generative world: "It is at my choice. The matter seems entirely arbitrary." Neither Cleanthes nor Philo can answer queries about the causes of their principles because they are equally arbitrary. That is why they have "agreed to forbear" asking such questions, and Cleanthes should stick to that agreement. Given immunity from questioning ultimate principles, Philo feels at liberty to promote his own choice of explanatory principles (generation), even though he has just held that all such choices are equally arbitrary. "Judging by our limited and imperfect experience, generation has some privileges above reason: For we see every day the latter arise from the former, never the former from the latter" (7.14.Philo to Demea). This "privilege" provides the only basis for his claim that Cleanthes' analogy (the world as machine) is "less striking" than his own analogy (the world as animal); only the possibility of reason arising from generation has "at least some faint shadow of experience" (7.15.Philo to Demea).

Philo rounds out his response to Demea's fifth question with two paragraphs that were inserted into our text in a late revision. The first brings forth ancient witnesses (Hesiod and Plato) to Philo's favored analogy but in a way that undermines itself, perhaps deliberately. "Hesiod and all the ancient mythologists" explained nature "from an animal birth, and copulation," while Plato, "so far as he is intelligible, seems to have adopted some such notion in his TIMEUS" (7.16.Philo to Demea). This is not exactly a ringing endorsement. Quite apart from the dubious support of "mythologists," the triple qualification in the description of Plato renders his backing slight and nebulous. But such weak authority is entirely consonant with the slight support provided by the "faint shadow of experience."

Finally, Philo summons forth a cosmogonic analogy more outrageous—but no less plausible, he thinks—than any previously mentioned.[13] Perhaps the world arose from the "bowels" of a giant spider and will be annihilated later by being reabsorbed. This theory "appears to us ridiculous; because a spider is a little contemptible animal, whose operations we are never likely to take for a model of the whole universe." But a planet of spiders might find it as thoroughly "natural and irrefragable" as our planet of humans finds design; and in the abstract, why couldn't a world "be spun from the belly as well as from the brain" (7.17.Philo to Demea)?

¶18: Cleanthes' reply

Cleanthes, who waits patiently, or at least quietly, while Philo and Demea talk about him and his principles, at last finds something to say in the concluding paragraph of Part 7. Rather than addressing Philo's arguments (or Demea in any way), however, Cleanthes speaks about Philo's person and also about himself. He first gently chides Philo for his "natural and unavoidable" skepticism: It is more amusing than dangerous. He next acknowledges that while he cannot "on a sudden" solve the difficulties Philo has raised, nonetheless he professes to "clearly see, in general, their fallacy and error." Cleanthes senses that bewildering vertigo many feel in the face of skeptical arguments—unconvinced by them yet unable to refute them or even to know how to go about refuting them. He thinks he can retain his reputation as an "accurate" thinker by clinging to what he regards as the truth in the face of unanswerable yet unbelievable doubts.

Interestingly, Cleanthes then goes one step further. Not only is he baffled yet unconvinced by Philo's "doubts and objections"; so too is Philo himself! "I question not," he says, "but that you are yourself, at present, in the same case," and this in three respects: Philo cannot solve his own objections; Philo must realize that "common sense and reason is entirely against you"; and the "whimsies" Philo has presented "may puzzle, but never can convince *us*" (7.18.Cleanthes to Philo; emphasis added). The last insinuation is unmistakable: Cleanthes trivializes Philo's objections (they are mere "whimsies"), and then reaches out to include him among those of "us" who are unconvinced by the objections. So Philo, in Cleanthes' eyes, is not an enemy of the design argument but rather a friend of Cleanthes in embracing design at some deep and natural level, despite all the skeptical difficulties. Cleanthes trusts Philo's argumentation less than he trusts his own sense of design, and he believes that Philo at heart has exactly the same conviction, however much he may delight in "raising doubts and objections" from his great "fertility of invention." There is, in Cleanthes' view, an asymmetry of natures: Cleanthes does not share Philo's bent for skepticism—it is an unusual trait, perhaps "natural and unavoidable" to Philo, but not so to the majority of mankind—even while Philo shares with Cleanthes and all humans the "common sense and reason" that remains unconvinced by skepticism (all 7.18.Cleanthes to Philo).

Part 7 has presented a novel form of dialogue—questions by Demea and answers by Philo about Cleanthes' principles—but, contrary to Philo's claim, there is no essentially "new idea." Rather, these familiar themes recur: On Cleanthes' own principles, theology should follow the best cosmological analogy. If generation, vegetation, or even extrusion is a better analogy to the world than design or reason, then the deity is more like an ostrich depositing its egg, a maple propellering its keys, or a spider spinning its web than it is like a human author acting with conscious intelligence. But even if generation, vegetation, and extrusion were no better analogies than design according to the "faint shadow of experience," they would at least be no worse, and we would then be faced with a welter of competing alternatives with no reasonable way of choosing among them. The only conclusion is that "The matter seems entirely arbitrary" (7.14.Philo to Demea). According to Cleanthes, however, this puzzling result is a function of Philo's "fertility of imagination," not a matter of "common sense and reason," which remains unconvinced even as it is unable to "solve regularly such out-of-the-way difficulties as you incessantly start upon me" (7.18.Cleanthes to Philo).

11

Part 8

All religious systems, it is confessed, are subject to great and insuperable difficulties.

—Philo to Cleanthes, Part 8.12

Structure:

¶¶1–2: Philo inventively revives the Epicurean hypothesis: an eternal return of order

¶3: Demea queries the absence of a first mover

¶¶4–9: Philo suggests a "new hypothesis": Unguided matter in motion may "revolve" into self-supporting, stable forms with all the appearance of contrivance

¶10: Cleanthes perceives "insuperable objections," namely the "conveniences and advantages" of things to us (and to "all animals"?)

¶¶11–12: Philo concedes imperfections in his hypothesis but points out equal "inconveniences" in all "religious systems"; these "insuperable difficulties" "prepare a complete triumph for the sceptic"

As we draw to the end of the first stage of Philo's extended examination of the "inconveniences" of Cleanthes' experimental theism,[1] Philo makes one last criticism by introducing yet another "system" (in several variations) to the competition. It is the old Epicurean hypothesis, suitably refurbished, of an endlessly recurring world, running on pure internal necessity yet with all the appearance of design. Cleanthes thinks this hypothesis has occurred to Philo "on a sudden in the course of the argument" (8.10; Cleanthes to Philo), but more likely it has long fermented within his inventive brain, for it is of all the alternatives he proposes the one most dear to his heart. Both Demea and Cleanthes voice their objections to this new hypothesis. Demea, anticipating the *a priori* argument he will introduce in Part 9, thinks the Epicurean world cannot run without a prime mover, but Philo replies that either motion beginning in matter or a beginningless eternity of motion is just as conceivable *a priori* as motion beginning "from mind and intelligence" (8.4.Philo to Demea). In addition, Philo imagines an intriguing variant—a universe that naturally selects for self-sustaining order, once it mutates that order.

Cleanthes then provides another line of "insuperable objections" to Philo's hypothesis: It ignores "the many conveniences and advantages" (chiefly to humans) of organs and other organisms—the world is remarkably "useful" to us. Philo concedes, unnecessarily, that this may be a weak spot in his hypothesis. But he will admit defects in the Epicurean hypothesis only so long as Cleanthes will admit equal imperfections in his own design hypothesis. If indeed "all religious systems . . . are subject to great and insuperable difficulties" (8.12.Philo to Cleanthes), then Philo can claim a "complete triumph for the sceptic." Whether the skeptic's triumph is complete will be considered more fully in Part 12. In the meantime (Parts 9–11), the discussion moves on to other topics.

¶¶1–2: Philo revises the Epicurean hypothesis

First, Philo reaches back to a comment Cleanthes made at the end of Part 7, that the objections Philo has raised spring only from "your fertility of invention" (7.18.Cleanthes to Philo). On the contrary, Philo replies, they are entirely due to "the nature of the subject." Where "the narrow compass of human reason" is adapted to the subject, usually only one view "carries probability or conviction with it." But where the subject permits a hundred hypotheses as equally likely, "invention has here full scope to exert itself." That is why Philo could "in an instant" propose many hypotheses that "would have some faint appearance of truth," however improbable.[2] Yet we should not be misled—as Cleanthes is (cf. 8.10)—by the apparently casual way in which Philo turns to "revive" the old Epicurean hypothesis, as if any old hypothesis would do equally well. This particular hypothesis is dear to Philo, even if he cannot claim to know that it is true. Philo has already made favorable references to Epicurean thought in Part 5 (5.2 and 5.11), and he will make more later (10.25); it is clear that he is well-acquainted with it.

Why is Philo so attracted to the Epicurean hypothesis?[3] In part because of the content of the hypothesis itself. It puts forth an all-encompassing naturalism, combining elements of chance and necessity in the "perpetual agitation" of nature (8.6.Philo to Cleanthes) while accounting for the appearance of contrivance.[4] But also, Philo is attracted to the *activity* of considering this hypothesis, or indeed any hypothesis that appears initially unpromising, in a field wide open to "invention." Philo delights in refuting seemingly plausible positions by conjuring up unsuspected counterexamples or neglected possibilities, and this is the role that the Epicurean hypothesis plays—a further "inconvenience" for Cleanthes' experimental theism.

Philo's delight is not just a disinterested pursuit of truth or even a love of argument for its own sake, though it is partially both of these. It is also central to Philo's self-affirmation, the joy that comes from exercising one's finest capacities to the fullest. Further, it is Philo's way of impressing others with his inventiveness and their inability to solve his conundrums; Philo displays his own strengths while exposing the weakness of others' arguments. In short, Philo is showing off. Without in the least discrediting Philo's *arguments,* therefore, we should also recognize that Philo's *arguing* has its own interest, at least to Philo.

But there is another factor involved. Recall that Philo, just as much as Demea and Cleanthes, aims to contribute to the education of young Pamphilus. Part of what Philo wants Pamphilus to learn is intellectual caution—not to swoon over a promising proposal until other alternatives have been inspected. More important, Philo hopes to show how cosmological speculation lies quite beyond "the narrow compass of human reason" (8.1.Philo to Cleanthes), so we are unable to decide among equally conceivable alternatives. "A total suspense of judgement is here our only reasonable resource" (8.12.Philo to Cleanthes). For all these reasons, Philo's proposal is not pure play, though playful it surely is.

But what is this initial hypothesis, and what "kind of imperfect analogy" (8.1.Philo to Cleanthes) does it preserve? Initially, Philo speaks of reviving "the old EPICUREAN hypothesis . . . with a few alterations" (8.2.Philo to Cleanthes). Only one such alteration is mentioned: supposing matter finite instead of infinite. But Philo also identifies "matter" with "particles," a modest emendation of Epicurus's "atoms." The explicit premises of this hypothesis are three:

1. Matter consists (exclusively?) of particles.
2. There is a finite number of particles.
3. Time is infinite ("an eternal duration").

From these assumptions, Philo wants to conclude that

4. "A finite number of particles is only susceptible of finite transpositions."

And hence that

> 5. "It must happen, in an eternal duration, that every possible order or position must be tried an infinite number of times." (all 8.2.Philo to Cleanthes)

Philo admits, indeed insists, that the three premises are dubitable—overall, the old Epicurean hypothesis "is commonly, and I believe, justly, esteemed the most absurd system, that has yet been proposed,"[5] and even as refurbished by Philo it hopes only for "a faint appearance of probability" (8.2.Philo to Cleanthes). One might have expected some premise about necessity or determinism, but it makes no difference whether the particles obey iron necessity or sometimes (though not often) leap from position to position, for over infinite time a merely finite number of positions or "transpositions" will necessarily recur, and indeed recur infinitely.

Surprisingly, Philo fails to realize that his conclusion doesn't follow from his three premises, because he has forgotten about space, in two respects: First, the extent of space: If space is infinitely large, a finite number of particles need never retrace a single position, much less a single order of positions. Second, the divisibility of space: If space is continuous or infinitely divisible, there will be an infinite number of positions, however infinitesimally distinct, in even the smallest patch of space. How might Philo repair these omissions? The first I think he could accommodate by simply stipulating a fourth assumption:

> 6. Space is finitely large.

The second is more problematic, and there are at least two ways out. One alternative is:

> 7a. Space is itself particulate or non-continuous.

Another is:

> 7b. Space is continuous, but differences in position below some limit make no causal difference.

In other words, 7b denies the modern notion of chaos theory, that imperceptibly small differences in initial conditions may have unpredictably large effects. For 7b, small differences in position have no effect at all, or only negligible effects, on the "order" of the world. Which of 7a or 7b would Philo accept? It does not really matter, since this whole kind of Epicurean hypothesis is not the kind that Philo goes on to develop. Instead, his attention is first diverted by a remark of Demea's.

¶3: Demea's query

Demea notes that Philo supposes "that matter can acquire motion, without any voluntary agent or first mover." Here Demea anticipates "the argument *a priori*" that he will give in Part 9; his answer also expresses a line of thought prominent from St. Thomas Aquinas to Samuel Clarke. But he is also encouraging Philo to make explicit one more premise implicit in his argument, that the particles of matter can and do change position—that they are in motion. Let us state this premise as follows:

8. Every particle is (actually or potentially) in motion.[6]

Of course, Demea does not want to assist Philo in his explication of the Epicurean hypothesis; rather, he wants to lodge an objection against its foundations: If motion of matter is universal, what can be motion's source, origin, or "first cause" except some "voluntary agent"? Demea need not hold that there are no purely mechanical or materialistic explanations for the motion of particles, only that these explanations are proximate, not ultimate. For Demea, the absolute beginning of motion, its true "first cause," must be a "voluntary agent," one with the powers of will and intelligence. If so, then no Epicurean hypothesis can be purely naturalistic; it must make reference to some superior agent, some designing cause, some personified Author of Nature. Without saying or intending so, Demea has given an *a priori* twist to the argument from design.

¶¶4–9: Philo's "new hypothesis"

Philo initially responds to Demea's challenge in two ways. First (8.4), he disputes Demea's view that matter cannot be the origin of motion; and second (8.5), he argues for the conservation of motion throughout eternity, regardless of its ultimate cause. The first point allows for the possibility of a purely naturalistic Epicurean hypothesis; the second allows for a deistic one.

On the first score, Philo argues that "every event,[7] before experience, is equally difficult and incomprehensible; and every event, after experience, is equally easy and intelligible." As far as experience goes, motion "in many instances" begins in matter "without any known voluntary agent," such that proposing an "unknown voluntary agent is mere hypothesis; and hypothesis attended with no advantages." "The beginning of motion in matter itself is as conceivable *a priori* as its communication from mind and intelligence" (all

8.4.Philo to Demea). Philo is clearly contesting Demea's presumption of agent causality over material object or event causality; *a priori* they are on equal footing. Moreover, experience shows us many phenomena with no known voluntary agent, so experience does not support Demea's contention. Thus, purely naturalistic Epicurean hypotheses (and, more broadly, non-theistic ones) are not ruled out from the very beginning; they are at least worth the energy of exploration and "invention."

On the second score, Philo claims that, quite independently of its origin, motion may still have been "propagated by impulse[8] through all eternity." Moreover, the total quantity of motion may be conserved over this time.[9] Once again Philo presents both *a priori* and empirical reasons for his view. On the *a priori* side, it is possible that "as much as is lost by the composition of motion, as much is gained by its resolution." Here by "composition" he means the uniting of two or more motions into one with the resulting motion having the same effect as the contributing motions combined; "resolution" is the converse operation, decomposing one motion into many, again to the same effect.[10] On the empirical side, Philo thinks that it is "certain, that matter is, and always has been, in continual agitation, as far as human experience or tradition reaches"[11] (all 8.5.Philo to Demea). On both sides, Philo wants to conceive a universe that runs on its own, with its own internal principles of operation; it permits a creator god, but only a deistic god who has no work to do once the world is made.[12]

Next, Philo modifies his Epicurean "hypothesis of cosmogony" in some quite interesting ways. He wants to permit both a "perpetual agitation" in the particles of the universe and a "constancy in the forms" produced by this agitation, a self-sustaining order of nature compatible with the "continual motion of matter."[13] His proposal is that the "transpositions" of matter must sooner or later result in a world with an apparent order such as ours, and when this order occurs, it "supports itself, for many ages, if not to eternity." Natural order evolves by natural selection. Remarkably, such a universe will "have all the same appearance of art and contrivance, which we observe at present" and which constitutes the ground of Cleanthes' design analogy. In such a world, parts have an apparently contrived relation to the whole, and the whole to the parts, because without such tight relations the order would disintegrate and matter would be "thrown into irregular motions and fermentations."[14] In such a case, "a chaos ensues" until such time as "some other regular form" appears (all from 8.6.Philo to Demea).

Philo then "refines" his Epicurean hypothesis even more while claiming merely to "vary the expression."[15] He begins this time not with an eternity of motion but rather with matter "thrown into any position, by a blind, unguided force"—not by choice or necessity, but by chance. Such an initial position, Philo thinks, must "in all probability" be the most chaotic and dis-ordered imaginable—and therefore the least like human contrivance, which possesses the three properties of symmetry of parts, adjustment of means to ends, and "a tendency to self-preservation."[16] From such an unpromising be-ginning, Philo proposes to evolve a world very much like our own, which does resemble human contrivance, through purely natural and mechanical processes. In short, Philo wants to grow (in thought) a universe like ours from chaos, without the assistance of an intelligent Author (all 8.7.Philo to Demea).

So Philo supposes that the initial "actuating force" continues to give "a perpetual restlessness to matter," such that the first position gives way to a second, the second to a third, and so on. For "many successions of changes and revolutions" these positions will be chaotic and disordered; any "glimpse or dawn of order" will be "instantly hurried away and confounded, by that never-ceasing force" (8.7.Philo to Demea). Yet, Philo urges, it is at least pos-sible that perpetually restless matter might "settle at last . . . so as to preserve an uniformity of appearance."[17] Indeed, Philo claims, this evolution of a settled state of the whole (with constantly changing parts) is "assured" because of "the eternal revolutions of unguided matter." Here Philo seems of two minds: The settled condition of matter is either "possible" or "assured." But the former claim depends on the assumption that the "blind, unguided force" impelling motion began acting at some finitely distant past time, while the latter presumes that the "revolutions of unguided matter" are "eternal" (all 8.8.Philo to Demea). It is as if Philo wants to secure the *possibility* that an apparently contrived universe evolves by *necessity* and then to reduce a possible necessity to a plain necessity. But perhaps the two modalities are of different kinds—the former epistemic (possible so far as we can tell) and the latter natural or metaphysical (necessary in itself).

Philo next moves from the whole to (some of) its parts:[18] If the universe could evolve its order blindly, then why not its parts such as "animals or vege-tables"? If so, then the "curious adjustment" of animal parts to each other and to the whole organism is no surprise, for "I would fain know how an animal could subsist, unless its parts were so adjusted?" (8.9.Philo to Demea). Here Philo stands on the brink of Darwin's discovery of evolution by natural selec-tion. Both parts and whole of the universe are subject to the same natural necessity that eventually produces a semblance—but only a semblance—of contrivance.[19]

¶10: Cleanthes' "insuperable objections"

Cleanthes now finds an opening to insert first an ad hominem comment and then a curiously weak objection—curious not simply because Cleanthes offers it in apparent seriousness but also because Philo seems to credit it with some force. The ad hominem remark is unpromising, taking Philo to have proposed the Epicurean hypothesis "on a sudden," on the grounds that the subtle, sifting Philo would not have seriously proposed a hypothesis subject to such "insuperable objections." But what if the objections are not "insuperable" but trifling and even comical? Then there would be no reason to suspect Philo of carelessness. Indeed, the very weakness of Cleanthes' "objections" lends a kind of backhanded support to Philo's hypothesis—if this is the worst that can be said against it, then it cannot be very incredible.

The "insuperable objections" Cleanthes has in mind are these: How, on Philo's hypotheses of natural necessity or chance, can there "arise the many conveniences and advantages, which men and all animals possess"? Here he mentions two kinds: (1) the utility of organs to their organisms, and (2) the utility of animals and vegetables to humans.[20] He goes on to discuss only the latter kind of "satisfaction and enjoyment" and trivializes his case by speaking as if camels had been put on the planet to propel humans "in the sandy deserts of AFRICA and ARABIA." He also injects an inappropriate further kind of case, not animal or vegetable but mineral: the lodestone, which was "framed to give that wonderful and useful direction to the needle" (i.e., the compass). Any one of these cases, Cleanthes avers, is "a sufficient proof of design, and of benevolence, which gave rise to the order and arrangement of the universe" (8.10.Cleanthes to Philo).[21]

Cleanthes' "insuperable objections" are clearly insupportable. On the first kind of "convenience," Cleanthes begs the question. Philo has claimed that natural necessity can produce results with the appearance of design because the parts or organs are essential to the survival of their organism. Cleanthes disputes this, saying that "two eyes, two ears are not absolutely necessary for the subsistence of the species." Does he mean that one eye and one ear suffice? But he gives no reason to suppose that this is true, nor that survival utility is an all-or-nothing affair (maybe two as opposed to one increase the *likelihood* of survival without making it "absolutely necessary"). But he does not indicate what human end (aside from survival) two eyes and ears do serve; the difficulty is to indicate a purpose that clearly points to intelligent (much less benevolent) design but does not equally conduce to survival. On the second kind of "convenience," human utility of animals and plants seems quite incidental to their existence. Philo could easily contend that useful animals and plants evolve, or are made, for some other end than human use, or perhaps for no end at all, and that only later are they recruited for human use. Human subsequent utility does not prove benevolent antecedent design. Only when humans breed existing species for human ends does the utility of animals and plants clearly prove benevolent design—but then of course the design is all too human and proves nothing at all about "the order and arrangement of the universe" (8.10.Cleanthes to Philo).

¶¶11–12: Philo's skeptical "triumph"

Philo does not bother to rebut Cleanthes' "insuperable objections." Instead, he lets them stand and accepts their conclusion: "At least, you may safely infer . . . that the foregoing hypothesis is so far incomplete and imperfect; which I shall not scruple to allow" (8.11.Philo to Cleanthes). Although his language is somewhat ambiguous,[22] clearly Philo cannot think the objections are telling, nor is he unable to imagine an adequate rebuttal. Instead, he readily concedes the limitations of his Epicurean hypothesis in order to address two other more important points: First, that every "system of cosmogony" is equally subject to "insuperable" objections, and second, that these difficulties in any case "prepare a complete triumph for the sceptic" (8.12.Philo to Cleanthes).

On the first point, Philo urges that we simply cannot expect to do better than an "incomplete and imperfect" hypothesis when it comes to such large subjects because our "experience of the analogy of nature"[23] is just too "limited and imperfect." This is Philo's old "great disproportion" theme, and it applies equally to Cleanthes' anthropomorphic hypotheses as to Philo's Epicurean ones. Still, Philo uses this rare confession of self-inadequacy to get in a few last licks at Cleanthes' anthropomorphism. "In all instances which we have ever seen," he says, "ideas are copied from real objects, and are ectypal, not archetypal," whereas Cleanthes' hypothesis reverses this priority.[24] Next, thought influences matter only where matter has "an equal reciprocal influence" on thought; there is an "equality of action and re-action" here, but Cleanthes' hypothesis implies an inequality. These (and many other[25]) difficulties should teach us all both "sobriety in condemning each other" and to avoid two errors of rashness: accepting a system simply "from a slight analogy" or rejecting one "on account of a small incongruity" (all 8.11.Philo to Cleanthes). Philo clearly thinks that Cleanthes commits both errors and that he, Philo, will avoid both by recourse to skepticism. To do so, however, he will have to commit a logical sleight-of-hand.

On the second point, Philo urges, "All religious systems, it is confessed, are subject to great and insuperable difficulties," such that every "disputant triumphs in his turn" while showing "the absurdities, barbarities, and pernicious tenets of his antagonist," but the whole exercise only prepares "a complete triumph for the sceptic."[26] The skeptic embraces no system, for the "plain reason, that no absurdity ought ever to be assented to with regard to any subject," and every system is absurd. Philo then seeks to draw Cleanthes into a kind of skeptical community: "A total suspense of judgement is here *our* only reasonable resource" (emphasis added). What kind of community Philo envisions is far from clear, for the skeptic is to be "with all mankind, on the offensive,"[27] hence is never "obliged to defend" any "fixed station or abiding city" (all 8.12.Philo to Cleanthes).

Note the odd course of Philo's argument. In 8.11, he says every hypothesis or system has some "small incongruity" or other and should not be rejected on this score; in 8.12, he says every system should be rejected, or at least suspended, because of its "absurdities, barbarities, and pernicious tenets." In the former paragraph, he counsels modesty in embracing a particular system and tolerance of other, different choices on the grounds of the "slight" support and "small" defects of every system; in the latter paragraph, he urges rejection of all systems and embrace of skepticism on the grounds of the suddenly vicious "absurdities" of those same systems. How can he move so rapidly from modest and tolerant dogmatism to confident and triumphant skepticism? There is a logical divide here, and Cleanthes and Philo stand on its opposite sides: Cleanthes firmly clinging to his anthropomorphism despite its defects and the allure of alternatives, Philo just as firmly eschewing all cosmological hypotheses despite his inability to conclusively prove or disprove any of the alternatives. Is there any way to bridge this kind of gulf? Perhaps, if there is a kind of community in which both can live together.

But Philo's triumphal skepticism only heightens the problem. In what kind of community can skeptics live if they have no "fixed station or abiding city"? Recall Philo's words from Part 1: In theology, "we are like foreigners in a strange country, to whom every thing must seem suspicious, and who are in danger every moment of transgressing against the laws and customs of the people, with whom they live and converse" (1.10.Philo to Cleanthes).[28] Likewise, the theological skeptic cannot participate in, nor perhaps understand, the life of religious communities whose "laws and customs" not only transcend but also transgress common human life. But common life itself is also suspect; the complete skeptic cannot account for "our vulgar methods of reasoning" and so must be "entirely guided by a kind of instinct or necessity in employing them" (1.10.Philo to Cleanthes). Where, then, can the skeptic live? The vital relation of skeptic to common life is at best problematic at the end of Part 8, and we will have to await Part 12 to see how the skeptic can join in community with the dogmatist, how Philo can live together with Cleanthes "in unreserved intimacy" (12.2.Philo to Cleanthes).

Let us pause to review the course of the long discussion in Parts 2–8 (over two-thirds of the *Dialogues*) of experimental reasoning concerning the deity's "natural" attributes. Cleanthes' "argument *a posteriori*" starts with the resemblance of human artifacts both to the whole world and to parts of the world such as organisms and organs and moves to the conclusion that the cause of the world, "the Author of Nature," is a designing intelligence "somewhat similar to the mind of man," though of course on a much grander scale. While Demea dissents from the piously troubling anthropomorphism inherent in arguments from human experience, Philo goes on to subject Cleanthes' reasoning to a blizzard of objections. Some objections question the "great disproportion"—whether we can fruitfully reason from our minute scene to such a vast whole, seeking to understand something so distant from common life. Others question the particular analogy Cleanthes employs to guide his reasoning (human contrivance), either by drawing the analogy more tightly than Cleanthes wants (making the Author of Nature too much like a human being, lacking the traditional perfections of divinity) or by attenuating it beyond usefulness (making the Author of Nature a blank mystery). Still others point out the multitude of alternative hypotheses based on different analogies: Once even remote analogies are permitted, it is not possible to stop seeing various likenesses with animals, plants, or insects, from which one can infer by Cleanthes' principles that the world's source differs remarkably (and sometimes comically) from intelligent design. More radical still, and closer to Philo's heart, are various naturalistic hypotheses, particularly variants of the old Epicurean hypothesis of eternal return, wherein the world possesses inherent order and needs no external explanation.

It appears, therefore, that there is scarcely an aspect of the design hypothesis that has not been severely tested and found wanting: its premises, its conclusion, its reasoning, its underlying analogy are all suspect. Had a reader only Parts 2–8 of the *Dialogues,* she might well conclude—as so many philosophical readers have in fact concluded—that Philo indeed "triumphs," that the design argument has breathed its last, and that Hume is happy to pronounce its valediction. But of course the *Dialogues* does not end with Part 8, just as it did not begin with Part 2, and no reader should suppose that the last words on design, natural theology, or natural religion have been said. We, along with Pamphilus, must continue to listen to *all* of the ensuing conversations before we can adequately learn what the *Dialogues* as a whole teaches about natural religion.

12

Part 9

Had we not better adhere to that simple and sublime argument *a priori,*
which by offering to us infallible demonstration, cuts off at once all doubt
and difficulty?

—Demea to Cleanthes and Philo, Part 9.1

Structure:
   ¶¶1–3: Demea presents an a priori *argument*
      ¶1: Demea touts the advantages of arguments a priori
      ¶2: Cleanthes refocuses Demea's attention on the argument
      ¶3: Demea states his "common" a priori *argument*
   ¶¶4–9: Cleanthes points out the "weakness" of Demea's argument (and inci-
   dentally undermines his own design argument)
      ¶4: "Metaphysical reasoning" little serves "the cause of true piety and
      religion"
      ¶5: Matters of fact cannot be proven a priori
      ¶6: The phrase "necessary existence" is meaningless or contradictory
      ¶7: If "necessary existence" is meaningful, it might apply to the ma-
      terial world
      ¶8: No first cause is needed for "an eternal succession of objects"
      ¶9: Explaining every part of a whole explains the whole; the whole
      is due to "an arbitrary act of the mind"
   ¶¶10–11: Philo reinforces Cleanthes' critique
      ¶10: Apparent design may be due to hidden internal necessity
      ¶11: A priori arguments are unsatisfying to most people "even [those]
      of good sense and best inclined to religion"

Part 9 is the shortest in the *Dialogues,*[1] its discussion of *a priori* arguments
seems oddly discordant with the other conversations, its insertion seems

poorly motivated, and the quality of argument is curiously weak. But we must not imagine that Hume was simply uninterested in *a priori* arguments and so did not bother to fashion a respectable argument deserving and receiving respectable critique.[2] On the contrary, Part 9 is rich in detail and matters of dialogic as well as philosophical interest; bad arguments abound, but understanding their inadequacies is instructive.

Part 9 begins as Demea finally tires of Philo's relentless cross-examination of Cleanthes' design hypotheses and introduces a totally different kind of argument, "that simple and sublime argument *a priori*"—actually a not-so-simple blend of various traditional cosmological and ontological arguments.[3] Cleanthes for once takes the lead in critique; he raises a variety of objections without noting (or noticing?) that most tell equally, if they tell at all, against his own design arguments. Philo for once plays the role of echoing accomplice, chiming in with two concluding paragraphs that oddly restate, but thereby reinforce, some points already made by Cleanthes. The roles and reasons of all three speakers in this Part deserve close scrutiny; it is no accident that Demea is the one who produces an *a priori* argument (he thinks it has certain religious advantages), or that Cleanthes and Philo join together in rebuttal (both rely on experience, not reason), or that Demea is so readily silenced (the true foundation for his piety lies elsewhere, as we shall see in Part 10).

¶1: Demea touts *a priori* arguments

Demea apparently takes to heart Philo's claim of "complete triumph for the sceptic" at the end of Part 8. If there are such difficulties attending "the argument *a posteriori*," he says, we should "better adhere to that simple and sublime argument *a priori*" (9.1.Demea to Cleanthes and Philo). Given his demonstrated lack of logical acuity, Demea would seem an odd proponent of *a priori* theological arguments with their notorious subtleties. But Demea's move to this form of argument is due less to the difficulties of Cleanthes' pet hypothesis, which Demea has opposed "from the beginning" (2.6.Demea to Cleanthes), and more to the promise of *a priori* argument: It supposedly yields "infallible demonstration," "cuts off at once all doubt and difficulty," and proves "the INFINITY[4] of the divine attributes" (all 9.1.Demea to Cleanthes and Philo).

It is plain that what attracts Demea to *a priori* argument is not some love of reason (he is the least rational of the three speakers) or a particular fondness for the details of this particular argument but rather an intense interest in securing absolutely firm footings for his own pious views. Demea will employ any method of arguing that promises to shore up his own religion, never mind inherent cogency or mutual consistency. But although he thinks this *a priori* argument matters to his religion, since it promises "certainty" and "assurance," he would readily abandon it the moment he found out that the promise can't be fulfilled, and he would switch allegiance in an instant to any other form of argument that pledges similar benefits. Since his attraction to *a priori* argument is so weak and external, therefore, it is no wonder that he produces so weak an instance of it. Demea wants to be convinced and assured, not to submit to the demands of logical rigor.

¶2: Cleanthes refocuses Demea

Cleanthes interjects. Demea has been touting the presumed "advantages and conveniences" of *a priori* argument. But there are two prior questions: Which particular *a priori* argument does Demea have in mind? And just how good is this particular argument? Cleanthes wants to ascertain the nature and value of the argument Demea proposes before examining its potential uses. But Cleanthes' reason for this order of inquiry is only partially (if at all) that of the pure logician who insists that only logically good (valid, sound, cogent) arguments should be used. Cleanthes cannot reject all appeals to useful consequences, since he will himself make an appeal to the moral utility of religion in Part 12. Demea, of course, goes further: What matters above all are the effects arguments have in shoring up his piety and himself. Even logically flawed arguments can yield good results—good from the standpoint of Demea's piety. The issue between Cleanthes and Demea is not so much a question of consistency (they agree that theology should cohere with piety) or even a question of priority (both agree that piety precedes theology and argument) but rather a question of piety (they live quite different religious lives). Cleanthes rejects Demea's appeal to the "advantages and conveniences" of his *a priori* argument most fundamentally because he rejects Demea's piety and does not wish it to draw support from any quarter. (Philo, as we shall see, shares Cleanthes' antipathy to Demea's kind of piety.)

¶3: Demea gives the *a priori* argument

Demea politely consents to produce his argument before assessing its usefulness. But we should not read his consent as implying that he thinks only logically good arguments should be used in support of piety. Demea is an incurable opportunist when it comes to argument: He will seize upon whatever line of argument or rhetoric will work to undergird his own religion and persuade others to commit themselves to the same path. This particular argument, he asserts, is "the common one." However, it turns out to be neither one nor common but instead an odd amalgam of *a priori* ingredients.[5]

One ingredient is familiar to supporters of the Principle of Sufficient Reason (PSR): "Whatever exists must have a cause or reason of its existence."[6]

This principle is applied by Demea to more than particular objects which begin to exist in time. Even an infinite "particular succession of causes" also requires a cause or reason why this sequence exists and not some other, or indeed none at all.

Another component is the sense of wonder at the heart of the cosmological argument, often expressed in the query "Why is there something rather than nothing at all?" If there is no "necessarily existent Being," then what could have "determined something to exist rather than nothing, and bestowed being on a particular possibility, exclusive of the rest"? Demea claims that neither "external causes," "chance," nor bare "nothing" can provide the appropriate explanation; only a necessarily existent being can do that.

Demea also folds in a certain line of thinking about what a "necessarily existent Being" is: One "who carries the REASON of his existence in himself; and who cannot be supposed not to exist without an express contradiction." Such a being provides the terminus to the threatening regress of cosmological explanations, is the reason why something exists rather than nothing, and satisfies the PSR by containing its own cause or reason for existence. Indeed, the very concept of necessary existence provides the germ of an ontological argument: Such a being "cannot be supposed not to exist without an express contradiction."

A fourth component explores causality and infinity in a very Aristotelian way. First, it is "absolutely impossible for any thing[7] to produce itself, or be the cause of its own existence"—a principle applicable to every member of any causal series of contingent beings and to any contingent series as well. The finite case is easy: Something outside the finite causal series must cause the existence of its first member and in doing so serve as the reason why this particular finite causal series exists. Similar reasoning applies to an infinite causal series that has a first member. But what about an infinite causal series where there is no first member? Each member of the series has a cause antecedent to it, but what about "the whole eternal chain or succession, taken together"? Either it has no "ultimate cause" at all, Demea contends, or there is an ultimate cause "that is necessarily existent."[8]

Combining all these strands, Demea concludes that "we must, therefore, have recourse to a necessarily existent Being." And further, this demonstrable Being is the object of religious affections: "There is consequently such a Being, that is, there is a Deity" (all 9.3.Demea to Cleanthes). The metaphysical first cause or necessary being is the very God Demea thinks he worships.

¶4: Cleanthes preempts Philo

Surprisingly, it is Cleanthes, not Philo, who springs to the attack. Cleanthes recognizes that "starting objections is his [Philo's] chief delight," yet he feels strongly enough about the present case to usurp Philo's customary critical role. He gives two reasons for his uncharacteristic intrusion: first, that Demea's argument "seems to me so obviously ill-grounded," and second, that Demea's argument is "of so little consequence to the cause of true piety and religion."[9] The first reason is the sole burden of his succeeding critical comments, but the second reason is clearly dearer to his heart. As we shall see, in the course of showing how "ill-grounded" Demea's argument is, Cleanthes unwittingly does damage to his own theological hypothesis of design, so his "venture" into criticism is costly indeed (all 9.4.Cleanthes to Demea).

But we must properly understand Cleanthes' concern about Demea's argument having "so little consequence to the cause of true piety and religion." One might suppose that this concern has chiefly to do with the abstract and abstruse nature of the "argument *a priori*" and its remoteness from concrete religious life and motivation; indeed, this is the very point Philo makes at the end of this Part (9.11). But Demea concedes this point in Part 10; in fact, he is eager to confess that feeling, not reasoning, is the true source of religion. If Cleanthes is concerned about the remoteness of argument from "true piety and religion," he will receive no quarrel from Demea. So there is reason to locate Cleanthes' worry about Demea's argument elsewhere.

To understand his concern, let us focus on "the cause of *true* piety and religion." Recall that Demea is enamored of the "simple and sublime argument *a priori*" because its demonstrative form produces "certainty" and "assurance." Doubt is the great enemy of Demea's piety, and Demea likes *a priori* argument because it supposedly "cuts off[10] at once all doubt and difficulty." But Cleanthes has tethered his religion to a totally different form of argument: His experimental theism argues by analogy and yields only likenesses and likelihoods. So Cleanthes' piety must tolerate doubt and uncertainty, and it must condemn any quest for absolute certainty. As a result, Cleanthes is more worried about Demea's righteous self-certainty than he is about the soundness of the argument *a priori*. In Cleanthes' eyes, Demea's piety needs less, not more, conviction and argumentative grounding. So here is Cleanthes' deeper need to "show the fallacy" of Demea's argument *a priori*: Cleanthes thinks Demea lacks true religion, and he wants to oppose any apparent support of Demea's piety (all from 9.4.Cleanthes to Demea and Philo).

There is one further point: Cleanthes is speaking not only, nor perhaps even primarily, to Demea, even though he is criticizing Demea's argument. There is the youthful and impressionable Pamphilus, of course, but there is also Philo. For the first, but not the last, time in the *Dialogues,* Cleanthes makes common cause with Philo. Philo has inveigled Demea into believing that he and Demea are allies because they both reject Cleanthes' "anthropomorphism" and support "mysticism." But they are not truly friends, much less co-religionists, and the gulf between them is unapparent only to Demea. A time of open rupture between the allies of convenience is approaching, a time when the friendship between Philo and Cleanthes can return to its accustomed "unreserved intimacy" (12.2.Philo to Cleanthes). In not leaving criticism of the argument *a priori* up to Philo, Cleanthes signals his alignment with Philo, in profound opposition to Demea's piety, and Philo reciprocates by echoing Cleanthes.

¶¶5–9: Cleanthes' criticisms

Cleanthes presents five criticisms of Demea's argument *a priori*. These criticisms seem impressive at first glance, but they are really surprisingly weak. For once, perhaps, Demea gets the better of an argument—or at least not the worst of one—but only by default.

1. First of all, Cleanthes argues that no "matter of fact" can be demonstrated or proved by *a priori* argument, and his reasoning is worth quoting in full:

> Nothing is demonstrable, unless the contrary implies a contradiction. Nothing, that is distinctly conceivable, implies a contradiction. Whatever we conceive as existent, we can also conceive as non-existent. There is no Being, therefore, whose non-existence implies a contradiction. Consequently, there is no Being, whose existence is demonstrable. I propose this argument as entirely decisive, and am willing to rest the whole controversy upon it. (9.5.Cleanthes to Demea and Philo)

This is as fine a *petitio principii* as you can find. Demea's claim (or rather, one of them) is that "a necessarily existent Being . . . carries the REASON of his existence in himself; and . . . cannot be supposed not to exist without an express contradiction" (9.3.Demea to Philo and Cleanthes). Cleanthes' crucial claim is that "whatever we conceive as existent, we can also conceive as non-existent," from which it follows that a necessarily existent Being, a being who "cannot be supposed not to exist without an express contradiction," cannot be conceived (9.5.Cleanthes to Demea). But what *argument* supports Cleanthes against Demea? None is given. Perhaps Cleanthes thinks his claim is self- evident, but it is not; it is far from obvious that a putatively "necessarily existent Being" *can* be conceived as non-existent without contradiction. The contention that all "matters of fact" are contingent is precisely the point at issue. Rather than providing an "entirely decisive" argument, Cleanthes has in fact presented only a question-begging counterclaim.

2. Cleanthes next argues that "the words . . . *necessary existence* have no meaning; or which is the same thing, none that is consistent." His argument here is subtle, but ultimately it is a non sequitur. Defenders of a "necessarily existent Being" try to explain necessary existence by saying that "if we knew

his whole essence or nature, we should perceive it to be as impossible for him not to exist as for twice two not to be four." In reply, Cleanthes holds that so long as "our faculties remain the same as at present," we can never grasp such necessity. We can always "conceive the non-existence of what we formerly conceived to exist; nor can the mind ever lie under a necessity of supposing any object to remain always in being" (all 9.6.Cleanthes to Demea and Philo).

Cleanthes' reply is puzzling. In effect, he concedes that the divine nature *could* exclude non-existence, as a matter of necessity, but that we, so long as "our faculties" remain unaltered, can never apprehend this necessity. It is not that God couldn't *be* a necessary being, just that we couldn't *recognize* or *conceive* this necessity. We are so built that we must be always able to conceive the non-existence of anything that we can conceive to exist; hence we are unable to conceive the necessity of a necessarily existent being, if such there be.

This constraint appears to be a brute matter of fact for Cleanthes, but it is thoroughly suspect. If it exists at all, it would seem to be a kind of psychological or subjective necessity, a universal contingent fact about humans. But how does Cleanthes claim to know that the inability "to conceive the non-existence of what we formerly conceived to exist" is part of our "essence or nature"? Does Cleanthes have better access into our nature than into God's nature? On his own principles, experience can never yield necessity. Even though we have tried and failed to conceive a necessarily existent being thousands of times, maybe we have not worked hard enough or thought about it in the right way. Further, argument *a priori* does not yield matter of fact, according to Cleanthes. He has just said "there is an evident absurdity in pretending to demonstrate a matter of fact, or to prove it by any arguments *a priori*" (9.5.Cleanthes to Demea and Philo). So Cleanthes is hoist on his own positivistic petard. In virtue of his presuppositions, he can no more gain insight into his own claims about human nature than can Demea into his claims about divine nature.

Cleanthes therefore misstates his conclusion. It is not that "necessary existence" lacks meaning, or consistent meaning, but rather that if it has any meaning we cannot correctly apply it, for any being which we can think to exist cannot be thought (by us) to be necessary, and any being which we can think to be necessary cannot be thought (by us) to exist. If God is a necessary being (and we have no way to rule this out), then according to Cleanthes' argument we can only conceive of God erroneously. In short, Cleanthes' conclusion is about us, not about God, and its support is weaker than he thinks.

3. Perhaps dimly perceiving the previous points, Cleanthes goes on to say that even if there is some way of explicating the phrase "necessarily existent Being" so that it is intelligible to us, why couldn't such a Being be the material

universe? Perhaps matter, "for aught we can determine" contains some properties that "would make its non-existence appear as great a contradiction as that twice two is five." Cleanthes here steps into dangerous waters, for he is putting forth an idea only recently essayed by Philo in criticism of the design hypothesis—the idea of a self-sufficient universe whose character and existence are internally necessitated. If such a possibility is credible, it counts as much against Cleanthes as against Demea.

But Cleanthes wades in deeper still. The only argument against the necessary existence of the world, he maintains, concerns the contingency of both the "matter" and the "form" of the world[11]—any part or particle of matter we may conceive not to exist, any form of matter we may conceive to be altered. The (unstated) implication is that if we may conceive every part to be contingent then the whole must also be contingent.[12] Now this very same argument, Cleanthes claims, "extends equally to the Deity." Insofar as we can conceive God's existence, we must be able to conceive God's non-existence (by the principle stated in point 2 above); if God's non-existence is impossible, it must be due to "some unknown, inconceivable qualities" (all 9.7.Cleanthes to Demea and Philo). But then, for all we know, why couldn't matter equally possess such unfathomable qualities? Here Cleanthes supports a supposition that Philo had earlier used and Cleanthes rejected as facing "insuperable objections" (8.10.Cleanthes to Philo). If, for all we know, matter could have such properties as necessary existence, then, for all we know, Philo's revived Epicurean hypotheses are as credible as Cleanthes' anthropomorphic theistic ones.

4. Cleanthes next inserts a sly but unexamined point about how temporality is essential to the notion of cause. The causal relation, he asserts, "implies a priority in time and a beginning of existence." A cause must temporally precede its effect, and any cause must have a beginning in time. Both claims are controversial. Whether there can be atemporal causes of temporal effects is unclear. But at the minimum, Cleanthes' former claim should be modified to say that a temporal cause cannot be later than its temporal effect (no "backward" causation), and he should recognize that his latter claim is independent of his former one. But Cleanthes requires both claims in order to hold that an "eternal succession of objects" doesn't need and indeed can't have "a general cause or first author,"[13] because such a cause would have to have a beginning in time and temporally precede all its effect(s). So there is no cause beginning in time that is prior to all the members of an "eternal succession of objects" (all 9.8.Cleanthes to Philo and Demea). Once again, Cleanthes does not seem to realize how this objection counts against his own design argument; if the universe is an "eternal succession of objects," there is no way to show it has a single original Author. Even a "finitely perfect"

Author of Nature such as Cleanthes later proposes (11.1) cannot save the thought of a single temporal Author of an everlasting Nature.

5. Cleanthes' final sally is more radical still: The world as a whole exists not in itself but only in the human mind. More precisely, the whole[14] is a "uniting of these parts" that is "performed merely by an arbitrary act of the mind, and has no influence on the nature of things." Such a uniting is "like the uniting of several distinct counties into one kingdom, or several distinct members into one body." From this radical claim, it follows, Cleanthes contends, that explaining the causes of all of the parts suffices to explain the cause of the whole, since the whole is only the result of "an arbitrary act of the mind." As he famously expresses it,

> Did I show you the particular causes of each individual in a collection of twenty particles of matter, I should think it very unreasonable, should you afterwards ask me, what was the cause of the whole twenty. That is sufficiently explained in explaining the cause[15] of the parts. (9.9.Cleanthes to Demea and Philo)

Cleanthes again seems oblivious to how this point undercuts his own design argument: Without a whole world to analogize to a human artifact, there is nothing for an Author of Nature to author.

Cleanthes, in criticizing Demea's argument *a priori,* has reiterated a number of points Philo had earlier urged against Cleanthes' own design argument. Is he blissfully unaware of the twin edges of the sword he wields? Perhaps, but more likely he thinks these criticisms count more decisively against Demea's argument *a priori.* An "experimental" or *a posteriori* argument requires weighing all the evidence, and no single consideration is conclusive, whereas an *a priori* demonstration is ruined by a single flaw or counterexample. But also, and more important, Cleanthes here intimates his deep bond with Philo; the two friends are in much greater agreement about what matters to them than might appear from their theological disputes in Parts 2–8.

¶¶10–11: Philo echoes Cleanthes

Cleanthes has finished his critique, but Philo "cannot forbear insisting still upon another topic." Not surprisingly, he actually touches on not one but two topics; quite surprisingly, both of these topics have already been mentioned by Cleanthes! Why does Philo essentially repeat Cleanthes' points while claiming he is saying something new? Philo does modestly augment Cleanthes' earlier points with a new analogy (on the first point) and a fuller depiction (on the second point), but, more important, by echoing these points he signals his alliance with Cleanthes, and by reinforcing the points he increases the likelihood that the reader (and the auditor!) will find the points impressive and convincing.[16]

Philo's first point is a mathematical analogy to the universe. Philo has learned from a French journal that "the products of 9 [when their digits are added together] compose always either 9 or some lesser product of 9." For example, 9 × 3 is 27, and 2 + 7 is 9. "To a superficial observer," Philo says, "so wonderful a regularity" appears due to "chance or design." But to someone who deeply understands the matter, it is all "the work of necessity," resulting from "the nature of these numbers." Philo then applies the analogy in a way that mimics Cleanthes' earlier inferences on behalf of design, but to a different conclusion: "Is it not probable, I ask, that the whole economy of the universe is conducted by a like necessity, though no human algebra can furnish a key, which solves the difficulty?" (9.10.Philo to Demea and Cleanthes). This is new backing for Philo's pet world hypothesis, the Epicurean self-sufficient universe.

Philo is speaking both to Demea and to Cleanthes. To Demea he says: "So dangerous is it to introduce this idea of necessity into the present question! And so naturally does it afford an inference directly opposite to the religious hypothesis!" (9.10.Philo to Demea). Demea has introduced the idea of necessity in putting forth an argument *a priori* that could yield an "infallible demonstration," an argument whose conclusion would follow of necessity from indubitable premises. But what little insight we have into necessity, thinks Philo, permits us to speculate that the world itself is the "necessarily existent Being" Demea seeks in the deity. Rather than lusting after certainty, Demea should more modestly content himself with probabilities. To Cleanthes, Philo cautions by the alarming leap he makes—and calls "probable"—from a small mathematical example to "the whole economy of the world." Such a leap, he implies, is no more fantastic than Cleanthes' vault from features of organisms resembling human artifice to the whole world. Philo's wildly unpersuasive use of a mathematical analogy should give pause to Cleanthes.

Philo's second point, concluding Part 9, in effect amplifies something Cleanthes mentioned earlier (9.4). Demea's argument *a priori,* Philo notes, "has seldom been found very convincing, except to people of a metaphysical head, who have accustomed themselves to abstract reasoning. . . . Other people, even of good sense and best inclined to religion, feel always some deficiency in such arguments" (9.11.Philo to Demea). Philo here takes several digs at Demea. First, Demea himself is certainly not "of a metaphysical head" accustomed to abstract reasoning, so he will not be—nor does he have the right to be—convinced by such an argument.[17]

Second, Demea does not even qualify as a "person of good sense and best inclined to religion"—*even such people* will find the argument *a priori* to be defective, while a religious fanatic such as Demea may still be attracted by its (spurious) aura of "infallible demonstration." In short, the argument *a priori* is not really religiously useful—that is, not useful to *true* religion and piety, however much it may seem useful to Demea's religion. Demea is therefore implicitly charged by Philo with lack of "good sense" and an inclination to religion that is not "the best." In fact, as we shall see, Demea's piety is downright dangerous.

Third, the fact that "people, even of good sense and best inclined to religion, feel always some deficiency in such arguments" constitutes "a certain proof, that men ever did and ever will derive their religion from other sources than from this species of reasoning" (all 9.11.Philo to Demea). But Demea would not disagree. Demea certainly derives his own religion from another source, as he will disclose in the very next Part: "Each man feels, in a manner, the truth of religion within his own breast" (10.1.Demea to Philo). But it is ironic that this point about the sources of religion—an *a posteriori* point—is the only "certain proof" that emerges from Part 9, the only one that all three speakers agree upon. Demea's argument *a priori* is in fact defective and unconvincing, but even were it to survive logical scrutiny, it would still not serve as a true "source" of religion; successful or faulty, the argument *a priori* proves only that "this species of reasoning" is not the ground or origin of true religion.[18]

The argument *a priori* has not fared well in Part 9, nor have the three speakers acquitted themselves well. Though Demea desires the argument's promised land of certainty and assurance, he makes a confused presentation of a mélange of considerations. Though Cleanthes wishes to rule out *a priori* theological arguments entirely, his critique is inconclusive and cuts just as deeply into his own favored design argument. Though Philo wants to add "another topic," he merely pads some points previously mentioned by Cleanthes and ends up reiterating a point with which Demea has agreed all along. What might a young listener such as Pamphilus learn from such a dialectical fiasco? Perhaps that no one of his elders is a completely reliable guide to theological argument and that both acceptance and rejection of the argument *a priori* bear critical scrutiny on psychological as well as on logical grounds. The *a priori* argument has by no means been breathed into life, but neither has it finally been laid to rest.

13

Part 10

It is my opinion, I own, replied DEMEA, that each man feels, in a manner, the truth of religion within his own breast.

—Demea to Philo and Cleanthes, Part 10.1

Structure:

¶¶1–2: Demea "owns" his true piety, and Philo ambiguously concurs
¶¶3–19: Demea and Philo wallow in human misery
> *¶¶3–5: Demea generalizes from his own experience of misery and dependency to "the people," the learned, and even to Cleanthes' library*
> *¶¶6–7: The exception of Leibniz only proves "the united testimony of mankind"*
> *¶8: "The whole earth . . . is cursed and polluted" (Demea)*
> *¶9: "The curious artifices of nature" only embitter life (Philo)*
> *¶¶10–12: Society surmounts real enemies (Demea) but introduces imaginary ones (Philo)*
> *¶¶13–15: Diseases of body and disorders of mind "render life ineligible" (Demea)*
> *¶¶16–19: Philo converses with an imaginary "adversary," whose attempted excuses only "still farther aggravate the charge"*
¶20: Cleanthes demurs: "I feel little or nothing of it in myself"
¶¶21–27: Demea and Philo offer rebuttals to Cleanthes
> *¶¶21–23: Demea appeals to authorities on "the greatness of human misery"*
> *¶¶24–27: Philo assails Cleanthes' anthropomorphism regarding the moral attributes of the deity (benevolence and mercy)*
¶¶28–31: Cleanthes strikes back
> *¶28: Philo has at last "betrayed" his true intentions*

¶29: Demea provides a theodicy of "larger views" of Providence

¶¶30–31: Cleanthes rejects Demea's "arbitrary suppositions" and seeks to "deny absolutely the misery and wickedness of man"

¶¶32–35: Philo answers Cleanthes

¶32: Pain outweighs pleasure in importance if not in frequency

¶33: Philo (ironically) admonishes Cleanthes for introducing "total scepticism"

¶34: What we find is not what one would expect from an infinite deity

¶35: Divine power is compatible with misery, but not derivable from it

¶36: Philo claims a qualified "triumph" regarding the divine moral attributes but recurs to faith and appeals to Cleanthes "to tug the labouring oar"

Following the long discussion in Parts 2–9 of the natural or metaphysical attributes of the deity (chiefly power and intelligence), Demea now steers the conversation in a different direction. The true roots of religion, he holds, lie elsewhere than in quasi-scientific evidence and inference; they are found instead within each person's heart, chiefly in "a consciousness of his imbecility and misery" that leads him to "seek protection" from the powers that bear down upon him (10.1.Demea to Philo and Cleanthes). Demea's soul-baring launches a complicated[1] discussion of the moral attributes of divinity (chiefly benevolence and mercy), with Cleanthes the optimistic foil to much wailing and gnashing of teeth by Demea and Philo. But these two are united only in their rejection of Panglossian optimism; they wallow in different kinds of misery, for different reasons, and intend quite different results. While Demea reveals his true piety, a religion of self-abasement and other-appeasement, Philo claims another "triumph" in using Cleanthes' own design argument to scout the divine moral attributes. But the piety of Philo and Cleanthes is also partially uncovered in their responses to Demea's self-disclosure; it will become a central topic of conversation between the two friends in Part 12.[2]

¶¶1–2: Demea owns his true piety, and Philo responds

Demea opens Part 10 with a passionate statement of his faith—it is not so much a profession of belief as an outpouring of feeling. Everyone, he claims, "feels, in a manner, the truth of religion within his own breast." Whether or not everyone feels this, it is at least Demea's own sincere and self-revealing cri de coeur; here at last Demea forsakes the arguments of others and divulges his own deepest views in his own proper literary form—confession. These feelings he "owns" quite personally and fervently, even though he speaks as if this attitude were a religious commonplace (all 10.1.Demea to Cleanthes and Philo).

Why does Demea only now expose the roots of his piety? Perhaps he is impatient with the lengthy examination of Cleanthes' experimental reasoning (in Parts 2–8); perhaps he is exasperated at the swift dismissal of his own *a priori* reasoning (in Part 9); perhaps he is frustrated at the overintellectualizing tendencies of both Cleanthes and Philo; or perhaps he realizes that he has little time remaining to inculcate proper piety in Pamphilus. But at any rate Demea does allow us to peer into the depths of his soul, a sight from which both Cleanthes (emphatically) and Philo (more subtly) recoil. Demea's piety is worlds apart from theirs. It is not just that Demea is rigidly dogmatic, or even that he values certitude above truth, but that the content of his piety is so appalling to them.

The "truth of religion" Demea feels within himself embraces six points: (1) We are led to religious conviction fundamentally not through reasoning but through feeling. The arguments for theism are not fundamental to piety. In saying this, Demea is not unaware that his position is self-contradictory— he relies upon universal human experience to witness for misery, even as he deprecates Cleanthes' experimental reasoning from universal experience of natural design. But Demea is willing to sacrifice even consistency for the sake of fervor. Demea, therefore, impatiently seeks to turn the conversation from theology to piety. (2) Our basic religious feeling is "a consciousness of [our] imbecility and misery," an unargued but deeply felt sense of our present overwhelming ignorance and unhappiness. We would not be in such desperate straits were we blissfully ignorant or knowingly miserable, much less happily knowledgeable. But, given both ignorance and unhappiness, "Wretched creatures that we are!"

(3) Our desperate condition prompts us "to seek protection from that Being, on whom [we] and all nature is dependent." Demea just assumes what has been at risk in the preceding dialogues: that nature does depend upon a divine Author. (4) Demea's religion is independent of his theism. While he does initially speak of "that Being," he shortly goes on to speak of "those unknown powers," suggesting that polytheism is as compatible with Demea's experience as theism. It is not theology that matters, but piety. (5) Human grasping for God or gods takes the form of futurity: Even "the best scenes" of present life are so wretched that we can only turn to another life to come. Future hope is enlivened by present misery. (6) What we can do now, in our present misery, is "to endeavour, by prayers, adoration, and sacrifice, to appease those unknown powers, whom we find, by experience, so able to afflict and oppress us." We need to atone for our sins and "appease those terrors,

with which we are incessantly agitated and tormented" (all 10.1.Demea to Cleanthes and Philo). So the hope for a future better life is chained not only to a sense of present torment but also to a demanding set of practices designed to ameliorate our condition by placating our tormentors. Appeasing higher powers is our only hope for avoiding misery.

Demea's piety lies here exposed in all its frightening implications. He is a fearful bully. His soul is tormented and cowering, terrorized by "unknown powers" causing uncontrollable distress on every hand. Man's lot on earth is fundamentally oppressive, miserable, and wretched, and the dark heart of religion seeks not so much solace for the sadly inevitable as escape into some better future life via abject prostration before the alien powers that now oppress us. This other-dependency is not passive, patiently waiting upon what will be. It takes the active form of seeking to "appease" the higher powers by "prayers, adoration, and sacrifice." These higher powers are inscrutable agents who need to be obeyed and appeased without reservation, however impenetrable their designs and arbitrary their commands. At the same time, appeasement is a stratagem, seeking to manipulate the higher powers to our advantage by giving them what they want. Demea has no doubt that he knows what divinity wants, hence what humans must do to appease their masters. Above all else, one must practice submission in all things in order to cultivate the subservient character especially pleasing to the higher powers. Quite naturally, then, Demea has no qualms about imposing his views on others; to those who are less powerful than he, such as the youthful Pamphilus, Demea must appear as one among the higher powers to be appeased. Here human religion mirrors divine despotism. Demea is fearful of arbitrary higher powers, and he is equally arbitrary in using his own power over others.

Philo's response at first hearing sounds like an echo. He is persuaded, he says, that "the best and indeed the only method of bringing every one to a due sense of religion is by just representations of the misery and wickedness of men." We require not argument but "eloquence and strong imagery"—not in order to prove what we feel but rather to make us feel it "if possible, more intimately and sensibly" (10.2.Philo to Demea and Cleanthes). But Philo's words are strongly ambiguous. He could be endorsing Demea's fearful view of the human condition. But what does he mean by "*just* representations"? Does Philo agree that the picture of human misery drawn by Demea is a "just" one? Why has Demea focused on "misery" but ignored "wickedness"? And what is "a *due* sense of religion"? Is it the same as Demea's piety, or has Demea exceeded what is due? We cannot be sure of Philo's meaning from the surface of his words. We will have to wait and see how he develops his thoughts, how he both reinforces and undermines Demea's views in the next 17 paragraphs (10.3–19).

¶¶3–15: Demea and Philo wallow in misery

Demea sets out to generalize from his own experience. "The people,"[3] he claims, "from their own immediate feeling and experience" are "sufficiently convinced" of "the miseries of life, the unhappiness of man, the general corruptions of our nature, the unsatisfactory enjoyments of pleasures, riches, honours" (10.3.Demea to Philo). Here Demea expands on the "imbecility and misery" of his opening statement, notably adding "the general corruptions of our nature."[4] His major claim is that "the people" share his own sense of misery and do not have to be argued into believing that human life is indeed an unhappy lot.

Demea's claim here differs significantly from Cleanthes' earlier similar contention that "the similarity of the works of nature to those of art" is "self-evident and undeniable" (3.1.Cleanthes to Philo). Cleanthes' "undeniable" claim serves as a premise for an "experimental" argument; the appeal to immediate experience aims to establish a fact about the world from which we can infer an Author. Demea works quite differently. His starting point is not an alleged fact about the world but one about ourselves: It is not so much that we *are* all miserable as that we all *feel* miserable. Further, Demea doesn't infer but presumes that there is some Author or authors of this misery. Demea's true concern is to move us to *do* something about our perceived misery—to appease those higher power(s) responsible for our miseries—and he wants to heighten our sense of misery in order to increase our motivation to appease. He thinks that what to do about our predicament will be obvious once we accept his diagnosis, but in doing so he begs the very point at issue in Cleanthes' design argument; namely, the nature and existence of an Author of Nature.

Philo chimes in that "the learned are perfectly agreed with the vulgar." The poets in particular speak with "the most pathetic[5] eloquence" on "the topic of human misery." Their agreement on this score is all the more authoritative because it has been reached from sentiment and not system and is therefore conformable to "the feeling and observation of each individual" (10.4.Philo to Demea). Not surprisingly, Demea construes Philo's claim as an appeal to authority,[6] so he hastens to pile on more immediate authorities: He points to the books surrounding them in Cleanthes' library. Outside of scientific tomes, Demea holds, all these works contain complaints of human misery: "No one author has ever, so far as I can recollect, been so extravagant as to deny it" (10.5.Demea to Philo).

But, Philo politely interjects, one person has indeed denied it: "Leibnitz" was the only, or at least the first, person to have "ventured upon so bold and paradoxical an opinion" (10.6.Philo to Demea).[7] Demea then is allowed to draw the obvious point[8] that Leibniz's exceptionalism is cause not for withdrawing the generalization about human misery but for taxing Leibniz: "And can any man hope by a simple denial (for the subject scarcely admits of reasoning) to bear down the united testimony of mankind, founded on sense and consciousness?" (10.7.Demea to Philo).

The whole conversation to this point in Part 10 has a paradoxical air. Why is so much time and effort being spent to insist upon what is supposed to be a truth so obvious to everyone that it "scarcely admits of reasoning"?[9] One reason, of course, is that Cleanthes is waiting in the wings to deny precisely this truth or to downplay its significance, and Demea and Philo are seeking to preempt him. But Demea and Philo are not really arguing a point. Rather, like the poets, they seek through rhetorical eloquence to heighten a pre-existent sense of misery, or perhaps to awaken this sense where it lies dormant, but not to provide rational support for its existence. Further, their dialogue on this topic accomplishes one of the ends of dialogue-writing, which is "peculiarly adapted" to obvious and important points of doctrine, "where the variety of lights, presented by various personages and characters, may appear neither tedious nor redundant" (PH.2–3).

Demea next delivers another extraordinary speech that reveals even more of his true piety: "The whole earth, believe me, PHILO, is cursed and polluted." Here Demea for once does not appeal to authority or abstract argument; he delivers a deeply personal credo, a confession of his own heartfelt faith. Demea's proclamation, however, is not gospel but bad news: Life is a constant warfare among the living, tormenting both strong and weak every moment of their lives, a sad litany of lack and lament, ending at last in "agony and horror" (10.8.Demea to Philo).

This confession adds two points to Demea's earlier self-revelation of his fearful piety. (7) Other human lives are not comforts and joys but competitors and threats; we are oppressed not just by the unaccountable acts of higher powers but also by the entirely understandable acts of our fellow creatures. We are locked in a perpetual power struggle with other humans, whom we can trust only to torment and distress us. Human sociability is at best a temporary stopgap against inevitable competition, at worse only another insidious form of struggle. (8) Life on earth is unclean ("cursed and polluted") and requires proper ritual purification; the basis for a religious sacrificial system is here laid down. Moreover, it is an easy implication that these sacrifices require specialists and experts, an entire priestly caste. Demea's piety finds its natural expression in an authoritarian, hierarchical, sacrificial religious system that will at once propitiate the gods, cleanse human pollution (so far as possible in this life), and dominate the people. This entire form of life is integral to Demea's piety.

Philo responds to Demea's credo with an argument that mirrors the first stages of Cleanthes' design argument, though with more worrisome implications. "Observe too," says Philo, "the curious artifices of nature in order to imbitter the life of every living being." Stronger prey on weaker, but weaker also "vex and molest the stronger" (consider the insects, he reminds Demea). So "every animal is surrounded with enemies, which incessantly seek his misery and destruction" (all 10.9.Philo to Demea). If there is an observable artifice in nature, suggests Philo, its aim is something more sinister than the benefit of living creatures; its purpose seems to be to "imbitter" life, not to enable and enrich it. Though Philo draws no conclusions from this premise, it is obvious that he wants Cleanthes to notice that an "experimental" argument of the form Cleanthes touts based on the evidence Demea feels leads inexorably to a natural theological conclusion quite contrary to what Cleanthes seeks: not a benevolent and beneficent deity but a malicious tyrant or indifferent beast.

Demea tries to soften the blow: Humans alone escape the war of species against species; by joining with others in society, humans "can easily master lions, tigers, and bears" (10.10.Demea to Philo). So there is room still to worship a benevolent deity. But Philo will not quit. Even if humans in society can overcome the real external enemies Demea mentions, there remain "*imaginary* enemies, the demons of his fancy, who haunt him with superstitious terrors, and blast every enjoyment of life" (10.11.Philo to Demea). It is easy to apply this picture of superstition to Demea's view of human life as "cursed and polluted." Rather than a true picture of our condition, Philo implies, Demea's view is a fantasy of fear projected onto the world. In fact, Demea requires superstition to shore up his fearful piety; without imagined enemies and terrors, this life might not seem to require the costly escape mechanisms Demea has in mind.

But there is more. Although society may well help us to "surmount those wild beasts, our natural enemies," Philo says, at the same time it introduces new enemies: "Man is the greatest enemy of man. Oppression, injustice, contempt, contumely,[10] violence, sedition, war, calumny,[11] treachery, fraud; by these they mutually torment each other." Only the fear of worse keeps people in society (12.12.Philo to Demea). How deeply does Philo believe all this? Certainly he is sensitive to social evils, but he expresses a more rounded view of social life in Part 12. For now he is baiting Demea to further reveal himself.

Demea has an amazing talent for selective listening. He ignores Philo's comments about superstition and fastens on the threats from animals and other people. These "external insults," Demea claims, are "nothing in comparison" to the internal woes of "the distempered condition of our mind and body," and he cites nine lines from Book XI of Milton's *Paradise Lost* cataloguing some of the maladies (all 10.13.Demea to Philo). Beyond this, the "disorders of the mind" are equally "dismal and vexatious": "remorse, shame, anguish, rage, disappointment, anxiety, fear, dejection, despair." The human lot, whether poor or rich, is utterly deplorable: "All the goods of life united would not make a very happy man: But all the ills united would make a wretch indeed" (all 10.14.Demea to Philo). In support of this view, he would show a visitor to our planet the ills of a hospital, a prison, a battlefield, a foundering fleet, "a nation languishing under tyranny, famine, or pestilence," and he could scarcely pretend that the "gay side of life"[12] is anything more than further "distress and sorrow" (all 10.15.Demea to Philo). The acuteness of this as a self-description is lost upon Demea; he imagines it to be the human condition.

¶¶16–19: Philo's imaginary dialogue

Philo next engages in a kind of dialogue new to the *Dialogues*—a conversation between himself and an imagined "antagonist" or "adversary," who, by providing four weak objections easily answered by Philo, further strengthens the case for human misery. (1) People complain about misery because of "their discontented, repining, anxious disposition." —But "such a wretched temper" is a "certain foundation of misery." (2) If people are so miserable, why don't they commit suicide? —But they are even more afraid of death; "We are terrified, not bribed to the continuance of our existence." (3) Only "a few refined spirits indulge" in excessive misery. —But they are the most sensitive ones, and they are most unhappy because they are more alive than the rest of us. (4) "Let men remain at rest," and then they will be content. —No![13] There is an "anxious languor" to rest, just as there is a "vexation" to activity (10.16–19.Philo to Demea). Here is one more instance of the "variety of lights, presented by various personages and characters" (PH.3), this time an internal dialogue with an imaginary interlocutor. All lights shine on one common subject. There is no escape from seeing the human condition as miserable and wretched.

¶20: Cleanthes demurs

Yet Cleanthes disagrees. In an extraordinarily subdued and compact pair of sentences, he first allows that "some others" might sense misery "something like" what Philo and Demea have presented, but then confesses that "I feel little or nothing of it in myself; and hope that it is not so common as you represent it" (10.20.Cleanthes to Philo and Demea). After all the varied and vivid depictions of misery by Demea and Philo, Cleanthes offers only a weak admission about others' sensibilities and an ambiguous avowal[14] about himself. Clearly his three weak lines will have little force against the nineteen thundering paragraphs of Demea and Philo. Yet Cleanthes is expressing his own piety, in his own quiet way, just as Demea has more expansively revealed *his* piety. Cleanthes' piety is not premised upon misery, and he can only hope that misery is not so widespread as Demea and Philo have portrayed it and that others will feel as he does, neither personally miserable nor overwhelmed by the misery of others. Whether Cleanthes' piety is complete Panglossism or something more balanced, we will shortly learn (in 10.30–31); even so, we will have to wait for Part 12 to gain a fuller picture of what Cleanthes considers "true religion."

¶¶21–23: Demea's rebuttal

Demea is startled, astonished, and a bit outraged by Cleanthes' confession. He cries out, with scarcely veiled sarcasm, to "congratulate" Cleanthes for "so happy a singularity" in not feeling human misery. Demea, without asking for clarification, seems to think that Cleanthes is not merely denying misery in himself but also not feeling it in others. Demea is indignant, and he cannot credit what he is hearing. He thinks Cleanthes must be disingenuous or naive in denying the sense of misery that is so fundamental to Demea's religiosity, and he wants to discredit the infidel as quickly as he can. Instinctively, therefore, he turns to authorities—the exemplary cases of others, "seemingly the most prosperous," who "have not been ashamed to vent their complaints in the most melancholy strains" (10.21–22.Demea to Cleanthes).[15] The unsubtle point is that Cleanthes must be just as miserable as his betters but is ashamed to admit the truth.

Demea then asks Cleanthes whether he or any of his acquaintances would relive the last ten or twenty years of their life. "No!" they will say, thinks Demea, even while they will hope for better in the future, inconsistently complaining "of the shortness of life, and of its vanity and sorrow." Demea concludes that "such is the greatness of human misery; it reconciles even contradictions" (10.23.Demea to Cleanthes).[16] Clearly the greatness of human misery is Demea's great theme; upon it he rests his piety, his theology, his very life. His arguments for his presumed "orthodoxy" are plainly secondary, a prop for what Demea passionately feels within his breast.

¶¶24–27: Philo's rebuttal

Philo takes a different tack with Cleanthes, questioning not his character but rather his argument that seeks to infer divine attributes from human evidence and hence ends up anthropomorphizing the deity. Even though he has a stronger sensitivity to human misery than Cleanthes, Philo basically enjoys life and is not personally threatened by Cleanthes' dismissal of human misery. He therefore doesn't have as much at stake as Demea, whose piety is based on a sense of misery and a desire to flee this unhappy life. So Philo patiently points out the difficulties misery creates for Cleanthes' natural theology without inserting his own piety or theology.

First off, Philo assails anthropomorphism directly. Given the vast evidence of human misery, how can one "assert the moral attributes of the Deity, his justice, benevolence, mercy, and rectitude, to be of the same nature with these virtues in human creatures?" Even if one allows that the deity's "natural" attributes of power and wisdom are infinite, what follows from the enormous mass of human misery? Only that the deity does not will "human or animal felicity." Nothing can be "more certain and infallible" than this inference, Philo maintains (10.24.Philo to Cleanthes).

Next, Philo raises "EPICURUS's old questions" and claims they are as yet unanswered: "Is he [i.e., God] willing to prevent evil, but not able? then is he impotent. Is he able, but not willing? then is he malevolent. Is he both able and willing? whence then is evil?" (10.25.Philo to Cleanthes). Philo deliberately does *not* turn Epicurus's old question into an indicative argument. No doubt an argument for atheism could be extracted from these queries,[17] but that is not Philo's intention. Philo does not seek to disprove God; he only wants to undermine Cleanthes' efforts to prove God, particularly a God with moral attributes resembling human morality.

Philo then concedes to Cleanthes a point he had earlier disputed: "You ascribe, CLEANTHES, (*and I believe justly*) a purpose and intention to nature" (10.26.Philo to Cleanthes; emphasis added). This is no small matter. Philo the skeptic is admitting that teleological thinking about nature is legitimate. The purpose of this concession, of course, is to allow Philo to depict natural teleology in a way contrary to Cleanthes: Nature's purpose need not be friendly to humans, as Cleanthes believes. But why does Philo add "and I believe justly" to Cleanthes' ascription of purpose and intention to nature? Is Philo merely being ironic, attempting to con Cleanthes, as he has deceived Demea, into believing he is on their side, "all the while erecting a concealed battery against" them (10.28.Cleanthes to Philo)? Or is he sincere, actually confessing his own genuine belief in natural teleology? Those who take Philo to be the all-destroying scourge of natural theology read his remarks here as ironic, but there is no reason to do so aside from a pre-determined view identifying Philo with Hume and importing guesses as to what Hume himself would believe on the matter. Part 12 will give us a clearer sense of Philo's religion; for now we do well to keep this question open.

If nature does have a purpose and intention, what is "the object of that curious artifice and machinery, which she has displayed in all animals?" Not the happiness of creatures, Philo urges, only "the preservation alone of individuals and propagation of the species." Philo gives two (incompatible) reasons: First, there is no special natural provision or "machinery" for creatures' "pleasure or ease." Second, even if nature does permit an "indulgence" or two, they are "over-balanced by opposite phenomena of still greater importance" (10.26.Philo to Cleanthes).

Philo's "spirit of opposition" (10.28.Cleanthes to Philo) has gotten the better of him, for the first point is not the one he truly means to make; it is too sweepingly absolute. Nevertheless, it is a fine rhetorical salvo and serves to prejudice the listener for the second point, which is the one Philo really wants to inculcate. Our sense of beauty is an "indulgence" of nature, yielding us pleasure "without being absolutely necessary to the preservation and propagation of the species"; yet this indulgence is dwarfed by the "racking pains" due to "small or incurable" "injury to the animal-machinery." Further, the "gratuitous satisfactions" of "mirth, laughter, play, frolic" are counterbalanced by the pains of "spleen, melancholy, discontent, superstition" (10.27.Philo to Cleanthes).[18] Given this "strange mixture of phenomena," anthropomorphites such as Cleanthes cannot infer divine benevolence. Either the evidence supports divine hostility (if misery overwhelms happiness) or it supports divine indifference (if the phenomena are balanced). Only "we mystics," Philo teases, can "account" for such mixed phenomena by "deriving it from attributes, infinitely perfect, but incomprehensible" (10.27.Philo to Cleanthes).[19]

Philo has given Cleanthes all the rope he needs to hang himself. Philo worked hard in earlier Parts to impugn natural teleology, particularly to deny that the order perceptible in the natural world even remotely resembles human artifice. Now he concedes that nature *is* like artifice, thereby granting the major premise of Cleanthes' argument. But what follows? Cleanthes had wanted to infer the divine "natural" attributes of power and intelligence, and perhaps Philo will concede that this inference is "just." But what about the divine "moral" attributes? How could they possibly be inferred from either the miserable world described by Demea or the mixed world portrayed by Philo? A designer with misery in mind must be malevolent, and one intending mixed phenomena must be indifferent to human happiness. Cleanthes' own form of "experimental" reasoning, given the evidence of this vale of tears, cannot point to a benevolent deity.

¶¶28–31: Cleanthes strikes back

Cleanthes replies, smiling:[20] "Have you at last . . . betrayed your intentions, PHILO?" Cleanthes had been somewhat surprised by Philo's "long agreement" with Demea, but now he sees that "you were all the while erecting a concealed battery against me" (10.28.Cleanthes to Philo). From Cleanthes' surprise we learn several things. First, Cleanthes thinks Philo's own personal —as opposed to his debating—position is not anywhere near Demea's. Since

Cleanthes is Philo's intimate, presumably he knows his friend's true views about such matters, and if he thinks agreeing with Demea is foreign to his friend, this is good evidence that Philo's true views lie elsewhere. But how much of Philo's agreement with Demea is suspect? We are not told, but we may surmise it includes the monopoly that misery has on Demea's thinking and perhaps even Demea's "mysticism" that traffics in inconsistent "accounts" of inexplicable matters.

Second, Cleanthes is not terribly interested in confuting Demea, but he is vitally concerned with responding to his good friend Philo's "concealed battery" argument. In fact, Cleanthes says, here at last is "a subject worthy of your noble spirit of opposition and controversy." Note that Cleanthes still admires Philo, still finds his spirit "noble," even as Philo cuts at the very roots of Cleanthes' piety. It is impossible to imagine Demea responding to inquiry threatening his piety with anything like this spirit of admiration. Demea would retaliate, not reply—the response of an insecure bully. Cleanthes is untroubled by his friend's questioning, and this implies that not only his piety but also their relationship of "unreserved intimacy" (12.2.Philo to Cleanthes) goes beyond, and beneath, theological disputation.

Third, Cleanthes clearly perceives the depth of Philo's latest thrust, for if it is not deflected it is fatal to his empirical theology. If Philo "can make out the present point, and prove mankind to be unhappy or corrupted, there is an end at once of all religion."[21] Religion is pointless without a moral deity, thinks Cleanthes, and divine moral attributes can only be established in the same way as divine natural attributes, from experienced phenomena via human analogy. But if the experienced phenomena show the human condition to be on balance miserable or mixed, then one can only infer a bad or amoral deity, and "to what purpose establish the natural attributes of the Deity, while the moral are still doubtful and uncertain" (all 10.28.Cleanthes to Philo)?

There is considerable ambiguity in Cleanthes' challenge to Philo, in at least two respects. First, does he require Philo to show that mankind is completely "unhappy or corrupted" in every respect or only that there is unhappiness or corruption on the whole or perhaps on average? The former, stronger claim is pursued by Demea but effectively abandoned by Philo in 10.26 in favor of the latter claim, which is somewhat easier to prove and yet equally threatening to Cleanthes' natural theology. Moreover, Cleanthes needs not universal happiness but only overall happiness for his argument. So why doesn't he simply worry only about the overall mixture or balance of pleasure and pain? Second, why does Cleanthes say "unhappy *or corrupted*"? The whole focus of Philo's paragraphs on "this strange mixture of phenomena" has been on human happiness and unhappiness, not on purity or corruption—it is a litany of pains and dissatisfactions, with only "superstition" marginally related to corruption. Besides, how could corruption threaten Cleanthes' theology,[22] since divine "purpose and intention" does not follow in any obvious way from human aims and ends?

Demea is also puzzled by Cleanthes' point, but in a different way. He finds it odd that Cleanthes should "take umbrage" at "opinions the most innocent, and the most generally received even amongst the religious and devout themselves." Moreover, he thinks that "all pious divines and preachers" have given a convenient solution to the problem of pain by enlarging our consciousness: "This world is but a point in comparison of the universe: This life but a moment in comparison of eternity. The present evil phenomena, therefore, are rectified in other regions, and in some future existence." On this "larger" view, Demea supposes with typically pious language, humans will "trace, with adoration, the benevolence and rectitude of the Deity, through all the mazes and intricacies of his providence" (all 10.29.Demea to Cleanthes). In short, orthodox piety either sees no problem because it is grounded on an experience of human misery, or it removes the problem by taking a "larger view" of things. So pains are no obstacle to piety; they are rather an opportunity for inculcating orthodoxy.

But Cleanthes will have nothing of Demea's pious theodicy. For once, he is vehement: "No! . . . No!," he responds. What is it that so disturbs him? Not so much Demea's "larger view" as the method he has used to arrive at that view. Demea has put forth "arbitrary suppositions" that are "contrary to matter of fact, visible and uncontroverted." He has conveniently supposed what cannot be proven from human experience, and Cleanthes is committed above all to the experimental method in natural theology. All that Demea can establish with his "conjectures and fictions" is "the bare possibility" of his views, not their truth or likelihood (all 10.30.Cleanthes to Demea).

Fair enough. But having restricted natural theological method to analogical inference from observable effects, Cleanthes realizes that to infer divine benevolence and providence, he must begin with premises about recognizably benevolent and providential phenomena. So he must "deny absolutely the misery and wickedness of man." Once again there is the ambiguity previously noted: Is there *no* misery and wickedness, or is it just outweighed by happiness and virtue? It must be the latter, as Cleanthes goes on to complain to Philo that "your representations are exaggerated. . . . Health is more common than sickness: Pleasure than pain: Happiness than misery." Indeed, according to Cleanthes, happiness outweighs misery *greatly*: "And for one vexation, which we meet with, we attain, upon computation, a hundred enjoyments" (all 10.31.Cleanthes to Philo and Demea). Cleanthes thinks that the moral attributes we can ascribe to the deity are directly proportional to the excess of human happiness over misery. If human happiness barely outweighed misery, that would imply only a niggardly benevolent deity; the happier the human, the better the deity.

There is also the second ambiguity encountered earlier: Cleanthes mentions "wickedness" as well as "misery," yet he instances only the latter, and Philo's forthcoming response does not even mention wickedness. Human wickedness is not really an issue for empirical natural theologians, for several reasons. First, it is harder to ascertain wickedness than misery. Wickedness is rooted in inner motivation and intention, and these are difficult to detect, not least in oneself, while the evidences of misery are plain to hand everywhere we look. Second, it is not clear how to weigh inner virtue and vice except in terms of the weal and woe produced. But then why not just measure happiness and misery directly? Third, no speaker in the *Dialogues*—not even Demea, that lover of misery—espouses a thoroughgoing doctrine of original sin as utter depravity. Such would be a non-empirical doctrine, constitutionally as well as methodologically unacceptable to Cleanthes.

So Cleanthes has put his empirical theology to perilous trial: If human happiness does not greatly outweigh human misery, then there is no way to infer divine moral attributes. Since he believes there is a deity with moral as well as natural attributes resembling (though greatly exceeding) human ones, he is committed to the position that human happiness must greatly outweigh human misery. If Philo or Demea can prove otherwise, Cleanthes' sunny theism is in deep trouble.

¶¶32–35: Philo answers Cleanthes

Philo rises to Cleanthes' challenge, scoring a series of points that culminate in a proclaimed "triumph" for the skeptic (10.36). His first point plays upon the meaning of "common" as both "frequent" and "vulgar, undistinguished, low and coarse." Even if Cleanthes were correct that "health is more common than sickness: Pleasure than pain: Happiness than misery," Philo believes that pain is "infinitely more violent and durable" than pleasure, to the degree that "one hour of it is often able to outweigh a day, a week, a month of our common insipid enjoyments." Pain is more impressive, significant, and weighty than pleasure. Pleasure rarely reaches "ecstasy and rapture" and cannot be sustained at that level. "But pain, Good God, how often!23 rises to torture and agony; and the longer it continues, it becomes still more genuine agony and torture." Often pain overwhelms our efforts at patience and courage, and "nothing terminates our misery but the removal of its cause, or another event, which is the sole cure of all evil, but which, from our natural folly, we regard with still greater horror and consternation" (all 10.32.Philo to Cleanthes). What counts is not just the relative frequency or number of pleasures and pains but also their relative importance and impact on our lives as a whole. Even if there are "a hundred enjoyments" to "one vexation," still that one may outweigh the hundred because of its intensity. Sometimes a pain so colors a life that only its cessation can make a life even of many enjoyments seem worth continuing. Not only quantity but also quality, intensity, and duration matter.

Philo next proceeds to "admonish" Cleanthes in a rather ironic fashion. By claiming that theology can only be empirical and that religion rests on a foundation of human happiness, Cleanthes has "unawares"[24] introduced "a total scepticism into the most essential articles of natural and revealed theology." For it is "contrary to every one's feeling and experience" to believe that our life "with all our present pains, infirmities, vexations, and follies" is "eligible and desirable." Moreover, it isn't possible "to compute, estimate, and compare all the pains and all the pleasures in the lives of all men and of all animals." Thus, at the very minimum, estimating happiness is a vastly uncertain affair (10.33.Philo to Cleanthes). Since Cleanthes' whole theology crucially rests on ascertaining overall happiness, it must likewise be incurably uncertain. So even if the evidence does not entail an uncaring or indifferent deity, it is so mixed and indeterminate that we cannot be sure what it does entail. Skepticism is the inevitable outcome of Cleanthes' experimental theology.

Further, even if "animal, or at least, human happiness in this life exceeds its misery" by any finite amount or multiple, and even if we could ascertain this amount or multiple, we would still be unable to infer divine infinity. Given an infinitely powerful, wise, and good God, we would not expect to encounter *any* misery at all (or at least not much relative to abundant good); so, given any considerable amount of misery, we cannot infer an infinite God. Here Philo puts forth an argument reminiscent of Epicurus's "old questions" (10.25.Philo to Cleanthes) but with two differences: This time Philo gives answers as well as questions, and his implied conclusion leans not toward atheism but toward agnosticism:

> Why is there any misery at all in the world? Not by chance surely. From some cause then. Is it from the intention of the Deity? But he is perfectly benevolent. Is it contrary to his intention? But he is almighty. Nothing can shake the solidity of this reasoning, so short, so clear, so decisive; except we assert, that these subjects exceed all human capacity. (all 10.34.Philo to Cleanthes)

In short, once theology is committed to an empirical approach, only a "total scepticism" (10.33.Philo to Cleanthes) is consistent with the mixed evidence.

Finally, even if "pain or misery in man is *compatible* with infinite power and goodness in the Deity," the former does not *entail* the latter. "You must *prove* these pure, unmixed, and uncontrollable attributes from the present mixed and confused phenomena, and from these alone. A hopeful undertaking!" (10.35.Philo to Cleanthes). So even if human misery is consistent with an infinitely powerful and good God, the mixed phenomena of this world cannot imply that there is such a Being.[25] Cleanthes' empirical theology, therefore, is doomed.

¶36: Philo's qualified triumph

And so Philo, for the third and final time,[26] proudly proclaims his triumph, although with significant qualifications. He triumphs only on the moral attributes of the deity. "Formerly, when we argued concerning the natural attributes of intelligence and design," Philo declares to Cleanthes, his triumph was illusory, or at least incomplete. Earlier Philo had to use all his "sceptical and metaphysical subtlety" to elude Cleanthes' grasp. Moreover, Philo says,

> In many views of the universe, and of its parts, particularly the latter, the beauty and fitness of final causes strike us with such irresistible force, that all objections appear (what I believe[27] they really are) mere cavils and sophisms; nor can we then imagine how it was ever possible for us to repose any weight on them.

But whereas natural teleology is irresistible and overcomes objections to inferring the divine natural attributes, this is not the case for the moral attributes of the deity. Absolutely "no view of human life or of the condition of mankind" implies the moral attributes, and we can "discover" such attributes, particularly in their infinite forms, only "by the eyes of faith alone" (all 10.36.Philo to Cleanthes).

What are we to make of this extraordinary paragraph? Is it a genuine confession of faith, or at least of natural theological belief? Or is it the teasing irony of a master debater? In particular, how committed is Philo to revealed theology and to natural teleology? On the former topic, it is unclear whether the appeal to "the eyes of faith" means anything more than Philo's frequent invocation of "mysticism" and the "great disproportion"—the view that "these subjects exceed all human capacity, and that our common measures of truth and falsehood are not applicable to them" (10.34.Philo to Cleanthes). Since Philo will have more to say about faith and revelation in Part 12 (especially 12.33), we shall not dwell on the topic here. But some comments on natural teleology are appropriate.

Throughout Parts 2–8, in doggedly pressing his criticisms of Cleanthes' design argument, Philo gave few hints of his own beliefs. Still, many assume that Philo's heart must lie upon his tongue, that he rejects any position he so effectively criticizes, and that he likewise rejects the attitude and approach toward the world that position represents. It is tempting to reason as follows: Philo thinks Cleanthes' design argument fails; therefore he doesn't believe that a powerful intelligent deity can be inferred from empirical evidences of design, and perhaps he does not believe that there *is* perceptible design or a Designer. On its face, however, Philo's speech in 10.36 overthrows these assumptions. Here he says he gives his own personal views, which he claims are also the shared views of all humans. Consider the first-person pronouns, singular and plural, in the sentence quoted above: "Strike *us* . . . *I* believe . . . can *we* . . . for *us*." It is hard to discern any irony in these words. Moreover, in Part 12, Philo will reiterate these views several times, again without perceptible irony.[28] So it is plausible to regard these words as straightforward expressions of Philo's genuine beliefs.

But why should Philo express his true beliefs here? In part because he is talking straight to his friend Cleanthes, not worrying about showing off for Demea (and Pamphilus), although he will have to wait until Demea leaves to fully speak his mind. But also because Philo wants to convey something very important to Cleanthes. Humans (Philo included) find the teleology in and of a beautiful natural world "irresistible"; the only question worth disputing in the end is how far this awareness enables natural theology to proceed. Philo does not really disagree in principle with Cleanthes about inference to the natural attributes of the deity; their difference is only over *degree* of *likeness*. But he does dispute any attempt to infer divine moral attributes, since "every one's feeling and experience" (10.33.Philo to Cleanthes) in this vale of tears discloses the lack of a *moral* teleology. We cannot ignore this great divide in human experience, nor can we overcome it by philosophical "cavils and sophisms." Our experience, as Philo sees it, implies some few divine natural attributes, but no acceptably friendly divine moral attributes.

So Part 10 ends with another powerful critique of Cleanthes' design argument: When applied to the question of the divine moral attributes, working from common human experience of misery in this world, this form of argument yields either a result contrary to piety (a malevolent or indifferent deity) or else no result at all (total skepticism). Philo now concedes "the natural attributes of intelligence and design" (10.36.Philo to Cleanthes), but there is no "view of human life" from which we can infer the moral attributes. Philo believes, in fact, that he has presented such a devastating case against moral design that it is now (at last!) Cleanthes' turn "to tug the labouring oar, and to support your philosophical subtleties against the dictates of plain reason and experience" (10.36.Philo to Cleanthes). The humor in this remark will emerge in Part 11, as Cleanthes rows for only one paragraph (to Philo's sixteen) and with precious little subtlety.

14

Part 11

But supposing the Author of Nature to be finitely perfect, though far exceeding mankind; a satisfactory account may then be given of natural and moral evil, and every untoward phenomenon be explained and adjusted.

—Cleanthes to Demea and Philo, Part 11.1

Thus PHILO continued to the last his spirit of opposition, and his censure of established opinions. But I could observe, that DEMEA did not at all relish the latter part of the discourse; and he took occasion soon after, on some pretense or other, to leave the company.

—Pamphilus to Hermippus, Part 11.21

Structure:

¶1: Cleanthes proposes a "finitely perfect" Author of Nature
¶¶2–17: Philo delivers what "occurs" to him
  ¶¶2–4: Conjectures are not inferences
  ¶¶5–12: The four "circumstances of evil," all apparently avoidable
    ¶5: Reflection on human limits and avoidability
    ¶6: First circumstance: The contingency of pain
    ¶¶7–8: Second circumstance: "general laws" versus "particular volitions"
    ¶¶9–10: Third circumstance: The lack of "powers and faculties"
    ¶11: Fourth circumstance: The inaccurate workmanship of nature
    ¶12: Conclusion: One can't infer a benevolent deity
  ¶¶13–15: Survey of possible hypotheses about the moral attributes of divinity, and Philo's preference
  ¶¶16–17: Moral evil

¶¶18–21: Demea realizes at last his true position in the company
    ¶18: Demea cries out betrayal
    ¶19: Cleanthes offers scant comfort
    ¶20: Philo continues "his censure of established opinions"
    ¶21: Demea departs and Pamphilus comments

There are really two parts to Part 11. The first part is a sequel to Part 10, considering a slightly altered hypothesis but with the same result. Invited to "tug the labouring oar" by Philo, Cleanthes expends minimal effort in suggesting a "new theory" to account for the world's misery: The "Author of Nature" is only "finitely perfect, though far exceeding mankind," so that the world's evils are due to circumstances beyond divine knowledge or control, not because benevolence is lacking (11.1.Cleanthes to Philo). He then turns over the rowing to Philo, who criticizes at length this new kind of anthropomorphic theology. Philo first proposes four "circumstances" on which natural evil depends and claims that they all appear avoidable, even by a finite deity: Hence, the mixed phenomena of the world, while consistent with the existence of a deity, certainly afford no valid inference to the moral nature of such a Being. He then suggests various alternative hypotheses about the moral qualities of "the first causes of the universe," and ventures that an indifferent first cause "seems by far the most probable" (11.15.Philo to Cleanthes and Demea).

The second part of Part 11 begins just as Philo is heating up his rhetoric against "anthropomorphism" in examining moral evil (11.16–17). Demea interrupts, flushed with emotion over what he is hearing (11.18). It is clear to Pamphilus "that DEMEA did not at all relish the latter part of the discourse," and "on some pretense or other," finally manages to "leave the company" at the very end of Part 11 (11.21.Pamphilus to Hermippus). A simple act, Demea's departure, but it is the single most important dramatic action in the entire *Dialogues,* so a reader must understand Demea's reasons for leaving. Even more important, however, is to understand the effect Demea's departure has on the dialogues. The conversations before and after Demea leaves have utterly different flavors, affecting both what is said, how it is said, and how it is meant. On this dramatic change (in both senses of "dramatic") rests not only an interpretation of Part 12 but a reading of the entire *Dialogues.*

¶1: Cleanthes proposes a "finitely perfect" deity

Philo concluded Part 10 with an appeal to Cleanthes: "It is your turn now to tug the labouring oar, and to support your philosophical subtleties against the dictates of plain reason and experience" (10.36.Philo to Cleanthes). Cleanthes does respond in Part 11, but with only a single tug, requiring little labor: He speaks but one cautious paragraph in suggesting a new hypothesis of a "finitely perfect" divinity to account for "the mixture of evil" we find in the universe. Cleanthes' caution seems well-advised, as his hypothesis soon encounters withering (though not necessarily fatal) criticism from Philo.

Cleanthes in fact invites Philo's lengthy comments ("without interruption") in order to learn if his "new theory" deserves any further attention.[1] Cleanthes is using Philo as a fast filter ("so prompt at starting views, and reflections, and analogies") for theological hypotheses to see if they should be taken seriously and developed into a systematic theology ("reduce it into form"). Cleanthes presents himself as not seriously committed to this new theory. We may, however, suspect Cleanthes' diffidence. Earlier (5.8–12), Philo had criticized empirical theology's inability to infer divine infinite attributes from finite experienced phenomena, and this criticism cuts as much against moral attributes as against natural ones. Cleanthes must either figure out a way to squeeze infinite attributes from finite evidence or develop some sort of finitistic theology. So his venture here into the "new theory" of a "finitely perfect" God (or god) is precisely what we should expect of an empirical theologian; this theory is dearer to Cleanthes' heart than his tentative manner suggests.

At any rate, Cleanthes has long suspected[2] that theologians' use of the word "infinite" is more "panegyric" than "philosophy" and that it would be better for both "reasoning" and "religion" to use "more accurate and more moderate expressions" lacking implications of infinity such as "*admirable, excellent, superlatively great, wise,* and *holy.*" Infinity, he thinks, "leads into absurdities" and "has no influence on the affections or sentiments." Moreover— and here he addresses Demea directly by name[3]—to invoke infinity is to "abandon all religion" by retaining "no conception of the great object of our adoration." Further, there is no way to reconcile a universe containing evil with "infinite attributes," much less to prove the latter from the former (all 11.1.Cleanthes to Demea and Philo).

Cleanthes' attack on infinity in religion is partly based on his own anthropomorphism and partly on the lessons he has learned from Philo in Part 10; but it also raises some new points that will prove crucial in Part 12. First, Cleanthes' experimental theology draws from experience not only conclusions and inferences but also meanings: Words have significance only as they are connected to experience. This is as true for theology as for science; one does not truly serve God by uttering meaningless words.[4] Second, Cleanthes adopts two arguments from Philo's critique in Part 10: "Any mixture of evil in the universe" is incompatible with an infinitely powerful, knowing, and good God;[5] and even if they were compatible, one could never "prove" an infinitely good deity from a mixture of good and bad phenomena (or, indeed, infer a Being infinite in any respect from merely finite evidence). Third, infinity "has no influence on the affections or sentiments." Cleanthes doesn't elaborate, but he implies that religious piety does and should involve affections or sentiments that energize actions and that a theology should enable and support such involvement. Theology should of course avoid "absurdities" and convince our minds of its truth, but it should also persuade our hearts of its importance—and infinity does neither (all 11.1.Cleanthes to Philo and Demea).

So Cleanthes has ample reason for seeking some alternative to a theology of the infinite. But the hypothesis he proposes is more than a little obscure: Let us suppose, he says, "the Author of Nature to be finitely perfect, though far exceeding mankind." What does it mean to be "finitely perfect"? How can perfection stop short of infinity? Further, does finite perfection affect all divine attributes or only some of them (and if so, which ones)? Cleanthes does not elaborate, but perhaps his position may be put in the following way: Let us say that a *finite theology* is any theology ascribing at least one finite perfection as a divine attribute. A *finite perfection* is any valuable or estimable quality raised to some finite level "far exceeding" its level in humanity. Any *finitely perfect being* has a compossible set of perfections, at least one of which is finite. An *Author of Nature* is an ultimate cause of the existence and/or character of the world. Cleanthes' "new theory," then, holds that there is one[6] Author of Nature inferable from the world we experience and it is a finitely perfect being, with at least the finite perfection of power. This is not a full finite theology, only a fragment of one, but it is all Cleanthes supplies.

But this suggestion raises a further problem. Cleanthes wants a deity somewhat limited in power, but perhaps not in intelligence, wisdom, or goodness, for "benevolence, regulated by wisdom, and limited by necessity, may produce just such a world as the present" (11.1.Cleanthes to Philo). It is unclear how his empirical method can restrict divine limitation to just one attribute,[7] but it is clear why Cleanthes would want this restriction: A being limited in intelligence and goodness is scarcely worshipful or even inspiring, though it may be feared on account of its power.[8] But a benevolent and wise being somewhat limited in power may still be revered even while excused for unfortunate results beyond its control.

One more puzzle: Why does Cleanthes "gladly" turn over examination of finite theology to Philo? Does he have nothing further to say on its behalf? Is he so uncommitted to this "new theory" that he silently drops it altogether following Philo's critique? On the contrary, I think that Cleanthes is deeply wedded to this view and that he believes Philo's criticisms do not count decisively against it. In fact, the view will reappear in Part 12 as something held in common by *both* Cleanthes and Philo![9] But for now, we follow Philo's critique.

¶¶2–4: Conjectures versus inferences

Philo sets out to "deliver what occurs to me, with regard to the present subject." The casual use of "occurs" suggests both that these objections are what comes to mind immediately, without careful reflection, and that they are not necessarily fully endorsed by Philo or even a part of his final view on the present subject.[10] Further, these quick criticisms may be questioned; the four "circumstances of evil" are fairly feeble objections to Cleanthes' finite theology.

Philo initially works not from the world to God but from God to the world. He asks what "a very limited intelligence" such as ours would conjecture in two contrasting cases. The first case is where the intelligence is "utterly unacquainted with the universe" yet "assured" that "a very good, wise, and powerful Being, however finite" has produced it. What the limited intelligence with a finite theology would conjecture about the world is, Philo claims, quite different from the "vice and misery and disorder" it would actually discover through experience. But surprise over the condition of the world would not entail giving up on God, for the intelligence would be "sensible of his own blindness and ignorance" and "must allow" that the reasons for divine production of this world "will forever escape his comprehension" (all 11.2.Philo to Cleanthes).

The second case, which is our actual case, is where the limited intelligence is not equipped with a prior belief in "a supreme intelligence, benevolent, and powerful" but must infer any theological beliefs from experience. Here, Philo maintains, the limited intelligence will never "find any reason for such a conclusion." Awareness of "the narrow limits of his understanding" will not help him to infer "the goodness of superior powers," since it would be an argument from ignorance, not from knowledge. The greater his ignorance, the more he will think "that such subjects are beyond the reach of his faculties" (all 11.2.Philo to Cleanthes). So given our limited intelligence and actual experience of the world, no inference to divine goodness will be plausible to us, and bemoaning our limitations encourages not religious belief but rather skepticism.

Philo next supplies an example of a "house or palace" inhospitable to its inhabitants:[11] "Where the windows, doors, fires, passages, stairs, and the whole economy of the building were the source of noise, confusion, fatigue, darkness, and the extremes of heat and cold; you would certainly blame the contrivance, without any farther examination." Moreover, you would also blame the architect: "If you find many inconveniences and deformities in the building, you will always, without entering into detail, condemn the architect" (all 11.3.Philo to Cleanthes). This is a dangerous topic. Philo is invading the home territory of the design argument. He is claiming first, that house is to architect as world is to Author of World and second, that the house is "inconvenient" to its inhabitants. From these premises follows blame for the architect. Adding the assumption that the world is likewise inconvenient to its inhabitants, we are drawn to the (unspoken) conclusion of blame for Author of the World. So far has finite theology led us that not only do we fail to infer the moral attributes of the deity, but we are led to assail the "skill and good intentions" of the world's presumed Author! If Cleanthes' empirical approach does lead to theism, it is to a God one can only blame and reject, not praise and worship.

In the next paragraph, Philo draws back from this heterodox implication. The world as we find it is not what we would expect "beforehand" to derive from "a very powerful, wise, and benevolent Deity" and hence, however consistent such a world may be with "the idea of such a Deity, it can never afford us an inference concerning his existence" (all 11.4.Philo to Cleanthes).[12] It is not so much that empirical theology leads to atheism, or to a deity one can only abhor, as that experience does not witness to a deity worthy of worship.

¶¶5–12: The four circumstances of evil

Next Philo explores what he calls the four "circumstances of evil." "Circumstance" is an underlying or background condition on which something else depends. All or most[13] evils, Philo claims, depend on just four general circumstances, and these circumstances, so far as we can tell, are "avoidable" —we can imagine a world in which they are significantly altered or absent. *So far as we can tell.* But our faculties are limited. What seems avoidable to us may in fact be necessary; still, we cannot assume or infer that there *is* such necessity forever hidden from us. Rather, recognizing our limitations, we should "be sceptical, or at least cautious," and not venture too far in our speculations (11.5.Philo to Cleanthes).

Philo will attempt to show, therefore, that the world's misery is, so far as we can tell, unnecessary and therefore avoidable—if not by us then by a sufficiently superior being.

The four circumstances and their means of avoidance are these:

1. Both pain and pleasure excite animals to action; why not "carry on the business of life without any pain"?

2. The world operates according to general law; why not operate by "particular volitions"?

3. All animals have a "great frugality" of "powers and faculties"; why not introduce a human propensity to industry instead of to idleness?

4. The "great machine of nature" seems inaccurately fitted and adjusted to the goal of human or animal happiness; why can't the "excess or defect" of natural means be moderated?

1. Both "pains, as well as pleasures, are employed to excite all creatures to action, and make them vigilant in the great work of self-preservation. Now pleasure alone, in its various degrees, seems to human understanding sufficient for this purpose." Pleasure seems as great a motivator as pain, or at least humans "might have been so constituted." In fact, why is there any pain at all? Animals can exist without pain for an hour, so why not for a lifetime?[14] Why couldn't animals exist without the present "contrivance of their organs" that produces the feeling of pain (all 11.6.Philo to Cleanthes)?

Now this is all quite dubious. To begin with, some pleasures either are the same as, or are unavoidably connected to, the cessation or diminution of pains, and some pains are similarly tied to pleasures. Second, it is not at all clear that pleasure could be as motivating as pain in all cases. Would a sudden great decrease in pleasure be as urgent an incentive to regain what pleases as a sudden sharp pain is to avoid what hurts? Could decreases of pleasures be as localized as pains so as to direct attention to the source of difficulty? Third, it is not clear whether the underlying "secret springs" of pleasure and pain are independent "contrivances of organs"; even if they are different mechanisms, perhaps they are jointly evolved or necessarily connected. So Philo's first circumstance of evil may not be avoidable.

2. The world is conducted by general laws, and this seems unnecessary "to a very perfect Being"[15] who could make everything occur "by particular volitions." Philo recognizes there would be costs to such an arrangement—for example, "no man could employ his reason in the conduct of life," because reason works via recognition of experienced regularities. But he thinks that the deity could "exterminate all ill" and "produce all good, without any preparation, or long progress of causes and effects" (all 11.7.Philo to Cleanthes).

Again, Philo has not thought through what "occurs" to him. He imagines a world where *everything* that happens is "conducted by particular volitions." Such a suggestion doesn't take seriously rational human autonomy or moral and intellectual virtue as goods producible only by the agent who acts. Moreover, what kind of character could be formed in a world where no predictions could be made except that whatever one did (or failed to do), only good would result? Philo is imagining a world in which there is only one agent; all other beings are mere passive recipients of benefits, and their "actions" would be the movements of puppets.

Perhaps recognizing such problems with his initial suggestion, Philo modifies it in the very next paragraph. Here the divine Being is not completely responsible by particular volitions for *every* event that occurs but only for influencing those many events that, within the mostly orderly "present economy of nature," have causes that are "unknown and variable" and so are considered "accidents." By knowing and influencing the "secret springs of the universe," such a superior Being could "turn all these accidents to the good of mankind, and render the whole world happy, without discovering himself in any operation." Such clandestine interventions would not "disturb the course of nature or confound human conduct" any more "than the present economy of things, where the causes are secret, and variable, and compounded." Perhaps there are good reasons for not intervening in this hidden way, but "they are unknown to us"; so while supposing such reasons may "*save* the conclusion concerning the divine attributes, yet surely it can never be sufficient to *establish* that conclusion" (all 11.8.Philo to Cleanthes).

Here Philo skates on the thin ice of ignorance. No doubt, "for aught we know," piecemeal improvements in the world could be made in this way; though for aught we know this is impossible (as it would be according to the necessitarian hypothesis Philo touted in 9.10). In this hazy realm of "imbecility" (10.1), it is no longer apparent that *any* circumstance of evil is contingent; the best conclusion we can form is that "for aught we know" is a poor guide to the "secret springs of the universe."

3. Given general laws and pain receptors in animals, "it scarcely seems possible but some ill must arise in the various shocks of matter." But a third circumstance makes such shocks more common than necessary: "the great frugality, with which all powers and faculties are distributed to every particular being." Indeed, each species has just enough capacity to preserve it from extinction.[16] Human beings are "of all others the most necessitous, and the most deficient in bodily advantages"; surely they at least could be provided with more talents than "their own skill and industry"? Nature is more like a "rigid master" than an "indulgent parent" in bestowing capacities that go no farther than the bare minimum needed for survival (11.9.Philo to Cleanthes).

Here Philo merges two complaints: First, there is no surplus of capacities for any purpose, including survival. But this complaint is canceled by Philo's admission that few if any species have gone extinct with the capacities they have; if the capacities are sufficient for survival, why ask for more? Second, these capacities don't "secure the happiness and welfare of the creature." Here Nature is too miserly and rigid *if* happiness of the individual is her purpose. At the very least, the Author of Nature could have made fewer (types of) animals and given them "more faculties for their happiness and preservation" (all 11.9.Philo to Cleanthes). Again, Philo's claims seem airily speculative: For one, he does not consider the costs of additional capacities, perhaps thinking there are none. "For aught we know," additional capacities for happiness might actually hinder survival. For another, he does not consider how a capacity might serve more than one function and how being barely adequate for one function might be a condition for excelling at another.

Philo next illustrates his general point with a human example. Why couldn't humans be endowed with "a greater propensity to industry and labor; a more vigorous spring and activity of mind; a more constant bent to business and application"? Doing so would "cure most of the ills of human life" because "almost all the moral, as well as natural evils of human life arise from idleness." Replacing idleness with industry is a "humble" request, thinks Philo, because "it is hard; I dare to repeat it, it is hard" to have to face "a world so full of wants and necessities" with an idle and lax "temper" (all 11.10.Philo to Cleanthes).

Once again, Philo's contentions are questionable. He seems to assume that "temper" is a product solely of nature, not also of human choice and nurture, and that it can be bestowed by a superior power quite independently of the agent whose temper it is. Moreover, he thinks that moral evil arises from "idleness," not from flawed volition or choice. But if an idle temperament is beyond our control, what becomes of human responsibility for moral evil—is it truly *wickedness*?

4. The last circumstance is "the inaccurate workmanship of all the springs and principles of the great machine of nature." Here Philo explicitly concedes the central contention of Cleanthes' earlier design argument: Nature is (very like) a "great machine" whose every part serves some purpose for the whole and where the "parts hang all together." Still, he claims, the parts are not "so accurately adjusted, as to keep precisely within those bounds, in which their utility consists; but they are, all of them, apt, on every occasion, to run into the one extreme or the other." It is as if "this grand production" has been made in outline and is unfinished in detail: Rains, heat, bodily humors, passions are all useful within limits, yet so often "they break their bounds" and become "pernicious" by "excess or defect." Such "irregularity" may never destroy a species, but it greatly inconveniences individuals (all 11.11.Philo to Cleanthes).

Here Philo's speculations, while they still float on a sea of ignorance, nudge against the shore of Cleanthes' presumed position. If we are to infer divine moral attributes, then there must be features of the experienced world that display divine concern; but how can we discern divine benevolence in our world? If human happiness is a divine concern and the "proper function" of the various parts of the great machine of nature, it follows from the lack of natural contrivance for human happiness that the deity is not much interested in our welfare. But the divine intent may be construed otherwise, in two directions. On the one hand, the deity may make and maintain the world-machine simply in order to promote *species* survival, with no concern for individual happiness; then the analogy of divine attributes to human moral attributes would be greatly diminished, if not removed. On the other hand, the deity may have moral ends other than happiness—for example, "soul making," in John Hick's sense[17]—and then the evidence of the world might be differently construed.

¶12: Conclusion from the four circumstances

Philo maintains that "all, or the greatest part" of natural evil[18] depends on the four circumstances, but he draws back from claiming that he knows they could all be altered. "This decision seems too presumptuous for creatures, so blind and ignorant." Instead, he concludes that "if the goodness of the Deity (I mean a goodness like the human)" could be proved *a priori,* these phenomena could be reconciled with it. But if one must infer divine goodness from the phenomena, "there can be no grounds for such an inference, while there are so many ills in the universe, and while these ills might so easily have been remedied, as far as human understanding can be allowed to judge on such a subject." In short, plentiful avoidable evils (avoidable "so far as we can tell") may well be compatible with divine moral attributes, but "surely they can never prove these attributes" (all 11.12.Philo to Cleanthes).

Philo is subtle. He does not seek to disprove Cleanthes' "finitely perfect" deity but rather (1) to show that Cleanthes cannot prove such a being from the world we experience (so far as we can tell, human or animal happiness is not a natural purpose, so the Author of Nature's moral attributes cannot be inferred); and (2) to widen the gap between any antecedently supposed or proved divine moral attributes and human moral qualities. It does not really matter, in the end, whether his "circumstances of evil" are avoidable (contingent) or unavoidable (necessary); the larger point is that while they may after all be consistent with the purposes of a good God, they do not imply such a being—nor, indeed, do they imply such purposes. Philo's real disagreement with Cleanthes, as we shall see in Part 12, is not over the existence or even the nature of the deity, but rather over the *degree of likeness* between human and divine attributes. The circumstances of evil, Philo thinks, show that if the deity has any recognizably moral concern for humans, it is very far removed from our own moral concerns. In short, Cleanthes' experimental anthropomorphism is no help to what Philo regards as true religion.

¶¶13–15: The divine moral attributes

In an appeal ironically reminiscent of Cleanthes' earlier design argument (cf. 2.5), Philo next[19] asks his listeners to "Look round this universe." What do we find? Certainly the "prodigious variety and fecundity" so admired by

Cleanthes. But look more closely at living beings: "How hostile and destructive to each other! How insufficient all of them for their own happiness! How contemptible or odious to the spectator!" This is the evidence from which, using Cleanthes' empirical methods, we are to infer the divine moral attributes. "The whole presents nothing but the idea of a blind nature, impregnated by a great vivifying principle; and pouring forth from her lap, without discernment or parental care, her maimed and abortive children" (all 11.13.Philo to Cleanthes). The language is overwrought, but Philo is trying to make an impression on his listeners, to call forth certain sentiments and attitudes toward the world.

One reaction to this evidence is Manichaean dualism, positing both good and evil principles; it seems "very specious"[20] in accounting for "the strange mixture of good and ill," but it implies a "combat" between good and evil that we do not (always) find in the world. We do discover sometimes "an opposition of principles," but this opposition assists, not interferes with, "all the operations of nature." "The true conclusion is, that the original source of all things is entirely indifferent to all these principles" (all 11.14.Philo to Cleanthes).

There are, Philo thinks, four possible hypotheses about the moral character of "the first causes[21] of the universe": (1) "they are endowed with perfect goodness,"[22] (2) "they have perfect malice," (3) they have "both goodness and malice," or (4) they have "neither goodness nor malice." The mixed phenomena of the world cannot lead to either (1) or (2), and the third hypothesis seems ruled out by "the uniformity and steadiness of general laws."[23] So the fourth "seems, by far the most probable" (all 11.15.Philo to Cleanthes). To some, divine indifference may seem a surprising conclusion from a teleological argument, but there is no antecedent reason to suppose that a superior being's purposes include care for creaturely welfare.

Are Philo's four hypotheses the *only* four that "may" be "framed"? Superficially they employ the logically exhaustive schema of a, not-a, both a and not-a, neither a nor not-a. But if pain, as Philo has argued in the first circumstance of evil, is not the logical negation of pleasure, and if divine purpose can include both promoting pleasure and removing pain, then divine good is not the simple negation of divine evil. So let us try again. Perhaps the four hypotheses follow this schema: a and not b, b and not a, both a and b, neither a nor b. But an important feature is missing: Goodness and malice come in *degrees*, with the divine case "perfect" as opposed to other, imperfect ones. As soon as we add this qualification we see there are other possibilities: Perfect a, perfect b, both perfect a and perfect b, neither perfect a nor perfect b, to be sure, but also perfect a or perfect b plus various degrees and kinds of imperfect b or imperfect a. Indeed, given "mixed" phenomena as evidence, one might equally plausibly infer various grades of imperfect goodness and malice in the Author of Nature as infer no goodness nor malice at all, for both are compatible with the negation of *perfect* goodness and malice. Philo's four hypotheses are the only possibilities only if we assume that goodness and malice, if present at all in the first causes of the universe, must be present as perfect goodness and perfect malice.

In addition, before assessing any of his four moral possibilities, Philo must make certain assumptions about the divine natural attributes of intelligence and power. Most important, he must assume that if there is evil in the world, the first cause(s) will notice it and be able to do something about it—the divine intelligence and power may be limited, but they cannot be greatly limited. Only on such a basis can Philo infer that the first causes are indifferent to creaturely good and evil.

¶¶16–17: Moral evil

Finally, Philo turns to moral evil in two short and puzzling paragraphs that precipitate Demea's departure. First, he claims that his remarks about natural evil also apply to moral evil, so that we have no more reason to think "that the rectitude of the supreme Being[24] resembles human rectitude than that his benevolence resembles the human." Further, there is even more reason to exclude from the Deity moral sentiments "such as we feel them," since moral evil outweighs moral good even more than natural evil outweighs natural good (all 11.16.Philo to Cleanthes).

The argument is very obscure, and Philo hedges his bets—he doesn't want to make this argument in his own voice and resorts to such distancing devices as "it will be thought" and "in the opinion of many." Is this because (1) the argument is not a very good one, (2) it is too good and therefore too dangerous in present company, or (3) it does not lead to Philo's own personal position? At the very least we should not credit Philo with a position until he claims it in his own voice, and then we should take note of his audience and intentions.

The argument is this: Although a supreme Being cannot be thought directly responsible for human moral evil, which is a human responsibility, still, such a Being is responsible for not preventing, mitigating, or eliminating such evil, if it can possibly do so. Any being with a moral sense resembling the human one would be appalled at moral evil and would seek to prevent, mitigate, or eliminate it so far as it could. But there is moral evil in great abundance in this world, greater (proportional to its matching good) even than the profusion of natural evils. So the supreme Being is at best indifferent, at worst malicious.

Philo then softens a premise: Even if vice doesn't outweigh virtue, a problem remains: "So long as there is any vice at all in the universe, it will very much puzzle you anthropomorphites, how to account for it." This is not the same problem as before, that of inferring divine attributes from mixed phenomena. Rather, it is a line of argument that borrows implicit premises from Demea's *a priori* argument in Part 9: Acts of moral evil require a cause just as any event does, and this cause [requires] another [cause]; so "you must either carry on the progression *in infinitum,* or rest on that original principle, who is the ultimate cause of all things" (all 11.17.Philo to Cleanthes). Here Demea heatedly breaks in, so we don't know exactly what Philo would have concluded. But it is clear that at least part of Demea's agitation is caused by Philo's apparent trajectory toward blaming the supreme Being for moral evil, in effect making the Deity no longer mysteriously good or even indifferent but rather vicious.

¶18: Demea cries out

"Hold! Hold!" cries out Demea, greatly agitated. Demea had thought Philo was his ally "in order to prove the incomprehensible nature of the divine being, and refute the principles of CLEANTHES, who would measure every thing by a human rule and standard." But now he finds Philo venturing into "all the topics of the greatest libertines and infidels, and betraying that holy cause, which you seemingly espoused." In fact, Demea plaintively asks, "Are you secretly, then, a more dangerous enemy than CLEANTHES himself?" (all 11.18.Demea to Philo). Demea's interjection marks a crucial moment in the *Dialogues,* and the last four paragraphs of Part 11 leading up to his departure constitute a climax to the conversations, the moment of highest dramatic urgency.[25]

Several aspects of Demea's cry deserve notice. First, Demea is very disturbed, in various ways. Obviously there is the public posture of indignant piety: Demea thinks of himself as the staunch upholder of orthodoxy, defending before Pamphilus the good name of religion against the dangerous libels of the free-thinking Philo. In addition, Demea feels betrayed. Since early in the conversations (cf. 1.2–3 and 2.1), Demea had considered Philo an ally against the enemy Cleanthes only to discover now that Philo is "a more dangerous enemy."[26] The betrayal is not only of "that holy cause" but also of himself. Also, on a personal level, there is embarrassment at being so slow in recognizing Philo's true allegiance.

Second, Demea had assumed all along that Philo's brand of "mysticism" was the same as his: After all, both severely delimit, even disparage, human knowledge and consider theological questions to lie beyond human comprehension. But this agreement is superficial. For Demea, "to prove the incomprehensible nature of the divine being" is to prepare the way for authoritarian religion, coupling dogmatic infinite theology to fearful and threatening piety. For Philo, to show that theology is beyond our grasp, if not quite our reach, is to equip us to dwell modestly and humanely in common life.

Third, what are the topics Philo is "running into" that Demea thinks are the territory of "the greatest libertines and infidels"? One, surely, is using evil not to bewail our condition and drive us to refuge in a superior power but rather to cast suspicion on the goodness of any such superior power. Holding that the divine is indifferent to our weal and woe is another, nearly as bad in Demea's eyes. Underlying both topics is Philo's evident willingness to adopt the methods of the "enemy" Cleanthes—drawing anthropomorphic inferences about the Deity from the evidences of human experience. But, most profound, it is Philo's reliance upon human thoughtfulness that is so threatening to Demea. Philo's willingness to "start," and to explore, all "views, and reflections, and analogies" (11.1.Cleanthes to Philo) is deeply subverting to Demea's foreclosed mind and rigid piety.

¶19: Cleanthes replies

Surprisingly, although Demea had been speaking directly to Philo, it is Cleanthes who replies. Cleanthes first twits Demea for being so "late" in noticing Philo's false friendship and then offers[27] Demea a new friendship, with himself, to replace what he has lost (or rather never possessed): "Your friend,[28] PHILO, from the beginning, has been amusing himself at both our expense." Cleanthes then diagnoses why Philo has been teasing them; the diagnosis is unflattering to Demea, although he probably doesn't notice. It is "the injudicious reasoning of our[29] vulgar theology," Cleanthes says, that has too easily allowed Philo opportunity for ridicule. Such theology dwells on "the total infirmity of human reason, the absolute incomprehensibility of the divine nature, the great and universal misery and still greater wickedness of men." These "principles"[30] are understandable in "ages of stupidity and ignorance" because they "promote superstition" and encourage "the blind amazement, the diffidence, and melancholy of mankind. But at present . . . " (all 11.19.Cleanthes to Demea).

Cleanthes is making important claims about superstition and true religion. The superstitious beliefs of "our vulgar theology" are connected to a groveling piety.[31] Perhaps such religion can be maintained during "ages of stupidity and ignorance" but not "at present," in an age where all beliefs, and particularly religious ones, need to withstand rational scrutiny and where the only appropriate religious piety is the very opposite of blind submission. "Superstition" is an important word for Cleanthes. It has for him the primary meaning of "an irrational religious belief or practice; a tenet, scruple, habit, etc. founded on fear or ignorance" (*OED,* sense 1b), with a secondary sense (now rare or obsolete) of "a false, pagan, or idolatrous religion" (*OED*, sense 2). Superstition is false religion because it is falsely *founded* religion: It is not so much that Demea's views are demonstrably false as that they are irrational, being founded not on evidence but rather on fearful feelings and slavish attitudes. What is opposed to "superstition" is not irreligion or no religion but rather true religion.

¶20: Philo continues his "censure of established opinions"

Cleanthes is unable to dilate on superstition and true religion, because he is interrupted by Philo. Philo wants to propound his pet theory as to why "these reverend gentlemen"[32] appear to be proponents of "ignorance": They are more cunning than ignorant because "they know how to change their style[33] with the times." Previously they did indeed maintain "that human life was vanity and misery" and did "exaggerate all the ills and pains, which are incident to men." But that was because it was "thought proper to encourage melancholy" when religion "stood entirely upon temper and education." But lately, as people have learned to think for themselves, "divines" are beginning to adopt another tack, "though still with some hesitation": Goods and pleasures outweigh evils and pains "even in this life." Further, in putting forth their views, they now make use of "such arguments as will endure, at least some scrutiny and examination" (all 11.20.Philo to Cleanthes). In short, religious rhetoric should not be taken at face value but should be examined for its underlying motives and ends.

It is tempting to view Philo as aiming exclusively at Demea. Certainly Demea views himself as a defender of orthodoxy, and he is eager to embrace any argument that he thinks will advance his cause and promote his power. Further, Demea wants to rely on "temper and education" to inculcate his religion, particularly in the young Pamphilus (cf. 1.1–2.Demea to Cleanthes and Philo). If Demea cannot cajole or coerce the present company, then he will give them arguments that he thinks will "endure . . . some scrutiny and examination."[34] But Cleanthes also seems sideswiped by Philo's charge that "divines" adapt their "style" to the times, for he is the one maintaining the fashionable experimental theology. Is Philo insinuating that Cleanthes has altered his religion, as well as his rhetoric, to fit the times? No doubt there is some kind of disagreement between Philo and Cleanthes on religion, but this is not it. The real issues will emerge only in Part 12.

¶21: Demea departs

The last words of Part 11 belong to young Pamphilus. Philo, he notes, "continued to the last his spirit of opposition, and his censure of established opinions" (11.21.Pamphilus to Hermippus). Does "the last" look back to the discussions with Demea present (to the end of Part 11), or does it also include all the discussions reported by Pamphilus (to the end of Part 12)? Philo can never shed his personal "spirit of opposition," so even in Part 12 he will continue to feel free to disagree with Cleanthes. Yet the spirit of their conversation changes markedly, from the sometimes contentious competition of Parts 1–11 to something more cooperative and friendly in Part 12. When Demea leaves, Philo is willing to acknowledge agreement and to search for common ground because he does not have to censure *Demea's* established opinions.

Pamphilus then adds, in his own voice: "I could observe that DEMEA did not at all relish the latter part of the discourse; and he took occasion soon after, on some pretense or other, to leave the company" (11.21.Pamphilus to Hermippus). This concluding sentence of Part 11 is key to understanding the central dramatic action of the entire *Dialogues*.

First, Demea finds some transparent "pretense" to leave at an unnatural juncture in the conversations. He has been offended, and he has lost all interest in remaining to listen, much less to contribute. He nurses a sense of betrayal by Philo. He has belatedly realized that he is the odd man out, and he is not placated by Cleanthes' offer of friendship. He is outnumbered in a fight over his religion cast among enemies, and his customary weapons are ineffective. So he leaves. This shows his deep contempt for the whole effort of Cleanthes and Philo to inquire rationally into natural religion and to induct young Pamphilus into civilized ways of living religiously. Demea cannot find reason to oppose reason's role in religion—or in inquiry into religion—so he irrationally rejects the whole inquiry. In the end, Demea is interested in conversation only as it reinforces his views; if a conversation turns against him, then he will give up talking and seek to enforce his views by other means, and if unable to do the latter, he will simply leave.[35]

Second, Demea leaves "the company." "Company" is a rich term, and many of its meanings intertwine, indicating both what Demea rejects and what he seeks. Company means "companionship, fellowship, society"; when one is "in company" one is "amidst other people, as opposed to *alone*" (*OED*, sense 1a). A company is "a number of individuals assembled or associated together" (sense 3), and while it may be only those "casually or temporarily brought into local association" (4a), it may also be those "with whom one voluntarily or habitually associates; companions or associates collectively, especially with reference to their character" (sense 4b), the sense in which company can be good or bad company—good or bad *for* one. A company can be "a gathering of people for social intercourse or entertainment; a social party; a circle" (sense 5) and so may have a festive air. Yet a company can also be "a body of persons combined or incorporated for some common object, or for the joint execution or performance of anything" (sense 6). Demea voluntarily rejects the companionship of Cleanthes and Philo because in their presence he is indeed alone. In doing so, he removes himself not simply from their sparkling conversation but also from their benign influences and their "joint execution or performance" of a certain way of life. In short, in leaving their company, Demea is rejecting their society, their religion, their way of life.

Third, it is easy to see why Demea leaves: He does not truly *belong* to the company, for his entire religion differs radically from that of Philo and Cleanthes. But why does he leave *now*? Pamphilus offers only the tantalizing hint that Demea "did not at all relish the latter part of the discourse." But how much of the discourse, and what specifically, did he not relish? There are (at least) six possibilities, ranging from less to more expansive.

1. Philo in 11.20 has criticized the changing "style" of "these reverend gentlemen," showing how they have adapted their arguments and appeals to the times. Does Demea suddenly feel exposed?[36]

2. Philo in 11.16–17 has implicated God in moral evil; on the moral evidence, and using an empirical method, it seems that the Divine is not so much indifferent as malicious. Demea's deity is supposedly neither (although his deity's harsh and arbitrary demands make this an arguable point).

3. In 11.13–15 Philo has argued for an indifferent deity—or rather deities—as the best explanation of the mixed good and evil phenomena in the world, while Demea's God is neither indifferent nor many.

4. In 11.1–12, Cleanthes proposes, and Philo criticizes, a "new theory" of a "finitely perfect" Author of Nature, while Demea's Creator is infinite in all respects.

5. Throughout 11.1–17, Philo has turned Cleanthes' empirical theology on its head and argued that the world's misery and evil imply that the deity or deities are not "perfectly" good but rather indifferent or even malicious. Demea worries not simply over the conclusion but also over the "anthropomorphism" of the method, using similarity to human experience as the theological touchstone.

6. Ever since the debacle of Demea's *a priori* argument in Part 9, Cleanthes and Philo have sought to examine the moral attributes of the deity via Cleanthes' empirical method, leading to conclusions that are progressively more threatening to Demea's presumed orthodoxy.

Any one "latter part of the discourse" offends deeply against Demea's religion and might suffice to provoke him to action; but surely all of them put together must stir him to leave. Add to these disagreements in religious views (theology) deep disagreements in practice and sentiment (piety), Demea's isolation in the present company, his recent awakening to his isolation, and his sense of betrayal by Philo, and we have a plenitude of reasons for removing himself from the company. In fact, Demea's departure is so thoroughly over-determined that it is inevitable, as any genuinely dramatic action must be. But Demea's departure is also momentous, for it allows Cleanthes and Philo to regain their accustomed "unreserved intimacy" (12.2.Philo to Cleanthes) so that they can at last speak their deeper minds.

15

Part 12

Notwithstanding the freedom of my conversation, and my love of singular arguments, no-one has a deeper sense of religion impressed on his mind, or pays more profound adoration to the divine Being, as he discovers himself to reason, in the inexplicable contrivance and artifice of nature.

—Philo to Cleanthes, Part 12.2

The proper office of religion is to regulate the heart of men, humanize their conduct, infuse the spirit of temperance, order, and obedience.

—Cleanthes to Philo, Part 12.12

Nothing ever made greater impression on me, than all the reasonings of that day.

—Pamphilus to Hermippus, Part 12.34

Structure:
   ¶1: Cleanthes and Philo continue the conversation in a new "manner"
   ¶¶2–4: Philo confesses his "sense of religion"
   ¶5: Cleanthes touts the advantages of theism and discounts skepticism
   ¶¶6–9: Philo expresses his "unfeigned sentiments"
      ¶¶6–7: The argument over theism is only a "verbal controversy" over degrees of likeness and analogy
      ¶8: Natural versus moral attributes—and a footnote
      ¶9: Philo's "veneration for true religion" and "abhorrence of vulgar superstitions"
   ¶¶10–12: Cleanthes has an "inclination" and Philo disagrees
      ¶10: Cleanthes: Corrupt religion is better than no religion

¶11: Philo: "Vulgar superstition" has "pernicious consequences"
¶12: Cleanthes: "The proper office of religion is to regulate the heart of men"
¶¶13–23: Philo discusses "true religion" versus "superstition or enthusiasm"
¶¶13–20: "The motives of vulgar superstition"
¶¶21–23: The "pernicious consequences" of "popular religions"
¶¶24–26: Cleanthes and Philo trade warnings
¶24: Cleanthes: Do not forfeit true religion's "great comfort" and support
¶¶25–26: Philo: Beware "the terrors of religion"
¶¶27–33: Philo sums up his view of religion
¶¶27–32: Piety
¶33: Theology
¶34: Pamphilus reviews the whole

Part 12 is the longest of the twelve Parts, and it is a sea change from what went before. Demea has left the conversation, and although he continues to serve as an object of discussion, his absence radically alters the interpersonal dynamics and tenor of discussion. Demea's piety and personality oppressed the earlier conversation: No one could speak honestly and openly because they were all constantly struggling against Demea's authoritarian personality and seeking to reject, controvert, or subvert his views. Conversation when Demea was around always had ulterior motives and purposes—it was in fact a politely veiled form of power play, where "winning" and "losing" had serious practical consequences.

But with Demea absent, both Cleanthes and Philo are free to confess their deeper views and attitudes, and their conversation alters fundamentally in "manner" and content. To be sure, Philo continues his "spirit of opposition" but with little interest in merely scoring debating points; where he is skeptical now, he is seriously so. But he also reaches for common ground with Cleanthes, not just in piety but also in theology; in particular, the two agree more on teleology and its role in natural theology than one might have suspected from the arguments of Parts 1–11. The two old friends are now at liberty to discuss new subjects ("verbal disputes"; religion and morality; enthusiasm and zeal) that were impossible with Demea present and to address old ones in a more profound way (evidence and theory; religious piety; "true religion" versus "superstition"; and skepticism).

In the end, a broader, more comprehensive view of natural religion[1] is illuminated and instanced—a view that is more honest and convincing to Cleanthes and Philo and to Pamphilus as well. They are finally able to discuss what truly matters to each of them about "true religion," particularly its un-avoidable impact on personal and public life, even as they live together "in company" in a way consonant with the views they express.[2]

¶1: A new "manner"

Pamphilus introduces Part 12 by underscoring the difference between Parts 1–11 and Part 12. "After DEMEA's departure, CLEANTHES and PHILO continued the conversation, in the following manner" (12.1.Pamphi-lus to Hermippus). It is all too easy to pass quickly over this sentence, con-struing "in the following manner" to mean merely "as follows." But the phrase is much more significant than that. "Manner" purposefully calls attention to the *way* the conversation continues, because that way differs significantly from the way of the preceding eleven Parts. It is not simply that the participants are down to two but that their conversation alters in *kind*.[3] What they talk about, how they talk about it, what they seek, and what they achieve all change. The subject becomes natural piety instead of natural theology, the tone is sincere expression instead of posturing for Pamphilus's benefit, the aim is agreement in company instead of winning a competition, and the result is a deeper understanding of true religion in contrast to superstition and enthu-siasm. So discerning the different "manner" of Part 12 is of utmost impor-tance in understanding the internal meaning of the entire *Dialogues*.[4]

Following Pamphilus's introductory sentence, Cleanthes opens the new manner of conversation with a gently chiding reference to the departed Demea: "Our friend . . . will have little inclination to revive this topic of discourse, while you [Philo] are in company" (12.1.Cleanthes to Philo). "Our friend" is of course a conventionally polite thing to say, and Cleanthes is nothing if not polite; *his* "manner" always includes "manners." But Cleanthes also signals solidarity with Philo and marks an important difference between two kinds of friendship: Demea divides the human world into friends and enemies on the basis of agreement or disagreement with himself, and his abrupt depar-ture means that he counts both Philo and Cleanthes as enemies because he finds they disagree profoundly with him, both in theology and in piety. But Cleanthes has in mind a different kind of friendship, one that permits contin-ued conversation even in the face of theological disagreement, a friendship based on caring tolerance and not fearful intolerance. Demea's type of friend-ship creates its own enemies—it could not exist without inimical others—while the friendship of Cleanthes and Philo does not. It is not Philo and Cleanthes who exclude or "banish" Demea from their "company" (contra Carnochan 1988, 522); Demea excludes himself.

At the same time, Cleanthes admonishes his true friend Philo for arousing Demea's animus, conveniently forgetting how Demea had ranged himself with Philo against the "anthropomorphism" of Cleanthes for nearly all the earlier dialogues.[5] The problem, he tells Philo, is "your spirit of controversy, joined to your abhorrence of vulgar superstition" that carries you to "strange lengths, when engaged in an argument." In fact, when caught up in controversy, "there is nothing so sacred and venerable, *even in your own eyes,* which you spare on that occasion" (12.1.Cleanthes to Philo; emphasis added). According to Cleanthes, when Philo is engaged in controversy—with Demea, to be sure, but also with Cleanthes, so long as Demea is present—we cannot credit his arguments as conveying Philo's true views, either in their (mostly negative) conclusions or in their (generally skeptical) bent. Thus, in particular, the details of Philo's controversial starting of cavils and objections in Parts 2–11 against Cleanthes' design argument must be taken with a grain of salt; they do not necessarily represent Philo's own true views. Demea's intolerant piety precipitates controversy, and Philo in controversy will say what it takes to win. Philo can finally speak his true mind only when, in Part 12, he is in non-combative conversation alone with his old friend Cleanthes.

Cleanthes continues: "To tell truth,[6] PHILO, I should rather wish to reason with either of you apart on a subject, so sublime and interesting." This is his way of marking the difference in "manner" Pamphilus has noted. When the three are together, the conversation is a competition, not a mutual sharing of heartfelt views, and Philo's "spirit of controversy" threatens to carry all before it. Still, Philo's controversial spirit is only one of the factors making for a difference in manner. Others include Demea's authoritarian personality and clumsy dogmatism; the general desire to win the affections and shape the piety of young Pamphilus; the antecedent friendship of Philo and Cleanthes, to which Demea appears an interloper; and the prior relationship of Cleanthes to his ward Pamphilus. Demea is in every respect the odd man out.

¶¶2–4: Philo's "sense of religion"

Philo agrees, in part. He does "confess"[7] that he is "less cautious on the subject of natural religion than on any other," but for two reasons quite other than those mentioned by Cleanthes. For one, "I know that I can never, on that head, corrupt the principles of any man of common sense." By implication, anyone whose principles are threatened by Philo's arguments lacks common sense: Demea but not Cleanthes is discomfited. For another, "No-one, I am confident, in whose eyes I appear a man of common sense, will ever mistake my intentions" (all 12.2.Philo to Cleanthes). Demea surely does not think Philo a man of common sense, nor does he understand what Philo is about; but then he is a poor judge of men and intentions. Cleanthes doesn't mistake Philo's intentions and doesn't differ from him in appealing to common sense (although they sometimes suppose common sense to affirm different things). So Philo appears to Cleanthes, though not to Demea, as "a man of common sense." But *is* he really such a man? Has Cleanthes correctly discerned Philo's motives or is Philo simply being ironic?[8]

Cleanthes is in a very good position to discern Philo's true intentions, and Philo admits as much in speaking of the "unreserved intimacy" in which he and Cleanthes live. There are no barriers between them to sincere expression of heartfelt views. Cleanthes has learned, through firsthand experience, who Philo truly is and what he truly believes, so he is not deceived by Philo's "spirit of controversy."

Here, then, in this condition of intellectual intimacy, is what Philo says is his true belief on the subject of natural religion:

> No-one has a deeper sense of religion impressed on his mind, or pays more profound adoration to the divine Being, as he discovers himself to reason, in the inexplicable contrivance and artifice of nature. A purpose, an intention, a design strikes every where the most careless, the most stupid thinker; and no man can be so hardened in absurd systems, as at all times to reject it. (12.2.Philo to Cleanthes)

This is an extraordinary confession, and it appears at first glance to constitute an extreme "reversal." Indeed, some commentators have called Philo's apparent change of mind "the primary problem" of interpreting the *Dialogues* (Jessop 1939 quoted in Pike 1970, 204). Those who view Philo as a total skeptic, naturalist, or outright atheist are most troubled and hence most tempted into imputing irony or deceit to Philo.[9] An ironic interpretation will gloss this passage somewhat as follows: "As he *discovers* himself to *reason*" (i.e., not at all), the "*inexplicable* contrivance and artifice of nature" (it cannot be a contrivance if it is inexplicable) "strikes every where *the most careless, the most stupid* thinker" (but not the more careful, sophisticated, intelligent reasoner).

But if we are not antecedently persuaded that we understand Philo's true position before we arrive at Part 12, if we take seriously Philo's numerous earlier admissions of the force of design arguments (cf. 10.26, 10.36, 11.11, 11.14), and if we do not ignore the changed "manner" of Part 12, then there is no obstacle to a straightforward reading. Philo, like anyone of "common sense," finds himself seized with an immediate sense of the natural world as somewhat like human contrivance and artifice, and he cannot help inferring that a "divine Being" somewhat like us is the world's original cause or Author, even if he cannot explain how or why such a Being acts. In an honest awareness of nature, not only the experimental theist Cleanthes but also the congenitally skeptical Philo has an intuitive apprehension of artifice.

Philo goes on to point out how this immediate sense is reinforced by the way humans ingenuously use design-like principles in other realms of thought. The "schools" believe "that nature does nothing in vain"; the Copernican system holds "that nature acts by the simplest methods, and chooses the most proper means to any end"; and "the same thing is observable in other parts of philosophy." So "all the sciences almost lead us insensibly to acknowledge a first intelligent author; and their authority is often so much the greater as they do not directly profess that intention" (all 12.2.Philo to Cleanthes). Again, it is possible to maintain that Philo is speaking ironically, piling up far-fetched resemblances only to attenuate the sense of natural artifice. But more likely he is speaking his true mind in attesting to natural teleology's irresistible, universal appeal: Even when humans do not have religion in mind, they cannot avoid a teleological apprehension of nature. From this apprehension, it is but a short step "to acknowledge a first intelligent author."

Next Philo introduces a most curious example: Galen's muscles.[10] Galen, he reports, says there are more than 600 different muscles in the human body, each with "at least ten different circumstances" relevant to achieving the body's ends. "So that, in the muscles alone, above 6000 several views and intentions must have been formed and executed." But then there are 284 bones, each with "above forty" distinct purposes, for an (uncalculated) total of over 11,360 skeletal purposes. "What a prodigious display of artifice, even in these simple and homogeneous parts?"[11] Add the "skin, ligaments, vessels, glandules, humours, the several limbs and members," and our astonishment can only grow. "The farther we advance in these researches, we discover new scenes of art and wisdom" even while we see "at a distance, farther scenes beyond our reach." So the sheer number and variety of apparent artifices in nature are very great indeed. If the infidel (i.e., non-Christian) Galen "could not withstand such striking appearances," then "to what pitch of pertinacious obstinacy must a philosopher in this age have attained, who can now doubt of a supreme intelligence?" (all 12.3.Philo to Cleanthes).

On its face, the question is rhetorical and the answer plain—that not even the skeptic Philo can bring himself truly to doubt of a supreme intelligence. Still, the speciously precise mathematics give pause to the modern reader, who easily suspects that Philo is concocting an underhanded critique of the design argument by elaborating *too* "prodigious" a "display of artifice." But we need not suspect Philo of insincerity, irony, or sarcasm. The argument is Galen's, and Philo does not rely upon its pseudo-quantitative side; he is not trying to arrive at a precise estimation of the probability of intelligent design. His points, rather, are that (1) science discovers an enormous number of unsuspected "ends" or "views and intentions" served by human bodies; (2) these "intentions" are multiplied in other animal bodies; (3) we also see "farther scenes [of teleology] beyond our reach"; and (4) contemplating all this teleology we cannot "doubt of a supreme intelligence" (all 12.3.Philo to

Cleanthes). In these points, the "skeptical" Philo concurs with the "infidel" Galen and the theist Cleanthes.

Further, Philo asks how a God "who did not discover himself immediately to our senses," and so whose every attribute could only be inferred by us,[12] could possibly "give stronger proofs of existence, than what appear on the whole face of nature?" What better clues to its character could such a Being give than what we already have in "the present economy of things"?— (1) some "artifices so plain, that no stupidity could mistake them," showing the divine purposiveness; (2) some "glimpses of still greater artifices," showing "his prodigious superiority above our narrow apprehensions"; and (3) concealment of many artifices altogether from creatures so "imperfect" as we. This evidence is doubtless weak, yet it is as strong as the nature of the case permits. Hence the "fact" of such a Being "must pass for undisputed" (all 12.4.Philo to Cleanthes).

Philo here expresses a view in tension with the previous paragraph touting Galen's myriad of natural purposes. He now claims that the evidence for a supreme intelligence is weak but as good as one could expect under the circumstances. These two views register the central dilemma of natural theology: strengthening the "prodigious" *evidence for* deity tugs against magnifying the "prodigious" *transcendence of* deity. The better we can argue to a deity, the less magnificent such a being becomes, and the more magnificent the deity, the less accessible it is. In the conversation of Parts 1–11, Cleanthes affirmed the strength of the evidence, while Philo and Demea upheld the deity's transcendence. Now in Part 12, Philo has implicitly endorsed *both* sides of the dilemma.

Philo has put the case for natural theology as plainly as he can, and he has confessed his own views as openly as Cleanthes could wish. He does not conceal his own sense of nature's teleology nor his thoroughly natural inference to "a first intelligent author" of nature. But he remains fully aware of how limited human understanding must be, given not only the prodigious nature of the deity but also the weakness of our faculties. The case for natural theology, therefore, is at once unavoidably compelling and utterly weak. The more we attend to nature, the more we learn of God; yet the more we learn of God, the more we know how little we know of God.

¶5: Cleanthes touts theism and discounts skepticism

Cleanthes says he concurs, but rather than accepting both sides of the tension Philo presents, he seeks solely to bolster the case for theism. Theism is "the only system of cosmogony which can be rendered intelligible and complete, and yet can throughout preserve a strong analogy to what we every day see and experience in the world." The analogy of the universe to human con-

trivance is "so obvious and natural" that it "must immediately strike all un-
prejudiced apprehensions, and procure universal approbation." No alternative
theory is sufficiently "precise and determinate," and skeptical "suspense of
judgment" is "in itself unsatisfactory" and cannot "be steadily maintained
against such striking appearances, as continually engage us into the religious
hypothesis." Humans could embrace a "false, absurd system" but they could
not eliminate all systems in opposition to theism, which is supported "by
strong and obvious reason, by natural propensity, and by early education" (all
12.5.Cleanthes to Philo).[13] Cleanthes seeks above all else a reasonable religion,
and what is reasonable is so by analogy with human experience of contrivance. Whereas Demea fears the world and distrusts reason, Cleanthes embraces the world and distrusts attempts to undermine reason; Demea's mis-
ology and misanthropy are countered by Cleanthes' anthropomorphism and
philanthropy.

But why does Cleanthes think only theism is both "intelligible and complete" and "precise and determinate"? Even if Cleanthes were justified in believing that Philo has done little more than "start doubts and difficulties"
without elaborating an alternative "system" (all 12.5), Cleanthes does not
support his own claims that theism is complete and precise. Moreover, Cleanthes mistakes the thrust of Philo's skepticism. Philo does not promote any
particular theological hypotheses but rather casts doubt on all such theories,
thereby weakening confidence in human ability to cope with such issues.
Cleanthes thinks that analogy "to what we everyday see and experience in the
world" will decisively settle the matter, but Philo has shown him ample reason
in Parts 2–8 and 10–11 to doubt that our experience and reason are up to
the task.

¶¶6–7: Philo on "mere verbal controversy"

Although Philo and Cleanthes agree that theism is the natural outcome
of natural theology, they still disagree. Cleanthes regards the evidence in
natural theology as quite strong, while Philo considers it extremely weak;
Cleanthes believes a great deal can be inferred about the divine attributes
from this evidence, while Philo thinks not very much at all. But what kind
of disagreements are these? Philo, as always, has an hypothesis. The controversy, he claims, is "somewhat of a dispute of words." All sides agree that the
"works of nature" are like "productions of art," and so, by "all the rules of
good reasoning," their causes are also alike. But nature and art also differ
considerably, hence so must their causes. So "the existence of a DEITY is
plainly ascertained by reason"; but the deity's nature is not so plain.[14] In particular, it is not clear that the deity so closely resembles a human mind that
one can use "mind" or "intelligence" as synonyms for "deity." Here, then,

according to Philo, is a "mere verbal controversy": Cleanthes uses, and Philo disputes the use of, human qualities to characterize the deity (all 12.6.Philo to Cleanthes).

Everyone of course is disgusted with merely verbal disputes, for which the only "remedy" is "clear definitions," precise ideas, and "strict and uniform use" of terms. But what if clarity, precision, and strictness are impossible in some areas due to "the very nature of language and of human ideas"? This is indeed the case, claims Philo in an inserted paragraph that is the longest in the entire *Dialogues*, in "controversies concerning the degrees of any quality or circumstance." For example, greatness, beauty, and praise come in degrees, and dispute over the exact degree can never be settled, because "the degrees of these qualities are not, like quantity or number, susceptible of any exact mensuration." Philo maintains that "the dispute concerning theism is of this nature, and consequently is merely verbal, or perhaps, if possible, still more incurably ambiguous" (all 12.7.Philo to Cleanthes). He makes his point by addressing first the theist and then the atheist.

The theist must not make the resemblance between human qualities and divine attributes too close. There is "a great and immeasurable, because incomprehensible, difference between the *human* and the *divine* mind." Moreover, the more pious the person, the greater will he magnify the difference: "He will even assert, that the difference is of a nature, which cannot be too much magnified" (all 12.7.Philo to Cleanthes).

The atheist is "only nominally so, and can never possibly be in earnest."[15] An atheist must concede "a certain degree of analogy among all the operations of nature, in every situation and in every age," even though the degree may be very "remote" indeed. Further, "the principle which first arranged and still maintains order in this universe, bears . . . also some remote inconceivable analogy to the other operations of nature," including human thought.[16]

The result, Philo cries out, is that the dispute between theism and atheism is cloudy at best. "The theist allows that the original intelligence is very different from human reason: The atheist allows that the original principle of order bears some remote analogy to it." Their "quarrel" about the deity is only "about the degrees" and "admits not of any precise meaning, nor consequently of any determination." Indeed, the antagonists may "insensibly change sides," the theist sliding into atheism by exaggerating the dissimilarity, the atheist moving into theism by magnifying the analogy.[17] Philo concludes with an admonition to both sides: "Consider then, where the real point of controversy lies, and if you cannot lay aside your disputes, endeavour, at least, to cure yourselves of your animosity" (all 12.7.Philo to Cleanthes).

Philo's characterization of the dispute between theism and atheism is inadequate.[18] On the one hand, questions of degree are not always unresolvable. No doubt qualifiers such as "very," "great," "little," and "remote" are somewhat vague when applied to resemblances, and disagreements concerning their application can be frustratingly interminable. Yet this is not always true of expressions containing "more," "less," "greater," and so forth; often these comparative judgments can be made with some precision and intersubjective agreement. So while it may not be possible to settle whether Hannibal is "great" or "very great," agreement may be easy when comparing the relative greatness of Hannibal and some other Carthaginian general. More generally, where ϕ is some degree predicate containing a qualifier such as "great," "little," "remote," and so forth, one must distinguish between asking *whether* x is more ϕ than y and asking *how much more* ϕ x is than y; the former can often be answered even when the latter cannot be.

On the other hand, not all unresolvable questions are matters of degree. Some questions may be resolvable in principle but empirically unresolvable because we lack the requisite time, means, or aptitude for settling them (e.g., exactly how many planets larger than the Earth lie within three AUs [one AU = the mean radius of earth's orbit] of all the stars in the Andromeda galaxy). Others may be unresolvable in principle but for different reasons: for example, because they involve infinity in a way that cannot be grasped by any finite being (e.g., writing out the complete decimal expansion of π) or because they involve an order of complexity beyond our particular finite capacities (predicting deterministic chaotic systems) or because the terms are incurably vague (a living wage) or arbitrarily applied (the strike zone in major league baseball).

Further, what is unresolvable need not be inconsequential. Something unresolvable in practice but not in principle may be quite consequential (will a very large asteroid strike the earth in the next ten years?). Similarly, in-principle unresolvability may also be consequential (the research programs of mathematical logicians before and after Gödel). More relevant to the *Dialogues,* disagreement in theology may concern the degree of likeness between human and divine attributes and still be quite consequential—it connects with other beliefs and attitudes and enmeshes one in divergent ways of life. After all, Demea and Cleanthes do live in two quite different social and moral "worlds," even if their theological disagreements are unresolvable.

So, for all these reasons, Philo's diagnosis of interminable theological disagreement is not very compelling. At the minimum it needs further work. But the ever-polite Cleanthes does not challenge Philo to do this further work, for the last thing the two friends need at this point is another interminable disagreement, especially one over the nature of interminable disagreement in natural theology! They need to move beyond theology to talk about the rest of religion and indeed what is for them the greater part of religion: piety.

¶8: Natural versus moral attributes

But first, Philo reiterates another point he had made earlier (in Parts 10–11) that cuts deeply into Cleanthes' position. Whatever absolute degree of resemblance the "works of nature" bear to human "art and contrivance," they resemble human art and contrivance comparatively *more* than they do human "benevolence and justice," hence "we have reason to infer that the natural attributes of the deity have a greater resemblance to those of man, than his moral have to human virtues." Philo now makes an astonishing inference, particularly in light of Part 11: "The moral qualities of man are more defective in their kind than his natural abilities," he holds, because "the supreme Being is allowed to be absolutely and entirely perfect," so that "whatever differs most from him departs the farthest from the supreme standard of rectitude and imperfection" (12.8.Philo to Cleanthes). But of course Cleanthes will not "allow" the premise, since the only divine attributes he accepts are those inferable from empirical evidence. On Cleanthes' terms, all we can justifiably believe is that divine moral attributes resemble human moral qualities less than divine natural attributes resemble human mental qualities—*not* that we are more defective in morality than in natural endowment.

At the end of 12.8, the reader encounters a mysterious footnote. In Hume's autograph manuscript, this note was written at the end of Part 12 with instruction for insertion here *as a footnote*. It extends Philo's theory of "merely verbal" disputes. "It seems evident," the footnote contends, that "the dispute between the sceptics and dogmatists is entirely verbal, or at least regards only the degrees of doubt and assurance, which we ought to indulge with regard to all such reasoning: And such disputes are commonly, at the bottom, verbal, and admit not of any precise determination." The dogmatist cannot deny the "absolutely insolvable" difficulties and the skeptic cannot deny the necessity to think, believe, and reason in the absence of certainty. "The only difference, then, between these sects, if they merit that name, is, that the sceptic, from habit, caprice, or inclination, insists most on the difficulties; the dogmatist, for the like reasons, on the necessity" (all 12.8.footnote).

It is initially tempting to read this footnote as a commentary on Philo the skeptic versus Cleanthes the dogmatist, for those are the roles they play. Philo, who abrades the arguments of Cleanthes in Parts 1–11, ends up admitting the bare vague truth of theism in Part 12, while Cleanthes, who stoutly maintains the experimental argument throughout, ends up (or should end up) admitting his argument's weakness on the moral attributes of the deity. Whether "from habit, caprice, or inclination," Philo chiefly insists on the "difficulties" of reasoning to a deity, while Cleanthes chiefly insists on the "necessity" of so reasoning. However, this reading is problematic at the margins. Philo does sweep his skepticism into every corner of life, but Cleanthes is not very dogmatic—even his commitment to experimental thinking is fallibilistic and probabilistic. If anyone has a dogmatic position (and personality) it is Demea, but his dogma rests not on reasoning but on faith and emotion.

But before we incorporate this footnote into our interpretation of the *Dialogues,* we must step back to address a larger issue: In this series of conversations, where every speech has a speaker, every word an author, who authors the footnotes?[19] Assigning authorship to any of the three principal speakers makes no sense at all; their speeches are recorded by Pamphilus and they are not editors of his text, so they get no chance to speak outside the body of the text. They are participants in the dialogues, not authors or editors of a record of the dialogues. Hermippus is likewise ruled out, because this "recital" of the conversations is delivered to him by Pamphilus (PH.6). So Pamphilus is the only named speaker who could possibly author the footnotes. Yet there are good reasons for thinking he cannot play this role. First, Pamphilus never refers to his own editorship, though he does discuss his role as "reciter." Second, why would Pamphilus edit his own recital, for whom, and to what end? Does Hermippus need to know these footnoted matters? Third, the content seems beyond Pamphilus. These footnotes are generally erudite, citing classical and contemporary authors with varying degrees of specificity, and displaying knowledge that would be unusual in one so young as Pamphilus, even if Cleanthes has given him quite a good education.[20]

So who could be responsible for these footnotes? Could there be some (anonymous) editor of Pamphilus's "recital" to Hermippus? This suggestion raises more problems than it solves. Should we then just accept the footnotes as directly from Hume? But that reintroduces all the contextual questions an internal interpretation brackets from the outset. It clearly intrudes an "author" neither named nor recognized in the text, and it adds a surd element that detracts from the text's "artfulness"—the footnotes would be irrational danglers to the *Dialogues,* like the "inaccurate workmanship" Philo finds in "the great machine of nature" (11.11.Philo to Demea and Cleanthes). An internal interpretation should credit Hume for the footnotes only as a last resort, if there is no alternative.

There are two more, faintly desperate, possibilities. One is that the footnote at 12.8 belongs in the body of the text as part of Philo's speech and that Hume has mistakenly asked that it be inserted as a footnote.[21] But while we may tolerate one such mistake, it scarcely seems credible that all fourteen footnotes are mistakes. Second, perhaps the footnotes belong completely "outside" the text of the dialogues altogether. This seems rather drastic, since the footnotes are so clearly part of Hume's *autograph text*.[22] Yet all the footnotes, save for the present one at 12.8, do not expand upon the body of the text; they contain the sort of information that an external commentator might provide but not the kind that an engaged participant or auditor would think necessary or even relevant to the issues at hand. So excision of these footnotes from the text—from the *dialogic text*, as we may call it—would be no great loss; indeed it would enhance the beautiful and purposive order of the *Dialogues*.[23]

None of these remedies is very satisfying. So why not adopt an external perspective and consider *Hume* to be speaking directly in the footnotes? If so, one should note *how little* of Hume actually surfaces in the *Dialogues* and how little difference it makes to the dialogues. As Malherbe says (1995, 223 n. 35), the footnote at 12.8 is some kind of "commentary on the text," but a commentary that does not materially advance the conversation.

¶9: Philo's "unfeigned sentiments"

Philo next makes an important personal statement that is vital to interpreting the entire *Dialogues*. He tells Cleanthes first that the foregoing "are my unfeigned sentiments on this subject" and second that "these sentiments, you know, I have ever cherished and maintained" (12.9.Philo to Cleanthes). In Demea's absence, Philo stresses that he speaks without pretense or sham, with no intent to deceive because there is no need to deceive. By implication, while in Demea's presence, Philo occasionally feigned or concealed his true beliefs. Further, Cleanthes knows all this; he knows Philo's views now are unfeigned because he has known Philo for a long time. This knowledge accounts for much of Cleanthes' otherwise puzzling silence in the face of Philo's criticisms in Parts 2–8 and 10–11: Cleanthes doesn't reply because he knows Philo is only inventing views that are not his own and that pose no threat to their friendship.

But what *are* Philo's unfeigned sentiments? Again, Philo makes two comments: first, that he has a "veneration for true religion" and second, that he has an "abhorrence of vulgar superstition." What "true religion" and its opposite mean will become clearer shortly (in 12.13–23). In the meantime, Philo confesses[24] "a peculiar pleasure" in pushing superstitious views over the brink, "sometimes into absurdity, sometimes into impiety." Upholders of superstition are "bigots" who have a greater aversion to impiety than to absurdity, yet nevertheless "are commonly equally guilty of both" (all 12.9.Philo to Cleanthes). The application to Demea is patent: Demea thinks of himself as a staunch defender of orthodoxy, but in Philo's eyes he is a bigot whose religion is vulgar superstition and wild enthusiasm. Demea is Philo's (and

Cleanthes') worst nightmare, embodying the irrational and destructive energy of superstitious enthusiasm.

¶¶10–12: Cleanthes' "contrary inclination"

Cleanthes responds curiously to Philo's "unfeigned sentiments." He first makes a general claim about religion and then introduces a particular religious doctrine heretofore undiscussed. "Religion," he claims, "however corrupted, is still better than no religion at all. The doctrine of a future state is so strong and necessary a security to morals, that we never ought to abandon or neglect it." Cleanthes seems to concede that this doctrine is (often) a superstition.[25] He defends it on the grounds not of truth but of utility:[26] It is a useful, indeed a "necessary," bulwark of morality, supporting moral rules by attaching "infinite and eternal" rewards and punishments that will have a greater effect than "finite and temporary" ones (all 12.10.Cleanthes to Philo). Cleanthes ranks true religion above superstitious religion above no religion at all, because even superstition's support may be useful for morality.

Cleanthes has entered dangerous territory, and Philo is quick to point out some of the perils. Throughout history, he notes, religion has had "pernicious consequences on public affairs," leading to "factions, civil wars, persecutions, subversions of government, oppression, slavery." In historical narration, the "religious spirit" leads always to "miseries" (12.11.Philo to Cleanthes). Philo's appeal to history is significant, whether or not he has the facts straight. Cleanthes has formulated a general hypothesis, to which Philo alleges *historical* counterexamples, confronting abstract "reasonings" with concrete "facts" (12.13.Philo to Cleanthes). Once one seeks to defend superstition by pointing to its salutary effects, one is at the mercy of the historical record.

Cleanthes, for once, has a ready reply, expressing his view of true religion in a famous passage. "The proper office of religion is to regulate the hearts of men, humanize their conduct, infuse the spirit of temperance, order, and obedience." When confined to this office, religion "is silent, and only enforces the motives of morality and justice"; it is therefore easy to overlook religion's influence and to confound it with other motives. Only when religion "acts as a separate principle over men" does it leave "its proper sphere, and ... become a cover to faction and ambition" (all 12.12.Cleanthes to Philo). Here Cleanthes gives a functional meaning not only to "religion" but also to "true religion" and "false religion": Religion is as religion does (its actual function and effects), so true religion is truly religion, doing what religion ought to do (its proper function); and false religion is what religion does but ought not to do (its improper function). The proper function of (true) religion is to prop up morality, and the improper function of (false) religion is to oppose and subvert morality.[27]

But this functional view of religion is a dangerous one for Cleanthes to hold in conjunction with his empirical theology, and it leads to his present endorsement of superstition. Experimental theology affirms only theological views supported by experience, while functional religion affirms any theological view supporting morality. But these two criteria may easily diverge, and in fact the doctrine of a future state fails the first test (it is therefore superstition) while passing the second (it is therefore useful or "true" religion). Perhaps Cleanthes wants to maintain the priority of the functional criterion over the empirical one, so that a morally useful superstition is preferable to a morally inert (or even harmful) theological truth. But this places Cleanthes uncomfortably close to Demea.

¶¶13–23: Philo on false and true religion

Philo wants to avoid Cleanthes' bind, so over the next eleven paragraphs he sets about providing a different characterization of "true religion" and its opposite, which now is said to have two parts: "superstition or enthusiasm."[28] It is important to recognize that Philo is moving on from *theology* to *religion*. Religion includes theology but theology is not all of religion, or even its greater part. The larger part of religion is *piety*, practical religion, how one lives as well as thinks and feels—a topic broached in Part 10 (Demea's fearful piety) but largely absent from the theological conversations in the other Parts. In this section of Part 12, Philo spends most of his time mounting a comprehensive attack upon pious "superstition or enthusiasm," yet embedded in his attack is a more positive view of religion. *Superstition* is "religious belief or practice founded upon fear or ignorance" (*OED*, sense 1) as well as "an irrational religious system" (sense 2); and *enthusiasm* (literally "god-possession") is "ill-regulated or misdirected religious emotion, extravagance of religious speculation" (*OED*, sense 2). By implication, their opposite, *true religion*, contains only theological beliefs rationally founded or bounded and only moderate emotions supporting moral common life. In short, Philo seeks a religion within the limits of common life alone.[29]

Philo's brief against false religion (and for true religion) contains five major points:

First, Philo specifically attacks the doctrine of a future state as superstition. It is an unnecessary support of morals, as natural inclination is a more powerful motive. Besides, a strong commitment to religion is generally at odds with morality, not in support of it. Cleanthes' argument for the afterlife—if "finite and temporary rewards and punishments have so great an influence, that therefore such as are infinite and eternal must have so much greater"—is invalid and its conclusion false. In fact, we have a time-biased set of desires; we are greatly attached "to present things" and unconcerned about "objects, so remote and uncertain" (12.13.Philo to Cleanthes).

Further, "divines"[30] who uphold Cleanthes' doctrine of the afterlife are guilty of a contradiction: On the one hand, when condemning "the common behaviour and conduct of the world," they view the principle of attachment to present things "as the strongest imaginable (which indeed it is)," while, on the other hand, when engaged in speculative controversy, they suppose "the motives of religion to be so powerful, that, without them, it were impossible for civil society to subsist." But the motive of the afterlife cannot be at once impotent and all-powerful (all 12.13.Philo to Cleanthes). In fact, says Philo,[31] "the smallest grain of natural honesty and benevolence has more effect on men's conduct, than the most pompous views, suggested by theological theories and systems." This is because "natural inclination" works "incessantly," as opposed to religious motives which "operate only by starts and bounds" and can barely become habitual.[32] Moreover, when religious principles run contrary to natural inclination, natural inclination can marshal all the forces of "wit and ingenuity of the mind," and in seeking to avoid religious duty, "it is almost always successful" (all 12.14.Philo to Cleanthes).

Second, Philo expands his view of true versus false religion. Philosophers don't need the reinforcement of religion since they "cultivate reason and reflection . . . to keep them under the restraint of morals." The vulgar, however, need motives other than reason and reflection, because they are incapable of the philosophical "pure" religion that "represents the Deity to be pleased with nothing but virtue in human behaviour." Instead, they attempt to appease and placate "the Divinity" with "frivolous observances, or rapturous ecstasies, or a bigoted credulity" (all 12.15.Philo to Cleanthes). Reasonable philosophers view the deity as fundamentally moral, while the enthusiastic vulgar view the Divinity as fundamentally uninterested in morality or more interested in something else. By implication, according to Philo, true religion is moral religion, false religion is amoral or immoral religion.

Even if "superstition or enthusiasm" is not directly opposed to morality, it does divert attention, raises up "a new and frivolous species of merit," and distributes praise and blame in a "preposterous way"; all of which weaken "men's attachment to the natural motives of justice and humanity" (all 12.16.Philo to Cleanthes). Consider religious ritual. Counting ritual purity as a human duty weakens moral commitment either by dilution (more duties to be fulfilled) or by diminution (fewer *moral* duties to be fulfilled). Further, religious motives are inconstant and "must be roused by continual efforts, in order to render the pious zealot satisfied with his own conduct, and make him fulfil his devotional task." Inevitable failure in this effort produces a "habit of dissimulation" to self and others. Hence the uniting of "the highest zeal in religion and the deepest hypocrisy" (12.17.Philo to Cleanthes). In addition, "the enthusiastic zealot" is led to promote "the interests of religion" even above morality (12.18.Philo to Cleanthes); for example, the whole-hearted pursuit of one's own eternal salvation "is apt to extinguish the benevolent affections, and beget a narrow, contracted selfishness" (12.19.Philo to Cleanthes). In sum, "the motives of vulgar superstition have no great influence on general conduct; nor is their operation very favourable to morality" (12.20.Philo to Cleanthes).

Third, false religion has an even darker side: the specter of powerful priests. Echoing his earlier words about "priestcraft" (cf. 1.19 and 11.20), Philo contends that "the greater number of priests, and their greater authority and riches will always augment the religious spirit," but that will produce only "pernicious consequences with regard to society" (12.21.Philo to Cleanthes).[33]

Fourth, Philo allows that "true religion . . . has no such pernicious consequences." But he is dealing with religion "as it has commonly been found in the world." Likewise, he has nothing bad to say of "that speculative tenet of theism," except that "as it is a species of philosophy" it must be "confined to very few persons" (all 12.22.Philo to Cleanthes). True religion is rare, while ordinary religion is pernicious.

Finally, Philo takes a curious detour—once fastened on making a critical case, he tosses in anything remotely relevant. The authority of oaths in courts of law does not stem from religion but rather from secular features such as "the solemnity and importance of the occasion, the regard to reputation, and the reflecting on the general interests of society" (12.23.Philo to Cleanthes). Actual religion's apparent good effects are due to something else.[34]

Here, then, is Philo's brief against false religion: The doctrine of a future state is an unnecessary and ineffective superstition which, far from supporting morality, actually opposes or subverts it; false religion destroys civil liberties and produces endless political disputes; false religion is much more common than true; and actual religion often adds nothing to socially useful institutions such as legal oaths. True religion, "the philosophical and rational kind," is a commendable prop of common life, but it is available only to a few and even then is less vital than inclination to "natural honesty and benevolence" (12.13.Philo to Cleanthes).

¶24: Cleanthes finds comfort in religion

Cleanthes is disturbed by Philo's sweeping case. "Take care," he twice warns Philo,[35] "push not matters too far: Allow not your zeal against false religion to undermine your veneration for the true." In particular, Cleanthes appeals to Philo not to "forfeit" the "genuine theism" that is "the chief, the only great comfort in life," the view that

> represents us as the workmanship of a Being perfectly good, wise, and powerful;
> who created us for happiness, and who, having implanted in us immeasurable

desires of good, will prolong our existence to all eternity, and will transfer us into an infinite variety of scenes, in order to satisfy those desires, and render our felicity complete and durable.

Our greatest happiness is to be under such a Being's "guardianship and protection" (all 12.24.Cleanthes to Philo).

Cleanthes retains to the end the natural teleology that is at the heart of his design argument: We are to see not only the natural world but even ourselves as the "workmanship" of a deity—even humans resemble human contrivances! In mentioning Philo's "zeal against false religion," Cleanthes is of course referring back to Philo's earlier "abhorrence of vulgar superstition" (12.9.Philo to Cleanthes), but he is also insinuating that Philo's aversion to religious zealotry (particularly in 12.17–18) is a sibling zeal and that its enthusiasm can easily do harm. Again Cleanthes appeals to the proper function of "genuine theism," but he extends its supposed effects. Genuine theism agreeably provides unsurpassable comfort and support in a life buffeted on all sides by "adverse fortune." Religion therefore not only supports morality but also comforts us when we fail morally and when morality fails us.

Cleanthes, Demea, and Philo have markedly different understandings of the deity and of our relation to the deity. For Demea, God is an arbitrary powerful being to be feared and appeased in abject submission, while for Cleanthes, this "Being" is a good and reasonable guardian of human happiness to be loved and enjoyed in moral service to others. Philo meanwhile admits a "divine Being" (12.2) in the form of a "principle" (12.7), "first and supreme cause" (12.6), "a supreme intelligence" (12.3), or "a God or Deity" (12.6). But he does not want to personify or anthropomorphize such a Being.

Cleanthes' language throughout 12.24 is finely wrought—elevated and almost liturgical. Perhaps Cleanthes wants to present not simply his own idiosyncratic creed but a confession to and for others as well. In particular, he makes it available to Philo, who at least pays it compliments (while withholding personal endorsement) in the very next paragraph.

¶¶25–26: The "terrors of religion"

Philo concedes that "these appearances . . . are most engaging and alluring; and with regard to the true philosopher, they are more than appearances."[36] However, his main point is no concession but rather an account of natural religion that is decidedly *un*alluring: "The greater part of mankind" is more considerably influenced by "the terrors of religion" (all 12.25.Philo to Cleanthes). Religious "devotion" is more often relied upon in adversity than in happiness: "Is not this a proof, that the religious spirit is not so nearly allied to joy as to sorrow?" (12.26.Philo to Cleanthes). Cleanthes demurs, citing religion's consoling effects on the afflicted[37] (12.27.Cleanthes to Philo). Philo concedes that there is indeed consolation in religion, but only "sometimes": For the most part, religion shows its darker side, so Philo dilates for the remainder of Part 12 on the nature and value of religion, both popular and philosophical, dwelling at length on piety (12.27–32) and briefly on theology (12.33).

¶¶27–32: Philo on religious piety

Humans form ideas of divinity ("those unknown beings") under influence of their "temper." It is not that religious "notions" are *only* projections of the personalities of their adherents but that we are predisposed to embrace concepts agreeable to our temper. Since most people's temper is one of "gloom and melancholy," it is only natural that "we find the tremendous[38] images to predominate in all religions." This is not just a problem for others: "We ourselves," he says to Cleanthes, exalt the deity and then "fall into the flattest contradiction, in affirming, that the damned are infinitely superior in number to the elect" (all 12.27.Philo to Cleanthes). An occasionally gloomy temper has made even Philo and Cleanthes susceptible to a doctrine of eternal damnation for the greater part of humanity.

But they are not alone. No "popular religion" has ever "represented the state of departed souls in such a light, as would render it eligible for human kind, that there should be such a state." By "eligible" Philo means "fit or deserving to be chosen or adopted" (*OED,* sense 3). These popular representations are ineligible because of the fate they predict for the majority of humanity: such shocking ideas as "Cerberus and furies; devils, and torrents of fire and brimstone" (all 12.28.Philo to Cleanthes).

Philo admits that "both fear and hope enter into religion" but maintains that fear predominates. When we are "in a cheerful disposition," we are "fit for business or company[39] or entertainment of any kind" in which we do not even think of religion. But when "melancholy, and dejected," we "brood upon the terrors of the invisible world," which only serves to deepen our "affliction." "Terror is the primary principle of religion" and always predominates over the "short intervals of pleasure" (all 12.29.Philo to Cleanthes). In fact, "fits of excessive, enthusiastic joy, by exhausting the spirits, always prepare the way for equal fits of superstitious terror and dejection." Here is the hidden link between superstition and enthusiasm: Both arise from excessive emotional states, not a "calm and equable" state of mind that is "happy" (12.30.Philo to Cleanthes).

Belief in a future state containing Heaven and Hell is profoundly disruptive of equanimity and "the ordinary frame of the mind." Such a belief actually undermines morality because it is "apt to make a considerable breach in the temper, and to produce that gloom and melancholy, so remarkable in all devout people" (all 12.30.Philo to Cleanthes). Terrors of the afterlife are "contrary to common sense," implying that "the Deity has human passions, and one of the lowest of human passions, a restless appetite for applause" as well as "a disregard to the opinions of creatures, so much inferior" (all 12.31.Philo to Cleanthes). The very doctrine Cleanthes had earlier urged as a "strong and necessary" support for morality (12.10.Cleanthes to Philo) Philo now excoriates as absurd, inconsistent, and immoral. Popular religion is the condition and effect of a troubled, unhappy mind.

Philo further flails away at "superstition" in the next paragraph. "Seneca" is quoted approvingly as saying "To know God is to worship him."[40] Ignorant worship is "absurd, superstitious, and even impious," degrading God to "the low condition of mankind, who are delighted with entreaty, solicitation, presents, and flattery," or even lower, to "a capricious demon, who exercises his power without reason and without humanity." Only "a very few, the philosophical theists" would merit divine favor because they "entertain or rather indeed endeavour to entertain, suitable notions of his divine perfections." Philosophical skeptics would be entitled to divine "compassion and indulgence" because of their "natural diffidence of their own capacity"[41] (all 12.32.Philo to Cleanthes).

Here, then, is Philo's view of religion: The great lot of religion—"popular" or "vulgar" religion—is rooted in, and yields, a melancholy frame of mind, drawing one away from the company of common life into the irrational beliefs of superstition and the irrational zeal of enthusiasm. Vulgar views of divinity (theology) are rooted in this irrational complex of mood and practice (piety). This is "false" religion, in contrast with the "true" religion of the philosopher, who maintains a morally adequate theology and an equable state of mind. But true religion is rare and false religion all too plentiful. For Philo, actual religion is so corrupted by superstition and enthusiasm that no religion is preferable to any religion at all.

Cleanthes and Philo do not differ a great deal on the nature of true (versus false) religion, and most of those differences are matters of degree. Their major disagreements are threefold: (1) How much true religion is there in proportion to false religion? (2) Does false religion have any redeeming features, such as supporting morality? (3) Is religion on the whole a good thing? The nature of these disagreements is unclear. Although Philo tends to see them as all-or-nothing issues, it is worth asking whether they also could be construed as matters of degree in the sense touted earlier by Philo (12.6–7). That is, (1) the relative proportion of true to false religion could be a matter

202 / Reading Hume's *Dialogues*

of "more or less," a higher or lower ration; (2) even false religion has *some* partially redeeming features; and (3) there are degrees of goodness and badness of religion. If this is the nature of their dispute, then Cleanthes and Philo can continue to argue about these subjects endlessly, even while maintaining their "company" and friendship. Also, such a discussion would be ripe for presentation as a dialogue—a "question of philosophy" that is "so obscure and uncertain" that "reasonable men may be allowed to differ, where no-one can reasonably be positive." Observing such discussion may well "afford an agreeable amusement" (PH.3–4).

¶33: Philo on natural theology

Having disposed of natural religious piety, Philo treats finally of natural theology in a famous paragraph that has spawned a host of interpretations. Philo first distills "the whole of natural theology" into "one simple" proposition, "*that the cause or causes of order in the universe probably bear some remote analogy to human intelligence*" (italics in the original). But before giving this proposition a very equivocal assent, Philo qualifies it heavily; these qualifications are italicized in the following summary, though not in the original:

(1) This distillation is what "*some* people *seem* to maintain."[42]
(2) What they seem to maintain is "one *simple*, though *somewhat ambiguous, at least undefined* proposition."
(3) This proposition is "that the *cause or causes* of order in the universe *probably* bear *some remote* analogy to human intelligence."[43]
(4) Assent to this proposition is subject to several qualifications:
    (a) the proposition is "*not capable of extension, variation, or more particular explication*"; that is, it does not ramify into a very extensive theology;
    (b) it "*affords no inference that affects human life, or can be the source of any action or forbearance*"; that is, there are no practical implications, no impact on piety;
    (c) the "*imperfect*" analogy extends to "human intelligence" but not "with *any appearance of probability,* to the other qualities of the mind."
(5) Assuming all three qualifications in (4), "the *most inquisitive, contemplative, and religious* man" can do nothing more than give "a *plain, philosophical* assent to the proposition" and "*believe*" that its support outweighs its objections.
(6) Even so, there will be "*some* astonishment" over the "greatness of the object: *Some* melancholy from its obscurity: *some* contempt of human reason, that it can give no solution *more satisfactory* with regard to so extraordinary and magnificent a question" (all 12.33.Philo to Cleanthes).

Clearly Philo is damning with extremely faint praise—or rather, disavowing with overqualified "assent." But what is his point? Is he condemning the whole of natural theology to irrelevance? Is he pointing out that his agreement with Cleanthes on natural theology is so slender, and so obscure, as to be practically meaningless? Is he reducing theism (*ad absurdum*) to atheism, or perhaps both theism and atheism to skepticism? Surprisingly, at this point in his last speech, the lengthy penultimate paragraph of the *Dialogues*, Philo himself ventures none of these rationales. Instead, he launches a famous (or infamous) appeal for revelation that is worth quoting at length:

> But believe me, CLEANTHES,[44] the most natural sentiment, which a well disposed mind will feel on this occasion, is a longing desire and expectation, that heaven would be pleased to dissipate, at least alleviate this profound ignorance, by affording some more particular revelation to mankind, and making discoveries of the nature, attributes, and operations of the divine object of our faith. A person, seasoned with a just sense of the imperfections of our natural reason, will fly to revealed truth with the greatest avidity: While the haughty dogmatist, persuaded, that he can erect a complete system of theology by the mere help of Philosophy, disdains any further aid and rejects this adventitious instructor. To be a philosophical sceptic is, in a man of letters, the first and most essential step towards being a sound, believing Christian. (12.33.Philo to Cleanthes)

Here Philo seems to abandon his "spirit of controversy" (12.1.Cleanthes to Philo) in order to urge a piety in tension with his earlier embrace of common life. He (rather proudly) contrasts his own humble skepticism about human theological capacities with Cleanthes' haughtily dogmatic (though modestly maintained) anthropomorphism and claims that only skepticism can prepare the way for a proper desire and hope for "some more particular revelation" (12.33.Philo to Cleanthes).

What on earth is going on in this paragraph? There are three major lines of interpretation:

First, taken at face value, Philo's philosophical skepticism pairs with his religious "mysticism": Human faculties of inquiry and comprehension are so limited, and theology's subject so immense, that we can neither comprehend nor begin to inquire into "the divine object." The best we can do is to remind ourselves of our necessary ignorance and to fervently hope that further knowledge of the divine be given to us by the deity. So skepticism about natural religion prepares the way for acceptance of revealed religion, that "adventitious instructor."

This straightforward interpretation has certain virtues: It does not require constant irony from Philo, and it connects with a long tradition of religious skepticism.[45] But the position it attributes to Philo seems radically unpalatable to the zealous foe of superstition and enthusiasm, for it entails admitting Demea into "the company" to proclaim his authoritarian views as a "more particular revelation" to be accepted entirely on faith. This is too high a price for Philo to pay: All his skepticism about rational natural theology would lead only to an embrace of irrational revealed theology.

Second, many want to view Philo as the "winner" or "hero" of the *Dialogues*;[46] they see this whole paragraph not as sincere confession of Philo's true beliefs but rather as ironic mockery of both Cleanthes and Demea. Philo's absurdly overqualified "simple" proposition, followed by his sudden and unexpected shift to revelation, are unsubtle indications that this whole speech is not to be taken at face value but in a contrary sense—his references to faith and revelation are merely "conventional and obviously insincere" (Boys Smith 1936). Philo really thinks the "one simple" proposition of natural theology is worthless for piety and uninteresting for theology. Moreover, his gesture toward "revelation" is empty, for he neither expects such revelation nor would he think we could rationally determine if we were in receipt of one. Philo's skepticism, therefore, is so thoroughgoing that it dissolves all theology, both natural and revealed, and likewise the two corresponding pieties. In short, skepticism destroys interest in *all* of religion.[47]

This interpretation makes considerable sense if one wants to identify Philo with Hume and claim that Hume is reacting against the severe Calvinism of his boyhood.[48] But there are severe difficulties: Why should Philo, who began Part 12 with a confession of sincerity to his intimate Cleanthes (12.2.Philo to Cleanthes), revert to irony at the end of Part 12 when he asks his longtime friend to "believe" him (12.33.Philo to Cleanthes)? Why would Philo deal this way not only with Cleanthes but also with Cleanthes' "pupil" Pamphilus, whose "education and instruction" Philo has been attempting to further all along (cf. 12.33)? What purpose could such heavy irony serve *within* the *Dialogues*?[49]

Third, Philo is neither opening the door to irrational revelation nor tossing religion out the window. His words do not drip with irony, but they are not completely straightforward either. Instead, while Philo speaks honestly and sincerely, he does not divulge all he believes. In particular, he does not develop a view of natural theology he shares with Cleanthes because they share a natural piety, including an "experimental" method, in their common life. Indeed, Cleanthes has already implicitly boiled down natural theology to the "one simple" proposition, by assiduous use of this empirical method, so all Philo has to do is point out its full implications. Philo, otherwise so critical, in the end has nothing negative to say about this method, because it harmonizes with his own understanding of reasoning as involving appeal to "common sense and experience" (1.9.Philo to Cleanthes and Demea). While Cleanthes thinks human reason can use this method to scale the heights of

Heaven, Philo has a dimmer view of "the weakness, blindness, and narrow limits of human reason" (1.3.Philo to Cleanthes and Demea). So Philo and Cleanthes differ on natural theology's results, not on its method.

Moreover, this disagreement in results is a matter of degree. The "one simple" proposition is about an *analogy* between "the cause or causes of order in the universe" and "human intelligence." The two friends agree on the analogy but see different degrees of likeness. Is the disagreement therefore a "merely verbal" dispute (cf. 12.6–7.Philo to Cleanthes)? Perhaps, though behind it lies a difference of perception. Philo sees certain features (chiefly differences) as more telling; Cleanthes sees others (chiefly resemblances) as more salient. All the facts are the same, and equally open to view, yet they are viewed differently; the "verbal" dispute tracks this difference in apprehension.

As to the "longing desire and expectation" for revelation (12.33.Philo to Cleanthes), again Philo need not be dissembling. He can truly want and await some particular revelation. But in doing so he need not surrender his rational capacity to scrutinize claimants. Learning about what transcends our finite capacities does not entail subverting those capacities. Philo's skeptical spirit is not checked at the door of the house of faith, and his closing recommendation of philosophical skepticism is a way of expressing his hope that skepticism will similarly take root in Pamphilus's character.[50]

In brief, despite all his cavils and objections to Cleanthes' arguments in earlier Parts, Philo has a natural theology of his own, and it is the same as Cleanthes' tepid theism—the "cause or causes of order in the universe" somewhat resemble human intelligence. Who would not hope to augment this meager knowledge with something more—if more could be received from the very thing one seeks to know? But amid his hopes, Philo can never surrender his skeptical bent, and there is no doubt that any putative revelation would receive from him as withering an examination of its credentials and content as he has given this day to the whole of natural theology.

Cleanthes and Philo, Pamphilus tells us, "pursued not this conversation much farther" (12.34.Pamphilus to Hermippus). Yet it is worth remembering how far they have already come: an inquiry into the whole of natural religion, both theology and piety. The "common life" these two intimates share both permits and encourages such wide-ranging and controverted conversation as enjoyment for themselves and as edification for youthful onlookers. They share a piety that seasons religion with reason, that places the highest value on moral conduct in society, and that is polite, civil, and refined.

¶34: Pamphilus reviews the whole

Pamphilus closes the *Dialogues* as he opened them, addressing to Hermippus some comments on the company.[51] He has been mightily impressed by "all the reasonings of that day" and feels compelled to "confess" a personal judgment based "upon a serious review of the whole."[52] In his personal view, "PHILO's principles are more probable than DEMEA's; but . . . those of CLEANTHES approach still nearer to the truth" (all 12.34.Pamphilus to Hermippus). Does this mean that Cleanthes has "won" the *Dialogues* after all? Not necessarily.

Most basically, we should question the presupposition that the dialogues are zero-sum competitions—whether for truth, for likelihood, or for allegiance—in which there are winners and losers. There are other, and more important, goals of human conversation, and Pamphilus has already indicated two of them: "study and society," or understanding and friendship, those "two greatest and purest pleasures of human life" (PH.4). Here the "winners" are those who understand and share intimacy, and the "losers" are those who do not or cannot participate in these great and pure pleasures. But neither understanding nor friendship are zero-sum competitions, and there is no requirement that anyone be excluded.

Of course there *are* argumentative competitions in the *Dialogues*. But Pamphilus is not necessarily their best judge. He is, after all, only an inexperienced youth. Moreover, he is the ward of Cleanthes, to whom he owes his education as "a man of letters." At the very least, he has learned the polite good sense of loyalty to one's mentor—and hence the need to judge publicly in his favor. So we have every reason to expect, and hence to suspect, Pamphilus's bias in favor of his guardian.

Third, we might question why Pamphilus's judgment should carry any more weight than those of the three principals in the *Dialogues*. Clearly, none of them would admit to "losing" the conversations. Although the note of "triumph" is lacking in Philo's speeches in Part 12, he speaks with such obvious assurance that he would doubtless claim that he has "won." Demea left the dialogues disgruntled, but more out of a sense of Philo's betrayal than of having lost an argument, so Demea wouldn't concede that he had "lost"—he might even think he had "won," or at least "won out," through surviving verbal persecution. Cleanthes is the most discrete of the trio, and he doesn't aggressively push his points by means of hard-edged arguments; yet he appears unshaken by all of Philo's brainstorms, so perhaps he has also "won" by virtue of steadfastly maintaining his "accurate" views to the end.

Finally, Pamphilus's judgment is not so much conclusion as provocation. Why does he award the palm of truth and probability to a man who has plainly lost most of the argumentative skirmishes in the book, if not perhaps the entire war? Who *does* come closest to the truth in these matters? To raise these questions is to continue the conversation Pamphilus has just recounted.[53] So we do well not to take Pamphilus's judgments as authoritative or conclusive, even though they are indeed the last words of the *Dialogues*. A discerning reader must decide for herself.

16

Conclusion

... its universal, its irresistible influences ...

—Cleanthes to Philo, Part 3.8

Many have tried to reduce the meaning of the *Dialogues* to a few straightforward points. All have failed. The work cannot be reduced, it can only be enlarged, because it is at once too complex and too unified, because it is an *organic unity*. All its subtle parts contribute to its complicated meaning, and none should be isolated or ignored. In particular, dialogic form is integral to natural religious content. The *Dialogues* is patently neither a bare string of positions nor a mother lode of arguments and refutations but rather a lively conversation, and conversational implications permeate and qualify the whole. All three characters' personalities and interactions provide not merely psychological intrigue and personal nuance but also philosophically interesting perspectives that shade everything and afford glimpses of penumbral forms of life.

Here is one more reason why no reading can displace its original: *Talking about* a harmony of form and content cannot substitute for *encountering* harmonized form and content. The *Dialogues* as a whole is like Cleanthes' design argument, in that it can work "its universal, its irresistible influence" even though it cannot be reduced to logically tidy form (3.8.Cleanthes to Philo). A respectful reading should not pursue a definitive interpretation but one that allows others to continue the conversation the text itself begins. In that light follow these concluding reflections on some important issues in the *Dialogues*.

1. Form, content, and hermeneutics

The literary form of the *Dialogues* is deeply ingredient in its philosophical content. A dialogue is wonderfully appropriate not only for "reciting" philosophical conversations on important but controversial and irresolvable questions such as natural religion but also for presenting views *in concreto,* as the beliefs, doubts, and fears of characters who approximate the complexity of real-life persons. By seeing how these characters variously hold, state, criticize, defend, and deflect various views and how these views connect with other things they hold dear, we learn of more than philosophical systems—we learn of life.

Moreover, written dialogues carry readers into conversation with the text in a particularly vital way, for we are constantly challenged not only by the ideas presented but also by the persons presenting those ideas. Modern philosophy can often seem distressingly remote and abstract—if not Hegel's "unearthly ballet of bloodless categories"[1] then a numbing swirl of numbered propositions or a playful pastiche of learned fragments. But absorption in a philosophical dialogue necessarily engages more concrete reflection—upon what others and oneself believe, to be sure, but also upon how one more fully relates to others, what moves one to act, and what form of life comports best with this reflection. The *Dialogues* both solicits and deserves such engagement.

To promote such engagement is a major reason why the present reading pursues an internal interpretation of the text. Too often writers on Hume are so concerned to defend some thesis or research program independently acquired and sustained that they fail to respond to the text as it actually functions on its own terms. This is a perverse form of reductionism, confining the full complexity of a text to some limited context. Here historicists are just as guilty as analysts. The latter, of course, aim to mine classic texts for propositions of current interest and have much less interest in how the text conveys its ideas on its own terms; analytic hermeneutics is reductive when it views its propositional mining operations as the only valid form of philosophical understanding. But historicism—planting works in their actual biographical and cultural milieus—also constricts a text by insisting that philosophical understanding remain within the ambit of historical significance. A truly philosophical spirit rebels, and rightly so, against either form of confinement.

Still, it might seem that an internal interpretation is equally confining, since it seems to truncate a text's context to itself. On the contrary:

(1) No interpretative approach, including an internal one, need be the only one. Let a hundred readings bloom; each insight may enrich all the others. Learning about how the issues appeared to Hume or to Hume's contemporaries, or how they may yield views precise and clear enough for current debate, can all be insightful—so long as no one of them seeks hermeneutical hegemony.

(2) Form and content are especially tightly connected in *this* text. Both

historicists and analysts fail to grapple with the full significance of this fact. Historicists think they have understood both form and content when the antecedents of the *Dialogues* are laid bare. Antecedents can indeed illuminate, but they cannot fully explain how form and content constitute a *particular* organic whole that conditions and qualifies both form and content. The *Dialogues* has something new to say on its own. Analysts, similarly, seek to extract the "philosophically interesting" content from its supposedly "incidental" literary form, but in ignoring the form they distort the content. An internal interpretation, however, is committed to letting the text speak for itself in all its ways of speaking—where actions, reactions, and character often speak louder than words and where words require above all a *speaker's* context. Letting a text speak for itself does not contract but expands its meaning.

(3) Any reading, but especially one with an internal hermeneutic, is a conversation with its text. When the text itself is a conversation, or set of conversations, then the reading becomes a *continuation* of a conversation. The reader is therefore no external observer but rather another character (and another *kind* of character) in an ongoing drama. Such engagement does not circumscribe the text but rather extends its significance by involving new views and new participants.

So the present reading takes note of both complex form and complicated content in the *Dialogues* as inextricable ingredients in its organic unity. Noticing and interrelating all these details is no infatuation with inessentials but an attempt to be faithful to the whole text, the text in its wholeness.

2. Authorship, irony, and Hume's intentions

Determining what David Hume means by the *Dialogues* has been a primary project of Hume scholarship for the last century. Often this quest has assumed the crude form of "Who speaks for Hume?" or "Who is Hume's mouthpiece?" or even "Who Is the Real Hume in the Dialogues?"[2] But there has been little examination of the premise behind this project—that the *Dialogues* actually were intended by Hume to express his own views via some character speaking directly or ironically. Given this premise, endless ingenuity has gone into discerning exactly what personal views Hume sought to convey in the *Dialogues*. This discernment may start either from outside the text (by first extracting Hume's undoubted personal views from more straightforward texts and then finding these views in the *Dialogues*) or from within the text (by first ascertaining which views win out and then affirming them as Hume's own views). But the mere fact that there is no generally agreed-upon outcome of this whole project should give one pause. Perhaps there is little consensus on who speaks for Hume (and on what, exactly, does he say) because of inattention to the dialogic form of the *Dialogues*.

Questions of meaning in and of a dialogue are complex. Simply listing the (putative) statements of each character ignores such vital considerations as why the character is saying this to that person (those persons) at this time, whether the character believes what he says, how and why he believes it, whether he wants others to believe that he believes it (and why), and how all these putative beliefs link up with the character's other beliefs, attitudes, desires, passions, commitments, projects, and relationships—in short, it ignores the inexhaustibly rich texture of life woven into the warp and weft of dramatic action. What a dialogue means is more than what it says; it is also what it shows and does—and what it gets a reader to think and see and do.

One misses far too much of what the *Dialogues* has to offer by relentlessly pursuing who speaks for Hume or its variants. Better to see where the *Dialogues* itself leads us. In speaking of natural religion, Demea, Cleanthes, and Philo offer to young Pamphilus not only views and arguments but also ways of life. Natural religion is far from being reducible to a set of natural theological propositions, much less to an epistemological meta-position about the availability of such propositions to human minds. Natural religion of course includes the well-cultivated field of natural theology, but it also includes the wilderness of natural piety. That is why the vastly different lives of Demea, Cleanthes, and Philo are very much on view. Which of our pieties do you find most attractive, the characters implicitly solicit: the fearful and fearsome authoritarianism of Demea, the sunny and unexamined "dogmatism" of Cleanthes, or the sifting and homeless "skepticism" of Philo? Of course, a reader may very well demur: "I choose none of the above; each character is inadequate, but they do not exhaust the options." Even so, one may stand to learn from this limited range of fragile views, flawed characters, and deficient forms of life.

Further, abandoning the misguided quest for Hume's mouthpiece can alter our appreciation of irony in the *Dialogues*. Irony as incongruity between what is straightforwardly said or done and its hidden significance is a handy but much-abused tool for construing a text that appears to say the opposite of what one thinks it ought to say.[3] Irony is a favorite hermeneutic tool of external interpreters of the *Dialogues*. When, for example, Philo several times in Part 12 voices his acceptance of the design argument (12.2–4, 12.6, 12.8, 12.33), someone who is antecedently convinced that Philo is Hume's mouthpiece and that Hume is an atheist, naturalist, or skeptic who gives no credence at all to design arguments must find some non-straightforward way of interpreting Philo's words, and irony is all too convenient. Philo does not really believe in natural design, they say, but is only teasing Cleanthes and placating Hume's eighteenth-century readers.[4]

It is important to distinguish two kinds of irony, one internal to a text and another external to it. Since irony is always *someone's* irony, *internal irony* belongs to one or another character within the text (internal narrator, character, etc.), while *external irony* belongs to someone outside the text (author, critic, reader). Internal irony does occur occasionally in the *Dialogues*. It is present, for example, in the way Philo sometimes talks to Demea, enlisting his participation with words superficially appealing to Demea but for ends that Philo and Cleanthes, though not Demea, recognize are contrary to Demea's deeper purposes. Such internal irony is signaled by one or more of the characters, and it does not require the superior perspicacity of an external observer. External irony, however, requires an onlooker who detects a subterranean meaning unremarked by *any* character. Typically, but not necessarily, the ironic interpreter thinks he is merely following the author's lead.

Many interpreters of the *Dialogues* form some view of what Hume believed and then run up against passages apparently maintaining something contrary. They then discount the discourse's face value; discern a hidden, more palatable meaning below the surface; and proclaim an instance of irony. E. C. Mossner is only blunter than most Humean ironists, not different in method, when he claims that there is a "veil of irony and delusion deliberately thrown over the *Dialogues* as a whole" (Mossner 1936, 348); indeed, he says, "irony is an indispensable factor of the Dialogues and holds, in truth, the key to its basic teachings" (Mossner 1977, 2). Mossner also differs from most in insisting magisterially that detecting this veil of irony requires "intimate knowledge of the mind of the author, as seen through *all* his publications, and of his character, his personality, as further seen through his correspondence, his autobiography, his unpublished papers, and possibly his biography" (Mossner, 1977, 12–13; emphasis in original).

Now Mossner is undoubtedly right that if one reads the *Dialogues* as Hume's recitation of his own opinions, with some character (typically Philo) as his chosen mouthpiece, then one will have to make liberal use of irony to make much sense of the text.[5] But such external irony is anathema to an internal interpretation, for it fundamentally distrusts the text. It uses something outside the text as a touchstone for reliable interpretation of the text, and it entails that a careful reader who attends only to the text itself can at best discern merely superficial significance—since what seems straightforward (or even ironical) within the text may nonetheless have an externally ironical undertow that only someone with "intimate knowledge of the mind of the author" can espy but yet that carries everything in its wake.

Of course, the external ironists may be right—after all, there are so many of them. But note that the plausibility of their irony rests on "intimate knowledge" of Hume's mind, not only in the form of general beliefs about the subject matter at hand but also in the form of *his particular intentions for this text*:

It rests on the assumption that Hume intended the *Dialogues* to convey and inculcate his own beliefs above all other purposes and that he intended to do so by putting these views into the mouth of one or another of the characters in the conversation. But there are other ways to think about Hume's particular intentions, and some of them, I would hold, are at least as plausible as the standard version. Here is one such way congruent with the present reading:

Perhaps Hume genuinely thought that natural religion was so deeply perplexing, so ultimately unfathomable by human thought, that rather than enforcing his own views on the subject he chiefly wanted to stimulate thought on the part of his readers. Perhaps Hume wanted an intelligent reader not so much to agree or disagree with *any* of the characters as rather to think hard for herself about these hard subjects. Perhaps Hume was himself more comfortable ranging over the *whole* logical space traversed by *all* his characters (or at least that homesteaded by Philo and Cleanthes) than settling down in only one of their particular territories. Perhaps, that is, Hume himself would above all have liked—and would want his readers—to inhabit a community of discourse that permits, enables, and even inspires a conversation such as his characters conduct without being forced in the end to take any one, much less all, of the positions they actually maintain.[6]

The *Dialogues,* therefore, may in fact be exactly what the title says: dialogues, not something in "the methodical and didactic manner" (PH.1). That is, they may be designed *not* to instruct us about Hume's views, much less to convince us of those views, but rather to engage us in a conversation that begins with overhearing (like Pamphilus), moves us into a set of discussions (like Cleanthes, Demea, and Philo), and continues with further reflection (like the present reading).[7] Perhaps, then, the *Dialogues* is not a didactic account of Hume's views but an artful effort to stimulate thoughtful reflection by Hume's readers about natural religion and their own ways of viewing and living it. In this way the form of the *Dialogues* would be much more ingredient in its meaning than external ironists have believed, and an internal interpretation of the text to that extent would be much more apposite.

3. Natural theology

The *Dialogues* brims with natural theology, but its detailed "hypotheses," "proofs," and "cavils" are best considered as each arises in the course of the discussion, and this we have already done. Here we consider how the text resolves two large issues in natural theology—teleology and true religion.

a. Teleology:

Teleology etymologically is the *logos* of *telos,* the logic of purpose or ends. It is understood quite differently by the three main characters, Cleanthes, Philo, and Demea.

For Cleanthes, teleology—especially natural teleology outside of human contrivance—lies at the heart of the design argument(s). Cleanthes' fundamental strategy is to move by analogy from recognition of natural teleology to the likely character of its "Author." Further, since all natural theology is "experimental," and since our best or only evidence from experience is teleological in nature, it follows that for Cleanthes without natural teleology there would be no natural theology, or none worth crediting.

Cleanthes recognizes teleology everywhere in nature, in the whole and in all its parts. "Look round the world," he appeals to Philo. "Contemplate the whole and every part of it" (2.5.Cleanthes to Philo). For him "the similarity of the works of nature to those of art" is "self-evident and undeniable" (3.1.Cleanthes to Philo), and all you have to do is to consider any of those works and "the idea of a contriver" will "immediately flow in upon you with a force like that of sensation" (3.7.Cleanthes to Philo). In the view of Cleanthes, everyone (including Philo) has a natural teleological sense, an ability (probably innate) to discern purpose and design in anything, if one observes it under the proper conditions. These conditions include such obvious factors as turning one's undivided attention to the object in question but also having an open mind not constricted by skeptical (Philo) or pious (Demea) blinders. Cleanthes holds that our natural teleological sense is a recognition of teleological reality, not a projection of human purpose or a fond imagining. For him, natural teleology is an actual property of natural things, not a property of our understanding of nature; we cannot help seeing teleology everywhere simply because it *is* everywhere and we are naturally equipped to discern its ubiquitous presence.

Recognition of natural teleology is rationally defensible only in a limited sense. There are no more primitive data from which, by "regular" logical rules, we can infer natural teleology; we either sense it or we do not, and if we do not sense it there is no argument that can substitute. The best one can do for those who do not notice natural teleology is to stimulate their inherent teleological sense or to direct their attention to its unavoidable operation.

Moreover, the teleology Cleanthes finds so pervasive has a certain character: It is not only intelligible, it is also friendly to us. Abstractly, of course, one could recognize the presence of purpose without understanding what that purpose is[8] or whether that purpose is on our behalf. But Cleanthes thinks all three properties (purpose, intelligibility, friendliness) are found throughout nature, in sufficient degree to permit us to infer plausible and comforting theological hypotheses: The Author of Nature is like us when we make things (contrivances, artifices, machines) for our own benefit.

Cleanthes can seem incredibly naive in his trust of our teleological sense. There are red flags waving on all sides: Philo warns him more than once of our excessive propensity to see, or rather to invent, order and purpose in everything, from the human uses of plants and animals to faces in the clouds. Modern science since Galileo has resolutely turned its back on teleological forms of explanation as not invoking "true causes" which are rather efficient or mechanical causes. Darwinian absolutists such as Daniel Dennett think they can explain how adopting an intentional stance to detect and predict the behavior of complex structures (not least other humans) might be evolutionarily useful and then explain how this stance might be used indiscriminately beyond its proper bounds.[9] Postmoderns find teleology itself a human construct, imposed on (our idea of) nature and ingredient only in the reality we conspire, in service of powerful interests, to create.[10] Against these powerful critiques, is there anything to say on Cleanthes' behalf? I believe there is.

First, there is a very widespread human tendency—close to a universal human disposition—to perceive teleology. For better or worse, we do, nearly all of us, most of the time, have a natural teleological sense. Our best option is not to deny this sense's existence or to seek to extirpate it from our apprehension of the world but rather to examine carefully its products and to use them cautiously.

Second, the reliability of this teleological sense in the realm of human affairs is extremely high, and no normal member of human society believes otherwise. Humans are very good at discerning when other humans behave teleologically, and we have an enormous vocabulary devised to discriminate among actions that are voluntary, intentional, deliberate, willing, witting, purposive, thoughtful, mindful, and the like. Such acuity is so useful to us because it is so accurate, even if that accuracy is not absolute.

Third, we often reliably extend our teleological sense beyond human behavior to objects and events we consider to be the effects of human purpose. We can normally successfully judge not only when some person is acting purposively but also when a complex object or event is (likely to be) the product of unobserved human purposive behavior.

Fourth, as Cleanthes' bizarre examples of the voice from the clouds and the vegetative library suggest, we trust our sense of teleology even when the object or event cannot be attributed to *human* purpose. We are confident we can recognize at least the existence of alien purpose, even when we cannot quite discern what that purpose is or how it is disposed toward us. Perhaps such confidence is unwarranted—it is possible, after all, that an alien intelligence might baffle our understanding, or even our recognition—but few would allow such skeptical possibilities to undermine greatly, much less to displace, our ordinary trust in our teleological sense.

Fifth, and most controversially, *if* there is a God who has designed and created the world, and if His purposes are not only present in the world but (occasionally and in part) accessible to us through faculties we naturally possess, then a sense of divine teleology may be reliable. If there is a divine purpose in the world written in a code we can (partially) recognize and decipher, then it is at least possible that some people apprehend that purpose. But Cleanthes wants more than this; he wants perception of divine purpose to count as *evidence* for the nature (and existence) of God, and here he seems to reverse logical priorities. It is not that recognition of divine purpose provides the basis for inference to God, but rather that, given belief in God, one can discern divine purpose in the world—one interprets or sees the world as containing divine purposes, as God's handiwork.[11] In brief, to extend a point of Philo's (10.35), while Cleanthes' natural teleology is *compatible* with his theism, it does not provide *evidence* for it. As a result, a sense for natural teleology cannot be all there is to a rationally defensible theology.

Much of what *Philo* has to say is deconstructive, designed to shake Cleanthes' confidence in his natural teleological sense. Among the various "inconveniences" he points out are a religiously dangerous anthropomorphism, explanatory impotence, a demotion of divine attributes, and a blinkered failure to canvass even a few of the many other possible analogies. But having poured all this critical acid on the design argument, Philo does not in the end forsake teleology altogether. In Part 12, he repeatedly confesses his own inability to avoid natural teleological apprehension: "No-one has a deeper sense of religion impressed on his mind," confides Philo to Cleanthes, "or pays more profound adoration to the divine Being, as he discovers himself to reason, in the inexplicable contrivance and artifice of nature" (12.2).

The key word, of course, is "inexplicable." Does Philo here ironically retract everything he seems so plainly to admit? On the contrary, Philo, like Cleanthes, cannot prevent himself from seeing the world as the "contrivance and artifice" of some powerful intelligent maker, even though he differs from Cleanthes in two crucial respects: (1) Whereas Cleanthes sees great similarity between human and divine "contrivance," Philo sees very little—some, but not very much. In short, the two intimates disagree over the *degree* of similarity, and this dispute, they agree, is intractable; there is no way for one friend to justify his position convincingly to the other, so each position is "inexplicable" to the other. (2) Philo is attracted to a different kind of divine purpose than Cleanthes when it comes to the "moral" attributes. Whereas Cleanthes thinks the phenomena of the world support divine benevolence, Philo thinks it is more probable that "the first causes of the universe . . . have neither goodness nor malice [i.e., that they are indifferent]" (11.15.Philo to Cleanthes and Demea).[12] What the Author of Nature's purpose is, and whether it is friendly, is "inexplicable" to us.

So it is not that Philo lacks a natural teleological sense or that in using this sense he perceives no purpose in the world. When he is not playing the role of skeptic, Philo is neither a complete atheist nor a pure naturalist but rather a natural theist. But what kind of God does Philo discern? Philo thinks such purpose as he can make out bears scant resemblance to human purpose (it is barely intelligible to us) and is in fact considerably closer to human indifference than to human benevolence (it does not seem at all friendly toward us). His theism therefore is a deism that is extremely "attenuated,"[13] "minimal,"[14] or even "anaemic."[15]

Demea professes disinterest in argument by analogy and in experimental religion in general. But he is blind to the ways in which his God—so powerful, awesome, demanding, and arbitrary—mirrors and resembles himself, as seen through a pious haze that transmutes difference in degree into difference in kind. When he uses the language of mysticism to exalt his deity above all human apprehension, Demea is still busily thinking in human-all-too-human terms, projecting his hopes and (mostly) fears onto his God.

Likewise Demea only *seems* uninterested in natural teleology. That is chiefly because Cleanthes' teleology implies recognizable (and friendly) purpose, while Demea claims the deity is inscrutable. But Demea's motives bear watching. It is not that Demea has had some compelling personal experience of the divine immensity that overwhelms into reverent silence; rather, he instinctively seeks to defend himself while describing his deity. The issue basically is one of power and control. If humans understand something, they can find ways to manipulate it to their advantage. The best way to safeguard power from human manipulation is to keep it hidden, and the more securely hidden the better—at the extreme, what cannot be comprehended cannot be controlled at all. But at the same time, divine mystery is a powerful tool for mystifying and controlling humans. Demea's God is powerfully inscrutable, and all one can do is to submit; likewise Demea himself has, or seeks, a dominating position among others who will unquestioningly obey his own powerful will.

So even Demea thinks teleologically (as all humans must, according to Cleanthes). His apparent disdain for natural teleology masks a deeper teleological interest—neither the friendly comfort descried by Cleanthes nor the cold indifference discerned by Philo but rather the essentially masked countenance of power. Demea does see the world in terms of purpose, even though the purposes of his overwhelmingly powerful deity are accountable only as unconditional demands for submission.

b. True Religion:

All three characters are vitally interested in true religion, but they do not agree on what it is, or on why it is valuable, or to whom.

Demea displays a "rigid inflexible orthodoxy," in the view of Hermippus

(PH.6), but his rigidity and inflexibility are much more apparent than his orthodoxy. Right at the outset of Part 1, Demea announces his interest in religion with a disconcerting *lack* of concern for truth or even for content: "To season their [his children's] minds with early piety is my chief care; and by continual precept and instruction, and I hope too, by example, I imprint deeply on their tender minds an habitual reverence for all the principles of religion." Demea's focus is on "*early* piety," "imprint *deeply*," and "*habitual* reverence": His idea is to impress "all the principles of religion" so firmly into the tender character of those under his power that they will never lose those principles. But which principles? For Demea, it is far more important to stamp a certain cast of mind than to inculcate any particular content; his chief concern is to "[tame] their mind to a proper submission and self-diffidence." True religion is not primarily a system, or even a disordered set, of true theological propositions; in fact, theology for Demea consists only of "the greatest mysteries," surpassing human ken (all 1.2.Demea to Philo and Cleanthes). What matters to him is a disposition of mind—utter submissiveness—and not its contents.

Insofar as Demea does dabble in theology, it is a confused and shifting display. On the one hand, he stubbornly clings to divine mystery, inaccessible to any native human capacity (2.1, 3.11), in order to protect the holiness and worshipfulness of God (6.1), or at least to ensure the proper attitudes of humility and reverence in us. Protecting such divine mystery is Demea's reason for his illusory temporary alliance with Philo against Cleanthes. But mystery is a dangerous refuge. Strictly speaking, mystery entails silence and undercuts any efforts to support orthodoxy: Where no beliefs at all are proper, "right belief" (i.e., "orthodoxy") is meaningless. It is "profaneness" and "temerity" to "pry" into the divine "nature and essence, decrees and attributes" (2.1). Such a judgment is the death knell of natural theology as well as of orthodoxy, for on its premise any "true religion" must be either natural piety (moral common life) or revealed religion (theological beliefs and practice somehow "given" to humans). Demea lacks the former and can only retreat to the latter; but what he would say in the latter's defense is not at all clear. Perhaps he would not even see that it needs defense.

On the other hand, Demea does proffer various kinds of arguments (ad hominem, appeal to authority, *a priori*, personal confession of feeling) that are uniformly weak and mutually inconsistent in support of various views that look at first glance to be vaguely orthodox: for example, for the "being of God, against the cavils of atheists and infidels" (2.1); the infinity and perfection of God (2.2); the "ineffable sublimity of the divine attributes" (3.13); the denial of "anthropomorphism" (3.12, 4.2, 11.18); the "perfect immutability and simplicity" of God (4.2); "the INFINITY of the divine attributes"

(9.1); the necessary existence of God (9.3); a sense of human "imbecility and misery" that drives us to seek "atonement" (10.1); divine providence (10.29); and, overarching all, the assurance of certitude (9.1). Defending all this Demea takes to be a "holy cause" (11.18), and he has only enmity and contempt for those who would oppose him.

But whether these views are orthodox seems not to trouble Demea. What matters to him is that these views be *authoritative,* in two senses: (1) commanding the complete and utter assent of believers, and (2) held on authority —putatively the authority of God, but also the authority of men like Demea. Investing these views with a semblance of high holiness, Demea wants Pamphilus, like his own children, not to understand but to accept; accepting these views is not so much believing *truth* as believing *him.* Here is the heart of "true religion" for Demea: It essentially consists in a certain form of piety, a life of submission and (especially) domination. Theological doctrines and arguments are measured by their utility in bolstering such piety, and their truth is incidental. True religion is unquestioning commitment to a basically coercive and fearful way of life, and theology is merely its properly submissive handmaiden.

At first glance, *Cleanthes* has a similarly utilitarian view of true religion, even if his religion is kinder and gentler. "The proper office of religion," he holds, "is to regulate the heart of men, humanize their conduct, infuse the spirit of temperance, order, and obedience" (12.12). Since these practical ends are so preeminent, and since religion is such an important and necessary means to these ends, it follows that religion is to be embraced whatever its defects: "Religion, however corrupted, is still better than no religion at all" (12.10). Further, religion, at least "genuine theism," is not only "the chief, the only great comfort in life" but also "the most agreeable reflection, which it is possible for human imagination to suggest" (12.24).

But "true religion" for Cleanthes, in addition to shoring up moral piety, does have that theological content he calls "genuine theism." Genuine theism

> represents us as the workmanship of a Being perfectly good, wise, and powerful; who created us for happiness, and who, having implanted in us immeasurable desires of good, will prolong our existence to all eternity, and will transfer us into an infinite variety of scenes, in order to satisfy those desires, and render our felicity complete and durable. Next to such a Being himself . . . the happiest lot which we can imagine, is that of being under his guardianship and protection. (12.24.Cleanthes to Philo)

Interestingly, few of these doctrines have been supported by Cleanthes during the course of the *Dialogues.* He has indeed argued for the existence of a good, wise, and powerful Being who has made us and all of nature and under whose guardianship and protection we may find comfort and security. But he has also seen that "perfectly" is unsupported on experimental grounds (hence his unclear tender of a "finitely perfect" deity in 11.1), and so is any indication of a purpose for which the Author of Nature has made us; in particular, evidence is totally lacking for both our longing for infinite and eternal felicity and divine satisfaction of this longing. At best, Cleanthes has made out an experimental case for only part of the "genuine theism" he favors, and his utilitarian or functional defense of religion in Part 12 is entirely too sketchy.

So "true religion" stands on two legs, according to Cleanthes: It is both experimentally warranted and practically useful (or even necessary). One suspects, however, that utility is more important than warrant. Cleanthes' ultimate commitment—that is, his *religious* commitment—is not to religion but to what religion properly serves: "to regulate the heart of men, humanize their conduct, infuse the spirit of temperance, order, and obedience, . . . [to enforce] the motives of morality and justice" (12.12). Clearly Cleanthes is a decent man, a reasonable, polite, sensible, gentle man; whether he is also a *Christian* gentleman is less clear.[16] Regardless of his particular religious affiliation, he is religious most fundamentally not because he is overcome by God's presence in the world but because he seeks to shore up his convivial and comfortable existence. Cleanthes is a pragmatic theist before he is an evidential deist.

Philo's view of true religion initially seems "still more incurably ambiguous" (12.7.Philo to Cleanthes). In Part 1, he claims that "no-one has a deeper sense of religion impressed on his mind" than he (1.2), and he seems to commend religion while condemning "this profane and irreligious age" (1.3); but at the same time he disparages the malign influences of "priestcraft" (1.19; cf. 11.20) and alleges "great and insuperable difficulties" for "all religious systems" or theologies (8.12). While allying himself with Demea in magnifying the transcendent mystery of God (2.3; cf. 1.3, 1.10; 2.15; 5.6), he seems equivocal in such comments as "the best and indeed the only method of bringing every one to a due sense of religion is by just representations of the misery and wickedness of men" (10.2). So it is hard to fathom his true and complete views over the first eleven Parts, while Demea is present. But in Part 12, when he is at last able to speak his mind directly to Cleanthes, it turns out that Philo has a fairly complex understanding of religion. He has "ever cherished and maintained," he says, both a "veneration for true religion" and an equal "abhorrence of vulgar superstitions" (12.9).

The true religion Philo venerates certainly includes theology—some version of the attenuated theism he shares with Cleanthes and explicates in 12.6–8 and 12.32–33—but theology is only the intellectual veneer of true religion. Religion includes piety as well as theology, and Philo agrees with

Cleanthes that "the proper office of religion is to regulate the heart of men" (12.12.Cleanthes to Philo). But Philo also thinks that true religion in fact regulates very few hearts—only those of "the philosophical and rational kind" (12.13.Philo to Cleanthes; cf. 12.22). Such rare individuals "entertain or rather indeed endeavor to entertain, suitable notions of his divine perfections" but do not present God as "a capricious demon, who exercises his power without reason and without humanity" (12.32.Philo to Cleanthes). The pure religion espoused by true philosophers "represents the Deity to be pleased with nothing but virtue in human behavior" (12.15.Philo to Cleanthes), and true philosophers endeavor to live in conformity to that representation—that is, to live virtuously as measured by "the natural motives of justice and humanity" expressed in common life (12.16.Philo to Cleanthes). True religion is for the few who are intelligent enough to conceive deity properly (a difficult task, in light of the limited evidence and our weak faculties) and self-controlled enough to allow religious piety only to reinforce, never to divert or undermine, common morality. True religion is as rare as it is commendable.

In most people, other forces are at work, and the results are unlovely: Their "vulgar superstitions" produce bigotry (12.9; 12.15), dissimulation and hypocrisy (12.17), selfishness (12.19), general resistance to the soothing principles of morality (12.16, 20), and "pernicious consequences on public affairs" (12.11, 21). For most people, superstitious beliefs combine with frenzied zeal to produce all the religious excesses so prominent in the historical record. While the true religion of true philosophers may be "most engaging and alluring" (12.25), the actual religion of the masses is the opposite of alluring—it is the fount of "endless disputes, quarrels, factions, persecutions, and civil commotions" (12.21).

Philo's primary example of a "vulgar superstition" with pernicious consequences is none other than Cleanthes' proffered bulwark of morality—belief in "the doctrine of a future state" (12.10). For Philo, this doctrine is rife with "dismal consequences" (12.11). Indeed, Philo declares a bit later, "There never was a popular religion which represented the state of departed souls in such a light, as would render it eligible for human kind, that there should be such a state" (12.28). The very thought of Hell is morally repugnant, and brooding "upon the terrors of the invisible world" plunges one into melancholy and dejection, rendering one unfit "for business or company or entertainment of any kind"—in short, unfit for any normal conduct of common life (12.29). But relief is scarcely better than the angst it supplants: The "cheerful prospects of futurity" promote "the other extreme of joy and triumph," but this exuberance is only a transitory respite before further "fits of superstitious terror and dejection." Not peace and equanimity but "gloom and melancholy" are "so remarkable in all devout people" (12.30).

So most religion—for most people, most of the time—is a bad thing, according to Philo, bad not only in its slipshod and repellant theology but most especially in its disturbing and destructive piety. True religion is both possible and desirable, but it is rare, and it exhausts itself supporting moral virtue.

How does Philo differ from Cleanthes? As we have seen, their theologies vary only by degrees, but what about their overall assessment of religion? There is more agreement than meets the eye. For both, true religion is a matter of non-superstitious (i.e., empirically supported) theology in pious support of common morality. Moreover, both profess to "venerate" true religion, wherever it may be found. Their disagreements lie in two areas: (1) how much of actual religion is true religion, and (2) whether actual religion, containing both true and false religion, is, all things considered, a good thing, "better than no religion at all," as Cleanthes puts it (12.10). Not surprisingly, both disagreements involve questions of degree.

On the first issue, Cleanthes, as usual, is more sanguine than Philo. He thinks that most religion is true religion, or at least more is true religion than Philo credits.[17] This conviction is largely based on religion's consequences. He focuses on "the doctrine of a future state" but doubtless believes other religious doctrines have a similar effect: "so strong and necessary a security to morals, that we never ought to abandon or neglect it." Religion's support for morality cannot be duplicated by any other human institution, and this great positive effect outweighs whatever evils religion engenders, though again Cleanthes thinks these evils are exaggerated by Philo. Philo, of course, has a contrary view, focusing on the "pernicious consequences" of actual religion, not only in the public sphere (12.11) but also in personal motivation and integrity (12.15–19). He denies that religious doctrines have much influence on human conduct, and when influential they rarely have the good effects Cleanthes claims (12.20–21). Most, if not quite all, of actual religion—"religion, as it has commonly been found in the world" (12.22)—is not true religion. So the issue between Cleanthes and Philo boils down to this: *How much* of actual religion is true religion? And their answers differ as "more or less"—a matter of degree.

On the second issue, Cleanthes warns Philo not to let his "zeal against false religion to undermine your veneration for the true" (12.24.Cleanthes to Philo), and he is willing to support even defective religion: "Religion, however corrupted, is still better than no religion at all" (12.10.Cleanthes to Philo). Philo, on the other hand, thinks actual religion on the whole has "pernicious consequences" for society and individuals alike; so no religion is better than some religion (of the actual sort). But once again the differences between Philo and Cleanthes are less than first appear. Cleanthes would not support a religion that did not increase adherence to common morality; he just thinks that the "proper office of religion" is by and large its actual performance. He does not deny that there are pernicious effects of religion but downplays their frequency relative to the welcome moral undergirding. Once again the disagreement is a matter of degree: Actual religion provides more (Cleanthes) or less (Philo) support for morality and less (Cleanthes) or more (Philo) disruption in society.

Since these disagreements are matters of degree, the friends agree that they cannot be rationally settled. But this meta-agreement is based more on intuition than on argument: When one inspects the full sweep of human affairs, *does* religion produce more good than evil? Cleanthes accentuates the positive, Philo the negative, but neither makes a serious effort to collect *all* the evidence, to think about how to weigh the positive and negative together, or to look at things from the other's perspective. The question of the overall value of religion is as irresolvable to Cleanthes and Philo as those other great questions in the *Dialogues*: whether the world is more like a human contrivance than an internally necessitated mechanism and whether good or evil predominates in the world.

4. Natural piety

Too often in philosophical writings the beliefs and arguments at stake seem utterly divorced from any form of life beyond scholarly disputation (if, indeed, scholarly disputation *is* a form of life). Propositions are carefully formulated and elaborate arguments and subtle refutations concocted, all with only the barest hand-waving about how accepting these propositions and arguments matters to anyone's life. But the *Dialogues* has a better way: It shows us how in natural religion the kind of concern one has for belief and argument intertwines with the kind of life one is concerned to live—in short, it portrays how theology and piety are intimately related.

In fact, piety is closer to the bone than theology for all the characters in the *Dialogues*; it is the core of everyone's "veneration for true religion" (12.9.Philo to Cleanthes). Yet the piety natural to Demea differs profoundly from that natural to Philo and Cleanthes. All agree that natural piety is rooted in a sense of radical dependence, an apprehension that all things, especially oneself, are contingent for their existence, character, and prosperity on other things—ultimately on divine things. But this common sense of creatureliness develops in strikingly different directions.

For Demea, creatureliness is a dismal and frightening lot. His initial instinct, "from a consciousness of his imbecility and misery, rather than from any reasoning," is "to seek protection from that Being, on whom he and all nature are dependent." Our present life is so uncertain and beyond our control that only "futurity is still the object of all our hopes and fears." All that we can presently do is to struggle "to appease those unknown powers, whom we find, by experience, so able to afflict and oppress us. Wretched creatures that we are!" (all 10.1.Demea to Philo and Cleanthes). This is a heartfelt cry of anguish. Demea is terrified to the core by the human condition, and his only hope lies far beyond us, in the unmerited and arbitrary gift of future bliss by superior powers. Out of his fundamental fear of present contingency grows his twinned hope and fear of futurity, and his entire theology and praxis are grounded in his frightened reaction to fundamental contingency. Demea's fearful natural religious piety issues in a coercive, hierarchical, authoritarian church that chiefly values "submission and self-diffidence" in its members (1.2.Demea to Philo and Cleanthes).

Demea's passion-driven piety seeks certitude in theology, an absolutely unshakeable conviction of the truth of some position definite enough to divide the sheep (his co-religionists) from the goats ("the greatest libertines and infidels" [11.18.Demea to Philo]). Anything less than complete certitude inordinately threatens Demea, and he will make any kind of appeal that reinforces his beliefs in the eyes of others or himself. He seeks reassurance that he is right and others wrong. That is why Demea is so attracted to the argument *a priori*—not because he finds it intrinsically interesting or convincing, and certainly not because he has a mind at all adequate to its subtleties, but rather because he covets its promised finality. He would like a precise proof of his piety, and he cannot tolerate divergent views. If he can persuade himself that he is certain, then (he thinks) he must be certainly right, and if he is certainly right, then all who disagree must be certainly wrong—wrong not only if they believe contrary to Demea, or withhold his beliefs, but wrong also if they believe what Demea believes with less than Demea's invincible certitude. It is part of Demea's "enthusiasm" to conflate certainty and truth: If a religious view is not certain it cannot be true, and if it is certain it must be true. Demea's authoritarian piety is reinforced by his theology of certitude.

Cleanthes and Philo share a very similar piety, they embrace the same form of theology, and these sharings are connected. Natural theology for them is not a sui generis kind of thinking but rather a familiar form of experimental reasoning, moving from the experience of teleology via principles of analogy to an Author of Nature. Of course they differ on the strength of the analogy between the presumed Author of Nature and a human artificer,[18] but this is a difference of degree, not a difference in kind, and their underlying agreements on the nature of theology ensure that their subsequent disagreements over degree will not rupture their friendship. Likewise, they both tolerate disagreement with each other because they are both comfortable with arguments that are irredeemably merely likely and hence uncertain to some degree. It is important to see that these various commitments are inter-connected. Their acceptance of the design argument, their agreement that teleological disputes are differences of degree, and their tolerance of ambiguity and uncertainty all dovetail, and this fit is at the heart of their common piety. Their friendship, in a civil and sociable common life, is reinforced by their views about God, the world, and themselves, as well as by their views about such views.

For Cleanthes, the highest power on which we depend is not an alien power afflicting and oppressing us, but rather a benevolent guardian and protector, who "created us for happiness" and will "render our felicity complete and durable" in a future life. True religion is "the chief, the only great comfort in life; and our principal support amidst all the attacks of adverse fortune" (all 12.24.Cleanthes to Philo). The proper response to our contingent status therefore is not fearful insecurity but trusting confidence. Cleanthes' natural piety not only provides assurance of future felicity, it also furthers present propriety by infusing that "spirit of temperance, order, and obedience" (12.12.Cleanthes to Philo) so useful to the kind of tolerant, civil, and peaceful community Cleanthes treasures.[19]

Philo's piety is more clouded than Cleanthes', though still not anywhere near Demea's frightened anguish. Philo worries that the hope for pleasant futurity may undermine commitment here and now to common human sentiments of "justice and humanity" (12.16.Philo to Cleanthes), and he clearly thinks that the religious piety the "Divine Being" would reward is possessed by only "a very few, the philosophical theists" (12.32.Philo to Cleanthes).

But Philo cannot affirm Cleanthes' sunny theology, for he is terminally conscious of the deep infirmities of human insight. For Philo, skepticism is not only a clear-eyed view of human capacity, it is also his instinctive reaction upon all claims that venture beyond common life and ordinary experience. In a sense, Philo is even more aware of human contingency than either Demea or Cleanthes, for he senses the limitations of our *understanding* of our situation, which prevents us from seeing deeply into our other dependencies. Philo may speculate that such self-reflective consciousness of contingency entitles skeptics to particular divine "compassion and indulgence" (12.32.Philo to Cleanthes), but in the end his skepticism must also infect this speculation about the religious value of speculation, preventing it from becoming even a modest hope like Cleanthes'.

So Philo's natural piety must remain in skeptical suspension, lacking not only hope and fear but also all conviction, unless and until it should be rescued by some power beyond human capacity to discern. That is why Philo alone of all the characters in the *Dialogues* voices the desire—and I believe it is a heartfelt, sincere desire—to transcend natural religion:

Believe me, CLEANTHES, the most natural sentiment, which a well disposed mind will feel on this occasion [seeing the poverty of natural religion], is a longing desire and expectation, that heaven would be pleased to dissipate, at least alleviate this profound ignorance, by affording some more particular revelation to mankind. . . . A person, seasoned with a just sense of the imperfections of natural reason, will fly to revealed truth with the greatest avidity. (12.33.Philo to Cleanthes)

This desire is, however, "the most natural sentiment" not for Demea (whose instinct is angst, and who would fear a "more particular revelation" as much as he fears the more general revelation of natural contingency) or for Cleanthes (whose desire for comfort is satisfied by the general revelation of nature), but only for Philo (who is neither frightened nor satisfied by natural religion).

The *Dialogues* presents, then, two irreconcilably different clusters of theology and piety, of theory and practice. For Philo and Cleanthes, experimental inquiry, analogical thinking, teleology, degrees of likeness and conviction, toleration of disagreement, and openness to inquiry all go together; while for Demea, the nexus includes rigid beliefs, optional arguments (used *ad libitum* for effect on self and others), a slightly desperate search for certitude (tinctured with a nagging sense of doubt), a passion for self-assertion, a willingness to submit or dominate, and the recourse to coercion should rhetoric fail. Moreover, the *Dialogues* does not so much discuss these clusters as it displays them; the careful reader sees them instanced and enacted in what the characters say and do and in how they say and do them. The consilience of argument and piety in people's lives is more vividly shown than abstractly mentioned.

The importance of natural religious piety for all three characters (and for Pamphilus as well) lies not only in its moral and eschatological implications but also in the ways it touches "common life"—life that is *common* in two senses, the life humans share with one another and the life that for most is ordinary. I will touch on two such aspects, education and friendship, which are highlighted in the very first sentence of Part 1, where Demea compliments Cleanthes "on the great care, which he took of my education, and on his unwearied perseverance and constancy in all his friendships" (1.1.Demea to Cleanthes). It is not just Cleanthes who takes great care of education and friendship; everyone in the *Dialogues* is equally concerned, though in different ways.

5. Education

Just as Pamphilus is youthfully eager to learn and finds that "nothing ever made greater impression on me" than this day's conversation (12.34.Pamphilus to Hermippus), so too each character in the *Dialogues* yearns to greatly impress Pamphilus—to *educate* him not only in theological belief but also in religious piety. Demea seeks to "imprint" an "early piety" of "submission and self-diffidence" (1.2.Demea to Philo); Philo constantly promotes a thorough-going sense of "the weakness, blindness, and narrow limits of human reason" (1.3.Philo to Demea and Cleanthes); and Cleanthes' protective guardianship of Pamphilus has instilled a loyalty not only to "true religion" (1.20.Cleanthes to Philo) but also to Cleanthes himself. But their methods warrant closer scrutiny, for implicit in the instructions each gives Pamphilus are three quite different pedagogies.

Demea's anxiety over his existential dependency manifests itself as a restless search for security, seeking certain beliefs and unquestioned command and obeisance. Just as he wishes "to appease those unknown powers" that "afflict and oppress us" (10.1.Demea to Philo and Cleanthes), so he cultivates submissiveness in those who must appease *him*.[20] He wants to teach his students how to submit unconditionally to authority, to surrender their own capacities for discernment and judgment. Within the context of the *Dialogues*, however, Demea has no effective opportunity to educate Pamphilus as he wants, for the conversations occur in Cleanthes' house with Cleanthes flanked by his old ally Philo; Demea is outnumbered, and Pamphilus belongs to Cleanthes. But clearly Demea would like to "imprint" his piety in Pamphilus just as he has brainwashed his own children (cf. 1.1), and he would seek to do so if he thought he could get away with it. Though pragmatic, Demea's piety is not negotiable; it brooks no opposition it can surmount, and it is not constrained by logic, reason, or fair play.

Congruently, Demea's pedagogy has a single overarching goal: fixing as firmly as possible, and by whatever effective means, Demea's "rigid, inflexible" views. The recipient of these views is both opportunity and obstacle: opportunity if tractable, obstacle if independently minded. That is why Demea seeks to remove resistance in his students, in order to inculcate a state of mind imbued with the "proper submission and self-diffidence" (1.2.Demea to Philo and Cleanthes).[21] Good instruction for Demea, therefore, is a form of manipulation and control of others, turning them into compliant vehicles for his own rigid views.

Philo's piety and pedagogy are poles apart from Demea's. Philo claims his entire performance throughout the *Dialogues* is for "the education and instruction" of Cleanthes' pupil Pamphilus (12.33.Philo to Cleanthes). Yet so far from seeking to "tame" his young student into abject submission, Philo wants to encourage him to be wilder and *less* tractable to dogma. Philo wants to liberate Pamphilus from others' opinions, to free him from the tyranny of authority and coercion. But Philo does not necessarily want to convert Pamphilus into a skeptic like himself; he wants Pamphilus to think for himself, to become an autonomous thinker. That is why Philo does not insist on his own views but uses his skeptical posture as an example to Pamphilus: By starting objections to all views—even to those Philo holds himself—he displays a spirit of clear and critical free thinking that radically undermines Demea's authoritarianism. Philo's display entices emulation. Proper education, Philo teaches by example, is developing one's own powers of thought, and his example moves Pamphilus only by inspiration, not by coercion or didaction.

Yet in a sense Philo does share Demea's goal of taming the mind, but with one absolutely crucial difference: The control comes from within, not from without. Both Philo and Demea want to rein in a certain natural human tendency to intellectual excess and hubris, yet by radically different means: self-diffidence and submission to others' authority for Demea, critical boldness and self-control for Philo. Despite the natural human desire to know things transcending our capacities, human reason is inescapably chained by "weakness, blindness, and narrow limits" (1.4.Philo to Demea and Cleanthes). What will keep us within those limits? For Demea, it is entirely a matter of will, submission of one's will to someone else's arbitrary command. Philo, however, puts his trust in the efficacy of rational self-critique. He thinks that reason can not only recognize its own limits but also control any tendency to transgress them. That is why Philo seeks to show, again and again, what goes awry when reason ventures out beyond its proper depth. Here is the true "triumph" of the skeptic, in showing our inability to settle speculative issues in theology and cosmogony—not that he reduces all human reasoning to naught, or that he can start objections no one can answer, but that we learn to be content with what we are competent to comprehend: the realm of common life and ordinary experience. Skeptical critique is not itself a way of life but the necessary preparation for one: "To be a philosophical sceptic is, in a man of letters, the first and most essential step towards being a sound, believing Christian" (12.33.Philo to Cleanthes).[22]

Cleanthes is comforted by his piety, and his education of Pamphilus is an initiation into these comforts. Near the end of Part 12, Cleanthes warns Philo: "Allow not your zeal against false religion to undermine your veneration for the true. Forfeit not this principle, the chief, the only great *comfort* in life; and our principal support amidst all the attacks of adverse fortune" (12.24.Cleanthes to Philo; emphasis added). True religion is life's greatest comfort for Cleanthes, so whatever supports true religion deserves allegiance. Cleanthes supports design arguments, and indeed experimental theology more generally, because they in turn support the true religion that brings him such comfort.

But how to entice others, particularly young others, into this comfortable embrace? First, expose them to its various comforts—simply bringing Pamphilus into Cleanthes' home is an initiation into the form of life that lodges there. Second, point out its principles where appropriate—using rational argument not as an end in itself but as a prop to perception or intuition. Third, provide a good example. Act toward others in a way that befits this comfortable form of life—be civil, gracious, kind, and generous; do not give offense; do not insist upon your views, your point of view, yourself. Education is therefore not a matter of subjection (Demea) nor of display (Philo) but of small kindnesses endlessly multiplied. One is induced to absorb views not through authoritative command or through intellectual virtuosity but because one has been treated kindly, over and over again. Clearly Pamphilus has been seduced by this gentle form of education, for his gratitude is evident in his loyalty to Cleanthes: not only in the comments Pamphilus makes (cf. 1.4, 3.10, and 12.34) but also in the way Cleanthes, unlike Philo and Demea, displays no solicitousness toward Pamphilus because he sees no need to compete for his affection. Cleanthes has been a kindly guardian to Pamphilus, a second father, and the youth's concluding ranking of Cleanthes over Philo (12.34) reflects as much his appreciation of Cleanthes' paternal protection as it does a disinterested judgment of argumentative merit.

6. Friendship

There are several kinds of friendship displayed in the *Dialogues;* three are instanced in the pairwise relationships of Demea, Cleanthes, and Philo.

Demea and Cleanthes: Demea neither comprehends nor experiences equal friendship; all his personal relations are implicitly contests of will, struggles to control others or to resist their efforts at controlling him. Yet he finds himself a guest in Cleanthes' country home, where convention requires at least the veneer of courtesy. How does Demea respond to this situation? He begins with flattery of his host but soon hands out unsolicited advice that contains an implicit critique of the kind of education Cleanthes has given Pamphilus (1.1.Demea to Cleanthes and Philo) and goes on to accept an alliance with Philo against Cleanthes (1.2.Demea to Philo and 1.3.Philo to Demea). Considered as a social player, Demea is rude: obsequious, insulting, and discourteous to his host.

Cleanthes does not repay Demea in kind; instead, he ignores the flattery and insult and jocularly seeks to ally Demea with himself against "this humorous sect of the sceptics" (1.5.Cleanthes to Demea; cf. 1.15). Moreover, he is mindful of his guest. While most of Part 1 is given over to a dialogue between Philo and Cleanthes on a topic about which Demea has nothing to say, Cleanthes more than once seeks to include Demea in the conversation, always explicitly (1.5, 1.7). This theme is repeated again and again in the *Dialogues*: Demea scants the social niceties, while Cleanthes insists upon them. Demea manipulates social convention in pursuit of personal advantage while Cleanthes responds in the conventionally proper way—a gracious host, a courteous conversationalist, a civil diverter of innuendo. Cleanthes treats Demea as graciously as he treats any guest, complying fully with all the norms of social propriety. Demea is a friend in view of personal advantage; Cleanthes is a friend by social custom that has become second nature.

Demea and Philo: Theirs is a utilitarian friendship, though with divergent views of the utilities. Their alliance in Part 1 against Cleanthes is the major dramatic tension of the *Dialogues,* and concern about its inevitable dissolution helps keep everyone interested in the intervening discussion: When, we wonder, will Demea wake up to his obvious deception?[23] Philo forges this alliance by ostensibly seeking to "improve and cultivate" Demea's principles of "the weakness, blindness, and narrow limits of human reason" (1.3.Philo to Cleanthes), and Demea implicitly assents to this "improvement." They are skeptical, while Cleanthes is dogmatic. But their alliance is paper-thin. Not only are Philo and Demea skeptical of Cleanthes' "experimental" natural theology in different ways, but they use this skepticism for diametrically opposed ends: Demea seeks to promote an authoritarian fideism, Philo a suspicion of such superstition and enthusiasm. They are utterly superficial friends, uniting only behind a skeptical slogan—a matter of apparently mutual convenience, not a shared form of life. Demea is duped by this shallow agreement, but Cleanthes sees that Philo is only stringing Demea along. Demea at long last in Part 11 awakens to Philo's transparent deception, and his dawning consciousness conveys both his dim understanding of their supposed "alliance" against Cleanthes and his aggrieved sense of betrayal: He now sees Philo as no friend but "a more dangerous enemy" (11.18.Demea to Philo). So both Demea and Philo have been using each other (though Philo is the more skillful user); their tenuous friendship is mutual manipulation, a kind of transaction founded on perceived self-interest.

Cleanthes and Philo: Their friendship is deeper than any other relationship in the *Dialogues.* They are old friends who "live in unreserved intimacy" (12.2.Philo to Cleanthes), who understand one another, and whose agreements ground, and permit, a variety of disagreements. Theirs is a friendship of equals, though each displays excellences and defects the other lacks. Philo is the superior dialectician and wordsmith, while Cleanthes recognizes that this talent has its dangers as well as its merits; it "carries you strange lengths, when engaged in an argument; and there is nothing so sacred and venerable, even in your own eyes, which you spare on that occasion" (12.1.Cleanthes to Philo). Cleanthes, on the other hand, lacks Philo's wit and invention, but he is unfailingly decent and resolutely venerates "true religion"—he seems to be one of those "very few, the philosophical theists, who entertain or rather endeavor to entertain, suitable notions of his divine perfections" (12.32.Philo to Cleanthes), even if he cannot always defend those notions against his brilliantly critical friend.

So they complement each other, these two old friends. But beyond that, they deeply trust and respect and like each other. They do not merely understand each other's subterfuges and strategies; they have no fear of divulging their deepest hopes and views to one another. They are, in a sense, transparent to one another, even though they do not see things from a single point of view. They live together in the same form of common life, and accept the same kind of fallibilist empirical natural theology compatible with that life, yet they calmly diverge on points of theology that seem to them irreconcilable and ultimately unarguable. Theirs is not an arrangement of convenience or domination; it is, to borrow George Fox's great phrase, a society of friends. This society, I believe, is intended to model for Pamphilus an enticing form of life, one that can explore the great issues of religion without erupting into superstition or enthusiasm—a form of life that can enfold deep difference and honest debate within its respect for persons. Their friendship epitomizes the natural religious piety that is the deepest concern of the *Dialogues*.

7. Concluding unscientific postscript

The *Dialogues* delights in so many ways that any account is necessarily incomplete. But we cannot conclude without mention of a primary delectation —Hume's wonderful language. Hume's artfulness is nowhere more evident than in the marvelous texture of his writing—the way expression is precisely tuned to thought, character, and situation; the exquisite choice of *les mots justes*; the lively use of quotations and references (real or imagined); the accessible presentation of abstruse arguments; the definitive phrases that capture philosophical positions in amber. Granted, Hume's eighteenth-century sentences are a bit lengthy for twenty-first-century-lite readers, yet they always parse, and, while they vibrate with variant meanings, they are rarely obscure. It is a pleasure to read them, and then to read them again and again. Truly this book "carries us, in a manner, into company, and unites the two greatest and purest pleasures of human life, study and society" (PH.4). In the end, therefore, the present reading is nothing more than a lengthy invitation to join in the pleasures of that studious society of friends.

NOTES

1. Introduction

1. A few writers have indeed sought to provide overall interpretations of the *Dialogues* in essays that accompany and introduce editions of Hume's text (Kemp Smith 1947; Pike 1970; Tweyman 1991); some books have focused on important themes in the *Dialogues* (Hurlbutt 1985; Tweyman 1986); and there have been welcome treatments of Hume's philosophy of religion as a whole in which the *Dialogues* is considered alongside Hume's other writings on religion (Gaskin 1988; Yandell 1990). But none are proper commentaries on all parts of Hume's text.

2. See, for example, Fogelin (1985) and Johnson (1995).

3. Stewart (1985), for example, caustically criticizes Rescher (1969) and Stove (1978), claiming that they engage in "ahistorical countermanoeuvres" that are "a *reductio ad absurdum* of the analytic method." He adds: "There are lessons here for anyone who still thinks philosophical argument exists in a timeless vacuum" (256).

4. See, for example, Jeffner (1966); Jones (1989); Livingston (1984); Prince (1992); Sprague (1988).

5. On skepticism, see especially the many works of Richard Popkin (for example, 1951, 1952, 1955–1956, 1980a, 1993). For other contexts, compare Hanson (1993, chap. 1); James (1979); Jeffner (1966); Jones (1982); Martin (1994); Norton (1982); Olshewsky (1991); Penelhum (1979, 1983a, 1983b, 1985); Price (1963, 1964, 1991); Stove (1979); Tweyman (1986); and Wright (1983, 1986).

6. The following also contain (mostly) internal interpretations: Bricke (1975); Carnochan (1988); Dancy (1995); Malherbe (1995); Prince (1992); Rohatyn (1983); Shapiro (1985); Simpson (1979); Tilley (1988); Vink (1986); White (1988); and Wieand (1985).

7. This presupposition resembles the hermeneutical "principle of charity," which is the assumption that the author "knew what he was doing and that he wrote exactly what he wanted to write" (Griswold 1999, 26). In Griswold's hands, this principle is not an attempt to divine the author's state of mind but rather "the supposition that the texts in question are unified products of design," possessing organic unity (ibid.). See also Griswold (1986, 1–16).

8. It should go without saying—but won't—that an internal interpreter need not *agree* with the text so interpreted. Thus, in opening up the *Dialogues'* rich treatment of "natural religion," I do not thereby necessarily endorse the views the text ultimately presents—in fact, I find these views too narrow and desiccated to be regarded as the definitive or last word on the subject. Even so, there is very much to learn about natural religion from Hume's *Dialogues*.

9. I am aware of only one "master text" that lacks singular terms altogether—the *Daodejing* (*Tao Te Ching*). While Hume's *Dialogues* mentions scores of particular people, places, and institutions, the *Daodejing* is silent about all spatio-temporal particulars ("The Dao" is in another category altogether).

10. Although I rely on Stanley Tweyman's excellent edition for citations of Hume's text (Tweyman 1991), I make references to the *Dialogues* independently of its numerous editions by using the following format: "Part.paragraph.speaker to audience." (There are

twelve Parts to the *Dialogues,* together with an opening section, "Pamphilus to Hermippus," that I have labeled "PH.") For example, "1.8.Philo to Cleanthes" refers to Part 1, paragraph 8, where Philo is speaking to Cleanthes; and PH.4 refers to "Pamphilus to Hermippus," paragraph 4, where, naturally, Pamphilus is addressing Hermippus.

11. J. C. A. Gaskin amusingly relates: "As an academic colleague of mine remarked about Hume, having just read the *Dialogues* for the first time, 'What does the dashed fellow actually *believe* in the end?'" (Gaskin 1993, xxiii). This puzzlement is natural, and its persistence may be a sign that this is the wrong sort of question to ask.

12. No one seems to hold that Demea in particular "speaks for Hume," except inadvertently, though he would of course be incidentally included in "everyone."

13. Keith Yandell (1990) provides a sterling example, filling out his claims fifteen years earlier that *The Natural History of Religion* "contains the key to Hume's position" and that the *Dialogues* must be read in its light (Yandell 1976, 111).

14. Hume to Adam Smith, August 15, 1776 (Greig 1932, vol. 2, letter 538). "Artfully" here means at least "very skillfully"; whether it also means "craftily" or even "deceptively" remains to be seen.

15. Surely Hume appreciated the irony of how his own intricate literary design might serve to undermine the appeal of the theological argument from natural design.

16. See Tweyman (1991), which devotes no pages to the preface and only 2⅓ pages to Part 1, where he mostly considers only the overall structure of the work and not specifically Part 1, the second longest Part. Tweyman, like many others, is so concerned with "the debate in the *Dialogues*" (his opening words, 1) that he misses the human drama which gives life and sense to that debate.

17. Why is the title plural? Doesn't Hume's book consist of a single sustained conversation—only one dialogue divided into twelve parts (and not "dialogues")? This puzzle is never discussed in the secondary literature, perhaps because it is assumed to be one of those "merely literary" questions unrelated to the text's philosophical meaning. For a contrary view, see Chapter 2 below.

18. Few commentaries on Plato's *Dialogues* are internal interpretations in the end, but all modern ones are first and foremost close readings of Plato's text, tracking the dramatic as well as the propositional dimensions of the various Socratic inquiries, fully conscious of how Plato seeks to draw the reader into the dialogic activity. But Humean philosophical scholarship has not often worried about "rhetorical," "pragmatic," and other "literary" matters (cf., however, Box 1990; Malherbe 1995; Morrisroe 1969b, 1970, 1974; Price 1965; Richetti 1983).

19. Here I stand firmly opposed to Manning's claim that the *Dialogues* can only or best be interpreted historically and contextually and not textually or intertextually (Manning 1990, 421).

20. Witness, for example, continuing sophisticated defenses of design arguments (Tennant 1928, 1930; Swinburne 1968, 1972, 1979), ancient but resurgent interest in the anthropic principle (Barrow and Tipler 1986; Tipler 1994), and various Big Bang cosmological speculations (Davies 1983, 1992). Thoughts of intelligent divine design are still present even in the study of life after Darwin, despite the efforts of Darwinian fundamentalists to scrub biology clean of teleology (cf., for example, Behe 1996). By citing these works, I do not mean to imply assent to their conclusions or viewpoints; rather, they serve to show only that design arguments are still intelligently advanced and vigorously argued well over two centuries after Hume's *Dialogues* supposedly discredited them.

21. The backing for this claim will have to await the detailed examination of the arguments in the actual dialogues.

2. Scene-Setting

1. The word "dialogue" is purposefully ambiguous among (1) an actual or imagined conversation, (2) a certain literary form which seeks to portray (1), (3) the activity of writing (2), and (4) the activity of reading (2). More about this ambiguity shortly.

2. The textual references are to "Part.paragraph(s)."

3. Hume to Gilbert Elliot of Minto, March 10, 1751 (Greig 1932, vol. 1, page 154, letter 72).

4. See also Pamphilus's prefatory comment to Hermippus that he "was present at those conversations" of Cleanthes with Philo and Demea (PH.6.Pamphilus to Hermippus), where "conversation" is a pretty fair synonym of "dialogue."

5. Gaskin (1988, 20) refers to the Parts as "Sections," perhaps unconsciously hearkening back to the structure of Hume's *Treatise,* a work with quite a different literary form.

6. See Austin (1985); Butler (1960); Manning (1990); Pakaluk (1984).

7. See Berkeley's "Three Dialogues between Hylas and Phylonus" (Luce and Jessop 1948).

8. *Webster's New World Dictionary of the American Language.*

9. The next two paragraphs are rather speculative and may be ignored by anyone who thinks "concerning" means nothing more than "about."

10. Philo does make passing references to an "Indian philosopher" (4.9), "the ancient pagan theology" (6.13), "Bramins" (7.17), and "Egyptian and Grecian superstitions" (12.15). But these belief systems are not seriously considered as religions.

11. David Pailin discusses eleven distinct notions or "forms" of "natural religion" in seventeenth- and eighteenth-century Britain. Unfortunately, the only kind he mentions as at stake in Hume's *Dialogues* is the conclusion of rational reflection—that is, natural theology, not natural piety (Pailin 1994, 201). But several other senses Pailin notes (the result of Adamic revelation, primarily a matter of morality, and the result of a distinct mode of human awareness) are also germane to the *Dialogues.*

12. The *Oxford English Dictionary* mentions eighteen main senses of the adjective "natural," with a number of sub-senses, and the 1971 supplement adds a nineteenth sense.

13. The terms "natural" or "naturally" occur six times in the six paragraphs of "Pamphilus to Hermippus."

14. Contrary to Prince (1992), who claims the *Dialogues* "may thus be considered a dialogue about the irrelevance of dialogue to religious belief" (285), resolutely views "dialogue" in an eighteenth-century external context (Shaftesbury and Berkeley), and ironically interprets the Preface.

15. Pamphilus does not say whether such interest is natural *only* to youth. If it were, then the only interest Cleanthes, Philo, and Demea could have in the conversations would be ulterior ones: their various interests in scoring against one another, in displaying rhetorical and argumentative skills, and, most important, in influencing Pamphilus. But Cleanthes and Philo do have an inherent interest in natural religion and in discussing it, even though Demea's piety prevents him from finding both subject and inquiry to be *intrinsically* interesting.

16. Philo and Demea assert this up front, while Cleanthes seeks to establish it; ostensibly the dialogues' quarrels are only over this being's (or these beings') "nature."

17. Michael Pakaluk (1984) views the characters not just as philosophical types but as "syndromes" (117), quasi-psychoanalytic diagnostic categories.

18. Norman Kemp Smith (1947) and Ernest Campbell Mossner (1936) have been widely influential in promoting the equations of Philo = Hume, Cleanthes = Butler, and Demea = Clarke, although other resemblances to Cleanthes and Demea are often noted (cf. Price 1963).

19. Michael Morrisroe (1970) emphasizes the "functions" of the characters as "rhetorical devices," but he wants to show how Hume used "the dramatic elements of the *Dialogues* as a tool with which he might move his audience to re-examine the argument from design" (107). This is too limiting.

20. Even so astute a reader as Gaskin (1988, 210) ascribes these "descriptions" to Pamphilus.

21. Note that Pamphilus views them as conversations of his mentor Cleanthes with Philo and Demea, not their conversations with Cleanthes; Pamphilus is clearly Cleanthrocentric.

22. As Morrisroe says, Cleanthes is "the dramatic center of the *Dialogues*" (Morrisroe 1969b, 968; cf. Morrisroe 1970).

23. He refers to Pyrrhonians and Sceptics (1.6–7; 1.17); Newton, Copernicus, and Galileo (1.12); Euclid (1.13); Arnauld (1.15); the Copernican system (1.16); Christianity and Christendom (1.17); Huet (1.17); and Locke and Bayle (1.17)—all in the first Part. Later on he mentions Copernicus again (3.1); "an ILIAD or ANEID" (3.4); Livy or Tacitus (3.6); Lucullus (6.10); and Columbus (6.11), as well as Constantinople (6.9); Asia and Europe (6.10); Greece, Spain, Italy (6.10); France, America, Europe (6.11); and Africa and Arabia (8.10). Cleanthes' name-dropping diminishes as the dialogues proceed, while that of Philo increases reciprocally, as if Cleanthes gradually loses, while Philo gains, self-confidence in what he thinks he knows.

24. Many assume that Demea is a clergyman, but the evidence is indirect and inconclusive: Demea's occasional liturgical-sounding language, oblique references by Cleanthes (11.19) and Philo (11.20) to clergy, and Demea's tendency to pontificate (Morrisroe 1970, 105). No matter. What counts in the *Dialogues* is not Demea's title or office but his character.

25. Why does Philo dupe Demea into thinking that they are allies in their uses of skepticism? Is he just being his usual playful self, setting the table for his prodigious skeptical appetite? Does he seek, like Socrates, to seduce his companion into inquiry in hopes of producing self-realization in an unreflective and self-deceived—hence dangerous —partner? Does he want to expose the inadequacies of Demea's piety in front of young Pamphilus to inoculate the youth against Demea's authoritarianism? Or does he simply want to get rid of Demea so that he and Cleanthes can converse honestly together? Perhaps all of these motivations are present. (See Carnochan 1988 for another, external alternative.)

26. There are exceptions; for example, his missing premises in revising the "old Epicurean hypotheses" in Part 8 and his almost parodic repetition of Cleanthes' criticisms of Demea in Part 9. Bricke (1975, 4–5) points out other instances of Philo's inconsistencies. Still, Philo's reasoning is almost always more rigorous than Cleanthes' or Demea's, and it is certainly more inventive.

27. See Hurlbutt (1988) for a reading of "careless sceptic" as "mitigated sceptic."

3. Pamphilus to Hermippus

1. For example, Tweyman (1991) says nothing at all about this preface but plunges straightaway into "an analysis of all twelve parts of the *Dialogues*" (vii), as if "all twelve parts" were the whole of the *Dialogues.*

2. Some differences between Cicero and Hume: Cicero is his own narrator, while Hume is absent from the *Dialogues* (we will treat the puzzling appearance of some footnotes in Chapter 15); the judgment at the end of Cicero's work is given both by the narrator and by one of the characters (Velleius) and not solely by the narrator; the meeting is in the house of the skeptic (Cotta), not that of the dogmatist (Balbus); the narrator is not a student of any of the speakers but is invited as an equal; there is reference to a prior debate "in an alcove"; and no one leaves the conversation, which is mostly a collection of set speeches from school texts.

3. The first five paragraphs are written in the third person; not until the sixth paragraph does Pamphilus speak of "I" and "you."

4. See Norman Kemp Smith's famous claim: "I shall contend that Philo, from start to finish, represents Hume; and that Cleanthes can be regarded as Hume's mouthpiece only in those passages in which he is explicitly agreeing with Philo, or in those other passage in which, while refuting Demea, he is also being used to prepare the way for one or other of Philo's independent conclusions" (1947, 59).

5. Note that Pamphilus did give Hermippus the "gist" of these actual conversations on an earlier occasion (PH.6) and that this prior sketch merely whetted Hermippus's thirst for a fuller depiction, a full-fledged *dialogic* recital.

6. Are there perhaps other obvious and important "truths" beside the Being of God

that are inculcated in the *Dialogues* (e.g., the value of conversation and company and the importance of shared piety) and perhaps other obscure but fascinating questions beside the nature of God (e.g., religious polity and the political effects and implications of religious piety)?

7. Pamphilus is the very first in a long line of commentators on the *Dialogues* to confuse natural religion with natural theology, because theological "dispute" is what catches his attention.

8. See 1.4 ("in Cleanthes' features I could distinguish an air of finesse"); 2.25 ("Philo was proceeding in this vehement manner, somewhat between jest and earnest, as it appeared to me"); and 3.10 ("Philo was a little embarrassed and confounded").

9. See two interesting variants in Plato's *Theaetetus* and *Symposium.*

10. I don't mean to imply that philosophers who follow Pamphilus in focusing solely on the propositional arguments they find in the *Dialogues* are childish or unsubtle. I merely wish to widen a reader's focus beyond what *Pamphilus* sees within *his* field of vision.

4. Part 1

1. As a prime example of the very "artful" design in these dialogues, we may note the effortless transition made by Pamphilus at the very beginning of his "recital" as he smoothly modulates attention from his reporting of the conversations to the conversations themselves: He incrementally shifts from his own past tense voice ("I joined the company, whom I found sitting") to his report first of Demea's actions in the past tense ("Demea paid Cleanthes some compliments") and then of Demea's words in the past tense ("the father of Pamphilus, said he"), and finally to Demea's own speech in the present tense, first in third-person comments ("The son is your pupil") and last in Demea's own distinctive voice, in the first person ("I am persuaded").

2. One small example: Demea later censures his host Cleanthes "before so young a man as Pamphilus" (2.10.Demea to Cleanthes).

3. Carnochan (1988) regards Cleanthes as sharing in Philo's "raillery or artificial malice" in order to play a "confidence game" or "sting" on Demea so they can drive him away and resume their friendship in Part 12. This is the "comic plot" of the *Dialogues,* according to Carnochan. I agree with Carnochan that Philo and Cleanthes are happier by themselves than together with Demea, although Philo does greatly enjoy the "raillery" Demea occasions. But I don't think Parts 2–11 are an organized confidence game; they have other purposes, such as the education of Pamphilus.

4. The note of ownership ("my own") and its implied sense of rightful control of others is a window on Demea's whole outlook.

5. Demea, as we shall see, really has *no* method in education or in natural theology.

6. Alternatively, perhaps he is simply and unknowingly inconsistent, a trait he frequently displays.

7. Philo's sarcasm lies in the fact that it is especially *Demea's* principles that "improperly" reared children—children whose minds are seasoned with a thinking piety—will reject, for Demea's principles rest on no other foundation than early, deep, and forceful imprinting; they are neither the fruition of our natural sentiments nor discovered and supported by our natural reason. Demea's authoritarian piety can rest only on an inculcated submissiveness.

8. Philo, for one, seems to accept this distinction and priority in the next paragraph, though with what degree of seriousness we cannot tell, as he quickly turns the subject to skepticism, ostensibly as a development of Demea's disparagement of reason.

9. These doubts are not explicitly broached here. Cleanthes must be speaking from memory of prior conversations.

10. Here, as often, Philo damns with faint praise: Philosophy's "exact and more scrupulous method of proceeding" will yield "greater stability, if not greater truth" (1.9.Philo to Cleanthes). Philosophy aims for truth but may have to settle for stability.

11. Philo uses two different kinds of metaphor in 1.3 to emphasize both the remote-

ness of the subject from ordinary experience and the limits, weakness, blindness, and frailty of our faculties. These are distinct disabilities—the one concerning the content of theology, the other our capacity for theology—but they conspire to the same result: Few theological claims can be backed by reason.

12. At least it undermines a self-reflective, consistent, and rational certitude. One may, of course, be "riveted" to certain beliefs, like Demea, by means of invincible ignorance, massive self-deception, or determined willfulness.

13. Cleanthes has five uninterrupted paragraphs here as against nine at the beginning of Part 3.

14. Certainly this is the eventual outcome of the forthcoming dialogues, as Cleanthes much later remarks: "Your spirit of controversy, joined to your abhorrence of vulgar superstition, carries you strange lengths, when engaged in an argument; and there is nothing so sacred and venerable, even in your own eyes, which you spare on that occasion" (12.1.Cleanthes to Philo).

15. Look how carefully Cleanthes sugars his tart comment: He "shall never assent" to Arnauld's "harsh" opinion, and he wants to affirm his own view, "I hope, without offense." Philo never displays such tender concern for the feelings of others, nor does Demea. Cleanthes does possess an "unwearied perseverance and constancy in all his friendships" (1.1.Demea to Cleanthes), especially to a friend so dear as Philo.

16. Their separate mention here is one more textual clue, if more were needed, that "natural religion" cannot be identified with "natural theology" in the *Dialogues*.

17. We shall see later what Cleanthes thinks these "obvious" arguments are (cf. 3.1–9) and whether Philo thinks the obstacles in their path are "artificial" (cf. 10.36 and 12.2).

18. See comments on 12.8fn for how Philo and Cleanthes regard disputes over "degrees," both in general and in the case of natural theology.

19. Why Demea? This question is addressed to him because it is a problem for him, for his kind of piety. He does not answer because he has no answer; the problem remains insoluble for him. Cleanthes' response on his behalf is more a host's graciousness than an actual rescue of Demea.

20. Only three paragraphs in the *Dialogues* mention the word "Christian" or its cognates: 1.17, 4.4, and 12.33. Since the topic is natural religion, particular revealed religions are not supposed to be at issue.

21. See Martin (1966, chap. 1).

22. See Wolterstorff (1996); Nuovo (1997); and Nuovo's introduction to Locke (1997).

23. Here is but one worry: Confirmation cannot be entailment, else a contradiction confirms, because it entails, *every* proposition.

5. Part 2

1. I use this somewhat awkward phrase to encompass the large family of resembling arguments, including arguments "from design," arguments "to design," and "teleological" arguments, that are engaged at one point or another in the *Dialogues*. Distinctions within this family will be made as needed.

2. 1st ed. 1674–1675, 6th ed. 1712. Hume's text has a footnote truncating Malebranche's title to the unaccented "Rechercher de la verite." The quotation comes from the concluding paragraph of Book Three, Part Two, Chapter Nine of Malebranche's work. For a modern translation, see Malebranche (1980). Demea's quotation is a fairly accurate rendition of Malebranche's original, with two interesting exceptions: (1) Demea inserts an emphasized "*any*" to Malebranche's denial of resemblance of divine spirit to human spirit, and (2) Demea omits Malebranche's clause, "since it is certain that matter is related to some perfection in God." Demea amends his own authority to say more emphatically what he, Demea, wants him to say: that there is no anthropomorphizing likeness of *any* kind between man and God. External authorities are useful for an authoritarian such as Demea only when they reinforce his real authority—Demea's will to believe as he wishes.

3. Demea later thinks Philo is guilty by association with Cleanthes (in 2.10); but Philo quickly protests his innocence, claiming he merely wishes to "argue with Cleanthes in his own way; and by showing him the dangerous consequences of his tenets, hope at last to reduce him to *our* opinion" (2.11.Philo to Demea; emphasis added). Philo is unlikely to be sincere and straightforward in these claims, but Demea nonetheless goes along until the end of Part 11.

4. "But as it is written, Eye hath not seen, nor ear heard, neither have entered into the heart of man, the things which God hath prepared for them that love him." (I Corinthians 2:9; Authorized [King James] Version)

5. "For since the beginning of the world men have not heard, nor perceived by the ear, neither hath the eye seen, O God, beside thee, what he hath prepared for him that waiteth for him." (Isaiah 64:4, Authorized Version)

6. "From of old no one has heard or perceived by the ear,
   no eye has seen a God besides thee,
   who works for those who wait for him." (Isaiah 64:4)

7. "Such things had never been heard or noted.
   No eye has seen [them], O God, but You,
   Who act for those who trust in You." (Isaiah 64:3)

8. "The eye of man hath not heard, the ear of man hath not seen, man's hand is not able to taste, his tongue to conceive, nor his heart to report, what my dream was" (*A Midsummer Night's Dream*, IV.i.218–221).

9. In germ, this is precisely the kind of *a priori* argument Demea uses and Philo criticizes in Part 9; by then, however, no one seems to remember this earlier indiscretion.

10. We will later see how uncomfortable Philo is with Demea's piety (Part 10) and how Philo himself explicitly criticizes not only the first of these two *a priori* arguments but also *a priori* arguments in general, noting that "men ever did and ever will derive their religion from other sources than from this [*a priori*] species of reasoning" (9.11.Philo to Demea).

11. Why does Cleanthes not respond directly? He gives us two clues: He doesn't want to "lose any time," either in "circumlocutions" with Demea or "in replying to the pious declamations of Philo" (2.5.Cleanthes to Demea and Philo). We have seen how rambling Demea's verbiage is—how unclear, inconsistent, confused, and unreflective—and how it cloaks his real purposes. But it would take Cleanthes more time than he wants to waste in order to clear up Demea's confusions, and Demea wouldn't understand anyway. Besides, Cleanthes is fundamentally concerned for *Pamphilus*'s education, not for Demea's. Likewise, Cleanthes doesn't take Philo's "pious declamations" too seriously. They may sound conventionally pious to Demea, but Cleanthes knows Philo well enough to believe they are stated here mostly for practical effect—the effect of luring Demea into continuing the conversations—than for their argumentative value. Cleanthes judges that the conversations will move forward if he escapes from the coils of negative theology and pious adoration of mystery to a more straightforward theological argument.

12. Cleanthes gives no examples of machines. His general characterizations could fit not only hardware such as carriages and clocks but also software such as science and stories—even the *Dialogues* themselves! Clearly there are *many* kinds of "productions of human contrivance."

13. For alternative attempts to construe the "logic" of Cleanthes' argument, see Barker (1983, 1989); Burch (1980); Cartwright (1978); and Salmon (1978, 1979).

14. We shall see in Part 12 that Philo and Cleanthes differ most intractably in perceiving degrees of analogy; we shall also see how both agree that while this disagreement is irresolvable, it nonetheless does not stand in the way of their friendship.

15. Ordinary uses of forms of "like" capture the connection (it is more than a pun): the *likeness* (similarity) of nature to human contrivance makes *likely* (probable) the *likeness* of the Author of Nature to human intelligence. What is like is likely—but *only* likely.

16. The implication, of course, is that Cleanthes is not sufficiently zealous or (more

dangerously) that he is no defender of religion. But Demea is foggy about what "perfect evidence" is. In 2.1, he held that the being of God is self-evident, although he was quite willing to support his view with an appeal to authority (2.2); but now he insists on "abstract arguments" and "proofs *a priori*" (2.6). What is vital for Demea is confirmation in certainty by any means available.

17. Demea will hang the label of "anthropomorphism" on Cleanthes' view in Part 4.

18. The "or" is curious. Philo apparently *equates* "order," "arrangement," and "the adjustment of final causes," but we have seen that they are not the same. Neither Cleanthes nor Philo clearly isolates the features of the world that serve as premises for "the" design argument: Just what is supposed to be the analogue to human "contrivances"? Here are some possible candidates: the spatial order or arrangement of parts or of the whole universe (hemoglobin, parts of bodies, galactic superclusters); the temporal order or sequence of parts or of the whole universe (diurnal succession, physical epochs since the Big Bang, biological evolution); specific natural laws (inverse square laws); fundamental physical constants (Planck's constant); the fact of natural lawfulness or determinism; the apparent teleology of particular spatial, temporal, or lawful structures or orders (the functions of organs, the usefulness of plants and animals, the evolution of primates); the apparent teleology of orderliness per se (the anthropic principle). Since there are so many possible design analogues, there will be quite a diversity of design arguments.

19. There is irony, or at least ambiguity, in these words. Does Philo count himself as a "sound theist"? Does he count Demea as such? Would Philo say the Biblical doctrine of human creation in the image of God (*imago dei*) is "unsound theism"? Perhaps the stress should be on degree ("*such* a degradation"), so that Philo's concern is not with *any* resemblance between "the Deity and human creatures" but with the *degree* of resemblance Cleanthes asserts between them, though Cleanthes in fact hasn't stated *how much* resemblance he believes there is. It is hard to determine how much Philo credits his own words and how much he is simply inveigling Demea to continue in the conversation.

20. Philo attributes this phrase to Demea, even though it is Philo's coinage. Demea did mention "mystery" (1.2) about the divine nature and expressed a need for humble adoration (2.1), but it is Philo who first puts these terms together (2.4.Philo to Cleanthes). Still, although Philo first *uses* the phrase, Demea really *owns* it, for it best expresses his piety: Adoring mystery is not something Philo has much use for, while it is the core of Demea's being—a fully mysterious being is the greatest authority of all precisely because it is literally unquestionable.

21. To this point Demea has spoken six paragraphs, Cleanthes twelve, and Philo sixteen.

22. Philo claims all but one of the remaining twelve paragraphs of Part 2, ten of fourteen paragraphs in Part 4, eleven of thirteen in Part 5, eight of thirteen in Part 6, twelve of eighteen in Part 7, and ten of twelve in Part 8, for a total of sixty-two out of eighty-two paragraphs—over 75 percent of the discussion on design arguments. Even when Part 3's thirteen paragraphs are added in, Philo still has nearly two-thirds of the discussion on design arguments. In addition, his paragraphs are usually longer, so he claims an even higher proportion of the words spoken and hence of the speaking time. Of course quantity is not everything; but Philo's qualitative advantage is at least as great as his quantitative edge.

23. Philo's three qualifications are worth noting: (1) He will not "*much*" dispute these things. Does this imply that he disputes them somewhat (cf. Part 9)? (2) He won't much dispute them "*at present.*" Perhaps he would do so on another occasion? (3) He won't presently much dispute them "*with you*"—presumably he is addressing Cleanthes. Would he dispute with others (whether or not they refuse these principles)?

24. Cleanthes has in fact previously mentioned only machines (2.5) and houses (2.9), and in the latter case he was just responding to a comparison first introduced by Philo (in 2.8). Ships and furniture (and houses as well) are *Philo's* examples of "productions of hu-

man contrivance" (2.5). Philo is good at putting words into others' mouths, however agreeable the taste.

25. For more on this topic, see comments below on Part 12.8fn.

26. How can a "limited" experience reveal an "infinite" *number* of springs and principles, much less infinite *kinds*? Cleanthes is too polite to remind Philo of his own distinction between "the precipitate march of the vulgar" and "the slow and deliberate steps of philosophers" (2.17.Philo to Cleanthes), though it well applies here.

27. Though how different could they be and still be called "intelligence, reason, or any thing similar to these faculties in men" (2.20.Philo to Cleanthes)?

28. By now the reader has begun to weary of Philo's unkind and denigrating insinuations. He certainly seems to strain the social niceties, and one can sense Cleanthes and Pamphilus—though not Demea!—growing steadily more upset as Philo careens along his skeptical course. It is a weakness in Philo's character to not know when to stop and to be as fond of clever insult as of solid argument. He lets his delight in disputation override his respect for others. Even so, Cleanthes remains his steadfast friend.

29. Perhaps both are equally but completely opposed to common speech; how does that help either of them?

30. See Temple (1992) on "the uniqueness objection."

31. Philo exaggerates. While Galileo may have used many analogies to break down the celestial/terrestrial dichotomy and to make comprehensible the Copernican system, there were other considerations: the massive observational data accumulated over centuries but recently improved by Brahe and, subsequently, the mechanical theoretical principles of Newton, more *a priori* than *a posteriori* in their genesis and application.

6. Part 3

1. More fully, Cleanthes says Philo's objections "are no better than the abstruse cavils of those philosophers, who denied motion" (3.1.Cleanthes to Philo). Now who might "those philosophers" be? There are two major possibilities: (1) Continuing in the vein of Copernicus and his opponents, they could be those natural philosophers who denied the motion of the earth about the sun. But this identification would not advance Cleanthes's argument, for the earth's motion is not "self-evident"; what seems evident to a human observer is that the celestial bodies move, not the earth, and it is the advocates of terrestrial motions who must use "abstruse" arguments to make their case. At best, Cleanthes could merely argue that once the analogy of celestial and terrestrial bodies is established, similarity of motion is clear in both cases. (2) It might be thought more convenient for Cleanthes to refer to Zeno and his "abstruse cavils" against all motion, for then one could claim it "self-evident and undeniable" that there is motion. But what Cleanthes wants to defend as self-evident and undeniable is an *analogy*, a likeness or resemblance, and motion per se is not an analogy but a directly observable phenomenon. So neither possible reference is very helpful to Cleanthes's argument, and maybe that is why he does not make his reference at all clear.

2. Or is he making two new arguments? Nelson Pike (1970) holds that Cleanthes' argument in Part 2 is a "scientific" version, while that (or those) in Part 3 is (are) "irregular." In Part 12, Pike argues, Philo accepts only the latter, not the former. But compare Wadia (1978) for criticism.

3. See Soles (1981).

4. Cleanthes also believes that God is speaking in Nature *to us*; God's language is one we can apprehend and understand, even if we cannot comprehend its full meaning. But Cleanthes doesn't stress *what* God is saying, just *that* (we recognize that) God is saying something.

5. Interestingly, Cleanthes does not mention "convey[s] some instruction altogether worthy of a benevolent Being, superior to mankind" as a difference between the imagined and the actual cases. Does he think that ordinary works of nature convey such instruction?

We shall see how divine benevolence fares as an inference from the works of nature in Parts 10 and 11.

6. See Tweyman (1982a) on "the articulate voice."

7. This is so even when we credit fully all reported theophanies. God spoke to Moses on the mountaintop, the Father spoke to Jesus at his baptism, Allah spoke to Mohammed in his heart, and so forth, but in none of these cases did God speak to *all* humans at the *same* time with the *same* statements in *all* dialects of the *entire* world. Cleanthes' case makes particular revelation completely universal; that is, it turns revealed religion into natural religion, or rather obliterates the distinction.

8. This is no dig at these authors; "Livy and Tacitus" represent the *best* of human authorship for Cleanthes.

9. See Tweyman (1979) on "the vegetable library."

10. See Sobel (1982) for enlightening commentary on this passage.

11. It is significant, I believe, that the text originally read "theological" instead of "religious." Cleanthes' discourse shifts from *theological argumentation*—attempting to prove the reliability of a certain kind of religious inference—to *religious presentation*—attempting to draw out and appeal to a certain religious sensitivity. Cleanthes moves from abstract inference toward religious perceptual practice.

12. These are not the only possible types. The reference to "an ignorant savage and barbarian" is not an omnibus explanation but the foil to Philo—"a state of mind very different from your sifting, inquisitive disposition, my ingenious friend" (3.9.Cleanthes to Philo). Perhaps we may also see an implicit rebuke of Demea: Is he not something of "an ignorant savage and barbarian" in Cleanthes' eyes?

13. Demea's problem is more radical: He may be *unable* to notice it in his zeal for certitude and authoritarian piety.

14. For example, one could ascribe it to a widespread but still erroneous human tendency to anthropomorphize the world. Hume himself wrestled with this problem as the crux of Cleanthes' case in his letter to Gilbert Elliot of Minto, written March 10, 1751, while working on the initial draft of the *Dialogues:*

> I cou'd wish that Cleanthes' Argument could be so analys'd, as to be render'd quite formal & regular. The Propensity of the Mind towards it, unless that Propensity were as strong & universal as that to believe in our Senses & Experience, will still, I am afraid, be esteem'd a suspicious Foundation. Tis here I wish for your Assistance. We must endeavour to prove that this Propensity is somewhat different from our Inclination to find our own Figures in the Clouds, our Face in the Moon, our Passions & Sentiments even in inanimate Matter. Such an Inclination may, & ought to be controul'd, & can never be a legitimate Ground of Assent. (Greig 1932, vol. 1, 155, letter 72)

In short, the difficulty lies in distinguishing between a subjective projection and an objective apprehension; only if the "Propensity of the Mind" toward anthropomorphizing were "as strong and universal" (and, we might add, as useful) as our belief in the reliability of our sense-experience could it escape skeptical censure. Concerning this difficulty, Hume apparently never received the "Assistance" he sought from Gilbert Elliot—nor do we from Cleanthes.

15. See Tweyman (1980) and Wadia (1979).

16. To be sure, Cleanthes and Philo disagree on the *degree* of likeness. Whether their agreement or their disagreement is more important we shall consider in Chapters 15 and 16.

17. In these three paragraphs, Demea never once speaks of "God" but uses the more impersonal terms of "the Deity" (four times), "a supreme existence," "a supreme intelligence," "the divine intelligence," and "the supreme Being" (once each). In this he follows

the typical practice of everyone in the *Dialogues*. It is hard to imagine any of them in a truly personal relationship with the God of Abraham, Isaac, and Jacob or with God the Father, Son, and Holy Spirit.

18. Demea once again echoes Scripture: "For my thoughts are not your thoughts, neither are your ways my ways, saith the LORD" (Isaiah 55:8, King James Version). But while these words might well imply incomprehensibility, it is difficult to extract perfection from them.

19. That Demea is willing to cite Plotinus so favorably is yet another reason for distrusting Hermippus's initial characterization of him as having a "rigid inflexible *orthodoxy*" (PH.6.Pamphilus to Hermippus; emphasis added). In fact, Demea's embrace of "mysticism" and divine incomprehensibility has quite other aims and motives than loyalty to orthodoxy.

20. Demea's allusions to the Bible indicate a fondness for received *language,* if not for received *doctrine.*

7. Part 4

1. Is Cleanthes sincere in referring to Demea's sincerity? Cleanthes certainly does not think that Demea's sincerity entails truth or other value, for Cleanthes' own sense of "true religion" is worlds apart from Demea's. I detect a lightly mocking tone to Cleanthes' words, a tone that may be what sets off Demea in the next paragraph, for his ire requires little provocation.

2. Demea delights in this unmeaning, for it seems to him to heighten the worthiness (and, not incidentally, reward) of piety to believe what is meaningless (to us, at least); it is laudable devotion to cling to what one cannot understand. For Cleanthes, on the other hand, religion is and ought to be minimally comprehensible; his God is the proper terminus of an intelligible inference from experience.

3. Cleanthes conflates atheists and agnostics: A skeptic may claim to believe either that God doesn't exist or that one cannot know whether God does or doesn't exist. Later on, Cleanthes will allow for such distinctions in our relation to the Author of Nature, but here he permits no middle ground between theist and atheist. Like Philo, Cleanthes is posturing while Demea is present, overstating his own position for his own purposes. His chief concern now is to disparage Demea's extreme brand of religion for Pamphilus's sake, not to recognize the more subtle differences between himself and Philo.

4. Why does Demea use the plural "us" here? Is it an attempt to embrace Philo in Demea's cause? Is it an effort to reassure himself that Philo is still on his side, conforming to Demea's self-conception as a defender of orthodoxy? Or is it the royal first person appropriate to Demea's sense of himself?

5. Demea is not merely expressing the views of others in a disinterested manner; these views are invested with authority for Demea. Even so, his concern is not to defend a *tradition's authority* but to justify *himself*; everything for him has a self-interested focus.

6. "Abuse of terms" has been alleged twice earlier in the *Dialogues*: (1) At the end of Part 3, Demea had pressed the very same charge against Cleanthes! There Demea argued that "our thought is fluctuating, uncertain, fleeting, successive, and compounded"; that these features belong to thought's "essence"; and that it would be an "abuse of terms" to call anything lacking these features "thought or reason." So far they are agreed; but their conclusions differ diametrically: Cleanthes concludes that since God essentially has thought or reason, the abuse of terms is to think that divine mind is completely simple, while Demea holds that since simplicity and immutability belong to the divine essence, the meaning of terms such as "thought or reason" as applied to God is "totally incomprehensible." Such terms only function to honor their recipient, so that "it appear[s] more pious and respectful" to retain them (3.13.Demea to Cleanthes). (2) Earlier still, in Part 2, Cleanthes had accused Philo of abusing terms in distinguishing improperly between reason and experience so as to put astronomical objects outside of what would ordinarily be re-

garded as experience (2.25.Cleanthes to Philo), though Philo meant no such implication by his distinction.

7. Cleanthes had urged a version of this appeal in Part 3 in presenting his "irregular" argument. Even if "the argument for theism" is "contradictory to the principles of logic," he said, it nonetheless has a "universal" and "irresistible influence" (3.8.Cleanthes to Philo). In effect, then, Philo is poking fun at *Cleanthes'* claim to universal consent: not that Cleanthes is wrong about the natural human tendency to anthropomorphize causality but that he is mistaken in thinking that a single consistent conception of divinity universally results from this tendency.

8. Presumably Demea would allow that the situation looks much the same, though with different exclusivistic conclusions, from the standpoint of belief in God$_C$ or belief in God$_P$—except that, Demea would doubtless maintain, these views are mistaken!

9. See Tweyman (1982b).

10. In an earlier paragraph scored out on the manuscript and replaced by the current 4.7, Hume had Philo making this point even more emphatically: "'Tis evident, then, that as far as abstract reason can judge, 'tis perfectly indifferent, whether we rest on the universe of matter or on that of thought; nor do we gain any thing by tracing the one into the other."

11. Philo seems to have in mind more some medieval Aristotelians than the ancient ones, but his critique holds for anyone who thinks postulating a capacity to do or bring about *x* explains how *x* is brought about.

12. An ambiguity here will return to plague Cleanthes in Parts 10–11: Just *how* does nature "bespeak" God? Does it declare anything more than God's bare being as creator and minimal nature as intelligent? Does it say anything about the contents of God's mind? Does it indicate *what* God is saying? If nature is designed by God, what *is* God's design?

13. Note that this is a question of relative distance, and therefore of more or less, not a matter of all or nothing.

14. These points replace an earlier draft passage where Philo concedes that Cleanthes' "answer [in 4.13] may, perhaps, be good . . . upon your principles, that the religious system can be proved by experience, and by experience alone; and that the Deity arose from some external cause," even while claiming that "these opinions, you know, will be adopted by very few." In the final text, Philo makes no such concessions, and pays no compliments, to Cleanthes' principles.

15. See 2.26.Philo to Cleanthes.

16. Philo's language betrays him here. He says that "naturalists indeed very justly explain particular *effects* by more general *causes*" while it is unsatisfactory "to explain a particular *effect* by a particular *cause*" (emphasis added). General causes do explain particular effects—but only in the plural, as a set or class of effects, not in the singular, as *this* particular effect. So general causes really explain general effects, not particular ones qua particular. Gravity explains the attractive acceleration of *bodies* (in general) but doesn't explain by itself the acceleration of *this body* (which requires mention of the fact that I dropped it as well as appeal to the law of gravity). That is why Philo talks about explaining "particular effects by more general causes," not about explaining "a particular effect by a more general cause" (4.14.Philo to Cleanthes).

8. Part 5

1. Perhaps we could view "like effects prove like causes" as a slogan summarizing a set of related principles. Here are three more: Since likeness is symmetrical, (1) "like causes prove like effects." Since likeness is a matter of degree, (2) "the more alike the effects, the more alike the causes" and (3) "the more alike the causes the more alike the effects." Philo's discussion makes use of (2) but not (1) or (3) because the argument is to and not from "the universal cause," "the Author of Nature."

2. How wide is this claim? Does Philo mean that this is the only experimental argument *for theism* or that this is the only experimental argument *for anything*? Surpris-

ingly, the latter: Philo ascribes to Cleanthes the very extensive claim that *all* (just, valid, proper) arguments from experience to any matter of fact or existence are founded on the principle of causal analogy. Theology, then, merely *applies* this universal principle of reasoning; it does not *alter* or *expand* it.

3. There is an unstated third contention: (3) All acceptable arguments concerning matters of fact and existence are experimental ones. This is implicit in Cleanthes' criticism of Demea's "*a priori* argument" in Part 9, where he holds that "there is an evident absurdity in pretending to demonstrate a matter of fact, or to prove it by any arguments *a priori*" (9.5.Cleanthes to Demea).

4. Further evidence that Philo is uncomfortable expressing the sentiments of this paragraph is that Hume seems to have been dissatisfied in writing them. On revision, Hume altered the language in a number of places, changing many words (e.g., "enlarged" for "extended") without changing the meaning. It is as if Hume—or Philo—cannot quite find the right words to express these points, simply because there is no conviction.

5. Here the triumph is noted by Pamphilus; later (8.12 and 10.36) it will be announced by Philo himself.

6. Only the first two of the five attributes are so marked in the text (by "First" and "Secondly"), but the others are obvious enough, especially when 5.7 and 5.9, which are later insertions, are bracketed.

7. See Tweyman (1983).

8. Philo expresses the point rather delicately: "The effect, so far as it falls under our cognizance, is not infinite" (5.5.Philo to Cleanthes). Perhaps he means to allow that the effect may be infinite but that we cannot, or do not, know this. Or perhaps he is making the Kantian point that all objects and events for us—as distinct from things in themselves—are always finite.

9. Here (5.6) "the deity" is uncapitalized, a rare occurrence. Is this just a careless error? Or does it mark the low esteem Philo has for a conception of God that does not require perfection?

10. Finitude does not entail imperfection, because something could be finite but "perfect of its kind" or perfect in some respects though not in all. Later Cleanthes will attempt to fashion a "finitely perfect" deity to solve the problem of evil (11.1.Cleanthes to Philo).

11. Presumably these "difficulties" are the natural evils to be discussed in Parts 10 and 11, but they might also be natural irregularities and anomalies that baffle human inquiry.

12. Here Philo finds it natural to employ an analogy: Just as when we are assessing whether there is one god or many gods simply on the basis of the created world all we know is that the maker or makers must have sufficient power to make the world, similarly, "where we see a body raised in a scale, we are sure that there is in the opposite scale, however concealed from sight, some counterpoising weight equal to it," although we cannot determine from this evidence alone whether there is "an aggregate of several distinct bodies, or one uniform united mass" (5.9.Philo to Cleanthes). Cleanthes cannot deny the appropriateness of such an analogy.

13. Philo uses this analogy more extensively in Part 6: Even though an animal body seems teleological, it is clearly not an artifact, so design by an external intelligent being is not at all apparent.

14. Philo does not mention the human psychological accompaniments of mortality and procreation—fear of death and sexual desire—but he does go on in 5.11 to speak of their material or bodily conditions.

15. Philo mentions "eyes, a nose, mouth, ears, &c," but with the previous point about reproduction in mind, we can add "organs of generation" as well, and more besides.

16. This statement foreshadows Philo's famous distillation of "the whole of natural theology" into a similar "somewhat ambiguous, at least undefined proposition" in 12.33.

17. Philo's language is ambiguous and probably ironically aimed at Demea: Philo

does not himself prefer a "wild and unsettled" theology to no theology at all. But does he prefer no theology at all to a "wild and unsettled" theology? Does he prefer any theology to no theology at all? What are the alternatives in his mind? Again, we must await Part 12.

18. Nor need they be Philo's views. Philo loves to imagine and explore possibilities he does not himself believe.

19. Cleanthes' indifference to theological specificity greatly assists an easy and unsurprising reconciliation with Philo in Part 12.

9. Part 6

1. This fact is unmentioned, but it is surely recognized by Philo and Cleanthes and perhaps even dimly comprehended by Demea. Demea's dawning recognition in Part 11 is largely what prompts his departure: He at last recognizes that they do not form a united "company."

2. Philo first says only that his alternative "must acquire an air of probability from the method of reasoning so much insisted on by Cleanthes," but he goes on to claim that "the universe resembles *more* a human body than it does the works of human art and contrivance" (6.4.Philo to Cleanthes; emphasis added). So Philo thinks his alternative is more probable than Cleanthes' hypothesis, on Cleanthes' principles of inference.

3. Philo overstates his case. He begins with the universe bearing "a great resemblance to an animal or organized body" but concludes "the world, therefore, I infer, is an animal, and the Deity is the SOUL of the world" (6.3). The unjustified slide from resemblance to identity should surprise only those who think that Philo is an absolutely impeccable thinker. But no character in this conversation is without defect: Demea is an authoritarian misologist, Cleanthes is without dialectical skill, and Philo lacks the proper humility his skepticism officially requires and his actual performance warrants.

4. Mereology is the mathematical, logical, or metaphysical theory of parts and wholes; the word is derived from the Greek *meros,* "part."

5. The use of "occur" instead of "occurs" is not a misprint, but a subtle subjunctive: It means roughly "If anything *should or were to occur* to you," as if Philo has no expectation that Cleanthes will think of something to say. (Of course he has *every* expectation!) And indeed something does immediately "occur" to Cleanthes. In fact, he had something in mind already, however inane, and gave every sign to Philo of wanting to say it.

6. Philo will later seize on this line of thought 7 as if it were "a new idea" of his own devising (7.1.Philo to Cleanthes and Demea), but in fact the idea is at least half due to Cleanthes.

7. Allegedly by Lucullus, Roman consul and general who lived 110?–57? B.C. But all Cleanthes' argument requires is that the trees were introduced by some person(s) at some time in the past.

8. Cleanthes does not consider the possibility that "the revolutions of human society" have affected not the *existence* of cherry trees but rather our *knowledge* of their existence—perhaps the trees have been present in Europe from eternity but records do not go back very far or are defective as far back as they do go.

9. Perhaps the latter grace explains the former: Philo does not want to embarrass Cleanthes by pointing out his intellectual inadequacies in front of Pamphilus.

10. Given Philo's inventiveness, Cleanthes should be grateful that Philo makes but a single point about catastrophism; one can only begin to imagine how many possibilities he might have suggested for why, even in an eternal world, species might fail to exist at some time in an environment for which they are naturally fitted. For example, the land may have moved; regional or global climate might have changed; species could be extinguished through disease, competition, predation, infertility, and many other causes; a species might be blocked from dispersing through non-human means; humans might have chopped down or burned all the trees; and so forth.

11. This view is compatible with but not identical to Philo's earlier hypothesis that "the Deity is the SOUL of the world" (6.3.Philo to Cleanthes), for the world's "eternal,

inherent principle of order" may reside in matter and/or mind—in the world's body and/or its soul.

12. Philo introduces a mildly jarring note when he says that "all of these systems, then, of scepticism, polytheism, and theism you must allow, on your principles, to be on a like footing" (6.13.Philo to Cleanthes). We should antecedently expect Philo to award skepticism the palm of triumph, as he does in Part 8: In the midst of equally plausible claims for competing systems, "A total suspense of judgement is here our only reasonable resource" (8.12.Philo to Cleanthes). Skepticism wins where no substantive hypothesis can gain the upper hand. But why then is skepticism here "on a like footing" with various substantive hypotheses? Perhaps because "skepticism" here does not have its customary meaning but is synonymous with "naturalism" or "materialism" (nature or matter having its own "original, inherent principle of order"), with the implied negation, and hence skepticism, of theism in its various forms (including polytheism). This view comports with the order of Philo's presentation (polytheism and theism in 6.13; naturalism or materialism in 6.12).

10. Part 7

1. Cleanthes will close Part 7 by remarking that he is "*unable*" to respond "on a sudden" (7.18.Cleanthes to Philo; emphasis added). Here is the contrast between their characters in a nutshell: Philo rushes in where Cleanthes fears to tell (cf. 6.7).

2. Philo explored one part of the analogy of the universe to an animal body in 6.3 (the deity as the world-soul), and Cleanthes suggested the vegetable analogy in 6.8.

3. Philo is noncommittal in this Part about the principles under discussion. Some of his earlier remarks seem opposed, and the consequences he draws seem untenable to him as well as to Cleanthes. But we should not foreclose the possibility that Philo in the end accepts Cleanthes' principles as the best of a bad lot—and even accepts Cleanthes' conclusion, however "lame and defective" (7.1.Philo to Cleanthes).

4. There are ironies aplenty in this seemingly innocuous remark. Cleanthes is their friend in quite different ways: an "intimate" to Philo, merely polite to Demea. Moreover, Philo and Demea have little in common, so the use of "our" is largely empty. And why does Philo choose to refer to Cleanthes at all by the distancing "our friend" instead of directly by "you"? Why is he turning Cleanthes into a spectator at the examination of his own principles?

5. Philo's terms are a bit misleading: "Generation" is the originating principle of animals and "vegetation" of plants. But in a more natural and traditional (Aristotelian) sense, Philo is really concerned with generation in both cases: "Generation" is a living being's principle of reproduction, its production of another living being of the same kind, while "vegetation" is its principle of growth and self-maintenance. "Spinning," or the extrusion of a non-living part, is something else altogether, and its disanalogy to "generation and vegetation" is perhaps why Philo introduces it almost as an afterthought in 7.17.

6. Here Philo thinks the animal and vegetable analogies are on a par, with neither having any "advantage" in resemblance (cf. 7.6.Philo to Demea). Later, however, he does claim a certain advantage for generation over vegetation: We learn from experience that generation sometimes produces reason, though reason never produces generation (and, though he does not say this, vegetation never produces reason nor reason vegetation) (cf. 7.14–15.Philo to Demea).

7. Recall that Cleanthes had earlier claimed—also without supplying evidence—that the world seems more like a plant than an animal (6.8.Cleanthes to Philo).

8. Which objects does Demea have in mind? Is he comparing animals against vegetables or animals and vegetables together against the world?

9. This paragraph and the next present a small but intriguing problem: In 7.7–8, Pamphilus reports what Demea "says" and what Philo "cries" with verbs in the present tense, whereas elsewhere in this Part, and indeed throughout the rest of the *Dialogues,* the verbs he uses are always in the past tense—"said," "replied," and so forth. Why? Is this

some slip of the dialogue-reciter Pamphilus or the *Dialogues*-writer Hume, or is it rather a clue to the text's meaning? On behalf of the last possibility, the sudden jar in verb tense does provide a kind of emphasis, precisely at the point where Demea and Philo agree, in their different ways, that there is not enough "data" to settle which, if any, cosmological analogy is best. Demea "says" this in four rhetorical questions, while Philo "cries" it out in three assertions and three rhetorical questions, but they are both fastening on the same key weakness in Cleanthes' whole procedure.

10. The similarities are either unclear or dubious. Perhaps Philo means merely that all four principles are causal principles or that they all produce material effects. But any clearer or closer likeness is problematic. Surely the effects are much more similar within the range of one principle (one plant's reproduction more or less resembles that of another) than they are across principles (plants reproduce differently from animals, and both work differently from minds and instincts).

11. We should not make too much of Philo's apparent concession here to the powers of *a priori* thinking, for his point is only hypothetical: Since experience cannot settle the issue, to avoid begging the question one would have to establish *a priori* that "order is, from its nature, inseparably attached to thought" and never to matter "of itself." But Philo is not committed to affirming the antecedent; indeed, he thinks the question can *only* be begged, never settled, whether *a posteriori* or *a priori*.

12. But what about Demea? Does Philo's point about the arbitrariness of ultimate principles apply to Demea as well as to Cleanthes? Philo does not say, for here he is concerned to present only two "sides"—his and Cleanthes'. But we will get a better glimpse of Demea's ultimate theoretical principle (absolute necessity) in Part 9.

13. He attributes the thought to "the Bramins," perhaps out of modesty or as a way of deflecting responsibility.

11. Part 8

1. This first stage of the examination (Parts 2–8), a consideration of the "natural" attributes of God, bulks considerably larger than the second (Parts 10–11), a consideration of the "moral" attributes of God. In both stages, Philo exposes many difficulties quite "inconvenient" for traditional theism as well as for Cleanthes' "anthropomorphism." The bulk of the *Dialogues* thus is given over to examination of "the" design argument—or, better, of various design-like arguments that seek to reason from a view of human experience to theological conclusions by extending analogies from the world we experience to a transcendent order we cannot.

2. Significantly, in a late textual revision ("either yours or"), Philo places Cleanthes' hypothesis alongside his own in mentioning the long odds against it (8.1.Philo to Cleanthes).

3. Or to the Epicurean *family* of hypotheses, for Philo develops several variations.

4. According to Philo, contrivance involves "a symmetry of parts," "an adjustment of means to ends and a tendency to self-preservation" (8.7.Philo to Cleanthes). Are these three properties independent of one another? Is each one necessary for contrivance, and are all three jointly sufficient? Philo does not say. Only the second feature is emphasized by Cleanthes in discussing human contrivances (2.5.Cleanthes to Philo and Demea); the first feature is optional, and the third is lacking altogether.

5. Does Philo himself genuinely believe that this is "justly" viewed as "the *most* absurd system that has yet been proposed"? Is he merely softening up Cleanthes or speaking ironically? Perhaps, but I see no reason not to take his words at face value. After all, what Philo goes on to elaborate is not the "old" Epicurean hypothesis but rather a new one with "a few alterations"—or rather, a family of altered versions that seek to repair various absurdities of the original Epicurean hypothesis. The final altered version may not be so absurd after all.

6. Philo claims that "there is not probably, at present, in the whole universe, one particle of matter at absolute rest" (8.5.Philo to Demea). But Philo wavers on the status of

this claim. Sometimes actual motion is necessary to matter, since matter has a "perpetual agitation, which seems essential to it" (8.6.Philo to Demea). At other times it takes experience to confirm that "every individual is perpetually changing, and every part of every individual" (8.8.Philo to Demea), even though composite wholes appear to remain (somewhat) constant. But regardless of the basis of Philo's universal claim, he need not hold that every particle is *actually* in motion, only that each is *potentially* so.

7. And every *sequence* of events, or at least every *causally ordered sequence* of events?

8. That is, by the contact and push of particles against one another.

9. Philo says "the same stock of it [motion], *or nearly the same*" (8.5.Philo to Demea; emphasis added). Why the qualification? If any motion is lost, then he needs to say why a finite quantity of motion should not dwindle to nothing in infinite time—unless there is replenishment of motion, and that would again raise Demea's worry.

10. The composition and resolution may be actual or merely conceptual.

11. Philo is willing to appeal to experience *and tradition*; he is not confined to his own personal experience, much less to a solipsism of the moment, for he can call upon the experience of others over time in a developed community with all the acquiescence in memory, testimony, authority, and the like that tradition involves.

12. Philo is perpetually attracted to the idea of a world in which no deity intervenes in particular ways, and if he contemplates a god at all, it is one who does not intervene in the world after creating it. This idea of something self-sufficient intrinsically or by gift is, I suggest, "the kind of imperfect analogy" at the heart of Philo's position, in contrast to Cleanthes' core analogy (also imperfect) of human contrivance and use. Plato's god, if he has one, is therefore a deistic one. In a deistic universe, there is little room for a deity save as remote, useless, and unfathomable "first cause."

13. Philo claims that "this is actually the case with the present world." This claim clearly begs the exact question at issue. Is Philo insinuating that this view of nature is, for all practical purposes, held by Demea and Cleanthes as well as by himself, despite their great theological differences?

14. Philo uses the word "fermentation" here in a special sense. In alchemy and pre-modern chemistry, fermentation involved an "internal effervescence or commotion," the production of heat, and an alteration in the substance (*OED*), but Philo simply seems to mean "irregular" internal motion with or without the production of heat.

15. These comments come in two paragraphs (8.7–8) added by Hume in a late revision.

16. See note 4 above.

17. Once again Philo begs the question in favor of his hypothesis by claiming that "this we find to be the case with the universe at present" (8.8.Philo to Demea [and Cleanthes]). Why does he introduce such an inappropriate appeal to experience in the midst of his cosmological speculations? At any rate, his friends do not protest his question-begging appeal.

18. Why isn't the move from whole to parts as generally fallacious as the move from parts to whole—the "fallacy of *de*composition," as one might term it?

19. There is irony in this argument. Philo, who had earlier taxed Cleanthes for thinking he could infer contrivance from parts to whole, here finds no difficulty in inferring natural necessity from whole to parts. Clearly Philo's own "imperfect analogy" (8.1.Philo to Cleanthes) is no better than Cleanthes'. But Philo would agree: No speculative cosmological hypothesis is better off than any other, and our only recourse is skeptical suspense of judgment.

20. Cleanthes does not mention a third kind: (3) the utility of humans to animals and vegetables (not only parasites, predators, and scavengers but also pets, livestock, and cultivated plants). His point of view is, as always, complacently anthropocentric: All the conveniences, and none of the inconveniences, are *for us*!

21. With the insertion of "benevolence," Cleanthes points ahead to Parts 10–11, where the so-called moral attributes of God are considered.

22. "You may safely infer" may mean either (1) Cleanthes' conclusion is true, (2) his argument is valid (the conclusion follows from his premises), or (3) his argument is sound (his argument is valid and premises true). Philo does accept Cleanthes' conclusion but not necessarily his argument, and so not necessarily his premises.

23. A sly allusion to Joseph Butler's extremely popular *The Analogy of Religion* (1736; 6th ed. 1764).

24. Here and in the next instance Philo conveniently forgets our experience of human contrivance—the very key to cosmology for Cleanthes—in his claims about "all instances" of experience. There is irony in Philo immodestly overstating his case to foster in Cleanthes a sense of modesty (about his own hypothesis) and tolerance (for hypotheses of others). But such irony is only another example of what Philo wants to affirm: that every hypothesis suffers from "a small incongruity" (8.11.Philo to Cleanthes). Such incongruity arises both in the hypotheses criticized and in the criticism of them.

25. Philo attributes to Cleanthes the view of divine mind or thought as "eternal, or in other words, an animal ingenerable and immortal" and hints at its difficulties. But Cleanthes has not explicitly committed to such a view.

26. Philo will proclaim triumph again in 10.36, in the first person. But here he speaks of "the sceptic" in the third person. Is he alienated from the skeptic as homeless vagabond? Does he want to put some distance between himself and the apparently null result of his testing of the design hypothesis (so that he can return to it in Part 12)?

27. The syntax is ambiguous: Is the skeptic in company *with* all mankind or is the skeptic *against* all mankind? Skepticism might seem to be contrary to general human common sense, but Philo would disagree; instead, he regards skepticism about matters transcending the bounds of human experience as both an implication and a safeguard of common sense and its community. What he said earlier about Stoicism applies also to skepticism: "The effects of the Stoic's reasoning will appear in his conduct in common life, and through the whole tenor of his actions" (1.8.Philo to Cleanthes).

28. Why "they" and not "we"? Have theological adventurers become foreigners to themselves?

12. Part 9

1. Part 9 has eleven paragraphs; Part 8 has twelve paragraphs; Parts 3, 5, and 6 have thirteen paragraphs each; and all the others are longer still. From another perspective, the attention lavished on "experimental theism" in Parts 2–8 (forty-one pages devoted to the "natural" divine attributes) and Parts 10–11 (twenty pages on the "moral" divine attributes) contrasts remarkably with that given to the "argument *a priori*": Part 9 has only four pages, less than a fifteenth of the pages devoted to arguments from experience.

2. As implied by, for example, Dye (1989); Morrisroe (1969a, 1969b, 1970); and Stove (1978).

3. See Calvert (1983); Campbell (1996); Dye (1989); Franklin (1980); Khamara (1992); Stahl (1984); Stewart (1985); and Stove (1978).

4. The word "INFINITY" is in capital letters, for speaker's emphasis. We may imagine Demea, red in face, dramatically raising his voice to stress these words, as if merely *attributing* infinity to divinity were itself an act of piety—as it doubtless is, on Demea's view of piety.

5. The argument has considerable but not complete affinities to the one offered by Samuel Clarke in his *Demonstration of the Being and Attributes of God* (1705). See Khamara (1992).

6. Does Demea think that causes are the same as reasons? Or that they are different but that the PSR covers both equally? Clearly Demea lacks interest in such niceties.

7. Clearly Demea must mean by "any thing" any *contingent* thing; that is, one which is neither necessary nor impossible. Otherwise a necessary being would be impossible, since it could not contain its own reason for existing. This is but one of many ex-

amples of Demea's logical laxity and another reminder that his concern is not for argument per se but for the reinforcement of passionately held beliefs.

8. Demea does not consider these complications: (1) Perhaps contingent series *a* is caused by contingent series *b*, and so on. (2) Perhaps the necessarily existent cause of series *a* is distinct from the necessarily existent cause of series *b*, and so on. Most likely he would insist that *every* regress must terminate in something that necessarily exists and that there can be only one such being.

9. Recall Demea's worry about the practical religious value of Cleanthes' experimental theology in Part 6.1. Cleanthes is just as exercised about the practical religious value of Demea's *a priori* theology.

10. The martial and potentially violent connotations of "cuts off" are significant and yield insight into Demea's character. Demea is willing, should reason fail, to resort to threat and violence in support of what he regards as "true religion."

11. Cleanthes waffles on the meaning of "matter." Earlier he used it as equivalent to "material universe," while here he uses it in quasi-Aristotelian contrast with "form," although there is atomistic thinking in some uses where he identifies "matter" with a part of the material universe; for example, a "particle of matter," and "form" with the order or arrangement of particles.

12. This is an invalid inference form in two respects, as Philo has often pointed out to Cleanthes (cf. 2.8, 2.18, 2.20, 2.22–23, 7.3, 7.11): (1) the inference from what we can conceive to what is the case is tenuous, and (2) not every property of parts, not even every property of each and every part, is a property of the whole. So even if each and every part of the universe is contingent, it doesn't follow that the universe as a whole is contingent. Perhaps, as Charles Hartshorne long argued, it is necessary that there be some world or other, though not necessary that there should be this particular world. See Hartshorne (1948 and 1964).

13. Presumably Cleanthes takes his phrase "general cause" in 9.8 to mean the same as Demea's "ultimate cause" in 9.3. But they may diverge: A general cause touches every effect, and not necessarily indirectly, while an ultimate cause reaches every effect *only* through intermediaries. Again Cleanthes may be "accurate," but he is not always precise.

14. Or "WHOLE," as Cleanthes expresses it, perhaps to emphasize its uniqueness.

15. Presumably Cleanthes means "causes," not "cause," for each of the twenty has a "particular" cause of its own.

16. See Pamphilus on the inculcation of obvious and important truths in PH.3.

17. But, of course, Demea is already convinced of his *position*. What he seeks is neither conviction nor justification but rather psychological reinforcement by any means available.

18. Note that Cleanthes can agree with this conclusion without conceding that all reasoning is useless as a "source" of religion, for he thinks that experimental reasoning is not subject to the same strictures as *a priori* reasoning.

13. Part 10

1. Part 10 is only the fifth longest Part (after Parts 12, 11, 2, and 1), but it has the largest number of paragraphs (thirty-six) and contains a number of twists and subplots.

2. See Tilley (1988) and Tweyman (1987) on the "Dialogues on Evil" in Parts 10 and 11. Other writers with interesting slants on these Parts include Beaty (1988); Capitan (1966); Pike (1963); Solon and Wertz (1969); and Stewart (1995).

3. Notice the distancing and even contempt in Demea's reference to "the people." Demea universalizes his own experience to gain a vantage point superior to everyone else.

4. Whether Demea intends this addition as a response to Philo's mention of "wickedness" in 10.2 is questionable, for Demea views human misery as something for which we are not responsible, except as by groveling we can escape it.

5. This sense of "pathetic," common in the eighteenth century, means "producing

an effect upon the emotions; exciting the passions or affections; moving, stirring, affecting" (*OED*).

6. Demea never stops to question the learned authoritativeness of poets (or anyone) who agree with him. Any concurring voice reinforces *Demea's* authority.

7. Hume added the following sentence to be inserted *as a footnote* at this point: "That sentiment had been maintained by Dr. King and some few others before Leibnitz [*sic*], though by none of so great fame as that German philosopher." Why does this significant qualification not appear in Philo's mouth? Why does Philo intentionally overstate his case? A similar episode occurs in Part 9, where Philo's grandiose claim that no single species "has yet been extinguished in the universe" is qualified by a marginal footnote instancing the authority of Caesar for a few "exceptions to the proposition here delivered" —but this latter footnote was scored out. In both cases Philo proposes glittering generalities that he knows require qualification. Is he merely being "careless" (PH.6) in the modern sense of lacking due care, or has he shrewdly pumped up his rhetoric to entice Demea into finally exposing his true colors? If the latter, then we need not credit Philo with full assent to Demea's sense of universal human misery; if he does share somewhat in this sense, he certainly does not agree with Demea's religious prescription. As we shall see in Part 12, Philo's own sense of piety is much closer to Cleanthes' than to Demea's.

8. The whole exchange in 10.3–7 has the air of a setup so transparent that even Demea can participate in it.

9. Cleanthes did not feel compelled earlier (2.5) to insist at such length upon a similarly supposedly evident and universal premise for the design argument.

10. "Insolent reproach or abuse; insulting or offensively contemptuous language or treatment; despite; scornful rudeness" (*OED*; Hume's 1762 *History of England* is the only eighteenth-century example cited).

11. "False and malicious misrepresentation of the words or actions of others, calculated to injure their reputation; libelous detraction, slander" (*OED*).

12. The only examples Demea gives for "the gay side of life" are a ball, an opera, and a court. He has no sense, perhaps no experience, of simpler or more commonplace pleasures. In particular, he has probably not enjoyed the present conversations with Cleanthes and Philo, save for the opportunity to harangue Pamphilus and wallow in misery.

13. Philo's fourth reply is emphatic. He will not permit escape from misery through inaction. Philo perhaps has in mind Demea's longing for a future exit from this life into heavenly gardens of rest. Philo does not believe there is such surcease, and he is as opposed to a religion of escape as he is to one of Panglossian false comfort.

14. What is the "it" of which Cleanthes feels "little or nothing"? Can it be (a sense of) human misery altogether? Or is it a sense of misery as infecting all of life and vastly outweighing all pleasures and goods? Clearly it must be the latter. Even for the sake of his beloved design argument, Cleanthes cannot plausibly deny the existence of *some* evils and miseries such as Demea and Philo point out. What he can deny, however, is that misery bulks so large as they have maintained. Cleanthes holds, in fact, that the goods of life greatly outweigh its miseries; but all he need claim at this point is that pains do not vastly outweigh pleasures. At issue is one more question of *degree*, of more or less. This is the disputed heart of natural theology, as we shall see in Part 12.

15. The alliteration of the names of his three examples—"Charles V," "Cicero," and "Cato"—with "Cleanthes" is no mere accident. Demea wants Cleanthes to feel the kinship.

16. Is this how Demea reconciles the contradictions in his own positions?

17. Nelson Pike (1963) notes that many have taken Philo in this passage to be purveying an *a priori* argument "against the existence of God." Although Pike thinks this argument is "quite unconvincing," he holds that there *is* an argument presented by Philo and that Hume is speaking through Philo as a mouthpiece. I think Philo is neither advancing nor considering an atheistic argument from evil; he has something else in mind.

18. Interestingly, "superstition" is the only ill repeated from Philo's earlier list. Clearly Philo thinks superstition is important as well as avoidable.

19. The tease is evident when we ask what kind of "account" and what kind of "derivation" we would have from something incomprehensible.

20. What sort of smile is on Cleanthes' face? Is it a dawning realization of the meaning of a long-puzzling situation? Is it a knowing smirk as Philo comes out of Demea's closet? Or is it the insider's grin of sharing a joke at another's expense? Pamphilus reports the smile but does not construe it.

21. He means, of course, his own or "true" religion—clearly Demea's religion is untroubled by universal human misery precisely because it is founded on such misery.

22. Some doctrine of deep-seated human corruption is required by Demea's religion. That makes it even stranger that Demea does not raise, much less insist on, this point. Everyone seems content to thresh out the question on the floor of happiness and unhappiness, worrying chiefly about pains that are beyond individual human control and not much at all about evils for which people are personally responsible.

23. Is Philo's cry the heartfelt anguish of a sincere believer in a good God contemplating the miseries of this world? Is it the cool irony of a non-believer, turning the emotional language of anguish into a mockery of theistic belief? Or is it simply the ghostly trace of a discarded belief, a merely conventional expression of emotion? Judgments of Philo's intention and sincerity must rely on an overall understanding of his role and positions in the *Dialogues*. My own view is that Philo's cry expresses genuine feeling but implies no developed view of divine providence.

24. Here Philo adds a secondary layer of admonishment: He chides Cleanthes not just for introducing total skepticism but for doing it "unawares"; he is both in error and ignorant of his error.

25. Philo says this result would hold even if the empirical phenomena were not mixed but "pure"—that is, containing only happiness and no misery—so long as the phenomena were not infinite but finite. With pure phenomena Philo stresses Cleanthes' inability to infer an *infinitely* good God, whereas with mixed phenomena Philo stresses his inability to infer an infinitely *good* God.

26. Also 5.5 and 8.12.

27. Hume replaced "perhaps" with "I believe" in a revision of the manuscript so as to underline Philo's commitment to this view. It is rare for Philo—in the presence of Demea—to express his own personal beliefs, as if doing so were difficult, distasteful, or dangerous.

28. I say "perceptible" since one can always impute irony as a way of making a recalcitrant text square with an interpretation antecedently assumed. An interpretation armed with omnipotent irony can never be refuted. Moreover, irony does comport well with the skeptical views and critical role of Philo. But there are other ways to interpret what Philo says and does without imputing irony, and a non-ironical internal *interpretation* emerges when passages such as the present one are taken as data, not as interpreted outcome.

14. Part 11

1. Actually, Cleanthes asks "if it deserve *our* attention" (emphasis added). He is (or wants to think he is) Philo's ally here, not his competitor, in the search for a defensible natural theology. Cleanthes hopes Philo will find this new theory as promising as Cleanthes does, and, despite his criticisms, Philo does have some sympathy for this view, as we shall see in Part 12.

2. Cleanthes' language is extremely circumspect and qualified: "I scruple not to allow . . . that I have been apt to suspect." Why is he triply indirect? Is he politely seeking to soothe Demea, whose orthodoxy is powerfully challenged by the thought of a finite Deity? If so, his indirection works, for Demea utters not a peep until Philo starts blaming God for moral evil (in 11.17).

3. Cleanthes' point here pertains only to Demea, not to Philo. Philo does not oppose the use of human analogy in thinking of the Deity—though he does differ from Cleanthes on the strengths of various likenesses—but Demea disagrees, since natural teleology affords no inference at all to the oppressive "unknown powers" he fears.

4. Cleanthes here echoes his earlier attack on Demea's "mysticism" (in 4.1): Our ideas of divinity are like all our other ideas; they derive their (valid) meaning solely from our experience.

5. See 10.34.Philo to Cleanthes. Philo there claims that "nothing can shake the solidity of this reasoning, so short, so clear, so decisive; except we assert, that these subjects exceed all human capacity," but Cleanthes' empiricist semantics blocks the latter exception. For Cleanthes, that way lies not true piety but unmeaning.

6. Cleanthes assumes there is exactly one such Author. But with finite perfections there is no guarantee of uniqueness, for we are in the realm of possible gods, not a necessary God. Still, monotheism versus polytheism is not a vital issue between Philo and Cleanthes; it is raised only once (in 5.8–9), and is not a bone of contention in Part 12.

7. Cleanthes is focused on the moral and not the natural attributes of the Deity, and he wants to safeguard divine benevolence and wisdom by limiting some other attribute. But there are no good *empirical* grounds for doing so; each and every divine attribute is at risk of limitation on Cleanthes' "experimental" approach.

8. One of the problems Cleanthes has with Demea, in fact, is his tendency to worship brute and arbitrary power at the expense of intelligible and caring purpose.

9. Neither stout criticism of a view nor silence in its defense means that one does not *believe* it!

10. What *is* the "present subject"? Is it (1) the "new theory" broached by Cleanthes, (2) any finite theology, or (3) the relevance of mixed phenomena to the moral attributes of divinity? The four "circumstances of evil" in 11. 5–12 have relevance to any finite theology as well as to Cleanthes' version. The survey of possible hypotheses about the divine moral attributes in 11.13–15 and the discussion of moral evil in 11.16–17 likewise have a wider purview. But perhaps Philo prefers an ambiguous understanding of "present subject" so that he may deliver *whatever* "occurs" to him without worrying about its precise salience.

11. There is an implicit assumption that the house is (designed) *for* the inhabitants. Philo wants to show that even with this design assumption, Cleanthes' finite theology falters.

12. Quite naturally, Philo deals with both existence and nature: We cannot infer that there *is* a Being of *this* nature.

13. Philo's agility in sliding from "all" to "most" (and back again) is remarkable. It gives credence to Hermippus's impression of "the careless scepticism of PHILO" (PH.6.Pamphilus to Hermippus), meaning not carefree but lacking due care. But perhaps Philo is more careful than he appears, even if he is annoyingly imprecise. The initial claim of "all" prepares the listener's mind; but "most" is all Philo needs for his claim that our world could be significantly improved by any superior being willing and able. The evils that would not be ameliorated or excised by altering the four circumstances are relatively few and insignificant. So Philo doesn't care about precision here because it doesn't matter.

14. A classically bad argument: If one can do without food for an hour, why should one ever need to eat? Philo, who is so rough on Cleanthes' inferences from part to whole concerning the world, here indulges himself in an equally dodgy part/whole inference about animal life.

15. Has Philo forgotten that his target is supposed to be a *finite* theology? No. Both he and Cleanthes tend to think of perfection (1) as a matter of degree, and (2) as not entailing infinity. So "very perfect" for them does not imply "infinite." But it does sound odd to speak of perfection as anything less than absolutely maximal.

16. No single species has yet gone extinct, claims Philo. A footnote instancing possible but dubious reports of extinctions from Caesar and Strabo, "and some few more instances," was written in the margin but then scored out. The rhetorical trick of bolstering

a generalization by allowing a few rare exceptions is not foreign to Philo, but it backfires here. After all, Philo's point would be helped, not hindered, if "great frugality" often led to extinction!

17. See Hick (1978).

18. Moral evil will be discussed shortly (in 11.16–17).

19. The paragraph is a later insertion, but it is no mere afterthought. It is precisely what is needed to shift the discussion from the four circumstances of evil to the more general issue of what evil implies about the divine moral attributes.

20. Philo has at hand the now-obsolete meaning of "fair or pleasing to the eye or sight; beautiful, handsome, lovely" as well as the more modern senses of "having a fair or attractive appearance or character . . . but in reality devoid of the qualities apparently possessed" and of being "fair, attractive, or plausible, but wanting in genuineness or sincerity" (*OED*, senses 1, 2, 3). The attractiveness of "the Manichaean system" need not be *merely* apparent; it can truly please in some respects, if not in all.

21. Note that it is "causes" in the plural, unlike the singular "original source" in the previous paragraph. We should not read too much into Philo's shift. He is merely asking what we can infer about whatever it is that causes the observable universe. Since these attributes are moral ones, they must belong to a personal being or beings. So Philo is asking about the motives or character of a Deity or deities.

22. Philo means that they are completely or purely good, without a trace of evil in their makeup, not that they are unsurpassably good; even so, "perfect" doesn't imply "infinite."

23. Philo seems to interpret the third possibility as equivalent to "the Manichaean system" in the previous paragraph. But there are other ways to understand it: For example, perhaps the first cause is moved by both good and evil, with or without a steady predominance of one over the other; perhaps only some kinds of good (and evil) appeal; or perhaps divine motivation is inconstant, so that first good then evil predominate in different situations. For an insightful commentary on Philo's argument here, see Jacquette (1985).

24. "Supreme Being" replaces "First Cause" from an earlier draft. In either case, Philo has shifted back from "first causes" to a unique author of nature. Is Philo suggesting that we have no good empirical way to ascertain *how many* divine beings there are?

25. The moment's significance is underlined by the way the speakers insert themselves into the conversation. Demea interrupts Philo, then Cleanthes takes it upon himself to respond to Demea on Philo's behalf, and then Philo interrupts him! These abrupt and impolite entrances indicate something crucial is at stake.

26. Demea doesn't seem to understand that Philo and Cleanthes are friends, not enemies, of each other. Demea must have a great many enemies, because his piety thrives on opposition, real or imagined, and the dichotomy of friend/enemy is a most fundamental way he sizes up people. Since friendship for Demea requires agreement in theology and piety, deviation in views implies lack of friendship; therefore, since Philo disagrees with Cleanthes in theology, they cannot be friends.

27. This gesture is more than terminal civility. Cleanthes is politely offering Demea friendship to soften the stinging criticisms he makes of Demea's theology.

28. This "your friend" should be in scare-quotes. Shared humiliation is too shallow a basis for true friendship. If a friend is one with whom one can "live in unreserved intimacy" (12.2.Philo to Cleanthes), then Philo is a friend of Cleanthes but not of Demea. Cleanthes has realized this all along, of course, while Demea believes what he wants to believe.

29. *Whose* "vulgar theology" is this? Is it Cleanthes' and Demea's? But they share little in theology, certainly not the characterization that follows. Is it the common theology of the day, "ours" only because Cleanthes and Demea are contemporaries with it? Is it orthodox theology at any time and place, "ours" only by courtesy or flattery? In the *Dialogues*, it is only Demea who holds all these "vulgar" views.

30. Searching for the right word here, Hume first wrote "arguments," then "doc-

trines," and only finally "principles." Why is it so hard to find the right word to characterize what Demea believes? Is it because he lives not by belief but by feeling and emotion?

31. Clearly Demea is the unnamed target: He alone in the *Dialogues* upholds the "strange topics" "so fondly cherished by orthodox divines and doctors."

32. Philo refers to the "orthodox divines and doctors" championing "our vulgar theology" mentioned by Cleanthes in 11.19.

33. Philo notes that this alteration in "style" is one with shifting religious uses of skepticism that he noted earlier (1.19); "These reverend gentlemen" will use whatever increases, or preserves, their power over others—the very opposite of adherence to principles.

34. Of course, the kinds of arguments Demea prefers—from authority or *a priori*— are unacceptable to Cleanthes and Philo, and the kind of argument they prefer—from experience, by analogy—is unacceptable to him. So Demea finds himself frustrated in this small society, unable to defend his theology and promote his piety in his accustomed manner.

35. Scott Davis contends that "Demea's departure is a sign of insight" and a "reasoned refusal" to accept Philo's and Cleanthes' "instrumental" canons of rationality (Davis 1991, 254). But this "reformed epistemology" account of Demea is thoroughly external— indeed foreign—to the text's actual portrait of a fearfully pious Demea.

36. But then why did he not feel equally exposed in 1.19, where Philo makes essentially the same point? Did Demea then not understand Philo as referring to *him*?

15. Part 12

1. Revealed religion is at least mentioned by Philo, so perhaps one could say that they discuss all of religion, both natural and revealed. But Philo's mention is more an expression of unfulfilled desire and faint hope than even the bare outline of a position. For Philo and Cleanthes in their comfortable "company," natural religion may be all the religion there is.

2. Whereas in Parts 2–11 the discussion is mostly about theology and rarely about piety, in Part 12 the proportions are reversed: Natural theology assumes a limited role within the context of a more-encompassing natural religious piety.

3. This meaning of "manner" (*OED*, sense 9a: "species, kind, sort") is presently archaic but would have been readily available in the eighteenth century.

4. Carnochan (1988) misperceives this new manner as an "air of casual unconcern," "negligence," and "unbuttoned ease" (521). He is also mistaken in thinking that intellectual "fervor" and rigor have departed with Demea; Demea's fervor is the very antithesis of intellectual rigor. Hendel (1963) is equally misguided in holding that "the argument droops; it becomes simply [!] a conversation between people who understand each other" (382), as if that were a small and uninteresting achievement. Both Carnochan and Hendel confuse controversy, disagreement, and passionate conviction with intellectual rigor.

5. Cleanthes deludes himself if he truly thinks he could "reason" with Demea in Philo's absence, although doubtless they could carry on a civil conversation. Demea's problem with the present "topic of discourse" goes beyond Philo's "spirit of controversy," and it includes fundamental objection to Cleanthes as well. Quite apart from theology, Demea's piety is necessarily intolerant of the tolerant piety Cleanthes shares with Philo.

6. Does "tell truth" instead of "tell the truth" signal that Cleanthes is not telling all the truth or only the truth but just some of the truth? Does he mislead if the phrase is taken for the whole truth?

7. In the changed "manner" of Part 12, we should take his confession at face value—not as more rhetorical posturing but as an honest statement of what Philo truly believes. For a cogent case that Philo's confession in Part 12 is not a "reversal" but a development of his earlier views, see Parent (1976b).

8. Many interpreters believe that Philo is a (barely) covert atheist, so in their view Philo must be dissembling, even to his intimate friend Cleanthes, whenever he expresses

something positive about religion. Henry Aiken, for example, holds that "it is hard to take very seriously the passages in which he [Philo = Hume] seems to avow an attenuated version of theism" (Aiken 1948, viii). On the contrary, there is every reason to believe that, following Demea's departure, Philo can at long last *drop* whatever irony and insincerity attends his earlier skeptical inquiries.

9. See Kemp Smith (1941, 1947); Austin (1985); Battersby (1979); Davis (1991); Hurlbutt (1988); Jessop (1977); Mossner (1977); Price (1965, chap. 4); Rivers (1993); Simpson (1979); and Sutherland (1983).

10. See Rivers (1993) for linkage of this example to John Wilkins' *Of the principles and duties of natural religion* (1675, 6th ed. 1710).

11. Why the question mark and not an exclamation mark? If it is not a typographical error on the part of Hume, does it mean that Philo ironically questions the artifice or its prodigiousness? Or does it mean that he is wonderingly exclaiming amazement?

12. This leaves out the possibility that the divine being could inform us directly by a "more particular" revelation. But this is a possibility of revealed, not natural, religion.

13. By implication, Demea's system is "false, absurd," while Philo seeks "no system at all." It follows, on Cleanthes' assumptions, that Philo's religion cannot be skepticism.

14. Recall Demea and Philo's early agreement that "the question is not concerning the BEING but the NATURE of GOD" (2.1.Demea to Cleanthes and Philo). Since then, all three participants have on occasion disregarded this agreement. Cleanthes held in Part 2 that his design argument proves "at once the existence of a Deity, *and* his similarity to human mind and intelligence" (2.5.Cleanthes to Demea and Philo; emphasis added). Demea's *a priori* argument in Part 9 seems aimed more at proving the existence than the infinite attributes of the Deity (9.3); and Philo's Epicurean worries about evil count as much against the existence as against the nature of a benevolent Deity (10.25). But in Part 12, there is no dispute between Cleanthes and Philo over the existence of the Deity, only over its attributes or nature—more precisely, over the degree of similarity of such divine attributes to human qualities of mind and morals.

15. The self-application to Philo is obvious. Despite what Demea and a host of commentators think, neither Philo's skepticism nor his mysticism entail atheism, although, as we shall see, Philo's alternative to atheism is by no means a full-blooded theism.

16. The atheist's "concession" and "retreat" are distinctly underwhelming. The degree of admitted analogy in both cases is so very remote that the atheist's "retreat" looks very much like an advance, conceding only nominal victory to theism (all 12.7.Philo to Cleanthes). But retreat and advance are also matters of degree.

17. Who are "the theist" and "the atheist"? Cleanthes and Philo? But Philo does not deny the Deity's existence. Demea and Cleanthes? Both profess theism. Perhaps Philo merely means to warn against any easy general distinction between theists and atheists.

18. See Andic (1974); Duerlinger (1971); and Steinberg (1987).

19. There are fourteen footnotes, at 1.1, 1.15, 1.17, 2.2, 5.2 (twice), 9.7, 9.10, 10.6, 11.9, 12.3, 12.8, and 12.23 (twice), and they fall into two groups. (1) The notes contain brief bibliographical citations of sources for quotations or allusions made by Cleanthes (four times), Demea (two times), and Philo (six times). Sometimes they simply name authors (1.17, 9.7), sometimes just titles (1.15, 2.2, 5.2 [twice], 9.10, 12.3, 12.23 [twice]), and sometimes both (1.1, 11.9). (2) These notes are more discursive and add something philosophical: 10.6 comments on "Dr. King" and "Leibnitz," 11.9 on possibly extinct species, and 12.8, by far the longest footnote, on skeptics and dogmatists. It is noteworthy that many references by the speakers are *not* footnoted; compare 1.12, 1.13, 1.17, and 3.1 for Cleanthes; 3.12, 10.13, and 10.21–23 for Demea; 1.8, 1.18, 2.24, 2.27, 5.10, 5.11, 6.13, 7.16, 10.4, 10.25, and 12.32 for Philo.

20. Can Pamphilus have done some homework? In 12.23, Philo refers to Euripides and adds "in a passage which I shall point out to you." Now the "you" primarily refers to Cleanthes, but there is no reason to exclude Pamphilus. So it is conceivable that Philo

gave Pamphilus the reference later and Pamphilus added it as a footnote to his "recital." But what about the references made by Demea? Can we suppose Pamphilus sought out Demea after he left or witnessed as Cleanthes spoke with Demea "apart" from Philo (cf. 12.1.Cleanthes to Philo)? This all seems too far-fetched.

21. See Battersby (1979); Bricke (1975); Malherbe (1995, 223 n. 35); Morrisroe (1974); Noxon (1964); Prince (1992); Shapiro (1985); Simpson (1979); Vink (1986); and Wieand (1985).

22. Moreover, we have accepted the title, "*Dialogues concerning Natural Religion*," as an important clue to the work's meaning; why not accept the footnotes as well? But while Pamphilus is a plausible author of the title of the conversations he "recites" to Hermippus, this is not the case for the footnotes, which have too much the earmarks of an erudite editor.

23. "The text" is as "incurably ambiguous" as Philo's "merely verbal" disputes: "The" autograph text exists in several layers of composition, addition, and emendation; each version or edition is therefore a different text. Further, a text differently contextualized is also a different text—different when the context is an eighteenth-century discussion and when it is a twentieth-century one, different when "winners" and "losers" are differently assigned, different when Hume's own personal views are sought in different speeches. Similarly, every reader sees a different text. So a dialogic text without footnotes would be just one text among many.

24. Again, the use of "confess" signals Philo's sincerity—but also perhaps a bit of contrition.

25. Three pieces of evidence: (1) Cleanthes makes no pretense of showing that experience supports this doctrine—support it must have, on his view of theology, in order to avoid being labeled a "superstition"; (2) this is how Philo interprets Cleanthes in the next paragraph, when Philo includes this doctrine as one "vulgar superstition" that is supposedly "salutary to society" (12.11.Philo to Cleanthes); and (3) Cleanthes does not dispute Philo's interpretation.

26. Note how this defense resembles the practice of Demea that Cleanthes had previously criticized (9.2). The major difference lies in the different pieties.

27. We can now see why it was so important to Cleanthes in Parts 10–11 to insist on a *moral* Deity: It ensures that his religion is true and not false religion.

28. See Passmore (1989).

29. To echo Kant's famous title, *Religion innerhalb der Grenzen der blossen Vernunft* (Königsburg 1793).

30. Philo's shift from "you" (Cleanthes) to "divines" means that Philo does not directly accuse Cleanthes of this contradiction. But is this because (as Philo believes) Cleanthes isn't guilty or because Philo, for once, is being politely indirect?

31. Philo here devises a clever ad hominem against Cleanthes by using his favorite court of appeal: This view, he claims, is "certain, from experience" (12.13.Philo to Cleanthes). He gives Cleanthes three options, all uncomfortable: (1) to loosen his grip on the appeal to experience, (2) to assert that the "facts" of experience differ from Philo's account of them, or (3) to abandon his view that religion's "proper office" is to "regulate the hearts of men."

32. Here Philo inserts an analogy from natural philosophy: Gravity may be a weak force, yet in the long run it will "prevail above a great impulse" because of its "constancy" (all 12.13.Philo to Cleanthes). Whatever real complaints Philo may have against Cleanthes' design argument, they cannot rule out human/natural analogies.

33. Philo puts his worries into a limited political form but doubtless would generalize: If "a wise magistrate" permits only one religion, he may gain "an uncertain prospect of tranquillity," but he sacrifices "every consideration of public liberty, science, reason, industry, and even his own independency." But if he permits "several sects, which is the wiser

maxim," he must be scrupulously neutral or else will face "nothing but endless disputes, quarrels, factions, persecutions, and civil commotions" (12.21.Philo to Cleanthes).

34. Philo takes this occasion to retail some racist jibes at "Greek faith," "Punic faith," and "Irish evidence." He chiefly wants to urge, contra Polybius, that the "infamy of Greek faith" is *not* due to the influence of Epicurean philosophy. These national slurs must be accounted for in other ways—presumably, in Philo's view, on the basis of deleterious *religious* effects.

35. The repetition is of course a matter of emphasis. But the use of "care" is more than emphasis. It hearkens back to Philo's "careless scepticism," in its several senses. Perhaps Cleanthes gives Philo a dual warning: "Be precise and scrupulous (not inexact in your thinking)! Be mindful and conscientious (not unconcerned about what really matters to you)!"

36. Why does Philo call them "appearances"? Cleanthes called them "the most agreeable reflection, which it is possible for human imagination to suggest" (12.24.Cleanthes to Philo); and "appearance" is softer than "imagining." But neither Cleanthes nor Philo offer any clue how a "true philosopher" would convert an "agreeable reflection" or "appearance" into something "more" (truth? reality? knowledge?).

37. It is fitting that Cleanthes' last words in the *Dialogues* are these: "But men, when afflicted, find consolation in religion" (12.27.Cleanthes to Philo). By "men," he surely means at least himself; Cleanthes *is* consoled by his religion, though it is not easy to imagine him much afflicted. In contrast, Demea is profoundly afflicted but little consoled; his authoritarian religion provides only a fragile sense of security. Philo is not afflicted and sees little need for consolation. Philo is as tone-deaf to the positive notes of religion as Cleanthes is blind to human misery.

38. "Tremendous" here means "terrifying, dreadful, horrible"; it is Rudolph Otto's *mysterium tremendum*.

39. Here is another clue as to why Demea has left "the company." He is not "fit" for it, not fitted to it, not suited to its requirements and rewards, because his heart is ruled by fear, not hope and cheer.

40. Scott Davis (1991) notes that this phrase is not found exactly in Seneca, but claims that for Seneca "worship is nothing other than the practice of stoic virtue" (252), from which it follows that on Philo's view, knowing God has chiefly a practical import.

41. It is hard not to see Demea, Cleanthes, and Philo as instances of these three types: Demea meriting divine offense, Cleanthes divine favor, and Philo divine compassion.

42. Who are these people, and why is their position a seeming one? Clearly it is Cleanthes' position, at the heart of his "most engaging and alluring" views. These views, however, are more than "appearances" only to "the true philosopher" (12.25.Philo to Cleanthes). Whether Philo counts Cleanthes or himself as a true philosopher is open to question.

43. This proposition is a more cautious restatement of Cleanthes' conclusion that "the Author of Nature is somewhat similar to the mind of man" (2.5.Cleanthes to Demea and Philo).

44. Why does Philo ask "Cleanthes" (not "you") to *believe* "me"? Is he worried that Cleanthes might *not* believe him? Is Philo about to utter something beyond the character Cleanthes has come to know? If so, is Philo speaking ironically? Or is he speaking sincerely, adding a conventional expression of conviction for the benefit of his conventional friend to drive home the seriousness of his appeal to revelation?

45. See Popkin (1955–1956, 1980a, 1980b).

46. Norman Kemp Smith (1941 and especially 1947) is *primus inter pares.*

47. Scott Davis (1991, 253) claims that for Philo = Hume, true religion reduces to natural science, so that Philo's gestures toward something more *must* be ironical.

48. See Kemp Smith (1947, 1–8).

49. Of course, a contextualizing interpretation could always claim that Hume was seeking to deflect criticism from the rabid clerics of his day by covering his tracks. But this makes little sense in a work planned to be published posthumously and then not anonymously. Explaining what goes on *inside* the *Dialogues* by what Hume thought would or might happen *outside* the work is unilluminating.

50. Incidentally, this parting bow indicates that Philo has been well aware, from the very beginning, of Pamphilus's presence. At no point have the conversations been merely theoretical; every participant has had in mind their rapt audience of one, and each has displayed his own view of how Pamphilus should be brought up. Pamphilus has been chiefly impressed by "all the *reasonings* of that day," yet we should not think that the discussants have sought only to develop his theology. They have also been concerned to instill by precept and example their own piety, the proper habits of living "in company" with like-minded others.

51. This time the judgments are Pamphilus's own, not reports of Hermippus's views.

52. This youthful judgment of relative probability has likely contributed greatly to thinking of the *Dialogues* as a competition in which there are "winners" and "losers." But why does Pamphilus make a judgment at all, much less *this* judgment? Why doesn't he just register the strong impression the conversations made on him without going on to evaluate the speakers? Has he absorbed Philo's philosophical skepticism, which is constantly judging positions and people? (Note that Pamphilus is impressed by the "*reasonings*" of the day.) Or is he attempting to reinforce the impressions Hermippus had gained from an earlier account of the conversations (cf. PH.6)?

53. I am grateful to Ed Craun for these points.

16. Conclusion

1. The gibe is from F. H. Bradley, *Principles of Logic,* vol. III, chap. 2, iv.

2. Basu (1978). A subsidiary project, after identifying Hume's persona, usually with Philo, is to identify the remaining characters with some actual individual of Hume's day or with an amalgamation of individual character traits: Whose mouthpieces are Cleanthes and Demea? But the subsidiary project makes sense only if the primary project makes sense.

3. A darker side of irony should not go unnoticed. As Lionel Grossman remarks, "Irony is preeminently an instrument of inclusion and exclusion, and its playful exterior disguises a certain repressiveness" (Grossman quoted in Siebert 1990, 179). There is a presumption of superiority by the one who understands the subversive double meaning and thereby gains ascendancy over those "left in the dark." Readers of irony imply they have insight superior to those in or out of the text who take things straightforwardly. But what about the ironist's own claims? Typically the ironist wishes to have a non-ironic last word or at least to keep his own views and values hidden; but in either case he claims a privilege not afforded the text. Irony's two-edged sword often maims its wielder.

4. In fact, there is little reason in the text to think that Philo is speaking ironically in these instances, since the wholly changed "manner" of conversation between Philo and Cleanthes in Part 12, with Demea no longer present to inject a spirit of competition, is one of openness and "unreserved intimacy" (12.2.Philo to Cleanthes). See Malherbe (1995, 208 and 222 n. 34).

5. There are two ways for external interpreters to maintain that Philo = Hume without resorting to irony: (1) argue that Philo doesn't change from Parts 1–11 to Part 12 (cf., e.g., Parent 1976a, 1976b; Priest 1985), or (2) hold that Philo does change, but to a position that more adequately represents Hume's mature views (cf., e.g., Penelhum 1979; in a later work, however, Penelhum worries that "perhaps we are all wrong in being as ready to identify Philo with Hume as we have been since Kemp Smith" [Penelhum 1983b, 179]).

6. Compare Siebert (1990, 176–177).

7. My effort to discern Hume's design of the *Dialogues* from within the text mirrors

a major topic in the *Dialogues* itself: discerning design in and of the world. The *Dialogues,* after all, is a (very skillful) contrivance of a human author, so—on Cleanthes' principles— its author's craft should have *some* analogy to the craft of the Author of the world. See Sessions (1998).

8. Think of the enigmatic parallelepiped in Stanley Kubrick's *2001: A Space Odyssey.*

9. Dennett (1996, 32) thinks Philo = Hume "caves in" because "he *just couldn't imagine* any other explanation of the origin of the manifest design in nature" than a theological one (emphasis in original).

10. See Foucault (1970, 1972).

11. On the other hand, from a naturalistic standpoint, one would see the world as having no purpose at all except for the behavior of intelligent beings in the world (and much of what appears purposive even there may well have other, better explanations).

12. Is there any difference between indifference and no purpose at all? (I owe this question to Jamie Ferreira.) In the end, very little, except that (1) Philo concedes, I think, that God is the kind of being concerning which it makes sense to attribute purpose, and (2) apparent divine indifference toward us may mask a deeper purpose, for all we know.

13. Gaskin (1976, 311; 1983, 171).

14. Collins (1967, 78); Hanson (1993, 77); and Penelhum (1983b, 179).

15. Penelhum (1983b, 169). Whether such attenuated deism is Hume's own view I leave to the external interpreters. I would only suggest that it need not be Hume's *only* view on these impenetrably obscure matters; he may well have had several views among which he was undecided, or he may have been unable to settle on any at all. External interpretative interest might do well to turn from "Who Speaks for Hume?" to "How do the *Dialogues* Reflect Hume's Inner Dialogues?"

16. Cleanthes mentions "Christian" and its kin "Christianity" and "Christendom" only four times, all in 1.17 where he is talking directly to Demea and the topic is the use and misuse of skepticism by Christianity, not Cleanthes' own personal religious affiliation. But Cleanthes is not alone, for no one in the *Dialogues* confesses personal Christian commitment (Demea doesn't even mention the word, and Philo twice speaks of Christians in the third person [4.4 and 12.33]). Why do they all keep Christianity at arm's length? Is it because they all presume any religion, or any "true religion," will be, or entail, Christianity? Is it because Christianity is a revealed religion, and revealed religion is off limits for these dialogues? Or is it because each has something (different) to hide, some secret about his own religious commitment? The text does not permit us to decide.

17. Note that Cleanthes' position on true religion exactly parallels his position on the existence and amount of evil in Part 10: There, he wants to "deny absolutely the misery and wickedness of man"; that is, to insist that good (greatly) outweighs bad (10.31.Cleanthes to Philo).

18. Actually, the crucial analogy is not one of proportion (between terms) but of proportionality (between relations); between the *relation* between God and the world on the one hand and the *relation* between a human maker and human artifacts on the other hand. But this distinction is unimportant here; the main point is that for both Cleanthes and Philo, analogical thinking is bedrock.

19. This is why Capaldi errs in claiming that "the message of *Dialogues* is that morality is *independent* of religion" (Capaldi 1975, 189; emphasis added). At times it does appear that natural piety empties itself into morality and other aspects of common life (cf., e.g., 12.12.Cleanthes to Philo). Yet religion *supports* morality, in Cleanthes' view, so morality *depends* on religion.

20. Of course, it is another matter whether appeasement ever does absolve Demea of his existential anxiety and produce the absolute assurance he so desperately craves.

21. Demea thinks that such submissiveness not only enables complete absorption of his instruction but also appeases those higher powers that "afflict and oppress" us (10.1.Demea to Philo and Cleanthes); Demea supposes his purposes are God's purposes.

22. See Tweyman (1981) on "The Sceptic as Teacher."

23. W. B. Carnochan considers this tenuous pact and its inevitable rupture to be "the comic plot of Hume's *Dialogues*" (Carnochan 1988). But Carnochan gives too much weight to this plot and its denouement; there are other structures and many shifting alliances throughout the first eleven Parts, and Part 12 is much more than an anticlimax.

LIST OF SOURCES

This list contains only works mentioned in the text, omitting a great many other items that were consulted in preparing this reading. For fuller bibliographies see Jessop 1938; Hall 1978; Livingston 1981; Gaskin 1988; Capaldi, King, and Livingston 1991; and Norton 1993.

Aiken, H. D., ed. 1948. *Hume's Dialogues concerning Natural Religion.* Hafner Library of Classics, 5. New York: Hafner.

Andic, Martin. 1974. "'Experimental Theism' and the Verbal Dispute in Hume's *Dialogues.*" *Archiv für Geschichte der Philosophie* 56: 239–256.

Austin, W. 1985. "Philo's Reversal." *Philosophical Topics* 13: 103–112.

Ayer, A. J. 1980. *Hume.* Oxford: Oxford University Press.

Barker, Stephen. 1983. "Hume on the Logic of Design." *Hume Studies* 9: 1–18.

———. 1989. "Reasoning by Analogy in Hume's *Dialogues.*" *Informal Logic* 11, no. 3: 173–184.

Barrow, John D., and Frank J. Tipler. 1986. *The Anthropic Cosmological Principle.* New York: Oxford University Press.

Basu, D. K. 1978. "Who Is the Real Hume in the Dialogues?" *Indian Philosophical Quarterly* 6: 21–28.

Battersby, Christine. 1979. "The *Dialogues* as Original Imitation: Cicero and the Nature of Hume's Skepticism." In *McGill Hume Studies,* edited by David Fate Norton, Nicholas Capaldi, and Wade Robison, 239–252. San Diego: Austin Hill Press.

Beaty, Michael D. 1988. "The Problem of Evil: The Unanswered Questions Argument." *Southwest Philosophical Review* 4: 57–64.

Behe, Michael J. 1996. *Darwin's Black Box: The Biochemical Challenge to Evolution.* New York: The Free Press.

Box, M. A. 1990. *The Suasive Art of David Hume.* Princeton: Princeton University Press.

Boys Smith, J. S. 1936. "Hume's *Dialogues concerning Natural Religion.*" *Journal of Theological Studies* 37: 337–349.

Bradley, F. H. 1922. *Principles of Logic.* Vol. 3. 2nd ed. London: Oxford University Press.

Bricke, John. 1975. "On the Interpretation of Hume's *Dialogues.*" *Religious Studies* 11: 1–18.

Burch, Robert. 1980. "Bayesianism and Analogy in Hume's Dialogues." *Hume Studies* 6: 32–44.

Butler, Ronald J. 1960. "Natural Belief and the Enigma of Hume." *Archiv für Geschichte der Philosophie* 42: 73–100.

Calvert, Brian. 1983. "Another Problem about Part IX of Hume's *Dialogues.*" *International Journal of the Philosophy of Religion* 14: 65–70.

Campbell, Joseph K. 1996. "Hume's Refutation of the Cosmological Argument." *International Journal for Philosophy of Religion* 40: 159–173.

Capaldi, Nicholas. 1975. *David Hume: The Newtonian Philosopher.* Boston: Twayne.

———. 1989. *Hume's Place in Moral Philosophy.* New York: Peter Lang.

Capaldi, Nicholas, James King, and Donald Livingston. 1991. "The Hume Literature of the 1980's." *American Philosophical Quarterly* 28: 255–272.

Capitan, William. 1966. "Part X of Hume's *Dialogues*." In *Hume,* edited by V. C. Chappell, 384–395. Garden City, New York: Doubleday Anchor.

Carnochan, W. B. 1988. "The Comic Plot of Hume's *Dialogues*." *Modern Philology* 85: 514–522.

Cartwright, Nancy. 1978. "Comments on Wesley Salmon's 'Science and Religion . . .'" *Philosophical Studies* 33: 177–183.

Collins, James Daniel. 1967. *The Emergence of Philosophy of Religion.* New Haven, Conn., and London: Yale University Press.

Dancy, Jonathan. 1995. "'For Here the Author Is Annihilated': Reflections on Philosophical Aspects of the Use of the Dialogue Form in Hume's *Dialogues concerning Natural Religion*." In *Philosophical Dialogues: Plato, Hume, Wittgenstein,* edited by Timothy J. Smiley, 29–60. Oxford: Oxford University Press.

Davies, P. C. W. 1983. *God and the New Physics.* New York: Simon & Schuster.

———. 1992. *The Mind of God.* New York: Simon & Schuster.

Davis, Scott. 1991. "Irony and Argument in *Dialogues,* XII." *Religious Studies* 27: 239–257.

Dennett, Daniel. 1996. *Darwin's Dangerous Idea: Evolution and the Meanings of Life.* New York: Simon & Schuster Touchstone.

Duerlinger, J. 1971. "The Verbal Dispute in Hume's *Dialogues*." *Archiv für Geschichte der Philosophie* 53: 22–34.

Dye, James. 1989. "A Word on Behalf of Demea." *Hume Studies* 15: 120–140.

Fogelin, Robert J. 1985. *Hume's Scepticism in the Treatise of Human Nature.* London and Boston: Routledge and Kegan Paul.

Foucault, Michel. 1970. *The Order of Things: An Archeology of the Human Sciences.* New York: Pantheon Books.

———. 1972. *The Archeology of Knowledge.* Translated by A. M. Sheridan Smith. New York: Pantheon Books.

Franklin, James. 1980. "More on Part IX of Hume's Dialogues." *Philosophical Quarterly* 30: 69–71.

Gaskin, J. C. A. 1976. "Hume's Critique of Religion." *Journal of the History of Philosophy* 14: 301–311.

———. 1983. "Hume's Attenuated Deism." *Archiv für Geschichte der Philosophie* 65: 160–173.

———. 1988. *Hume's Philosophy of Religion.* 2nd ed. London: Macmillan Press. (1st ed. London: Macmillan, 1978.)

———, ed. 1993. *David Hume: Principal Writings on Religion including Dialogues concerning Natural Religion and The Natural History of Religion.* Oxford: Oxford University Press.

Greig, J. Y. T. [Hohn Carruthers], ed. 1932. *The Letters of David Hume.* 2 vols. Oxford: Clarendon Press.

Griswold, Charles L. 1986. *Self-Knowledge in Plato's Phaedrus.* New Haven, Conn.: Yale University Press.

———. 1999. *Adam Smith and the Virtues of Enlightenment.* Cambridge: Cambridge University Press.

Hall, Roland. 1978. *Fifty Years of Hume Scholarship: A Bibliographical Guide.* Edinburgh: Edinburgh University Press.

Hanson, Delbert J. 1993. *Fideism and Hume's Philosophy.* New York: Peter Lang.

Hartshorne, Charles. 1948. *The Divine Relativity.* New Haven, Conn.: Yale University Press.

———. 1964. *Man's Vision of God.* Hamden, Conn.: Archon Books.

Hendel, Charles. 1963. *Studies in the Philosophy of David Hume.* 2nd ed. Indianapolis and New York: Bobbs-Merrill. (1st ed., Princeton: Princeton University Press, 1925.)

Hick, John. 1978. *Evil and the God of Love*. Rev. ed. New York: Harper and Row.

Hume, David. 1980. *Dialogues concerning Natural Religion and the Posthumous Essays*. Edited by Richard H. Popkin. Indianapolis and Cambridge: Hackett Publishing Company.

Hurlbutt, Robert H. 1985. *Hume, Newton, and the Design Argument*. Rev. ed. Lincoln: University of Nebraska Press.

——. 1988. "The Careless Skeptic—the 'Pamphilian' Ironies in Hume's Dialogues." *Hume Studies* 14: 207–250.

Jacquette, Dale. 1985. "Analogical Inference in Hume's Philosophy of Religion." *Faith and Philosophy* 2: 287–294.

James, E. D. 1979. "Scepticism and Religious Belief: Pascal, Bayle, Hume." In *Classical Influences on Western Thought A.D. 1650–1870*, edited by R. R. Bolgar, 93–104. Cambridge: Cambridge University Press.

Jeffner, Anders. 1966. *Butler and Hume on Religion: A Comparative Analysis*. Stockholm: Diakonistyrelsens Bokforlag.

Jessop, T. E. 1938. *A Bibliography of David Hume and Scottish Philosophy*. London: A. Brown, Hull.

——. 1939. "Symposium: The Present-Day Relevance of Hume's *Dialogues concerning Natural Religion*." Aristotelian Society Supplementary Volume 18, 218–228.

——. 1977. "Hume's Response to the Pressure to Conform in Religious Beliefs." *Southwest Philosophical Studies* 2: 95–101.

Johnson, Oliver A. 1995. *The Mind of David Hume: A Companion to Book I of A Treatise of Human Nature*. Urbana: University of Illinois Press, 1995.

Jones, Peter. 1982. *Hume's Sentiments: Their Ciceronian and French Context*. Edinburgh: Edinburgh University Press.

——, ed. 1989. *The 'Science of Man' in the Scottish Enlightenment: Hume, Reid and their Contemporaries*. Edinburgh: Edinburgh University Press.

Khamara, Edward J. 1992. "Hume versus Clarke on the Cosmological Argument." *Philosophical Quarterly* 42: 34–55.

Livingston, Donald W. 1981. "The Hume Literature of the 1970s: Philosophy of History and Philosophy of Religion." *Philosophical Topics* 12: 167–192.

——. 1984. *Hume's Philosophy of Common Life*. Chicago: University of Chicago Press.

Locke, John. 1997. *The Reasonableness of Christianity: As Delivered in the Scriptures*. Introduction by Victor Nuovo. South Bend, Ind.: St. Augustine's Press.

Luce, A. A., and T. G. Jessop, eds. 1948. *The Works of George Berkeley, Bishop of Cloyne*. Vol. 2 of 9. Edinburgh: Thomas Nelson.

Malebranche, Nicolas. 1980. *The Search after Truth*. Translated by Thomas M. Lennon and Paul J. Oscamp. Columbus: Ohio State University Press.

Malherbe, Michel. 1995. "Hume and the Art of Dialogue." In *Hume and Hume's Connexions*, edited by M. A. Stewart and John P. Wright, 201–223. University Park: Pennsylvania State University Press.

Manning, Robert John Sheffler. 1990. "David Hume's *Dialogues concerning Natural Religion*: Otherness in History and in Text." *Religious Studies* 26: 415–426.

Martin, J. A., Jr. 1966. *The New Dialogue between Philosophy and Theology*. New York: The Seabury Press.

Martin, Marie. 1994. "Hume as Classical Moralist." *International Philosophical Quarterly* 34: 323–334.

Morrisroe, Michael, Jr. 1969a. "Rhetorical Methods in Hume's Works on Religion." *Philosophy and Rhetoric* 2: 121–138.

——. 1969b. "Hume's Rhetorical Strategy: A Solution to the Riddle of the *Dialogues concerning Natural Religion*." *Texas Studies in Literature and Language* 11: 963–974.

——. 1970. "Characterization as Rhetorical Device in Hume's *Dialogues concerning Natural Religion*." *Enlightenment Essays* 1: 95–107.

——. 1974. "Linguistic Analysis as Rhetorical Pattern in David Hume." In *Hume and the Enlightenment: Essays Presented to Ernest Campbell Mossner,* edited by W. B. Todd, 72–82. Edinburgh: Edinburgh University Press and Austin: University of Texas Humanities Research Center.

Mossner, Ernest Campbell. 1936. "The Enigma of Hume." *Mind* 45: 334–349.

——. 1977. "Hume and the Legacy of the *Dialogues.*" In *David Hume: Bicentenary Papers,* edited by G. Morice, 1–22. Austin: University of Texas Press and Edinburgh: Edinburgh University Press.

Norton, David Fate. 1982. *David Hume: Common-Sense Moralist, Sceptical Metaphysician.* Princeton, N.J.: Princeton University Press.

——, ed. 1993. *The Cambridge Companion to Hume.* Cambridge: Cambridge University Press.

Noxon, James. 1964. "Hume's Agnosticism." *The Philosophical Review* 73: 248–261.

Nuovo, Victor, ed. 1997. *John Locke and Christianity: Contemporary Responses to The Reasonableness of Christianity.* Bristol: Thoemmes Press.

Olshewsky, Thomas M. 1991. "The Classical Roots of Hume's Skepticism." *Journal of the History of Ideas* 52: 269–287.

Pailin, David. 1994. "The Confused and Confusing Story of Natural Religion." *Religion* 24 (July): 199–212.

Pakaluk, Michael. 1984. "Philosophical Types in Hume's Dialogues." In *Philosophers of the Scottish Enlightenment,* edited by V. Hope, 116–132. Edinburgh: Edinburgh University Press.

Parent, W. A. 1976a. "An Interpretation of Hume's *Dialogues.*" *Review of Metaphysics* 30: 96–114.

——. 1976b. "Philo's Confession." *Philosophical Quarterly* 26: 63–68.

Passmore, John A. 1989. "Enthusiasm, Fanaticism and David Hume." In *The 'Science of Man' in the Scottish Enlightenment: Hume, Reid and their Contemporaries,* edited by Peter Jones, 85–107. Edinburgh: Edinburgh University Press.

Penelhum, Terence. 1975. *Hume.* New York: St. Martin's Press and London: Macmillan.

——. 1979. "Hume's Skepticism and the *Dialogues.*" In *McGill Hume Studies,* edited by David Fate Norton, Nicholas Capaldi, and Wade Robison, 253–278. San Diego: Austin Hill Press.

——. 1983a. *God and Scepticism.* Dordrecht: Reidel.

——. 1983b. "Natural Belief and Religious Belief in Hume's Philosophy." *Philosophical Quarterly* 33: 160–181.

——. 1985. "Scepticism, Sentiment and Common Sense in Hume." *Dialogue* 24: 515–522. (Review of Norton 1982 and Jones 1982.)

Pike, Nelson. 1963. "Hume on Evil." *Philosophical Review* 72: 180–197.

——. 1970. "Hume on the Argument from Design." In David Hume, *Dialogues concerning Natural Religion,* edited and with a commentary by Nelson Pike, 125–238. Indianapolis: Bobbs-Merrill.

Popkin, Richard H. 1951. "David Hume, His Pyrrhonism and His Critique of Pyrrhonism." *Philosophical Quarterly* 1: 385–407.

——. 1952. "David Hume and Pyrrhonian Controversy." *Review of Metaphysics* 6: 65–81.

——. 1955–1956. "The Skeptical Precursors of David Hume." *Philosophy and Phenomenological Research* 16: 61–71.

——. 1980a. *The High Road to Pyrrhonism.* Edited by Richard A. Watson and James E. Force. Studies in Hume and Scottish Philosophy. San Diego: Austin Hill.

——, ed. 1980b. "Introduction." In *Dialogues concerning Natural Religion and the Posthumous Essays,* by David Hume. Indianapolis and Cambridge: Hackett Publishing Company.

——. 1993. "Sources of Knowledge of Sextus Empiricus in Hume's Time." *Journal of the History of Ideas* 54: 137–141.

Price, John Valdimir. 1963. "Empirical Theists in Cicero and Hume." *Texas Studies in Literature and Language* 5: 255–264.

———. 1964. "Sceptics in Cicero and Hume." *Journal of the History of Ideas* 25: 97–106.

———. 1965. *The Ironic Hume*. Austin: University of Texas Press.

———. 1991. *David Hume*. New York: Twayne.

Priest, G. 1985. "Hume's Final Argument." *History of Philosophy Quarterly* 2: 349–351.

Prince, Michael B. 1992. "Hume and the End of Religious Dialogue." *Eighteenth Century Studies* 25, no. 3: 283–308.

Rescher, Nicholas. 1969. "An Argument of Hume's." In his *Essays in Philosophical Analysis*, chap. VII. Pittsburgh: University of Pittsburgh Press. (A revised and somewhat expanded version of "Logical Analysis in Historical Application," *Methodos* 11 [1959], 81–89.)

Richetti, John J. 1983. *Philosophical Writing: Locke, Berkeley, Hume*. Cambridge, Mass.: Harvard University Press.

Rivers, Isabel. 1993. " 'Galen's Muscles': Wilkins, Hume, and the Educational Use of the Argument from Design." *Historical Journal* 36, no. 3: 577–597.

Rohatyn, Dennis. 1983. "Hume's Dialogical Conceits: The Case of *Dialogue* XII." *Philosophy and Phenomenological Research* 43: 519–532.

Salmon, Wesley C. 1978. "Religion and Science: A New Look at Hume's *Dialogues*." *Philosophical Studies* 33: 143–176.

———. 1979. "Experimental Atheism." *Philosophical Studies* 35: 101–104.

Sessions, William Lad. 1998. "Author! Author! Some Reflections on Design in and beyond Hume's *Dialogues*." Paper presented at the Twentieth World Congress of Philosophy, Boston.

Shapiro, Gary. 1985. "The Man of Letters and the Author of Nature: Hume on Philosophical Discourse." *The Eighteenth Century* 26: 115–137.

Siebert, Donald T. 1990. *The Moral Animus of David Hume*. Newark: University of Delaware Press and London and Toronto: Associated University Presses.

Simpson, David. 1979. "Hume's Intimate Voices and the Method of Dialogue." *Texas Studies in Literature and Language* 21: 68–92.

Smith, Barry. 1991. "Textual Deference." *American Philosophical Quarterly* 28: 1–12.

Smith, Norman Kemp. 1941. *The Philosophy of David Hume: A Critical Study of Its Origins and Central Doctrines*. London: Macmillan and New York: St. Martin's Press.

———, ed. 1947. "Introduction." In David Hume, *Dialogues concerning Natural Religion*, 2nd ed., edited and with an introduction by Norman Kemp Smith, 1–123. Indianapolis: Bobbs Merrill.

Sobel, Jerry E. 1982. "Arguing, Accepting, and Preserving Design in Heidegger, Hume, and Kant." In *Essays in Kant's Aesthetics*, edited by Ted Cohen and Paul Guyer, 271–305. Chicago: University of Chicago Press.

Soles, Deborah Hansen. 1981. "Hume, Language and God." *Philosophical Topics* 12: 109–120.

Solon, T. P. M., and S. K. Wertz. 1969. "Hume's Argument from Evil." *The Personalist* 50: 383–392.

Sprague, Elmer. 1988. "Hume, Henry More and the Design Argument." *Hume Studies* 14: 305–327.

Stahl, Donald E. 1984. "Hume's Dialogue IX Defended." *Philosophical Quarterly* 34: 505–507.

Steinberg, Eric. 1987. "Hume on Liberty, Necessity and Verbal Disputes." *Hume Studies* 13: 113–137.

Stewart, M. A. 1985. "Hume and the 'Metaphysical Argument *A Priori*.'" In *Philosophy, Its History and Historiography*, edited by A. J. Holland, 243–270. Dordrecht: D. Reidel.

———. 1995. "An Early Fragment on Evil." In *Hume and Hume's Connexions*, edited by M. A. Stewart and John P. Wright, 160–170. University Park: Pennsylvania State University Press.

Stove, D. C. 1978. "Part IX of Hume's Dialogues." *Philosophical Quarterly* 28: 300–309.
———. 1979. "The Nature of Hume's Skepticism." In *McGill Hume Studies,* edited by David Fate Norton, Nicholas Capaldi, and Wade Robison, 203–225. San Diego: Austin Hill Press.
Sutherland, Stewart R. 1983. "Penelhum on Hume." *Philosophical Quarterly* 33: 131–136.
Swinburne, Richard G. 1968. "The Argument from Design." *Philosophy* 43: 199–212.
———. 1972. "The Argument from Design—A Defence." *Religious Studies* 8: 193–205.
———. 1979. *The Existence of God.* Oxford: Clarendon Press.
Temple, Dennis. 1992. "Hume's Logical Objection to the Argument from Design Based on the Uniqueness of the Universe." *Religious Studies* 28: 19–30.
Tennant, Frederick Robert. 1928, 1930. *Philosophical Theology.* 2 vols. Cambridge: Cambridge University Press.
Tilley, Terence W. 1988. "Hume on God and Evil: Dialogues X and XI as Dramatic Conversation." *Journal of the American Academy of Religion* LVI, no. 4: 703–726.
Tipler, Frank J. 1994. *The Physics of Immortality.* New York: Doubleday.
Tweyman, Stanley. 1979. "The Vegetable Library and God." *Dialogue* (Canada) 18: 517–527.
———. 1980. "Remarks on Wadia's Philo Confounded." *Hume Studies* 6: 155–161.
———. 1981. "The Sceptic as Teacher." *Spindrift* 1: 16–28.
———. 1982a. "The Articulate Voice and God." *Southern Journal of Philosophy* 20: 263–275.
———. 1982b. "An Inconvenience of Anthropomorphism." *Hume Studies* 8: 19–42.
———. 1983. "The 'Reductio' in Part V of Hume's 'Dialogues.'" *Southern Journal of Philosophy* 21: 453–460.
———. 1985. "An Enquiry Concerning Hume's Dialogues." In *Early Modern Philosophy,* edited by Georges J. D. Moyal and Stanley Tweyman, 155–175. Delmar, N.Y.: Caravan Books.
———. 1986. *Scepticism and Belief in Hume's Dialogues concerning Natural Religion.* The Hague: Martinus Nijhoff.
———. 1987. "Hume's Dialogues on Evil." *Hume Studies* 13: 74–85. (Reprinted in *Scepticism and Belief in Hume's Dialogues concerning Natural Religion,* edited by Stanley Tweyman, 187–195 [The Hague: Martinus Nijhoff, 1991].)
———, ed. 1991. *David Hume: Dialogues concerning Natural Religion in Focus.* London and New York: Routledge.
Vink, A. G. 1986. "The Literary and Dramatic Character of Hume's Dialogues concerning Natural Religion." *Religious Studies* 22: 387–396.
Wadia, Pheroze S. 1978. "Professor Pike on Part III of Hume's Dialogues." *Religious Studies* 14: 325–342.
———. 1979. "Philo Confounded." In *McGill Hume Studies,* edited by David Fate Norton, Nicholas Capaldi, and Wade Robison, 279–290. San Diego: Austin Hill Press.
———. 1987. "Commentary on Professor Tweyman's 'Hume on Evil.'" *Hume Studies* 13: 104–112. (Reprinted in *Scepticism and Belief in Hume's Dialogues concerning Natural Religion,* edited by Stanley Tweyman, 104–112 [The Hague: Martinus Nijhoff, 1991].)
White, R. 1988. "Hume's *Dialogues* and the Comedy of Religion." *Hume Studies* 14: 390–407.
Wieand, Jeffrey. 1985. "Pamphilus in Hume's *Dialogues.*" *The Journal of Religion* 65: 33–45.
Woltersorff, Nicholas. 1966. *John Locke and the Ethics of Belief.* Cambridge: Cambridge University Press.
Wright, John P. 1983. *The Sceptical Realism of David Hume.* Minneapolis: University of Minnesota Press.
———. 1986. "Hume's Academic Skepticism: A Reappraisal of His Philosophy of Human Understanding." *Canadian Journal of Philosophy* 16: 407–436.

Yandell, Keith E. 1976. "Hume on Religious Belief." In *Hume: A Re-evaluation,* edited by Donald W. Livingston and James T. King, 109–125. New York: Fordham University Press.

———. 1990. *Hume's "Inexplicable Mystery": His Views on Religion.* Philadelphia: Temple University Press.

INDEX

a posteriori: argument, 11, 53, 54, 60, 63, 65, 66, 74, 83, 119, 134, 137, 144; point, 146

a priori, 52, 58, 65, 217; argument, 12, 17, 59, 66, 88, 119, 126, 129, 130, 136–138, 140–142, 144–146, 176, 180, 223; argument vs. *a posteriori* argument, 16; demonstration, 144; ingredients, 138; proofs, 63, 122; theology, 103

Abelard, 49

absolutists, Darwinian, 214

absurdities, 47, 135–136, 142, 166, 167, 194

Acts, 49

Africa, 132

afterlife, 196, 197, 201

agnosticism, 161

Aiken, Henry D., 6

America, 114

analogy, 22, 54, 58, 61, 62, 69, 70, 71, 79, 93, 104, 117, 140, 144, 145, 166, 173, 177, 182, 188–190, 205, 213, 215, 223; alternative, 118; argument by, 216; argument from, 76; causal, 106; Cleanthes', 122; cosmogonic, 123; cosmological, 124; design, 130; disguised, 61; to the entire universe, 121; experienced, 121; to human intelligence, 202; imperfect, 127, 202; inconceivable, 190; human, 103, 158; limited, 111; mathematical, 145; of nature, 133; particular, 135; Philo's, 123; remote, 135; rules of, 66; slight, 133; weak, 63; world-vegetable/ world-animal, 120

analyst, 208, 209

analytic hermeneutics, 208

analytic vs. historicist tradition, 2

anatomy, 101

Andromeda, 191

animism, 112; cosmic, 112

annihilation, 84

Anselm, 49

anthropocentrism, 70

anthropomorphic hypothesis, 72, 133

anthropomorphism, 53, 70, 84, 87, 91, 96–98, 108, 133–135, 140, 147, 156, 165, 166, 180, 185, 189; dangerous, 215; denial of, 217; dogmatic, 203; experimental, 173

anthropomorphite, 87, 89, 96, 105, 157, 176

Apologists, 49

Aquinas, 49, 123

Arabia, 132

Arnauld, 48

arrogance, 41

artifice, 35, 76, 186, 188, 213; apparent, 187; display of, 187; human, 68, 100, 145, 157, 186; of nature, 29, 147, 153, 156, 157, 182, 186, 187, 215

artificer, 76, 111; human, 223; of nature, 82

Asia, 114

astronomy, 53, 64, 75, 101, 120

atheism, 49, 87, 90, 156, 161, 169, 190, 203

atheist, 50, 54, 55, 87–91, 186, 190, 210, 216, 217

Athenagoras, 49

Augustine, 49

Author of Nature, 10, 11, 15, 23, 54, 61, 62, 81, 83, 93, 99, 106, 135, 171,

160, 197; argument, 113; prejudice, 112; views, 201

West, 114
Whitehead, 4
wickedness, 148, 150, 159, 160, 172, 177, 219; human, 160
workmanship of nature, 164
world, 5, 10, 12, 60, 61, 63, 68, 70–72, 78, 81, 87, 88, 90–94, 103–109, 112, 114, 119–124, 126, 130, 131, 144, 151, 159, 165, 167–175, 180, 189, 213, 215, 221, 222, 224; actual, 77, 79; -analogy, 113; as animal, 110, 113, 117, 119, 120, 122; as contrivance and artifice, 215; celestial, 73; condition of, 168; divine, 93; economy of, 145; endlessly recurring, 125; eternity of, 113; everyday, 77; experienced, 172, 173; formation of, 79; as God's body, 111; God's presence in, 219; human,

184; hypothetical, 77; hypothesis, 145; ideal, 92; invisible, 200, 220; -machine, 61; as machine, 122, 173; -making, 103; material, 87, 91–94, 116; matter and form of, 143; mental, 91, 96; mental vs. material, 91, 92; mysterious, 94; natural, 77, 94, 157, 163, 186, 199; order of, 91, 92, 128, 135; orderly, 81; origination, 71; perfect, 103; physical, 96; present, 92; progeny, 120; purpose in, 215, 216; religious, 18; social and moral, 191; -soul, 111, 116; -soul hypothesis, 111–113; -system, 96, 108; teleological, 77; as vegetable, 113, 117, 119; whole vs. parts of, 62, 69, 134, 144

zeal, 81, 183, 197–199, 201, 220, 221, 227
zealot, 197
zealotry, 199

William Lad Sessions is Ballengee 250th Anniversary
Professor of Philosophy and Chair of the Philosophy
Department at Washington and Lee University.
He is the author of
The Concept of Faith: A Philosophical Investigation.